Since the great financial debacle of 2008, a blizzard of analyses has buried critical understanding beneath drifts of moral righteousness and pleas for regulatory rescue. This book clears a crucial path toward a comprehensive framework. It provides an incisive mapping of the conceptual foundations for the prevailing heterodox approaches that treat finance as merely parasitical rent. It also advances a radical Marxist understanding of the intrinsic role that finance plays in contemporary capitalism. Sotiropoulos, Milios, and Lapatsioras plow a technically nuanced opening to the deeper significance of derivatives as a form of abstract risk that embodies productive social relations. As storms continue to gather on the horizon, you'll want to have this book with you.

Randy Martin, Chair and Professor of Department of Arts and Public Policy, Tisch School of the Arts, New York University, USA

Sotiropoulos, Milios, and Lapatsioras have undertaken the ambitious task to rethink and revitalize Marx's ideas on finance and use them to decipher the nature of contemporary capitalism and the crisis emerging from it. Their argument is important and provocative, the fruit of long years of involvement in research and political activism. Their major achievement is to have constructed a unique and distinctive interdisciplinary analysis – a real analytical contribution – in the burgeoning contemporary literature on that subject. Their study is both theoretically profound and politically compelling, and especially relevant in the present critical period.

Alexis Tsipras, Head of SYRIZA and Leader of the Greek Parliamentary Opposition

Most "Marxist" analyses of the contemporary crisis suffer from an overly simplified understanding of value and money. By contrast, this study focuses on what distinguishes Marx's critique of political economy from both classical political economy and modern heterodox approaches: value form analysis and the theory of fetishism. The authors not only use the full theoretical apparatus of all three volumes of *Capital* (which rarely takes place), but offer exciting theoretical enhancements such as demonstrating the connection between fictitious capital and fetishism. They also show how to make such theoretical innovations fertile for a critical analysis of the Euro crisis. In sum, this is a really thrilling piece of modern Marxist critical analysis.

Michael Heinrich, University of Applied Sciences, Berlin, Author of *An Introduction to the Three Volumes of Karl Marx's* Capital

A Political Economy of Contemporary Capitalism and its Crisis

The recent financial meltdown and the resulting global recession have rekindled debates regarding the nature of contemporary capitalism.

This book analyzes the ongoing financialization of the economy as a development within capitalism, and explores the ways in which it has changed the organization of capitalist power. The authors offer an interpretation of the role of the financial sphere, which displays a striking contrast to the majority of contemporary heterodox approaches. Their argument stresses the crucial role of financial derivatives in the contemporary organization of capitalist power relations, suggesting that the process of financialization is in fact entirely unthinkable in the absence of derivatives.

The book also uses Marx's concepts and some of the arguments developed in the framework of the historic Marxist controversies on economic crises in order to gain an insight into the modern neoliberal form of capitalism and the recent financial crisis. Employing a series of relevant international examples, this book will be essential reading for all those with an interest in the financial crisis, and all those seeking to comprehend the workings of capitalism.

Dimitris P. Sotiropoulos is Lecturer of Economics at Kingston University, London, UK.

John Milios is Professor of Political Economy and History of Economic Thought at the National Technical University of Athens, Greece.

Spyros Lapatsioras is Lecturer of the History of Economic Thought at the University of Crete, Greece.

Routledge frontiers of political economy

1 **Equilibrium Versus Understanding**
Towards the rehumanization of economics within social theory
Mark Addleson

2 **Evolution, Order and Complexity**
Edited by Elias L. Khalil and Kenneth E. Boulding

3 **Interactions in Political Economy**
Malvern after ten years
Edited by Steven Pressman

4 **The End of Economics**
Michael Perelman

5 **Probability in Economics**
Omar F. Hamouda and Robin Rowley

6 **Capital Controversy, Post Keynesian Economics and the History of Economics**
Essays in honour of Geoff Harcourt, volume one
Edited by Philip Arestis, Gabriel Palma and Malcolm Sawyer

7 **Markets, Unemployment and Economic Policy**
Essays in honour of Geoff Harcourt, volume two
Edited by Philip Arestis, Gabriel Palma and Malcolm Sawyer

8 **Social Economy**
The logic of capitalist development
Clark Everling

9 **New Keynesian Economics/Post Keynesian Alternatives**
Edited by Roy J. Rotheim

10 **The Representative Agent in Macroeconomics**
James E. Hartley

11 **Borderlands of Economics**
Essays in honour of Daniel R. Fusfeld
Edited by Nahid Aslanbeigui and Young Back Choi

12 **Value, Distribution and Capital**
Essays in honour of Pierangelo Garegnani
Edited by Gary Mongiovi and Fabio Petri

13 **The Economics of Science**
Methodology and epistemology as if economics really mattered
James R. Wible

14 **Competitiveness, Localised Learning and Regional Development**
Specialisation and prosperity in small open economies
Peter Maskell, Heikki Eskelinen, Ingjaldur Hannibalsson, Anders Malmberg and Eirik Vatne

15 **Labour Market Theory**
A constructive reassessment
Ben J. Fine

16 **Women and European Employment**
Jill Rubery, Mark Smith, Colette Fagan and Damian Grimshaw

17 **Explorations in Economic Methodology**
From Lakatos to empirical philosophy of science
Roger Backhouse

18 **Subjectivity in Political Economy**
Essays on wanting and choosing
David P. Levine

19 **The Political Economy of Middle East Peace**
The impact of competing trade agendas
Edited by J.W. Wright, Jr.

20 **The Active Consumer**
Novelty and surprise in consumer choice
Edited by Marina Bianchi

21 **Subjectivism and Economic Analysis**
Essays in memory of Ludwig Lachmann
Edited by Roger Koppl and Gary Mongiovi

22 **Themes in Post-Keynesian Economics**
Essays in honour of Geoff Harcourt, volume three
Edited by Claudio Sardoni and Peter Kriesler

23 **The Dynamics of Technological Knowledge**
Cristiano Antonelli

24 **The Political Economy of Diet, Health and Food Policy**
Ben J. Fine

25 **The End of Finance**
Capital market inflation, financial derivatives and pension fund capitalism
Jan Toporowski

26 **Political Economy and the New Capitalism**
Edited by Jan Toporowski

27 **Growth Theory**
A philosophical perspective
Patricia Northover

28 **The Political Economy of the Small Firm**
Edited by Charlie Dannreuther

29 **Hahn and Economic Methodology**
Edited by Thomas Boylan and Paschal F. O'Gorman

30 **Gender, Growth and Trade**
The miracle economies of the postwar years
David Kucera

31 **Normative Political Economy**
Subjective freedom, the market and the state
David Levine

32 **Economist with a Public Purpose**
Essays in honour of John Kenneth Galbraith
Edited by Michael Keaney

33 **Involuntary Unemployment**
The elusive quest for a theory
Michel De Vroey

34 **The Fundamental Institutions of Capitalism**
Ernesto Screpanti

35 **Transcending Transaction**
The search for self-generating markets
Alan Shipman

36 **Power in Business and the State**
An historical analysis of its concentration
Frank Bealey

37 **Editing Economics**
Essays in honour of Mark Perlman
Edited by Hank Lim, Ungsuh K. Park and Geoff Harcourt

38 **Money, Macroeconomics and Keynes**
Essays in honour of Victoria Chick, volume one
Edited by Philip Arestis, Meghnad Desai and Sheila Dow

39 **Methodology, Microeconomics and Keynes**
Essays in honour of Victoria Chick, volume two
Edited by Philip Arestis, Meghnad Desai and Sheila Dow

40 **Market Drive and Governance**
Re-examining the rules for economic and commercial contest
Ralf Boscheck

41 **The Value of Marx**
Political economy for contemporary capitalism
Alfredo Saad-Filho

42 **Issues in Positive Political Economy**
S. Mansoob Murshed

43 **The Enigma of Globalisation**
A journey to a new stage of capitalism
Robert Went

44 **The Market**
Equilibrium, stability, mythology
S.N. Afriat

45 **The Political Economy of Rule Evasion and Policy Reform**
Jim Leitzel

46 **Unpaid Work and the Economy**
Edited by Antonella Picchio

47 **Distributional Justice**
Theory and measurement
Hilde Bojer

48 **Cognitive Developments in Economics**
Edited by Salvatore Rizzello

49 **Social Foundations of Markets, Money and Credit**
Costas Lapavitsas

50 **Rethinking Capitalist Development**
Essays on the economics of Josef Steindl
Edited by Tracy Mott and Nina Shapiro

51 **An Evolutionary Approach to Social Welfare**
Christian Sartorius

52 **Kalecki's Economics Today**
Edited by Zdzislaw L. Sadowski and Adam Szeworski

53 **Fiscal Policy from Reagan to Blair**
The left veers right
Ravi K. Roy and Arthur T. Denzau

54 **The Cognitive Mechanics of Economic Development and Institutional Change**
Bertin Martens

55 **Individualism and the Social Order**
The social element in liberal thought
Charles R. McCann, Jr.

56 **Affirmative Action in the United States and India**
A comparative perspective
Thomas E. Weisskopf

57 **Global Political Economy and the Wealth of Nations**
Performance, institutions, problems and policies
Edited by Phillip Anthony O'Hara

58 **Structural Economics**
Thijs ten Raa

59 **Macroeconomic Theory and Economic Policy**
Essays in honour of Jean-Paul Fitoussi
Edited by K. Vela Velupillai

60 **The Struggle over Work**
The "end of work" and employment alternatives in post-industrial societies
Shaun Wilson

61 **The Political Economy of Global Sporting Organisations**
John Forster and Nigel Pope

62 **The Flawed Foundations of General Equilibrium Theory**
Critical essays on economic theory
Frank Ackerman and Alejandro Nadal

63 **Uncertainty in Economic Theory**
Essays in honor of David Schmeidler's 65th birthday
Edited by Itzhak Gilboa

64 **The New Institutional Economics of Corruption**
Edited by Johann Graf Lambsdorff, Markus Taube and Matthias Schramm

65 **The Price Index and its Extension**
A chapter in economic measurement
S.N. Afriat

66 **Reduction, Rationality and Game Theory in Marxian Economics**
Bruce Philp

67 **Culture and Politics in Economic Development**
Volker Bornschier

68 **Modern Applications of Austrian Thought**
Edited by Jürgen G. Backhaus

69 **Ordinary Choices**
Individuals, incommensurability, and democracy
Robert Urquhart

70 **Labour Theory of Value**
Peter C. Dooley

71 **Capitalism**
Victor D. Lippit

72 **Macroeconomic Foundations of Macroeconomics**
Alvaro Cencini

73 **Marx for the 21st Century**
Edited by Hiroshi Uchida

74 **Growth and Development in the Global Political Economy**
Social structures of accumulation and modes of regulation
Phillip Anthony O'Hara

75 **The New Economy and Macroeconomic Stability**
A neo-modern perspective drawing on the complexity approach and Keynesian economics
Teodoro Dario Togati

76 **The Future of Social Security Policy**
Women, work and a citizens' basic income
Ailsa McKay

77 **Clinton and Blair**
The political economy of the third way
Flavio Romano

78 **Marxian Reproduction Schema**
Money and aggregate demand in a capitalist economy
A.B. Trigg

79 **The Core Theory in Economics**
Problems and solutions
Lester G. Telser

80 **Economics, Ethics and the Market**
Introduction and applications
Johan J. Graafland

81 **Social Costs and Public Action in Modern Capitalism**
Essays inspired by Karl William Kapp's theory of social costs
Edited by Wolfram Elsner, Pietro Frigato and Paolo Ramazzotti

82 **Globalization and the Myths of Free Trade**
History, theory and empirical evidence
Edited by Anwar Shaikh

83 **Equilibrium in Economics**
Scope and limits
Edited by Valeria Mosini

84 **Globalization**
State of the art and perspectives
Edited by Stefan A. Schirm

85 **Neoliberalism**
National and regional experiments with global ideas
Edited by Ravi K. Roy, Arthur T. Denzau and Thomas D. Willett

86 **Post-Keynesian Macroeconomics**
Essays in honour of Ingrid Rima
Edited by Mathew Forstater, Gary Mongiovi and Steven Pressman

87 **Consumer Capitalism**
Anastasios S. Korkotsides

88 **Remapping Gender in the New Global Order**
Edited by Marjorie Griffin Cohen and Janine Brodie

89 **Hayek and Natural Law**
Eric Angner

90 **Race and Economic Opportunity in the Twenty-First Century**
Edited by Marlene Kim

91 **Renaissance in Behavioural Economics**
Harvey Leibenstein's impact on contemporary economic analysis
Edited by Roger Frantz

92 **Human Ecology Economics**
A new framework for global sustainability
Edited by Roy E. Allen

93 **Imagining Economics Otherwise**
Encounters with identity/difference
Nitasha Kaul

94 **Reigniting the Labor Movement**
Restoring means to ends in a democratic labor movement
Gerald Friedman

95 **The Spatial Model of Politics**
Norman Schofield

96 **The Economics of American Judaism**
Carmel Ullman Chiswick

97 **Critical Political Economy**
Christian Arnsperger

98 **Culture and Economic Explanation**
Economics in the US and Japan
Donald W. Katzner

99 **Feminism, Economics and Utopia**
Time travelling through paradigms
Karin Schönpflug

100 **Risk in International Finance**
Vikash Yadav

101 **Economic Policy and Performance in Industrial Democracies**
Party governments, central banks and the fiscal–monetary policy mix
Takayuki Sakamoto

102 **Advances on Income Inequality and Concentration Measures**
Edited by Gianni Betti and Achille Lemmi

103 **Economic Representations**
Academic and everyday
Edited by David F. Ruccio

104 **Mathematical Economics and the Dynamics of Capitalism**
Goodwin's legacy continued
Edited by Peter Flaschel and Michael Landesmann

105 **The Keynesian Multiplier**
Edited by Claude Gnos and Louis-Philippe Rochon

106 **Money, Enterprise and Income Distribution**
Towards a macroeconomic theory of capitalism
John Smithin

107 **Fiscal Decentralization and Local Public Finance in Japan**
Nobuki Mochida

108 **The 'Uncertain' Foundations of Post-Keynesian Economics**
Essays in exploration
Stephen P. Dunn

109 **Karl Marx's *Grundrisse***
Foundations of the critique of political economy 150 years later
Edited by Marcello Musto

110 **Economics and the Price Index**
S.N. Afriat and Carlo Milana

111 **Sublime Economy**
On the intersection of art and economics
Edited by Jack Amariglio, Joseph W. Childers and Stephen E. Cullenberg

112 **Popper, Hayek and the Open Society**
Calvin Hayes

113 **The Political Economy of Work**
David Spencer

114 **Institutional Economics**
Bernard Chavance

115 **Religion, Economics and Demography**
The effects of religion on education, work, and the family
Evelyn L. Lehrer

116 **Economics, Rational Choice and Normative Philosophy**
Edited by Thomas A. Boylan and Ruvin Gekker

117 **Economics Versus Human Rights**
Manuel Couret Branco

118 **Hayek Versus Marx and Today's Challenges**
Eric Aarons

119 **Work Time Regulation as Sustainable Full Employment Policy**
Robert LaJeunesse

120 **Equilibrium, Welfare and Uncertainty**
Mukul Majumdar

121 **Capitalism, Institutions and Economic Development**
Michael Heller

122 **Economic Pluralism**
Robert Garnett, Erik Olsen and Martha Starr

123 **Dialectics of Class Struggle in the Global Economy**
Clark Everling

124 **Political Economy and Globalization**
Richard Westra

125 **Full-Spectrum Economics**
Toward an inclusive and emancipatory social science
Christian Arnsperger

126 **Computable, Constructive and Behavioural Economic Dynamics**
Essays in honour of Kumaraswamy (Vela) Velupillai
Stefano Zambelli

127 **Monetary Macrodynamics**
Toichiro Asada, Carl Chiarella, Peter Flaschel and Reiner Franke

128 **Rationality and Explanation in Economics**
Maurice Lagueux

129 **The Market, Happiness, and Solidarity**
A Christian perspective
Johan J. Graafland

130 **Economic Complexity and Equilibrium Illusion**
Essays on market instability and macro vitality
Ping Chen

131 **Economic Theory and Social Change**
Problems and revisions
Hasse Ekstedt and Angelo Fusari

132 **The Practices of Happiness**
Political economy, religion and wellbeing
Edited by John Atherton, Elaine Graham and Ian Steedman

133 **The Measurement of Individual Well-Being and Group Inequalities**
Essays in memory of Z. M. Berrebi
Edited by Joseph Deutsch and Jacques Silber

134 **Wage Policy, Income Distribution, and Democratic Theory**
Oren M. Levin-Waldman

135 **The Political Economy of Bureaucracy**
Steven O. Richardson

136 **The Moral Rhetoric of Political Economy**
Justice and modern economic thought
Paul Turpin

137 **Macroeconomic Regimes in Western Industrial Countries**
Hansjörg Herr and Milka Kazandziska

138 **The Political Economy of the Environment**
Edited by Simon Dietz, Jonathan Michie and Christine Oughton

139 **Business Ethics and the Austrian Tradition in Economics**
Hardy Bouillon

140 **Inequality and Power**
The economics of class
Eric A. Schutz

141 **Capital as a Social Kind**
Definitions and transformations in the critique of political economy
Howard Engelskirchen

142 **Happiness, Ethics and Economics**
Johannes Hirata

143 **Capital, Exploitation and Economic Crisis**
John Weeks

144 **The Global Economic Crisis**
New perspectives on the critique of economic theory and policy
Edited by Emiliano Brancaccio and Giuseppe Fontana

145 **Economics and Diversity**
Carlo D'Ippoliti

146 **Political Economy of Human Rights**
Rights, realities and realization
Bas de Gaay Fortman

146 **Robinson Crusoe's Economic Man**
A construction and deconstruction
Edited by Ulla Grapard and Gillian Hewitson

147 **Freedom and Happiness in Economic Thought and Philosophy**
From clash to reconciliation
Edited by Ragip Ege and Herrade Igersheim

148 **Political Economy After Economics**
David Laibman

149 **Reconstructing Keynesian Macroeconomics Volume 1**
Partial perspectives
Carl Chiarella, Peter Flaschel and Willi Semmler

150 **Institutional Economics and National Competitiveness**
Edited by Young Back Choi

151 **Capitalist Diversity and Diversity within Capitalism**
Edited by Geoffrey T. Wood and Christel Lane

152 **The Consumer, Credit and Neoliberalism**
Governing the modern economy
Christopher Payne

153 **Order and Control in American Socio-Economic Thought**
Social scientists and Progressive-Era reform
Charles McCann

154 **The Irreconcilable Inconsistencies of Neoclassical Macroeconomics**
A false paradigm
John Weeks

155 **The Political Economy of Putin's Russia**
Pekka Sutela

156 **Facts, Values and Objectivity in Economics**
José Castro Caldas and Vítor Neves

157 **Economic Growth and the High Wage Economy**
Choices, constraints and opportunities in the market economy
Morris Altman

158 Social Costs Today
Institutional analyses of the present crises
Edited by Wolfram Elsner, Pietro Frigato and Paolo Ramazzotti

159 Economics, Sustainability and Democracy
Economics in the era of climate change
Christopher Nobbs

160 Organizations, Individualism and Economic Theory
Maria Brouwer

161 Economic Models for Policy Making
Principles and designs revisited
S. I. Cohen

162 Reconstructing Keynesian Macroeconomics Volume 2
Integrated approaches
Carl Chiarella, Peter Flaschel and Willi Semmler

163 Architectures of Economic Subjectivity
The philosophical foundations of the subject in the history of economic thought
Sonya Marie Scott

164 Support-Bargaining, Economics and Society
A social species
Patrick Spread

165 Inherited Wealth, Justice and Equality
Edited by Guido Erreygers and John Cunliffe

166 The Charismatic Principle in Social Life
Edited by Luigino Bruni and Barbara Sena

167 Ownership Economics
On the foundations of interest, money, markets, business cycles and economic development
Gunnar Heinsohn and Otto Steiger; translated and edited with comments and additions by Frank Decker

168 Urban and Regional Development Trajectories in Contemporary Capitalism
Edited by Flavia Martinelli, Frank Moulaert and Andreas Novy

169 Social Fairness and Economics
Economic essays in the spirit of Duncan Foley
Edited by Lance Taylor, Armon Rezai and Thomas Michl

170 Financial Crisis, Labour Markets and Institutions
Edited by Sebastiano Fadda and Pasquale Tridico

171 Marx and Living Labour
Laurent Baronian

172 A Political Economy of Contemporary Capitalism and its Crisis
Demystifying finance
Dimitris P. Sotiropoulos, John Milios, and Spyros Lapatsioras

A Political Economy of Contemporary Capitalism and its Crisis

Demystifying finance

Dimitris P. Sotiropoulos, John Milios, and Spyros Lapatsioras

Routledge
Taylor & Francis Group
LONDON AND NEW YORK

First published 2013
by Routledge
2 Park Square, Milton Park, Abingdon, Oxfordshire OX14 4RN

Simultaneously published in the USA and Canada
by Routledge
711 Third Avenue, New York, NY 10017

First issued in paperback 2014

Routledge is an imprint of the Taylor & Francis Group, an informa business

British Library Cataloguing in Publication Data
A catalogue record for this book is available from the British Library

Library of Congress Cataloging in Publication Data
Sotiropoulos, Dimitris
A political economy of contemporary capitalism and its crisis: demystifying finance / Dimitris P. Sotiropoulos, John Milios, and Spyros Lapatsioras.
pages cm
Includes bibliographical references and index.
1. Capitalism. 2. Financial crises. 3. Finance. I. Milios, John. II. Lapatsioras, Spyros. III. Title.
HB501.S777 2013
330.12'2–dc23 2012049792

ISBN 978-0-415-68408-8 (hbk)
ISBN 978-1-138-90111-7 (pbk)
ISBN 978-0-203-77129-7 (ebk)

Typeset in Times New Roman
by Wearset Ltd, Boldon, Tyne and Wear

Contents

Illustrations

Figures

Tables

Acknowledgments

This book owes debts to several people who in international meetings and conferences (both political and academic) have assisted in the development of our arguments when they were still in the making. We would also like to thank the Political Economy Research Group (PERG) at Kingston University (Paul Auerbach, Iren Levina, Simon Mohun, Engelbert Stockhammer, and Julian Wells) for suggestions and criticisms that have contributed to the improvement of the quality of our work. Finally, our students – an audience willing to discuss and challenge our ideas at their very first stage – are gratefully acknowledged. A special mention is also owed to David Gorman for having improved the style of the manuscript.

Introduction

The recent financial crisis is without precedent in the post-war period, a fact acknowledged by the majority of economists. At the same time, the crisis is a "marginal moment," which unveils and helps us rethink the workings of contemporary capitalism. The latter is mostly grasped under the term of financialization in relevant discussions.

A crucial aspect of almost all contemporary heterodox approaches is the idea that the hegemony of neoliberalism, and of the globalized financial sector of the economy, produces a peculiarly predatory version of capitalism, one with inherent tendencies towards crisis. In the relevant economic literature the term financialization denotes the phenomenon of the increasing importance of financial markets, financial motives, financial institutions, and financial elites in the operation of the economy and its governing institutions, both at the national and international level.

Hence, for a Keynesian-like argumentation, neoliberalism is an unjust (in terms of income distribution), unstable, anti-developmental variant of capitalism whose direct consequence is a contraction of workers' incomes and proliferation of speculation. This general perspective also seems to be prevalent in Marxist discussions. For a number of theoreticians influenced by Marxism, two strains have been present: either neoliberal capitalism has not succeeded in restoring the profitability of capital (the rate of profit) to high levels, that is to say to levels satisfactory for dynamic capitalist accumulation or, contrarily, it has gone too far in this direction (high profits), leaving the working class with incomes insufficient for consuming the social product. In this fashion, capitalism appears to be entrapped (either since the mid 1970s or at some later point) in a perennial crisis, the end of which is not readily visible. The result of this process is that large sums of capital are unable to find outlets for investment, thus either engendering "bubbles," or underpinning ineffective policies of forced accumulation that depend on lending and debt.

In this book, we intend to embark upon a comprehensive assessment of the above-mentioned views; to specify their analytical origins and their capability for interpreting reality. Marx's analysis is revisited in an effort to show that his original system of categories can serve as a comprehensive framework for the interpretation of the developments in contemporary financial markets.

We intend to show that the great majority of heterodox approaches, although they doubtless reflect significant aspects of present-day capitalism, are unable to provide a sufficiently inclusive account of the reasons for the neoliberal reforms and the resulting financialization of capitalist societies. Their basic weakness – and it is at the same time the link that holds them together – is that they represent the neoliberal formula for securing profitability of capital not as a question of producing profit, but as an issue concerned with income redistribution – one pertaining essentially to the sphere of circulation. In this approach, it appears that the developmental "ineptitude" and the instability of present-day capitalism are the result of certain "insatiability," or at any rate of bad regulation, in the relations governing income distribution.

In this book, we treat financialization as an organic development, and not as a distortion within capitalist production: the concomitant analysis here of the treatment of labor and capital in contemporary capitalism will be in sharp contrast to typical heterodox approaches. Modern finance is not unrealistic, hypertrophic and dysfunctional. In this sense, we clearly differentiate ourselves from those who believe that the current global financial situation is about speculation and then express concern at the growing separation of finance from the "real" economy. Perceiving financialization as an innately capitalist process, we intend to explore the ways in which it serves as a context for the organization of capitalist power relations.

Financialization and derivatives markets are not only about intensive assessment and information gathering. The valuation process carried out by financial markets has important consequences for the organization of capitalist power relations. From our viewpoint this is the basic message of Marx's theory. Financialization has to do with how this valuation reinforces and strengthens the implementation of the tendencies of capital. Financialization has been developed as a power technology, to be superimposed on social power relations for the purpose of organizing them and reinforcing their strength and effectiveness.

When Marx attempted to describe the social nature of financial markets, he introduced the concept of "fictitious capital" and spoke of fetishism. He wanted to draw our attention to the fact that capital assets are reified forms of appearance of the social relations of capital. They are in effect structural representations of capitalist relations, objectified perceptions which obscure the class nature of capitalist societies while, at the same time, signaling and calling forth the proper mode of behavior required for the effective reproduction of capitalist power relations.

Financialization embodies a range of institutions, procedures, reflections, and strategies that make possible the accomplishment (not without contradictions) of fundamental targets in the context of existing social relations. This is just another way of expressing Marx's discussion of the commodification of social relationships. Financial markets have the dual function of assessing and effectively organizing individual economic actors *and* at the same time promoting a particular form of financing. Derivatives and all "exotic" modern financial devices and innovations are the necessary precondition for the implementation of financialization. They introduce a formative perspective on actual concrete risks, making them commensurate with each other and reducing their heterogeneity to a singularity. Their reality as values – the very fact that they are commodities with a price, that is to say economic objects always already quantifiable – makes possible the commensuration of heterogeneous concrete risks. In other words, their reality as commodities secures an abstraction from the real inequality of concrete risks, reducing them to expressions of a single social attribute: abstract risk. In this sense, they monitor and control the terms and the reproduction trajectories of the contemporary capitalist relation, evaluating and endeavoring to predict (albeit imperfectly) the course of the class struggle, forestalling events that would be unfavorable from the viewpoint of capital.

Financialization is thus not the result of some fatal and persistent inability of capitalism to restore profitability or to realize surplus-value. The contemporary crisis is in fact the outcome of an active unfolding of the class struggle within the confines of contemporary social forms. The explosion of financial derivatives and the innovating forms of risk management have helped to fuel the crisis. If financialization and derivatives are to be regarded as independent determinants of changes in the contemporary world, they should rather be seen as innovations engendering new kinds of rationality for the promotion of exploitation strategies based on the circuit of capital, rather than as aberrations or dysfunctional developments impeding the development of the "real" economy. The new rationalities of financialization presume an attitude of compliance with the laws of the capitalist system. Strange to say, these new rationalities systematically push for an underestimation of risks. Contemporary capitalism is caught in this exhausting tension between the need to be "efficient" and the underestimation of risks.

In Part I of the book ("The long tradition of finance as a counter-productive activity in heterodox thinking: a Marxian appraisal") we propose to conduct a critical review of the major approaches to finance as a point of departure for the formulation of our own theoretical analysis. The outline of this part demonstrates to some extent the intentions of our analysis in this book. It traces in Ricardo's intervention patterns of thinking and lines of reasoning, which were to be rediscovered by Veblen and Keynes in light of new institutional developments that accompanied capitalism during the Great Depression of 1929. The same outline also sums up an interpretation of capitalism, which characterizes many recent radical approaches. The idea of "the absentee owner who appropriates income from the productive industrial community in the form of rent based on the legal condition of private property" summarizes the basic insight that is common to the above-mentioned tradition.

Chapter 1 ("The parasitic absentee owner in the Keynes–Veblen–Proudhon tradition") includes a critical presentation of a long heterodox tradition, whose roots are to be traced in the nineteenth century on the role of finance. Chapter 2 ("Ricardian Marxism and finance as unproductive activity") critically discusses the Ricardian interpretation of Marx's monetary theory of value and capital, focussing on Rudolf Hilferding's writings. In Chapter 3 ("Is finance productive or 'parasitic'?") we introduce the main thesis of our theoretical research in the context of Marx's oeuvre, namely that finance is not a sophisticated kind of usury, but a development in line with the spirit of capitalism.

In Part II of the book ("Financial innovation, money, and capitalist exploitation: a short detour in the history of economic ideas") we embark on a critical interrogation of fundamental theses posited by the heterodox, mainstream, and Marxist theoretical approaches to the role of finance. We examine the potential of each approach to provide an insight into the historical and contemporary tendencies of capitalism. We further focus on Marx's unique theoretical problematic, which introduced a new research field that allows us to understand the social nature of contemporary changes in the financial sphere. By contrast, mainstream economic reasoning always finds it difficult to think seriously about finance properly, incorporating it into economic theory in general, and specifically into explanations for instability and crises in capitalism.

Chapter 4 ("Derivatives as money?") challenges Rudolf Hilferding's early approach according to which derivatives shall be regarded as a new form of money. Chapter 5 ("Finance, discipline and social behavior: tracing the terms of a problem that was never properly stated") revisits certain works of Proudhon, Hayek, von Mises, Lange, and Keynes in order to highlight the role of finance for the consolidation of capitalist power. Our main conclusion is that finance is not so much about forecasting the future but about disciplining the present, even if the latter passes through the estimation of future outcomes.

Part III of the book ("Rethinking finance: a Marxian analytical framework") draws upon the argumentation of the two previous parts in order to theoretically systematize the analysis of contemporary capitalism. It shows how financialization reinforces and strengthens capitalist power and how it establishes competitive conditions for the valorization of capital and the organization of neoliberal finance. At the same time, we investigate its immanent contradictions and we explain why instability and efficiency are but two different sides on the same coin in contemporary capitalism.

Chapter 6 ("Episodes in finance") revisits major episodes in the development of financial markets. The chapter provides some preliminary illustrations of the crucial role of the state in consolidating the workings of the financial sphere. Chapter 7 ("Fictitious capital and finance: an introduction to Marx's analysis [in the third volume of *Capital*]") analyzes developments in contemporary capitalism in light of Marx's category of fictitious capital. The latter is "fictitious," not in the sense of imaginary detachment from real conditions of production, as is usually suggested, but *in the sense that it reifies capitalist production relations*: *it is capital's form of existence*. From this point of view, contemporary capitalism comprises a historically specific form of the organization of capitalist power wherein governmentality through financial markets acquires a crucial role. In Chapter 8 ("Financialization as a technology of power: incorporating risk into the Marxian framework") we discuss why securitization of debt has become an important process and how it has contributed both to the emergence of the contemporary credit system and to its current crisis. We further explain how financialization and derivatives markets have made possible a thorough "scrutiny" of financial assets by establishing a *universal way* of interpreting and understanding reality from the viewpoint of risk. In this context, we defend the thesis that the function of finance is to represent and make commensurate a series of class conflicts and other events (already identified as risks), which are involved in the capitalist valorization in general.

Part IV of the book ("The crisis of the Euro area") focusses on the Euro area as an illustrative example of the workings of contemporary capitalism, thus clarifying the argumentation of the previous parts. The strategy of the euro is analyzed as a mechanism for continuously exerting pressure for the reorganization of labor in the various member-countries. In this context, we show how tensions in the financial markets have consolidated and focussed neoliberal reactions to issues surrounding capital–labor relations and how the presence of these financial structures at their present level of sophistication has aided state power in the implementation of policies favoring the interest of capital.

Chapter 9 ("Towards a political economy of monetary unions: revisiting the crisis of the Euro area") deals with the structure of the Euro area. Our analysis defends the thesis that the persistent imbalances within the latter are primarily financial account imbalances. They are the result of high growth rates in the "peripheral" European economies, accompanied by both a rapid reduction in the cost of domestic borrowing and a significant inflow of foreign savings to these countries: the imbalances do not result from any fundamental deficit in competitiveness. In the last instance, current account imbalances are the result of the development of class struggle in the context of a set of symbiotic relations within the EMU (European Monetary Union). Chapter 10 ("European governance and its contradictions") concludes this last part of the book by focussing on the class character of the neoliberal agenda in the European unification process.

Finally the "Conclusion" completes the book by recapitulating our theoretical argument. We focus especially on the tension between Marx's theoretical system of the Critique of Political Economy and the views that emerge out of the major heterodox discourses on crisis and finance. We also sketch the outline of a general political agenda.

Part I

The long tradition of finance as a counter-productive activity in heterodox thinking

A Marxian appraisal

1 The parasitic absentee owner in the Keynes–Veblen–Proudhon tradition

1 Introduction

This chapter is an introduction to the main theme of this book. It discusses how the workings of finance are treated within the non-Marxist heterodox tradition of Keynes, Veblen and Proudhon. It returns to the original sources in order to sketch the general outline of their analytical problematic.

The idea of "the absentee owner who appropriates income from the productive industrial community in the form of rent based on the legal condition of private property" summarizes the basic insight that is common to the above-mentioned interventions. This insight is also widely accepted in contemporary discussions of the nature of capitalism that do not explicitly refer to or draw upon the above authors. At the same time, the very same idea can be easily ascribed to the approach of Ricardo. In this sense, Veblen, Keynes and/or Proudhon can be seen to apply already established arguments in the field of political economy to the analysis of financial development and innovations of the first quarter of the twentieth century.

The argument of this chapter also points out that many of today's radical ideas, both in theory and politics, may simply be trivial replicas of much older patterns of thinking. It also summarizes the trains of thought, which cannot be considered as particularly Marxian in origin. This will help clarify the analysis of the subsequent chapters of this book.

2 Reloading Ricardo

Not many scholars in the history of economic thought have been proved to be so seductive as David Ricardo. He continued a line of reasoning which was first developed by Adam Smith, based on the labor theory of value (we should mention that the work of Smith was richer and more integrated as theoretical intervention but with more contradictions and ambivalences with regard to the labor content of value).[1] To be brief, the concept of value in its Smithian version of "labor expended" (on the production of a commodity) can be summarized in the following theses.

- Thesis 1: Labor is the only source of value (throughout the history of humankind).[2]

  The Ricardian interpretation takes labor to be the transhistorical source of social wealth (see Postone 2003: 59). This insight is analytically substantial and has many crucial implications for the organization of the discourse of classical political economy. Value is considered as an *organic property* of all commodities (a qualitative feature of them), which derives from the fact that they are the products of human labor. This has an immediate outcome:
- Thesis 2: The possessing classes (i.e., capitalists and landowners) appropriate a part of the value produced by the laborer.

  Smith was indeed more explicit than Ricardo about this consequence.[3] The incomes of the possessing classes are derived from the value of the totality of commodities produced by the laborers during a certain period of time. This suggestion implies a critique of the capitalist system (a critique that neither Smith nor Ricardo was brave enough to push it to its limits), which focuses on the mode of distribution and appropriation of labor and its products. This is so because both capitalist profit and ground rent have the same social nature: deductions from expended labor to the benefit of an economic agent *external* to the production process. Like Smith, Ricardo devoted many pages in his writings to analyzing the different distributional economic mechanisms and "laws" that characterize the magnitudes of profit (uniform rate of profit) and rent (absolute or differential rent).[4] Nevertheless, the social base of both profit and rent remains apparently the same: the expropriation of labor. Neither does the landowner nor the capitalist make any "real" contribution to the production process. If rent is created by a monopoly over a scarce factor of production, then in quite the same manner, profit is created out of the monopolization of the means of production. It turns out that the criteria that distinguish capitalist profit from ground rent are much less evident than is normally believed. In an alternative formulation we can thus remark that:
- Thesis 3: Capitalist profit has the form of an *absolute rent* expropriating a share of the wealth produced by others.

  Absolute rent is the potential economic outcome of the landowner's legal proprietorship of the land. In this sense, capitalist profit is indeed a form of absolute rent since it can be seen as the potential economic outcome of the capitalist's legal proprietorship of means of production. It is quite clear that in this line of reasoning, "the social relations that characterize capitalism are seen as extrinsic to labor itself" (Postone 2003: 58). The power of capitalists emanates from, and is kept in place by, the particular legal structure of the property relations. The core of the capitalist organization of society is the legal institution of private property. In this sense, profit and rent are the results of the income (labor) redistribution that characterizes the era of private property (and every form of it):
- Thesis 4: The essence of profit and ground rent emanates from and is interlinked with the institution of private property.

To finish our general sketch of the Ricardian problematic,[5] there still remains a final point. It is rather evident in the above remarks that capital and land have become scarce resources, from the very fact that they bear a price. We have to stress that this category of "scarcity" is different from the neoclassical one. Capital and land are scarce due to the institution of private property, which enables the possessing classes to appropriate as income a part of total social labor. The greater the social strength of these classes, the greater the quantity of expropriated labor, and the greater the scarcity of capital and land. This is a form of scarcity that stems from the conflicting nature of income distribution and from the fact that social relations are conceived as extrinsic to labor. Smith and Ricardo never explicitly refer to this type of scarcity. This is not a natural scarcity but a socially acquired one, regardless of whether capital or land are limited in quantity or subjected to other subjective restraints (willingness to save etc.).[6] This is our final remark:

- Thesis 5: Rent and profit (itself a particular kind of rent) render the means of production (capital and land) scarce. This is a socially imposed type of scarcity, which results from the conflicting nature of income distribution.

The outline of this section demonstrates, to some extent, the intentions of our analysis in this book. In Ricardo's intervention it traces patterns of thinking and lines of reasoning, which were to be rediscovered by Veblen and Keynes in the light of the new institutional developments that accompanied capitalism during the Great Depression of 1929. The same outline also sums up an interpretation of capitalism that characterizes many recent radical approaches, such as those of Negri (2010), Hardt (2010) and Zizek (2012) (according to these, contemporary capitalism is marked by a shift from profit to rent). It seems that the Ricardian framework in its most general reading is far more influential in the field of political economy than is usually thought.

3 Veblen and Keynes in the era of common stock finance

3.1 The "cult" of common stocks

What is actually missing from the above Ricardian framework is some explicit reference to the workings of the financial system. Ricardo was actively engaged in the monetary debates of his time regarding the Restriction Act of 1799 on the side of the bullionists (the monetarists of the period).[7] Nevertheless, his general problematic, as presented above, can be easily detached from his monetarist arguments. It is not at all accidental that the majority of his faithful followers (many of them under the name of neo-Ricardians) explicitly adopted the Keynesian conception of effective demand.[8] It is not our intention here to get involved in the details of the relevant debates on Ricardo's thinking. We want, rather, to emphasize that his general problematic fits easily with other heterodox interpretations of finance. In this sense, both Veblen and Keynes were not left untouched by his theoretical seductiveness.

The financial system in the first decades of the nineteenth century was highly developed, especially in Great Britain. It contained a variety of characteristics, financial products and innovations that still dominate contemporary markets. For instance, stock options were not unusual contracts in trades and in fact concentrated a significant part of the financial transactions on the stock exchange; although they "were unenforceable at law, the broker's pledge – 'my word is my bond' – was deemed sufficient" (Chancellor 2000: 97). Indeed, brokers noted that the options trade was so prevalent in 1821 as "to constitute the greater part of the business done in the house."[9] The financial markets were powerful and state officials were more or less unwilling to curtail them. In our example, the Committee of the Stock Exchange decided not to ban options trading "after several brokers threatened to establish a rival exchange" (ibid.). Ricardo was certainly aware of these developments. He succeeded in making a real fortune as a famous and respectful financial broker before his early retirement, which allowed him to pursue a second career as an economist and member of Parliament.[10] During the Napoleonic Wars, Ricardo "amassed over half a million pounds" from loan contracting and speculation in the sovereign bond market (Chancellor 2000: 98; Neal 1990: 223–224). He built a delayed theoretical and political carrier upon this professional background, yet he did not focus on the theorizing of financial issues.

Finance found its place at the heart of the discussions of political economy at the start of the twentieth century. This was the era of the so-called big capitalist enterprise, which was associated with a growing interest in corporate common stock trading. Anonymous equity markets emerged in many capitalist centers worldwide. Prior to the twentieth century, US companies relied almost exclusively on bonds and preferred stock for raising capital (Miller 1992: 6; Baskin and Miranti 1997). The new period made clear the difference between shares and bonds as the former turned into a major investment vehicle, especially after the 1920s. This transition to a broader common stock ownership did not pass unnoticed in economic discussions (indeed, it became the main theme in the interventions of Hilferding, Veblen and Keynes). Nevertheless, other aspects of the financial innovation of the same period were left analytically untouched (see Chapter 4).

It was Chandler who coined the term "managerial capitalism" to describe this economic phase (Baskin and Miranti 1997: 167). Some of the data of the New York Stock Exchange (NYSE) highlight this qualitative trend:

> the increasing importance of equity is reflected in NYSE statistics: total annual share turnover rose from 159 million in 1900 to 1.1 billion at the height of the 1929 boom; the value of preferred and common stocks underwritten amounted to $405 million in 1910 and increased to $9.4 billion in 1929; and Standard and Poor's Composite Common Stock Index [...] zigzagged upward from 6.15 in 1900 to 26.02 in 1929.
>
> (Ibid.)

At the same time, in the developed capitalist world, the labor process underwent a profound transformation. This included: the increasingly widespread application of scientific knowledge in production, the concentration and centralization of capital, the reduction of the specific weight of non-capitalist sectors of the economy (especially in the production of consumer goods), the rise of domestic markets, the growth of big cities, and the numerical expansion of the new lower-middle class. The expansion of capitalist production in all the developed capitalist countries led to a corresponding expansion of foreign trade. All these changes in the labor and production processes were linked to corresponding transformations at the political and ideological level.[11]

This period was also characterized by the development of financial innovations primarily linked to the stock exchange. As we shall discuss in Chapter 4, developments in the stock exchange were not the only institutional innovation to be experienced by developed capitalist societies; organized derivative transactions were gaining ground but failed to attract theoretical interest, with a few remarkable exceptions. Developments in the stock exchange, combined with the creation of a small number of gigantic industrial enterprises in most industrial sectors (bringing together a large part of the production and in this way acquiring the capacity to function for a greater or smaller period of time as monopolies in the Marxist sense of the term – chiefly artificial monopolies[12]), led to the widespread belief that the high degree of separation of ownership and control in the big corporation had given birth to a brand new social class, the managerial class or the "captains of industry" (to use Carlyle's famous expression which had become common in that period). The analytical viewpoint that the managerial class comprises a distinct social class still remains a dominant idea in the heterodox discussions.

At the same time, the business world was gradually accepting the idea that developed capitalist economies had entered a new era of limitless prosperity (Chancellor 2000: 191, Hoffman *et al.* 2007: 57). This "new era" was believed to be solid and based on the ground of new neoclassical economic thinking and related institution building: the business cycle had been effectively tamed by the establishment of the Federal Reserve System in 1913;[13] a new "scientific" style of corporate management brought improvements in the productivity of the labor process and lowered the levels of inventory stocks;[14] the increase in corporate efficiency and wealth would induce investors to seek profit from these developments by focusing on corporate equities; and new specialized financial intermediaries were ready to insulate some of the risks of equity ownership "by offering financial management expertise and the chance to invest in diversified portfolios" (Baskin and Miranti 1997: 168).[15]

By the 1900s, the two mainstream schools of thought regarding the financial markets were already in place.[16] On the one hand, there were the adherents of what was to be called, many years later, the efficient market hypothesis (EMH). This hypothesis argues that all important information is incorporated in the movement of asset prices, while these prices are independent of any past historical trends (the random walk hypothesis in the sense that security prices have "no memory," and therefore no one is able to take advantage of pre-specified price patterns). This idea became a benchmark in modern financial theory when it merged with the statistical formulation of the random walk hypothesis; but, it was a dominant belief in the workings of finance long before. For instance, in 1881, a stockbroker (named Henry Clews) gave testimony to a legislative committee arguing: "speculation is a method for adjusting differences of opinions as to future values, whether of products or of stocks" (cited in Chancellor 2000: 187). On the other hand, there were those who followed "chartist" procedures to predict stock prices through close examination of the fundamental economic data or past price behavior.[17] For instance, Roger Babson, a famous investor who graduated in 1898 from MIT, believed that "by looking carefully enough at the information available on industrial production, crops, construction, railroad utilization, and the like [...] one could predict where the economy and thus the stock market were headed" (cited in Fox 2009: 17). At the same time, William Peter Hamilton, editor of the *Wall Street Journal*, was arguing that the stock market predicted the economy, not the other way around: "the market represents everything everybody knows, hopes, believes, anticipates" (cited in Fox ibid.: 17).

The timing was perfect for a systemic failure, which came in 1929. The development of financial markets, along with the outstanding nature of financial innovations, when combined with the belief that capitalism had reached a new era of limitless prosperity (at least on the other side of the Atlantic) would sooner or later cause a financial crash. This period provided the contour of the liberal form of capitalism. Despite the long break of the nationalist conflicts of the 1930s and the economic experiments in national "self-sufficiency," the Second World War and the little more than two decades of the Bretton Woods era, "financialization" of economic life became again the most significant trend in contemporary societies.

3.2 A brief comment on the nature of capitalism after the end of nineteenth century

All these stylized elements of so-called managerial capitalism were just some manifestations (important as they were for the organization of the circuit of capital) of a more radical shift in capitalist economies. For the developed capitalist countries, the turn of the century marked the passage from the historical stage of the *capitalism of absolute surplus-value* to the historical stage of the *capitalism of relative surplus-value.*[18] In brief, this historical phase (which begin about in 1870) brought about a number of decisive transformations in all the countries of developed capitalism. It signaled the end of a whole historical period during which capitalist accumulation had been based decisively on the mechanism of absolute surplus-value (lengthening of the working day, employment of women and children for extremely low wages, etc.). This capitalism of absolute surplus-value reaches its limits with the end of the nineteenth century, giving way gradually to the capitalism of relative surplus-value (profit maximization strategies based mainly on the production of relative surplus-value, i.e., through the increase in the productivity of labor the purpose of which is "to cheapen the worker himself,"[19] despite increasing popular consumption). The transformations accompanying this shift pertain not only to the production process but also to social reproduction as a whole, including the political and ideological levels. These transformations distinguish the form of capitalist domination even in the first period after the Industrial Revolution in the nineteenth century (the capitalism of absolute surplus-value) from the later form of this domination (the capitalism of relative surplus-value). Nevertheless, we must stress that *what was transformed was not the "laws" of capital accumulation corresponding to the capitalist mode of production (in other words, the structural characteristics of capitalist relations at all social levels), but the conditions and forms of appearance of capitalist relations in the historical perspective.*[20] In other words, it is a question of the historical transformation of the power balance and accordingly of the organizational forms of power in developed capitalist social formations.

The majority of the analyses of that period missed the basic point. The entrance into the era of the capitalism of relative surplus-value was perceived as a major departure from the capitalism of the nineteenth century, a *structural shift* in the workings of the capitalist system.[21] A variety of different analytical determinations were introduced to this end: managerial capitalism, the imperialist stage of capitalism, monopoly capitalism, etc. This perspective is still dominant in most heterodox discussions. Nevertheless, what was actually involved was the reorganization, through the historical process of class struggle, of the (economic, political, and ideological) capitalist relations of production, which are interwoven with the simultaneous expansion of capital.

3.3 Finance and the domination of the absentee owner in Veblen's analysis

We believe that Veblen's theoretical intervention is some sort of an *analytical prototype* upon which many contemporary analyses explicitly or implicitly draw. The above-mentioned elements of the Ricardian problematic are discernible in Veblen's type of reasoning as well.

There is one essential point in the understanding of Veblen's approach to the financial system: capitalism is necessarily associated with the institution of absentee ownership. This point is clear enough in Veblen's latter writings.[22] To summarize his argument, capitalism is indelibly marked by the institutions of private property and the wage relation. This argument indicates an unresolved cleavage between society's productive powers ("industrial work": making goods and services) and the organization of "business enterprise" (pecuniary profit seeking). With the development of capitalism this cleavage can only widen, denoting the detachment of business enterprise from the creation of "real" wealth. More precisely, this division became visible enough after the Industrial Revolution, when the capitalist owner, instead of a "master workman, [...] became a business man engaged in a quest of profits" (Veblen 1997: 58). As a major consequence, "industrial business became a commercial enterprise, and the industrial plant became a going concern capitalized on its earning-capacity" (ibid.: 59). The outcome is the emergence of a social regime that favors absentee owners and financial intermediaries. The social role of the absentee owner finds its complete form in the joint-stock company (which, as we mentioned above, was the dominant form of capitalist enterprise of the period). Now the production of the real wealth continues to be subordinated to the quest for profit, not from the revenues from commodity sales but from increases in the capitalized property and maximization of financial values:

> The goods market, of course, in absolute terms is still as powerful an economic factor as ever, but it is no longer the dominant factor in business and industrial traffic, as it once was. The capital market has taken the first place in this respect. The capital market is the modern economic feature which makes and identifies the higher "credit economy" as such. In this credit economy resort is habitually had to the market as a vent for accumulated money values and a source of supply of capital. *Trading under the old regime was a traffic in goods; under the new regime there is added, as the dominant and characteristic trait, trading in capital.*
>
> (Veblen 1958: 75, emphasis added)

We do not intend here to go into the details of Veblen's argument.[23] It is far richer and far more complex than presented here. Nevertheless, the mark of the Ricardian problematic is clear enough. Veblen adopted the latter, mostly emphasizing points 3 and 4 (see Section 2.1). He attempted to analyze the consequences stemming from the gradual development of the institution of private property. We could indeed say that he pushed the Ricardian argument to its furthest limits. If the development of the institution of private property gradually gave birth to corporations and absentee ownership, then capitalization and finance become central themes in economic theory.[24]

According to this line of thought, the dominance of the absentee owner imposes limits upon capitalist production, thus repressing the true productive potentialities of industrial organization. This is the so-called process of *sabotage*. Because of the underconsumption, which in Veblen's view necessarily accompanies capitalism (Veblen 1997: 111), the full utilization of society's productive capacities would lead to such prices and production levels that would annihilate profits and security values. This is why businessmen curtail the level of output, reduce the rate of utilization and sustain unemployment up to a certain level (ibid.: 97). At the same time, the *right* to sabotage production is the crucial social precondition which enables the legal owners to satisfactorily impose their terms upon the industrial community (ibid.: 66–67). Rather sarcastically, Veblen argues that "ownership would be nothing better than an idle gesture without this legal right of sabotage" (ibid.: 66). In this sense, he understands capitalist profit (the earnings of the absentee owner) as a form of an *absolute rent* – or *financial rent*, because capitalist earnings are a type of financial earning in the era of capitalization.[25] Since the absentee owner remains generally external to the production process and does not belong to the "industrial community," their income emanates from the expropriation of the "workmanship" of this industrial community as long as they retain "the power of sabotage at a distance, by the help of the constituted authorities whose duty it is to enforce the legal rights of citizens" (ibid.: 66). This type of rent is the outcome of the capitalist economy as long as the world of finance (capitalization and security trading) retains its power over the industrial community.[26]

Veblen's line of reasoning perceives the rise of *finance* as the *dominance of the absentee owner* (the legal owner of capital) that represses the productive capacities of industrial community (workers and technicians). In order for finance to function likewise there must exist a fundamental presupposition: *security prices must be totally disengaged from the real trends of capitalist production.* This is quite clear when Veblen sets out his critique of the shareholder's value maximization approach, which was dominant in the discussions of his time (see Veblen 1997: 86). In this context, the financial system, much more than carrying out a particular way of organizing the investment process, "interprets" capitalist reality in a way that systematically diverges from the real conditions of the capitalist production. Or to put it differently, the maximization of financial values is based on an arbitrary interpretation of capitalist reality that brings about unemployment and undercapacity of production factors:

> Accordingly, the amount of the business capital of a given concern, or of the business community as a whole, varies in magnitude in great measure independently of the mechanical facts of industry [...]. The market fluctuations in the amount of capital proceed on variations of confidence on the part of the investors, on current belief as to the probable policy or tactics of the business men in control, on forecasts as to the seasons and the tactics of the guild of politicians, and on the indeterminable, largely instinctive, shifting movements of public sentiment and apprehension. *So that under modern conditions the magnitude of the business capital and its mutations from day to day are in great measure a question of folk psychology rather than of material fact.* [...] But the earning-capacity which in this way affords ground for the valuation of marketable capital (or for the market capitalization of the securities bought and sold) is not its past or actual earning-capacity, but its presumptive future earning-capacity; so that the fluctuations in the capital market – the varying market capitalization of securities – turn about imagined future events.
>
> (Veblen 1997: 77, 79 emphasis added)

As will become evident below, this line of reasoning was to be found in Keynesian approach, as well.[27] In order to summarize it, we shall resort to Luhmann's analytical formulations.

According to Luhmann, with the aid of a developed financial sphere, "the economy is in a position to observe itself from the view-point of risk; that is to say to choose a highly specific form of self-observation" (Luhmann 2003: 183). This widespread process of self-observation is crucial and absolutely necessary for the valuation of the financial securities of different types – i.e., of property in Veblen's terms. In other words, we cannot have financial values in the absence of strategies for the representation of capitalist reality from the viewpoint of risk. In the above-mentioned context, the fully-fledged disengagement of the valuation of property from the "real" industrial conditions is based on the fact that the dominant representation strategies are "in great measure a question of folk psychology than of material fact [...] about imagined future events" (see above passage). Therefore, the detachment of property price from the underlying industrial conditions is the result of the organic inability of forecasts and interpretations to capture the "material facts" of production. This argument is in line with Luhmann's analysis. In the latter, as the financial system becomes more complex and opaque to itself with the institutional development of new innovations (let's say because of the rise of absentee ownership), investors have no other choice than turn to "observing observers" in order to estimate anticipated future events (ibid.: 187). This "observation of observation of the market is guided more and more by the prognoses of others and not only by the form in which it calculates its own business results" (ibid.: 185). The financial system begins thus to operate in the fashion of "second-order observation," where:

> everyone sees everything from this vantage point, bigger risks are incurred as participants imitate the willingness of others to take risks – although precisely this factor raises total indebtedness and thus total risk.
>
> (Luhmann 2003: 179)

Financial prices are potential sources of capital gains (or losses) without any direct relation to underlying "real" investment and profitability prospects. Economic life becomes fully subordinated to the fashion of *second-order-observation*, which also adds to the overall risk (leverage). In Veblen's argument, this development not only results in an unstable economic milieu but, most importantly, it reproduces an inefficient usage of society's productive capacities.

This analytical framework reflects the Ricardian problematic. To be sure, Veblen was not a follower of Ricardo. His writings adopted the institutionalist viewpoint attempting to grasp the nature of industrial organization in the beginnings of the twentieth century in the light of the new financial innovations. Nevertheless, the key points of the Ricardian problematic are apparent in Veblen's analytical speculation. He saw capitalist power as deriving from the institution of private property, capitalist profits as a type of absolute rent, and finance as a form of the sabotage of workmanship based on the financial pattern of second-order-observation. In other words, he offered a perception of finance which is very strong even in the contemporary discussions on financialization: the rise of finance is primarily apprehended as unrealistic, hypertrophic, and dysfunctional, a true distortion of some ideal capitalism.

3.4 Keynes and the parasitical "third" class: scarcity as social power

We will argue that within Keynes' argumentation too there is a strong Ricardian moment, in the sense described above. The limitation of space does not allow us to embark upon a thorough examination of Keynes' ideas. It is not our intention to add another chapter to the discussions of the importance of Keynesian "revolution" in economic theory. We will thus isolate the aspects of the Keynesian theory that have to do with the subject matter of this chapter and provide a general outline.

Keynes' reasoning converges with Veblen's insights. Modern finance becomes complex and invites second-order-observation. In this fashion, rentiers are spontaneously attracted by speculation without this being "the outcome of a wrong-headed propensity" (Keynes 1973: 155). Financial prices are potential sources of capital gains or losses without any direct relation to real underlying economic trends.

The *General Theory* was a product of the "red thirties": with "the Great Depression making the weakness of capitalism self-evident, thorough-going socialism was very prominent on the agenda of possible resolutions of the crisis" (Minsky 1975: 156). Nevertheless, Keynes explicitly rejected socialism as unnecessary, arguing for a "wise" alternative economic policy, which could deliver full employment within a capitalist regime. At the same time, contrary to the discussions that followed among the ranks of his followers after his death (we are referring here to the trend of post-Keynesian thinking), the general context of the labor theory of value evoked his sympathy.[28] Of course, he did not discover in the context of the labor theory a reliable method of price determination. He was also rather reluctant to explicitly admit that profits are the outcome of appropriation of the wage workers' labor contribution. However, he explicitly expressed his sympathy:[29]

> with the pre-classical doctrine that everything is *produced* by *labour* [...]. It is preferable to regard labour, including, of course, the personal services of the entrepreneur and his assistants, as the sole factor of production, operating in a given environment of technique, natural resources, capital equipment and effective demand.
>
> (Keynes 1973: 214)

Keynes found in the labor theory a simple way to link the changes in effective demand to the level of employment without the mediation "of vague concepts, such as the quantity of output as a whole, the quantity of capital equipment as a whole and the general level of prices" (ibid.: 43). He seems to understand very well the problem with the aggregation of these economic variables (which was to become the central theme in the debates over capital in the 1960s between neoclassical and heterodox economists – a debate that was triggered by the intervention of Sraffa).[30] Labor as a "physical" unit can measure the level of employment and associate it with variations in output quite independently of income distribution and the pace of economic growth (ibid.: 214). Hence, from the viewpoint of employment:

> to predict how entrepreneurs possessing a given equipment will respond to a shift in the aggregate demand function it is not necessary to know how the quantity of the resulting output, the standard of life and the general level of prices would compare with what they were at a different date or in a another country.
>
> (Ibid.: 44)

Keynes' general economic philosophy converged on that of Veblen. He respected the entrepreneur. He detested the absentee owner, whom he called the *rentier*, because they were a "functionless investor" whose income "rewards no genuine sacrifice" (ibid.: 376). He further viewed "the inequality of income that results from enterprise (mainly capital gains) as desirable, but the inequality of income that results from 'pure' ownership of wealth (the income of rentiers) as undesirable" (Minsky 1975: 151). In the *Tract on Monetary Reform* (1971: 4) (and subsequently in the *General Theory*), Keynes similarly conceives of rentiers (the "investing class" or the financial capitalists) as constituting a discrete unproductive social class, bracketed together with the other two "productive" classes, the entrepreneurs or top managers (the "business class") and the workers (the "earning class"), in a tripartite class stratification. The functionless rentier retains the "cumulative oppressive power" to exploit the scarcity-value of liquid capital (Keynes 1973: 376). Like Ricardo's landowner, the rentier enjoys incomes that do not correspond to any "real productive" contribution. In Keynes' own words "the owner of capital can obtain interest because capital is scarce, just as the owner of land can obtain rent because land is scarce" (ibid.). The rentier is furthermore believed to be mostly a newcomer to economic life. According to Keynes, a new configuration of capitalism emerged in the late nineteenth century. The large corporation, which is supposedly structured around a radical separation between ownership of the means of production and management of the production process, gave a new role to rentiers and financial institutions (ibid.: 147–150).

As mentioned above, Keynes did consider labor as the sole production factor (including in it the performance of managers). In his viewpoint, capital is not productive and returns yield to its proprietor because of its "scarcity":

> It is much preferable to speak of capital as having a yield over the course of its life in excess of its original cost, than as being *productive*. For the only reason why an asset offers a prospect of yielding during its life services having an aggregate value greater than its initial supply price is because it is *scarce*; and it is kept scarce because of the competition of the rate of interest on money. If capital becomes less scarce, the excess yield will diminish, without its having become less productive – at least in the physical sense.
>
> (Keynes 1973: 213)

The above argument may appear somewhat strange to those who are more or less unfamiliar with Keynes' analysis: How can the rentier be identified with

Ricardo's landowner as though he were in possession of a "scarce" production factor? Land scarcity may be taken as given, but capital does not come to resemble a scarce production factor unless the proprietor is achieving high returns on the battlefield of income distribution.[31] In this regard, capitalist profit is just a form of *absolute rent* as far as it is expropriated by the absentee rentier. It is the ruling role of the latter in the economy that renders capital scarce. In an economy in which capitalist enterprise is carried on largely with borrowed capital, "the payment of interest to the rentier-capitalist acts as a brake to progress" (Dillard 1942: 68). Keynes' speculation is rather straightforward: In an environment of high interest rates, *ceteris paribus*, the marginal efficiency of capital matches them before full employment is achieved. Therefore, capital is kept scarce and labor unemployed. This trend can only be reversed if lower interest rates bring the "euthanasia" of the rentier.[32]

This line of reasoning provides a picture of finance that is not different from Veblen's conception. Of course, Keynes' account of finance is much more complex and finally incomplete. Many key aspects regarding finance were left essentially implicit, subjected to "allusion rather than detailed argumentation in *The General Theory*. [...] The missing step in the standard Keynesian theory was the explicit consideration of capitalist finance within a cyclical and speculative context" (Minsky 1975: 129). Nevertheless, despite its incomplete character, the message of Keynes' analysis is clear: "it is finance that acts as the sometimes dampening, sometimes amplifying governor of investment" (ibid.: 130).

For Keynes, the role of financial markets tends to be complex in modern economies where the ownership of big corporations is separated from management: "they sometimes facilitate investment but sometimes add greatly to the instability of the system" (Keynes 1973: 150–151). Of course, it is on instability that the emphasis is placed. To understand the argument one must distinguish between *speculation* as "the activity of forecasting the psychology of the market" (i.e., the purchase of securities for resale at a different price), and *enterprise* as "the activity of forecasting the prospective yield of assets over their whole life" (i.e., the purchase of securities for long-term income) (ibid.: 158). Enterprise activity focuses on the observation of the real dynamics of economic fundamentals. Nevertheless, economic investors *are well aware* of the complexity of advanced financial markets: present information cannot be a reliable guide for future trends. According to Keynes (ibid.: 149) "our knowledge of the factors which will govern the yield of an investment some years hence is usually very slight and often negligible." It is thus entirely unrealistic to assume that the expectations embodied in investment decisions could be efficient in the mainstream sense. They depend on *animal spirits*, not on "the outcome of the weighted average of quantitative benefits multiplied by quantitative probabilities" (ibid.: 161).

Although the concept of "animal spirits" in the context of finance was not properly developed by Keynes, it is obvious that it is an extreme case of a structural heuristic rule. It can be better explained by Luhmann's analysis. *Since modern finance has become complex and opaque, second-order-observation emerges as the dominant pricing and investment pattern.* This is in line with Keynes' much cited description of the newspaper beauty contest.[33] If readers are asked to select the six prettiest faces from a sample of printed pictures, the average reader will decide on the basis of what they think the average opinion will be. As the financial system generates complex financial instruments, the monitoring of real trends becomes impossible because market behavior is guided more and more by general psychology. Exactly as happens in the story of the beauty contest.

3.5 Proudhon: a short digression to the history of the idea of the functionless investor

Keynes and Veblen (or even Hilferding; see Chapter 2) were not the first to highlight and criticize the figure of the absentee owner. This idea is much older in the history of economic thought. We do not intend here to embark upon a theoretical genealogy of the term (although it is of a great importance). Nevertheless, we must stress the long existence of a theoretical tradition which sees money (ownership) and its mismanagement as the root of all social evil.[34] We shall make just one crucial stop in the tradition: this will be Proudhon's intervention.[35] In what follows, we shall briefly focus on the aspects of his analysis that concern the content of this chapter.[36]

Proudhon experienced the revolution of 1830 in France and the revolutions of 1848 but not the Parisian Commune. He was a typographer, and a self-educated and very ingenious person. A highly influential figure in the socialist politics of this time, he became one of the fathers of contemporary anarchism. In his short debate with Bastiat between the end of 1849 and the beginning of 1850, Proudhon did not hesitate to challenge the latter's scientific authority, stating to him that "when you speak of Capital and Interest, [you] do not touch the question! [...] No, Monsieur Bastiat, you do not understand political economy" (letter 3.§15, letter 11.§3). In fact, it was the mainstream political economy of the time that invoked Proudhon's critique. Proudhon did believe that the existence of interest (along with any other *property income* such as rent) is the fundamental force driving the market economy away from the unity of interests and social harmony (letter 11.§47). Therefore, "the formula of revolution" is the abolition of the unearned income of interest and rent and the establishment of an economic order based on market competition and private property. This project of social reform would include "the organization of circulation and credit" in a way that absorbs "the function of the Capitalists in that of the Laborer" (letter 3.§2).

The essence of his insight is to make every product of labor equivalent to ready money, overcoming thus the scarcity of money and credit. According to Proudhon's thinking, this project would replace the Bank of France with a "Peoples' Bank" reducing the cost of credit.[37] Proudhon:

> did not propose to eliminate the private enterprise system. Market competition was to continue to regulate the prices of commodities. What he

> proposed to do was to set up the necessary conditions prerequisite to the smooth functioning of competitive forces.
>
> (Dillard 1942: 67)

For him, the major economic problem of capitalism was to be discovered in the workings of financial sphere.

In many respects, Proudhon's speculation resembles the thinking of Keynes and Veblen. The capitalist is regarded as a person external to production – as some sort of a functionless investor or a parasitic absentee owner. Proudhon did not object to private ownership of the means of production, only to the receipt of property income. *The problem is not the existence of capital* per se *but the very fact that it bears a price associated with interest payments*. This makes the mechanism of lending a robbery, a true distortion of the harmonic social relations. This is so because in the transaction of lending, *capital is not actually exchanged*. The owner never ceases to be the proprietor; and in addition to that, they still receive an extra income: interest. The latter represents "no positive product" on the part of capitalist; it "costs no labor" to them.[38] This is true for every type of property income, and for every type of rent. Profit is a type of absolute rent and the connection to the above-mentioned Ricardian frame is apparent. Accordingly, every form of rent is a robbery and capitalism thus should be approached as a well organized "conspiracy of Capitalists against Laborers" imposing an artificial scarcity upon money and capital assets (letter 5.§43).

This line of reasoning is very similar to Keynes' and Veblen's formulations. Capitalism is a robbery of laborers because absentee proprietors have rendered capital scarce by imposing an absolute rent on lending. The same principle holds for every type of property income, with Proudhon usually comparing the capitalist with the landlord (letter 7.§45). Interest derives from no genuine sacrifice, it is "*a premium on idleness*, the primary cause of misery and the inequality of wealth" (letter 3.§24; emphasis added). The owner of liquid capital lends it because:

> he neither intends nor is able to make it valuable to him personally, – because, if he should keep it in his own hands, this capital, sterile by nature, would remain sterile, whereas, by its loan and the resulting interest, it yields a profit which enables the Capitalist to live without working.
>
> (Proudhon: letter 3.§21)

This line of reasoning departed from the dominant abstinence or productivity theories of interest of the period and comes close to the Keynesian conception of liquidity preference.[39] In Proudhon's thinking, interest is not a reward for some productive contribution but a payment for not hoarding, *a reward for parting with liquidity*. In this interest price, the capitalist offers something that is useless for her. This income permits capitalists to live sumptuously without the slightest effort.

This conception of capital and interest perceives capitalism as an exploitation regime, which allows capitalists to spend a luxurious and effortless life on the basis of the productive contribution of the working class. Moreover, the payment of interest does not stimulate saving and accumulation. On the contrary, it restrains the economic development and capital accumulation:

> this Interest [...] is the identical grand forger which, in order to appropriate, fraudulently and without labor, products that it does not create and services that it never renders, falsifies accounts, enters surcharges and suppositions upon the books, destroys the equilibrium of trade, carries disorder into business, and inevitably brings all nations to despair and misery.
>
> (Proudhon: letter 11.§62)

Proudhon's remedy for the resolution of income inequalities was a capitalism with property, but without the income attached to it. Here is where his famous "People's Bank" comes into the picture (see letter 11). Gratuitous credit was the solution because it would abolish interest (we shall revisit this issue in Chapter 5). The connection of this argumentation with Keynes' system is more than obvious. Both writers "see in money and in the credit structure built upon them the principal cause of" economic inequalities and deficiencies (Dillard 1942: 67). They both "hold that private property in the means of production is fundamentally sound, and both feel that the" imposition of scarcity upon capital is the real root of the economic problem (ibid.). *The exploitative character of capitalism comes from the nature of profit as absolute rent, which renders capital assets as scarce.* The Ricardian problematic is once more effective in this line of thought.

4 Ricardo on Wall Street and the effect of second-order-observation

4.1 Ricardo on Wall Street

Ricardo experienced for himself the so-called Industrial Revolution. These were also the years of important changes in the financial markets. London replaced Amsterdam as the financial center of Europe (Neal 1990: 223; Acworth 1925: 81–82).[40] As already mentioned, Ricardo was at the heart of these institutional changes in finance as a successful broker. The Industrial Revolution was the beginning of a great economic expansion for England that also "changed corporate finance in fundamental way" (Baskin and Miranti 1997: 127). During the nineteenth century, markets for corporate debt were becoming anonymous (i.e., liquid) and corporate securities markets were becoming more cohesive and integrated (ibid.: 131). These developments considerably helped the capital-intensive industries of the period – the most important example here is the railroad industry. Nevertheless, this was not yet the era of the joint-stock company. The limited liability, which gave birth to the modern form of corporation, was to come many years later in 1855. Ricardo made a fortune speculating in the markets of British government debt during the Napoleonic Wars, but he was not familiar with the workings of the stock exchanges of London and Wall Street 100 years later. Neither was he familiar with so-called managerial capitalism.

Hence, Ricardo's capitalist was a person somehow involved in the production process. As Veblen would put it (and Keynes would agree), the "businesslike management of industrial concerns" has not shifted yet from "a personal footing of workmanship" (i.e., from a "footing of workday participation in the work done") to that of "absentee ownership and control" (Veblen 1997: 58, 59). In other words, the capitalist has not yet become a "functionless investor"; although distinct from worker, the capitalist is seen as an "internal" character in terms of the process of production. The "interiority" of the capitalist is due to the fact that there is not a high degree of separation of ownership and control: hence, the roles of the owner and that of entrepreneur or manager coincide to some extent. This does not change the nature of profits – if we are to accept the problematic of labor theory of value – as a form of "political" rent. But it does differentiate the capitalist from the landowner, since the former has a part in the organization of production and the expansion of productive capacity of the firm while the latter just exploits the scarcity of land to their own benefit.[41]

This argument was not formulated by Ricardo himself. It can be seen as an extension of his reasoning in order to grasp the changes of managerial capitalism. It fails to give a decisive answer as to why capitalist income differs in principle from that of landowners. The capitalist as manager has a productive contribution superintending the creation of use value and typically earns a wage-income. But at the same time, they still remain the owner who receives income for not a "genuine sacrifice" (as Keynes would argue). Why is this profit-income different from that of the landowner? Ricardo's answer was that capitalists *save*. Unlike landowners, they do not waste their wealth in luxurious consumption. They retain and reinvest their profits. And according to Say's Law, savings become investments and, as such, play a positive role in capitalist growth. Landowners were identified with unproductive consumption. Even the underconsumptionists of the period, such as Malthus, were unable to attack this grounded belief. Therefore, they rejected Say's Law by defending the usefulness of landlords' unproductive consumption (along with the consumption of civil servants and foreigners).

But what if rich landlords invest part of their wealth in financial markets? After all, it is impossible to consume all their income. In Ricardo's day, landlords used to invest a large proportion of their revenues from their lands in making cultivation more productive.[42] But it was rather unusual for them to commence an industrial enterprise, thus changing over to another social class. Nevertheless, in the era of common stock finance they could buy shares or other corporate securities, which "serviced" the investment of others. Their savings could easily find their way to production (or to "productive" consumption) through developed finance without the landlord being involved in the production process. In that case, landlords would become owners as money capitalists.

Absentee or functionless owners would look like Ricardo's landlords and vice versa; their incomes would not be any "real contribution" to production. In this regard, Veblen and Keynes do continue Ricardo's argument, expanding the latter so as to deal with the developments of their period. They actually endeavored to place Ricardo on Wall Street.

However, it is rather obvious that a sophisticated underconsumptionist critique of Say's Law could not be based any more on the conservative defense of landlords and priests (Malthus) or on the neo-mercantilist plea of the so-called "third persons" (Sismondi). What was needed was a new conception of investment and finance. More or less, both Keynes and Veblen moved in this analytical direction. In this, the former was more explicit than the latter. According to his comments, the old underconsumptionist "school of thinking" laid too much emphasis "on increased consumption" while there was "much social advantage to be obtained from increased investment" (Keynes 1973: 325). As the stock of capital increases, the latter becomes less scarce to the disadvantage of rentiers.

The new conception of finance had to rely on a criticism of the neoclassical theory of financial markets. It is from this period that two fundamental opposite discourses about finance emerge. The conflict between them embraces the underpinnings of contemporary debates as well.

4.2 The fundamental tension with regard to finance in the non-Marxian context

It may sound awkward, but the fundamental difference (the point of departure) between the mainstream neoclassical conception of finance and the heterodox one (which was presented in this chapter) *lies in the character of capitalist production.* Common ground in all the heterodox discussions so far was the fact that every class, which lives within the borders of the capitalist firm (belonging to the "industrial community"), is productive and useful socially while every "external" class has necessarily a counter-productive and parasitic role to play. In other words, heterodox approaches along the lines of Keynes, Veblen, or Proudhon firmly believe in the productive "spirit" of the industrial community (workers, technicians, or even managers) which, if left alone without being wrenched by any external intervention, could deliver the optimum economic outcome.

Davidson (2002: 188) is absolutely right to point out that according to Keynes' argumentation, only completely illiquid markets (that is to say, in the absence of finance) could be "efficient." In that case, owners would not be absentee, but attached to the industrial community; and "once investment was committed, the owners would have an incentive to use the existing facilities in the best possible way no matter what unforeseen circumstances might arise over the life of plant and equipment" (ibid.). Mainstream neoclassical thinking strongly rejects this viewpoint: according to it, the absentee owner enhances the productive capacity of society.

In the neoclassical universe,[43] most people do not work for money alone but for the creation of use values. Nevertheless, bankers, brokers, and absentee investors unfortunately do. This fact has important consequences for them because the outcome of their effort is not visible to them. They do not produce use values and they get no "ethical" reward and motivation out of this. Neither the broker (who sells, for instance, corporate bonds issued by an industrial firm that produces cars) nor the investor (who puts these bonds in their portfolio) actually sees the cars, and therefore they are deprived of the feeling of creating something tangible and useful to society (*sic*). In fact, they do not really care about the final product. The most direct measure of this financial sector's contribution is the money it makes in terms of profits and returns. According to the mainstream thinking, "this is where both the merits of arm's-length financial system and its cost arise" (Rajan 2010: 124).

Continuing in the mainstream thinking, the car-maker capitalist or the manager of a joint-stock company produces a useful thing along with profit. In this "real" sector of the economy the making of profits is directly linked to the making of use values. Many authors, from a heterodox point of view, use the Marxian formula: $M-C-M'$ (M stands for money and C for commodity), to make a similar point: the use value C as a mere mediator becomes subservient to increasing the initially invested money capital M. Money and use value need to travel on parallel trajectories in order to deliver employment, social coherence, and stability. Nevertheless, for the heterodox side of the story, this ideal image is deranged by the workings of finance. The financial sphere is captured by the dimension of $M-M''$: seeking for profits without the necessity of any mediation from the production of use values. The financial broker and the capitalist investor are at a distance from the production of use values and hence from the "real" consequences of their economic actions. *Their profits are the only indicator that society will benefit from their economic activity.* On a regular basis:

> competitive market mechanisms keep the search for profits on a track that also ensures it enhances value to society. This is the fundamental reason why free-market capitalism works and why bankers usually do good even as they do very well for themselves.
>
> (Rajan 2010: 126)

Nevertheless, this is not always the case since "the finely incentivized financial system" can "derail rapidly" (ibid.).

The practice of short-selling (many times banned in the wake of the 2008 financial meltdown) is a nice illustration that clarifies the mainstream line of reasoning. If a trader feels that a listed company is being mismanaged (and, thus, its internal industrial community underperforms to the cost of society), they can make a profit selling short its stock (in the jargon of mainstream finance they try to take advantage of the mismatch between the share price and the underlying economic fundamentals; see Chapter 7). In other words, they borrow and sell stock they do not own, "anticipating the price will go down" and that they "will be able to buy the stock back later at a lower price to close out his position at a tidy profit" (Rajan 2010: 124). While this trader's actions may be considered as speculative and aimed at making more money out of money in the fashion $M-M''$, mainstream theory thinks this trader's role is socially valuable in a double sense: they deprive poorly run companies of resources and at the same time make financial markets efficient by signaling that prices are not close to fundamentals (this is the basic premise of the famous efficient market hypothesis, EMH[44]). If the guess of the trader is correct and the company is being mismanaged, its stock price will be higher than its "intrinsic" value. Many other traders will take the same position, thus pushing the price down to its "real" value. The share prices will plummet and the company will no longer be able to raise equity or debt to finance its inefficient projects (and it could even be forced to close down or let itself be taken over):

> The trader who shorts the stock does not see the workers who lose their jobs or the hardship that unemployment causes their families; all he sees are the profits he will make if he turns out to be right in his judgment.
>
> (ibid.: 124)

Nevertheless, it is the traders' detachment from real production, their "very oblivion to the larger consequences" of their trades, that makes them effective and links their personal gains to the social benefit. With their intermediation, savings finally reach the "good" enterprises and the discrepancies between actual prices and intrinsic values are narrowed down. In this sense, financial prices reflect as a tendency all available information, and actual prices wander randomly about their intrinsic values.

On the other hand, if the trader is wrong, they cannot harm the firm. Other traders will take the opposite "bets," thus making the short seller lose money. Only when a short seller's belief reflects the economic fundamentals of the firm will they be widely shared, causing the share price to fall. Here is, therefore, the basic message of the mainstream theory:

> mismanagement is the source of the firm's troubles; the trader merely holds up a mirror to reflect it. Indeed, the more disconnected the trader is from the people in the firm, the more reliable a mirror he is able to provide.
>
> (Ibid.: 125, emphasis added)

This is indeed the big lesson of mainstream theory: quite contrary to the heterodox discourse, the distance between the absentee owner and the industrial community of the firm is the precondition of economic efficiency. The workings of finance make sure that there is always a close distance between prices and economic fundamentals. The socially useful role of absentee owners is based on their detachment from the "real" economy. This detachment sometimes causes and aggravates economic crises, but this is just an unavoidable side effect. The competition between different traders makes new information about economic fundamentals accessible to everyone by making it reflected in actual prices. The distance of finance from "real" use value production in the pattern of $M-M''$ is by no means a problem for society; on the contrary, it is the fundamental premise that assures the congruence of the distanced investor's interests with those of any other economic agent in a harmonious universe.

This illustration highlights the differences between the above-mentioned heterodox tradition and mainstream thinking. It primarily clarifies a crucial point: *the non-Marxian heterodox tradition cannot be assimilated by the neoclassical tradition only if the financial domain does not successfully mirror the economic fundamentals*. In other words, the heterodox analysis cannot make a self-standing analytical case in the absence of a "second-order-observation" type of reasoning. In the context of the above illustration, the pattern of second-order-observation would render short-selling as highly deranging, and the liquidity of the market as the ground for economic inefficiency.

5 Epilogue

In the rest of the book, we shall stress the uniqueness of the Marxian problematic, which does not fit into the debate described above. Finance will still remain our theme. Marx puts forward a different conception of finance because he has a radically different understanding of capitalist production. To put this differently, we shall argue that the non-Marxian heterodox tradition fails to grasp the essence of finance (and therefore of contemporary capitalism) because it lacks a proper theory of capital.

We have explained elsewhere that Marxian theory is immanently conflictual in the sense that it cannot exist and be developed except as an inherently schismatic discipline.[45] In fact, the existence of Marxism has always been interwoven with the formation of a variety of Marxist trends or schools, which, as a rule, are constructed on the basis of contradictory and opposed theoretical principles, positions, and inferences. This phenomenon is universal and observable in all countries where Marxism has taken root. However, we cannot recognise, as currents in Marxism, interventions that do not retain as a fundamental point of reference the theoretical problematic introduced into the field of thought by Marx. In other words, interventions which treat Marxism as a mere moment of differentiation within broader systems of thought (e.g., Keynes, Ricardo, Hegel, etc.), aspiring in this way to concoct an official genealogy, should not consider themselves as Marxian. In this regard, this chapter can be considered as a useful guide.

2 Ricardian Marxism and finance as unproductive activity

1 Marx's monetary theory of value and capital: a general outline

As has been argued elsewhere (Heinrich 1999, 2009, Milios *et al.* 2002, Arthur 2002, Postone 2003), Marx's theory of value does not constitute a "modification" or a mere "correction" of the classical political economy theory of value but rather establishes a new theoretical proposition, prefiguring a new theoretical object of analysis. Marx's notion of value does not coincide with Ricardo's concept of value as "labor expended." It involves a complex conjoining of the specifically capitalist features of the labor process with the corresponding forms of appearance of the products of labor, making it possible in this way for the capital relation to be deciphered. Value becomes an expression of the capital relation. The capitalist mode of production (CMP) emerges as the main theoretical object of Marx's analysis.

Marx constructed a new theoretical discourse and a new theoretical paradigm. He showed that the products of labor become values because they are produced within the framework of the capital relation (i.e., as "products of capital"). He further showed that value necessarily manifests itself in the form of money.[1] Money is thus the manifestation *par excellence* of (value and thus of) capital.

As "products of capital," useful objects (use values) are the bearers of value. They become commodities, property, which acquire material existence and are actualized in the market through the exchangeability of any commodity with any other, i.e., precisely through their character as commodities with a specific (monetary) price on the market. From the *Grundrisse* (1857–1858) (Marx 1993: 776ff.), to *Capital* (1867) (Marx 1990: 174), Marx insisted that value is an expression of relations that characterize exclusively the capitalist mode of production. Value registers the *relationship of exchange* between each commodity and *all other* commodities and expresses the effect of the specifically capitalist homogenization of the labor processes in the CMP (production for exchange and production for profit) (Milios *et al.* 2002: 17–23).

According to Marx, value is determined by abstract labor. But abstract labor is not an empirical magnitude that can be measured using a stopwatch. It is an "abstraction" constituted (i.e., acquiring tangible existence) in the process of exchange:

> Social labour-time exists in these commodities in a latent state, so to speak, and becomes evident only in the course of their exchange. [...] Universal social labour is consequently not a ready-made prerequisite but an emerging result.
>
> (Marx 1981: 45)

Marx starts by developing his theory of value (and of the CMP) out of an analysis of commodity circulation. To be able to decipher the form of appearance of value as money he introduces the scheme of the "simple form of value" in which, *seemingly*, a quantity of a commodity is exchanged for a (different) quantity of another commodity (x commodity $A=y$ commodity B). Classical economists regarded this scheme as barter; they further believed that all market transactions can be reduced to such simple acts of barter (which are facilitated by money because its mediation dispenses with the requirement for a mutual coincidence of needs).

Marx shows that what we have in this scheme is not two commodities of pre-existing equal value being exchanged with each other.[2] What we have is *one commodity* (the commodity occupying the "left-hand position," i.e., the *relative value-form*) whose value is measured in units of a different use-value (namely the "commodity' which occupies the position of the *equivalent* and so serves as the "measure of value" for the commodity in the relative form). The second "commodity" (in the position of the equivalent: B) is not an ordinary commodity (unity of exchange value and use-value); it plays the role of the "measure of value," of "money," for the first commodity. The value of the relative (A) is expressed *exclusively* in units of the equivalent (B). The value of the latter (of B) cannot be expressed, as it does not exist in the world of tangible reality:

> But as soon as the coat takes up the position of the equivalent in the value expression, the magnitude of its value ceases to be expressed quantitatively. On the contrary, the coat now figures in the value equation merely as a definite quantity of some article.
>
> (Marx 1990: 147)

In other words, the simple form of value tells us that x units of commodity A *have the exchange value of* y units of the equivalent B, or that *the exchange value of* a unit of commodity A *is expressed in* y/x *units of* B. The "simple form of value" as propounded by Marx measures only the exchange value of commodity A in units of the equivalent B.

From the analysis of the simple value-form, Marx has no difficulty in deriving the *money form*. He utilizes two intermediate intellectual formulae for this purpose: the *total or expanded* and the *general* form for expressing value. The latter form in this developmental sequence (the *general* form of value) is characterized by one and only one equivalent in which all commodities express their value. These commodities are thus always in the position of the *relative* value-form. Only one "thing" has come to constitute the *universal equivalent form of value* (Marx 1990: 161). In this sense, the first feature of money is its "property" of being *the general equivalent*. Thus the relation of general exchangeability of commodities is expressed (or realized) only in an indirect, *mediated* sense, i.e., through money, which functions as general equivalent in the process of exchange, and through which all commodities (having been inserted into the relative position) express their value.

Marx's analysis does not therefore entail reproduction of the barter model (of exchanging one commodity for another), since it holds that exchange is necessarily mediated by money. Money is interpreted as an intrinsic and necessary element in capitalist economic relations:

> Commodities do not then assume the form of *direct mutual exchangeability*. *Their socially validated form is a mediated one.*
>
> (MEGA II.5: 42)

In Marx's theoretical system there cannot be any other measure (or form of appearance) of value.[3] The essential feature of the market economy (of capitalism) is thus not simply commodity exchange (as asserted by mainstream theories) but monetary circulation and money:

> The *social* character of labour appears as the *money existence* of the commodity.
>
> (Marx 1991: 649)

Having defined value as a social relation, Marx argues that money does not only play the role of a "means" or a "measure," but also tends to take on the role of an "end in itself." Here we encounter a preliminary definition of capital, with the (provisional and "immature") introduction of the concept of *capital*: money functioning as an end in itself.

In order to be able to function as an end in itself, money has to move in the sphere of circulation in accordance with the formula $M–C–M$, where M stands for money and C for commodity. Due to the homogeneity of money, however, this formula is meaningless unless the contingency is one of quantitative change, i.e., increase in value. The circulation must involve the creation of surplus-value, in which case the formula would become $M–C–M'$ where M' stands for $M+\Delta M$.

But money can function as an "end in itself" only when it dominates the sphere of production, incorporating the latter into its $M–C–M'$ circulation, i.e., when it functions as (money) capital by implementing the capital relation. The exploitation of labor power in the production sphere constitutes the actual presupposition for this incorporation and this movement. *In the Marxist theory of the capitalist mode of production both value and money are concepts that cannot be defined independently of the notion of capital.* They contain (and are contained in) the concept of capital. *Being a monetary theory of value, Marx's theory is at the same time a monetary theory of capital.*[4]

The motion of money as capital *binds* the production process to the circulation process, in the sense that commodity production becomes a phase or a moment (albeit the decisive moment for the whole valorization process) of the total *circuit of social capital*: $M\!-\!C(=Mp+Lp)\ [\rightarrow P \rightarrow C'']\!-\!M'$, where C stands for the input-commodities: means of production (Mp) plus labor power (Lp), C'' for the output-commodities of the production process (P), which is finally realized in "more money" (M').

> Value therefore now becomes value in process, money in process, and, as such, capital. [...] The circulation of money as capital is [...] an end in itself, for the expansion of value takes place only within this constantly renewed movement.
>
> (Marx 1990: 256, 253)

Capitalist exploitation is not perceived as a simple "subtraction" or "deduction" from the product of the worker's labor but is seen as *a social relation*, necessarily expressing itself in the circuit of social capital and in *the production of surplus-value, which takes the form of making (more) money.* The question of the "measurement of value" can only be stated at the level of its forms of appearance, i.e., in monetary terms.[5]

Furthermore, the Marxian monetary theory of value allows for the comprehension of the social "endogeneity" and non-neutrality of money in capitalism. Money is not the representative of a commodity or a formal "symbol of value" (exogenously issued by a certain authority) but the "embodiment" of the capital relation. In terms of quantity, it is thus created in accordance with the process of expanded reproduction of this relation. Surplus-value is also conceived as a social relation, a result of (and prerequisite for) capitalist exploitation, which necessarily takes the form of (more) money, as the increment in value brought about by uniting the process of production with the process of circulation. This theoretical framework allows us to comprehend the functioning of the financial sphere as a process of "money creation" in accordance with the dynamics of the expanded reproduction of social capital, and also the fact that capital exists as a financial security, or, to use a Marxian terminology, the pure form of capital is fictitious capital. We shall elaborate on these issues in the following chapters of the book.

2 The prevailing "Ricardian Marxism" and Marx's ambivalences towards classical political economy

Despite the radical rupture of Marx's theoretical system (his monetary theory of value) with the classical labor theory of value,[6] the prevailing Marxist tradition portrays Marx's value theory as a continuation and completion of the classical one, specifically in the version formulated by David Ricardo. The assumption is that Marx's most important contribution to the labor theory is his analysis of the exploitation of the laboring classes by capital (appropriation of surplus labor) through the introduction of the notion of labor power and the elaboration of what makes it distinct from labor. It is characteristic that two of the historically most prominent Marxist theoreticians and political leaders, Lenin and Gramsci, had pointedly affirmed this alleged theoretical continuity between Ricardo's and Marx's value theory: "Adam Smith and David Ricardo laid the foundations of the labour theory of value. *Marx continued their work.* He rigidly *proved and consistently developed this theory*" (Lenin 1913, emphasis added). Moreover, "It seems to me that in a certain sense we can say that the philosophy of praxis [meaning Marxism] equals Hegel+David Ricardo [...] Ricardo is to be conjoined with Hegel and Robespierre" (Gramsci 1977: 1247–1248).

In the context of this tradition, value is defined as the quantity of (socially necessary) labor contained in a commodity, and surplus-value as the quantity of labor appropriated by the ruling classes after the laborer has been remunerated in keeping with the value of his/her labor power. It is worth mentioning here that the classical concept of value as a quantity of expended labor is by no means incompatible with the idea of exploitation, understood as the deduction to the benefit of the non-laboring classes (capitalists and landlords) of a portion of the value produced by the worker and contained in commodities (see also our comments in Chapter 1). Following Adam Smith, economists in the tradition of classical political economy had portrayed exploitation as *surplus labor* long before Marx formulated his own theory:

> There can be no other source of profit than the value added to the raw material by the labour [...]. The materials, the buildings, the machinery, the wages, can add nothing to their own value. The additional value proceeds from labour alone.
>
> (Thompson 1824: 67)

This dominance of the Ricardian notion of value among Marxists did, though, leave room for an alternative Marxist tradition that comprehends value and surplus-value as historically specific social relations: namely as the specific form assumed by economic relations, exploitation, and the products of labor in societies based on commodity production, i.e., capitalism. This alternative tradition emphasizes Marx's analysis of the *value-form* and money, above all in Section 1 of the first volume of *Capital*; an analysis which seems to have been neglected by all classical approaches to Marxian value theory. According to it, value and surplus-value are not transhistorical essences but historically specific social relations expressed and measured only through their forms of appearance: prices and profit. The approach is one of a "relationship interior in its effects" (Althusser and Balibar 1997: 188) or "causality through relations" (Roberts 1996, 119ff.):

> The fact that surplus-value is not a measurable reality arises from the fact that it is not a thing, but the concept of a relationship, the concept of an

existing social structure of production, of an existence visible and measurable *only in its "effects*."

(Althusser and Balibar 1997: 180)

By the same token, "value is not determined separately from, prior to, or independent of, its forms" (Roberts 1996: 119).[7]

Far before the intervention of Althusser, this alternative tradition is expressed in the works of Rubin from the 1920s (Rubin 1972, 2012). It can also be traced in the work of a number of Marxist authors writing prior to the consolidation of Stalinism in the late 1930s.[8] Nevertheless, we shall not elaborate on this issue.

The prevalence of Ricardian value theory (in its various forms) among Marxists is, to some extent, due to Marx's own theoretical ambivalences towards classical political economy that can be traced in his mature economic writings. At certain points of his works, mainly in Volume 3 of *Capital* (especially when dealing with the "transformation of values into prices of production"), Marx distances himself from the implications of his own theory (non-commensurability between value and price), making quantitative comparisons between values (measured in labor time) and production prices. Through mathematical calculations he attempts to "transform" the former into the latter. In this way, however tacitly, he retreats into the classical viewpoint according to which values are qualitatively identical to, and therefore quantitatively comparable with, prices. He accepts the problematic that two individual capitals utilizing the same amount of living labor, but different amounts of constant capital, will produce an output of equal value but (given the general profit rate) unequal (production) price. He then claims that in order to justify the theory of value, one has to prove that, at the level of the economy as a whole, the sum of values equals the sum of commodity prices, while at the same time the total surplus-value should be equal to the total profit (the so-called "double invariance principal"). The "transformation of values into production prices" aimed at providing that proof.

Marx now assumes a double system of measurement: (a) a unit of measurement of value (e.g., the labor-hour) which (b) is commensurate with the unit of measurement of prices (dollars or any other currency). In other words, exactly like the classics of political economy, he accepts that value can be measured independently of its forms, i.e., independently of (and abstracting from) money. The implication is that abstract social labor belongs to the world of empirically measurable objects, exactly like money. Thus, there emerges a second discourse in Marx's writings, one which adheres to the classical tradition of political economy.[9] Between the two discourses there exists a conceptual gap; they are incompatible with each other.

Few Marxists are, however, ready to accept the possibility of such contradictions in Marx's mature economic writings.[10] Contrary to Marx's monetary theory, the Ricardian version of value as "labor expended" cannot come to grips with the Janus-existence of capital as production means and as financial securities. It thus comprehends the financial sphere in terms of speculation, detached from "real" economy.

3 Finance as parasitism: Rudolf Hilferding's *Finance Capital*

One of the main implications of abandoning Marx's monetary value theory in favor of the classical (Ricardian) problematic of value as "labor expended" is the comprehension of finance as a parasitic activity. This result will be further clarified in the light our argument in Part III of the book. But in brief, we can understand it as follows. As the pricing of securities cannot be ascribed to the "quantity of labor expended in production," financial assets can only be grasped as mere vehicles of speculation and redistribution of existing wealth to the benefit of big (financial) enterprises. The deviation between market prices and labor values is seen as a distortion of the whole economic process adding to the instability of the system. At the same time, interest rate payments attached to financial securities are also seen as a deduction in the form of rent from the already expended labor value. As wages secure the subsistence of employees, the interest rate mostly squeezes profits and therefore is against "normal" capitalist activity (investment). This pits industrial capitalists or managers against the financial fraction and makes these two forms of capital quite asymmetrical.

This problematic which has overwhelmed heterodox discussions for more than a century can be traced in the intervention of Hilferding, whose well-known book, *Finance Capital* (1909), has been celebrated as a major contribution to Marxist theory. Hilferding's own intention was to deliver the fourth volume of *Capital* to the public. As already discussed extensively elsewhere,[11] Hilferding's line of reasoning radically departs from Marx's problematic in *Capital*. This theoretical effect has major implications for the analysis of the dynamics of capital.[12]

3.1 The abandonment of the concept of social capital

In plain terms, social capital is the concept of capital at the level of the capitalist economy as a whole. It is a complex term introduced no earlier than the third volume of *Capital* to embrace the hidden causal determinations of the capitalist system (the capitalist mode of production). These immanent causal relations of capitalist production – the structural *determinations* of capital – that govern the capitalist economy, transform the totality of enterprises ("individual capitals," in Marx's terminology) into elements of social capital in the sense that they situate the individual capitals within an economic milieu which then exercises a conditioning influence upon them. In this procedure, the role of competition is crucial and takes a very important twist. It becomes a determination immanent in the social nature of capital. This is very different from the concept of competition in the approach of classical political economy where it is rather a technical condition that regulates the flow of capital between spheres of different profitability. In Marx's analysis, competition makes it possible for the separate individual capitals to constitute themselves and function as social capital. Through their structural interdependence, that is to say their organization as social capital, the individual capitals, or fractions of capital, together acquire the status of a social class and function as uniform social force that opposes and dominates labor.[13]

By introducing the idea of "the elimination of free competition among individual capitalists by the large monopolistic combines" (Hilferding 1981: 301), Hilferding embarks upon a microeconomic approach, according to which the characteristics of the "dominant form" of enterprise (individual capital in the form of a big joint-stock firm) *shape* the whole capitalist system (the social capital), determining its patterns of evolution and change. This amounts to a reversal of the flow of cause and effect in the relationship between social capital and individual capital, constituting a *paradigm shift* within Marxian economic theory. What is important in this line of reasoning is not merely the details of Hilferding's analysis. The conception of competition as an unsound convention totally external to the capital relation, which furthermore can be eliminated by the combined action of the dispersed individual enterprises,[14] breaks the ground by sketching a radical departure from Marx's problematic. We encounter here a different diagram of the organization of capitalist power obviously dissociated from Marx's argument regarding social capital. This shift opens up the appropriate theoretical space for a different theorization of the capitalist phenomena similar to the general institutionalist problematic to be found in Weber, Veblen, Schumpeter, and Galbraith.[15] In what follows, we shall touch upon the consequences for the understanding of finance.

3.2 *Industry seized by finance*

Hilferding implicitly rejects the concept of social capital and hence embarks upon different questions and analytical priorities. In this regard, he posits himself safely within the historicist problematic. In *Finance Capital*, different fractions of capital are analyzed as pre-existing their unity as a ruling capitalist class. They are profoundly governed by *distinctive* logics and imperatives.

Commercial capital absorbs the operations of circulation from industrial capital; it becomes an independent section of aggregate capital; and, it yields "an average profit, which is simply part of the profit generated by industrialists in the process of production, that is, a *pro tanto* (proportional) deduction from the profit which would otherwise accrue to industrialists" (Hilferding 1981: 170). Circulation also requires a series of financial transactions most of which, along with the "business of keeping accounts," have been taken over by the banks. In this sense, the bank embodies the so-called money-dealing capital and the bank capital, which is the total loan capital available (ibid.: 170–174). According to Hilferding, "industrial, commercial, and money-dealing capital are distinct parts of social capital, which at any given moment *must have a definite relation to each other*" (ibid.: 176; emphasis added). At the same time, bank capital is "the money form of productive capital," which has been originated by bank loans.

The usage of the term social capital by Hilferding simply denotes the numerical sum of all individual capitals in the economy. This term has no other meaning and, of course, it is deprived of the theoretical content that Marx himself had given the concept. On the other hand, not all three capital fractions "produce profit" and, hence, they have different modes of functioning. Given this assumption, it becomes a primary theoretical target to discern the "definite relation" among them because *their unity cannot exist unless one is hegemonic over the others*. In fact, Hilferding was clear from the beginning that "the understanding of present-day economic tendencies" can only be accomplished when someone deals properly with the hegemonic unity between the different fractions of social capital (this is how we should read the introduction to *Finance Capital* in the light of the consequent analysis).

Without going into details, the basic idea of Hilferding's intervention runs pretty much as follows. During the "monopoly phase of capitalism," industrial concentration and the concentration of banking reinforce each other (ibid.: 223). As management has been separated from ownership – we must not forget that Hilferding lives and writes in the period of so-called managerial capitalism (see Chapter 1) – industrial and commercial capital tend to be completely owned by the depositors who are represented by the bank. According to this argument, bank capital becomes finance capital: precisely, "finance capital develops with the development of the joint-stock company and reaches its peak with the monopolization of industry" (ibid.: 225). This development amounts to a new hegemonic configuration within the "social" capital, this time rather counter-productive. We can see how this line of reasoning approaches other heterodox traditions of the same period (Veblen and Keynes).

Hilferding's point can be better understood when we focus on his marginal comments, which describe the transition of capitalism to its "latest phase." With the dominance of financial capital a cycle in the development of capitalism appears to be completed: Finance capital dominates as a *parasitic form of capital*, enjoying great income transfers from the profit-earning capacity of "productive" capital while repressing the latter (ibid.: 226). But industrial capital was not always the dominant form. It is only with the dissolution of mercantilism that "usurer's capital becomes subordinated to industrial capital" (ibid.: 226). We do not intend here to check the historical validity of these observations. We just want to present their economic reasoning. During this "subordination," money-dealing capital and bank capital perform typical functions of money and credit appropriate for the well-being of industry. We encounter here a unity in social capital under the profound hegemony of industrial capital. Nevertheless, things radically changed with the extension of finance and the new wave of financial innovation at the end of the nineteenth century. This development puts the money capitalist in a different position, undermining the above-mentioned nature of unity and challenging the hegemony of industry:

> The mobilization of capital and the continual expansion of credit gradually brings about a complete change in the position of the money capitalists. The power of the banks increases and they become founders and eventually rulers of industry, *whose profits they seize for themselves as finance capital, just as formerly the old usurer seized, in the form of "interest," the produce of the peasants and the ground rent of the lord of the manor*. The Hegelians spoke of the negation of the negation: bank capital was the negation of the

> usurer's capital and is itself negated by finance capital. The latter is the synthesis of usurer's and bank capital, and it appropriates to itself the fruits of social production at an infinitely higher stage of economic development.
>
> (Hilferding 1981: 226; emphasis added)

In the same manner, Hilferding also argues:

> In a developed capitalist system, the rate of interest is fairly stable, while the rate of profit declines, and in consequence the share of interest in the total profit increases to some extent at the expense of entrepreneurial profit. In other words, *the share of rentiers grows at the expense of productive capitalists*, a phenomenon which does indeed contradict the dogma of the falling interest rate, but nevertheless accords with the facts. It is also a cause of the growing influence and importance of interest-bearing capital, that is to say, of the banks, and one of the main levers for effecting the transformation of capital into finance capital.
>
> (Hilferding 1981: 103–104; emphasis added)

For the reader of this book so far, the sound of these passages is quite familiar. Finance is declared to be a predator that exercises its repressive function over the fruits of industry; its revenue is further compared to ground rent; its social nature is described as parasitical, resembling a form of neo-usury. And most importantly, finance *rules over* industry, accomplishing a different configuration of hegemony that ensures a different type of unity of the social capital. Over-extension of finance becomes synonymous with the ascendancy of its dominance over the productive capacity of society. It is here that Hilferding meets Veblen, Keynes and Proudhon in a context similar to the Ricardian one. Nevertheless, one can discover other aspects about finance in Hilferding's writings that are closer to Marx's argumentation. We shall return to this issue in Chapter 5.[16]

4 Developments upon Hilferding's argument

The argument that Hilferding's analysis was restricted to a very particular paradigm of finance – both temporally and geographically specified: Germany and continental Europe before World War II – is rather common in the literature. After all, in continental Europe, besides the trend towards monopolies in production (individual capitals being able to ensure for some time period an above average rate of profit, mostly artificial monopolies according to Marx's terminology, see Milios and Sotiropoulos (2009; Chapter 6)), it was indeed the era of J. Pierpont Morgan and Rothschilds, to mention two of the most famous bankers.[17] The "monopoly trend" encompassed banks as well, but there was also another important reason for the dominant presence of the big banks that escaped Hilferding's attention. The huge internationalization of capital and the ascendance of finance, which developed after the end of nineteenth century, made urgent the management of emerging new risks in a complex international milieu.

Where markets were restricted, successful banks were taking steps to safeguard their clients. Gaining reputation and winning investors' trust, they could organize a reliable risk management and make profits. They could mobilize capital from distant lands or funnel it to new industries; they could take over and reorganize old industries or create curtails; they could finance foreign governments; or they could sell protection during the repeated severe financial crises of the period.[18]

To use Hilferding's terminology, finance's control over industry can take two alternative routes as regards property relations: absentee owners can be represented either by banks or by themselves in open markets (Hilferding 1981: 224–225). Hilferding did not believe the second route had many chances; it turned out that he was wrong. Nevertheless, one could still use his line of reasoning with a slight twist in order to analyze contemporary finance and its putative predatory dominance over industry and/or labor incomes. There is, indeed, a group of Marxist scholars who are working in that direction.

Fine (2010), for instance, draws heavily upon Hilferding's reading of Marx. In brief, he commences from the thesis that besides industrial capital, the other forms of capital (namely, merchant capital and interest bearing capital) are defined by their *not* producing surplus-value (ibid.: 110). As each form of capital retains its innate functioning and objectives, prior to and outside their unity as social capital, their concrete articulation cannot be taken for granted but will always be a matter of hegemony. Fine does not formulate this explicitly, but it is pretty obvious in his line of thought. He sees contemporary capitalism as the result of a "disproportionate expansion of capital in exchange, through extensive and intensive proliferation of financial derivatives but also the extension of finance into ever more areas of economic and social reproduction, of which personal finance is a leading example" (ibid.: 112). Therefore, converging on Hilferding's reasoning as analyzed so far in this chapter, he comprehends neoliberalism as the capitalist regime that places great significance upon the "financial-speculative activities as opposed to industrial investment as an increasingly important source of profit" (ibid.: 113). In short:

> financialisation is underpinned by the quantitative expansion of interest bearing capital and its extension across the economy at the expense of restructuring of industrial capital both directly and indirectly through the broader modes of neoliberal impact upon economic and social reproduction.
> (Ibid.)

Fine understands financialization as the subordination of industrial investment to speculation and income expropriation, a regime wherein the domination of "unproductive" forms of capital have made economic activity prone to the search for profits in the sphere of circulation (commercial or financial), thereby shifting away from production (repressing the productive capacities of society). If there is an imaginary continuum that includes productive, commercial, money-dealing, and interest bearing capital, then neoliberalism is approached as the increasing shift of economic activity towards the "right" end, that is to say towards the auspices of finance.[19]

The same notion of finance as a predatory social process is dominant, in a slightly different line of reasoning this time, in the interventions of Lapavitsas and Dos Santos (see Lapavitsas 2009, Lapavitsas and Dos Santos 2008). Financialization is seen as having been developed in the background of the poor real accumulation since late 1970s. As a result, the capitalist class, and banks in particular, have relied on financial expropriation (mostly of workers) as an additional source of profit that originates in the sphere of circulation (see Lapavitsas 2009: 114, 126, 131, 140). The economic basis of this financial expropriation is not properly developed by the authors, but it seems that Lapavitsas tends to conceive it in terms of the informational asymmetries pertaining to the financial system. The "institutional framework, the legal arrangements, the informational flows and the social power of banks" over workers put financial firms in a position, in principle, "to squeeze the borrower and extract usurious returns" (Lapavitsas 2008: 15). This summarizes a catastrophic picture of financial capitalism, in line with the view of Hilferding, that identifies finance with usury. The "mediocre" and "precarious growth" of capitalism has deteriorated the labor incomes, which are further squeezed by the predatory activities of modern finance (expropriation as a substitute for exploitation).

As will become clear in the rest of the book, we think that these approaches fail to grasp the essence of modern financial innovation and the nature of contemporary capitalism. Finance is something much more than a sophisticated kind of usury. It is not a distortion but rather a development in line with the spirit of capitalism. Strangely enough, this conception of finance can also be found in Hilferding's writings, as we shall point out in Chapter 4.

3 Is finance productive or "parasitic?"

1 Finance as the seizure of others' income

Let's summarize what we have discussed so far in the two previous chapters. First, the idea of the capitalist as an absentee and functionless proprietor who receives income in the form of absolute rent by taking advantage of the scarcity of capital can traced back to the original work of Ricardo. Second, this divorce of the capitalist owner from the production process paves the way for the approaches that conceive of them as inhabitants of the financial sphere who benefit by making profit through the seizure of income created in "real" production. In this sense, the absentee capitalist owner functions like an old fashioned usurer, circumventing the accumulation of use values in the search for profits in the sphere of circulation (both seizure and speculation). By and large, this is how a significant part of literature reads the Marxian formula $M\!-\!M''$.

According to this approach, profitability in capitalism can be derived through two distinctive routes: a productive one ($M\!-\!C\!-\!M'$, where M stands for money, C for commodities and $M'=M+\Delta M$) and a parasitic or speculative one ($M\!-\!M''$, with $M''=\Delta M'$). Ricardo, of course, never came to this conclusion or categorization. Nevertheless, the latter can be seen as an immediate consequence of his reasoning if this reasoning is extended to grasp the developments of contemporary finance. In this regard, one can suggest that if the absentee owner becomes dominant in the organization of capitalist life, the "productive" aspects of the latter are repressed, putting speculative and predatory activities in a dominant position. This would be the case because the preponderant motive of capitalism would amount to the seeking of profits in the sphere of financial circulation, i.e., appropriating the profits created by other fractions of (productive) capital, or even the income of (productive) workers. Circulation becomes the principal means of absorbing profit previously generated by production; all this would cause stagnation and instability in production of use values.

Especially in the traditional (Ricardian) Marxism, all labor processes in the spheres of circulation and finance are regarded as non-productive, which means that the profits gained by individual capitals in these spheres are considered simply as income transfers from the productive (industrial) capitalist activities.[1] Nevertheless, industrial production has ceased to be the heart of our capitalist world. A significant part of the recent literature takes this conclusion as a point of departure for the further analysis of contemporary capitalism as unreasonably predatory and dysfunctional.

In this chapter we will challenge this line of reasoning in two ways. Capitalist investments to set up financial firms are definitely not "non-productive." At the same time, equally wrong is the assumption that the logic of so-called finance capital is independent from, contradictory to, and dominant over, the logic of industrial capital. In other words, we will defend the thesis that the development of finance cannot be considered as dysfunctional to, and repressive of, the productive capacities of the economy. This chapter will be the introduction to an alternative reading of Marx with regard to the role of finance that will be further developed in the rest of the book.

2 Marx's monetary approach to capital: what is *Capitalist* production and who is productive?

Summarizing what we have developed in Chapter 2, we could argue that one comprehensive introductory definition of capitalism and capitalist production could be the following: a historically specific social relation that expresses itself in the form of "money as an end in itself" or "money that creates more money," in accordance with the formula $M–C–M'$ (where M stands for money and C for commodity; note that in our viewpoint this formula describes the circuit of *every* individual capital regardless of the faction to which it belongs). Marx has shown that this formula of money circulation is actually the expression of capitalist economic and social relations, incorporating as it does the process of direct commodity production, which now becomes production-for-exchange and production-for-profit. In the context of capitalist economic and social relations, the movement of money as capital binds the production process *to* the circulation process: commodity production becomes a phase or moment (and indeed, for the whole valorization process, the decisive moment) of the circuit of social capital:

$$M–C^{LP}_{Mp} \ldots P \ldots C' \ldots M' \tag{1.1}$$

The capitalist appears on the market as the owner of money M, buying commodities C, which consist of means of production Mp and labor power Lp. In the process of production (P) these commodities C are productively used up so as to generate an output of other commodities, a product C', whose value should exceed that of C. Finally, she sells that output to recover a sum of money M' higher than M.

Following the above analysis, it is of little theoretical worth to pose the trivial question "what human labor is *generally* productive," which usually gets the equally trivial and repetitive answer that only "useful labor" (labor producing useful things or use values) is 'productive.' This answer further insinuates that certain ethical or other moral criteria should be posited as regards what should be considered to be "useful" and what should not. The question about productive and non-productive labor has, instead, to be tackled as a question concerning capitalist production: What is productive *for* and *in the framework of* the capitalist relations of production?

Stated this way, the answer is rather straightforward: all forms of labor that produce surplus-value are productive, in other words all labor being exchanged with (variable) capital and thus producing profit for capital. On the contrary, capitalistically non-productive are all forms of labor that are not being exchanged with (variable) capital: non-renumerated labor (e.g., household labor producing use values for one's own consumption), remunerated labor exchanged not with capital but with private income (e.g., servants, gardeners, housekeepers, etc. in private households), public servants or government employees in state apparatuses that do not sell goods or services (e.g., ministries, the police, public schools etc.), self-employed producers who sell "simple" commodities (i.e., commodities that are not being capitalistically produced and thus do not contain surplus value to be realized in the market). As Marx states:

> Since the direct purpose and the *actual product* of capitalist production is *surplus value*, only *such labour* is *productive*, and only such an exerter of labour capacity is a *productive worker*, as directly *produces surplus value*. Hence only such labour is productive as is *consumed* directly in the production process for the purpose of valorising capital. [...] And only the bourgeoisie can confuse the question of what are *productive labour* and *productive workers* from the standpoint of capital with the question of what *productive* labour is in general, and can therefore be satisfied with the tautological answer that all that labour is productive which produces, which results in a product, or any kind of use value, which has any result at all.
> (Marx 1990: 1038–1039, the trans. compared with the German original and slightly altered)

We would like to insist on one point, clearly formulated in Marx's analysis. Every capitalist enterprise is identical with *any other* as the locus of a money creating activity, as "value in process, money in process." The use values involved in the process of capital valorization are only a means for the accomplishment of an aim, which does not depend on their specific features. This point is obvious in the following rather long quotation:

> Capitalist production is not merely the production of commodities, it is, by its very essence, the production of surplus-value. The worker produces not for himself, but for capital. It is no longer sufficient, therefore, for him simply to produce. He must produce surplus-value. That only worker who is productive is one who produces surplus-value for the capitalist [...]. If we may take an example from *outside the sphere of material production*, a schoolmaster is a productive worker when, in addition to belabouring the heads of his pupils, he works himself into the ground to enrich the owner of

> the school. That the latter has laid out his capital in a teaching factory, instead of a sausage factory, makes no difference to the relation. The concept of a productive worker therefore implies not merely a relation between the activity of work and its useful effect [...], but also *a specifically social relation of production.*
>
> (Marx 1990: 644, emphasis added)

Every capitalist is always at the same time a "trader" or "merchant" (who as a money owner buys commodities, the enterprise's input: means of production and labor power, in order to sell commodities, the produced output) and "manager"of a labor and production process, which makes it possible for trading to be effective. They establish such a price for the bulk of the commodities sold (the enterprise's output) that is not only higher than the expenditure on the commodities bought (the enterprise's input) over the same time period, but is also to that extent higher, so as to ensure an "average" increment of the money quantity advanced by the enterprise at the beginning of the whole process (an average rate of profit).

The above insights mean that every capitalist enterprise, regardless of the economic sector in which it is active (primary, secondary, circulation, finance) is equally a process of buying commodities ("creating costs"), i.e., a means of production and labor power, in order to sell commodities of a different form and use value (included are *sui generis* financial commodities, as we will argue below). It is a process of unifying production and circulation in the unique capitalist production as a whole.[2] As Marx writes in the *Grundrisse*:

> However, in so far as circulation itself creates costs, itself requires surplus labour, it appears as itself included within the production process.
>
> (Marx 1993: 524)

Finance "creates costs." It employs labor power and means of production to create and sell certain (*sui generis*) commodities (exchange values that are at the same time use values for others). In other words, financial intermediation may take different forms and encompass different types of institutions but each case is linked to a particular set of financial services, which are in fact capitalist commodities. We will not get involved in the discussions concerning the functions of financial intermediaries. But, in general, the latter intermediates the investment process under particular terms which follow the institutional trends of the capitalist economies.[3] This intermediation is a *sui generis* service itself and is therefore a productive activity striving for profit maximization, like any other sector of the capitalist economy. It shall thus be regarded as a productive activity.

3 A brief digression. Marx's second discourse: productive is only the creation of "material" use values

The above analysis of Marx (on productive labor) coexists, however, with another discourse in his mature writings, especially in the third volume of

Capital. According to this second discourse, a capitalist production and valorization process is productive only if it ends up in the creation of tangible material products. Thus, labor cannot be conceived as productive in the services sector, especially in commerce and finance. In this part of his work, Marx distances himself from his own analysis that capital is "self-valorising value" regardless of the economic sector or the sphere of its activity, and declares that "commercial capital [...] creates neither value nor surplus-value" (Marx 1991: 392). Consequently, "since the merchant, being simply an agent of circulation, produces neither value nor surplus-value [...] the commercial workers whom he employs in these same functions cannot possibly create surplus-value for him directly" (ibid.: 406).

We have already discussed in Chapter 2, that these ambivalences in the writings of Marx do not solely concern the issue of productive and non-productive labor in capitalism. In fact, in Marx's mature writings two theoretical discourses, each of which is incompatible with the other, are present. On the one hand, there is the theoretical system that he named "critique of political economy" (which includes the monetary theory of value and capital). On the other, we encounter a sophisticated version of the classical (mainly Ricardian) political economy of value as "labor expended," which is to be found mainly in sections of Volume 3 of *Capital* and at other points in his 1861–1865 manuscript writings. In other words, Marx's writings have two souls and the accounts with classical political economy have not been decisively settled.[4] It is the existence of these conceptual contradictions in his writings that has given rise to different tendencies among his followers. This fact reflects the difficulty, but also the significance and the range, of Marx's theoretical revolution and it is common in every theoretical rupture of the kind – even in the natural sciences, i.e., in every attempt to create a new theoretical discipline on the basis of the critique of an established system of thought.

In some parts of his texts on the issue of productive and non-productive labor, Marx seems to have temporarily "inherited" from classical economists a physiocratic element that is very often present in their analyses. According to this, a capitalist process of value and surplus-value production can take place only when it creates a palpable use value, a physically tangible product! In what follows, we are going to base our analysis on Marx's non-Ricardian monetary theory of value and capital, distancing ourselves from the classical or physiocratic elements that inhabit certain parts of his work. It is most important, however, to stress the fact that many Marxists behave as if they are unaware of Marx's contradictions, and further, that most of them present Marx's second discourse (his ambivalence towards classical labor theory and Physiocracy) as the only genuine Marxist approach.

4 The historicist reading of Marx and its critique

One of the basic points of this book is that Marx's argument about interest bearing capital does not refer to a mere fraction of the capitalist class, but it captures the most concrete form of capital itself. We have already discussed this idea in the context of Chapter 2 and shall return to it in this chapter. A proper analysis in the light of recent financial developments will take place in Part III of this book.

According to Marx's monetary theory of value, money is the independent form of the appearance of value. As such it potentially becomes capital and thus expresses the capital relation itself. In this manner, new analytical determinations and categories are introduced within the existing conceptual domain. They do not negate or reverse the content of the old ones. They enhance the analytical meaning of the already introduced categories and provide a more integrated determination of the concept of money, so that the latter can fully grasp the complexity of the financial sphere phenomena. From this point of view, the circuit of interest bearing capital, $M-[M-C-M']-M''$, captures the more developed form of capital in a capitalist society.

We shall return to this idea in the next section, but as has become evident from our comments in Chapter 2, many Marxist or non-Marxist scholars do not share this viewpoint.[5] It is quite common in Marxist discussions to understand the concept of interest bearing capital on the grounds of a misinterpretation of Marx's argument in the second volume of *Capital*.[6] Of course, this misinterpretation is associated with a particular conception of Marx's logic of exposition, but we shall not elaborate on this issue.[7]

At the beginning of the second volume of *Capital*, Marx focuses on the general circuit of capital as a process, which comprises the unity of three moments or individual circuit forms. These moments are depicted in Figure 3.1. The historicist reading of Marx argues that each single moment of the whole process epitomizes, constitutes, and coheres a particular fraction (industrial, commercial, and financial) of the capitalist class (indicated by the left side of Figure 3.1) as opposed to the rest.

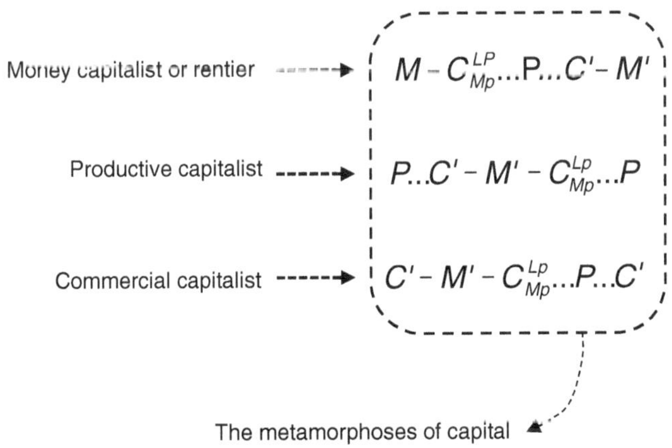

Figure 3.1 While Marx describes the three "metamorphoses" of capital, the historicist reading of his text perceives each single moment as a separate fraction.

According to the same line of thought, the "point of departure" and the "point of return" of every independent fraction of capital play a crucial role in the definition of particular (intra-capitalist class) interests, economic patterns, strategic perspectives, and experiences. For instance, the fraction of financial rentiers or intermediaries ("money" capitalists as opposed to "industrial" and "commercial" capitalists) is based on the circuit form $M–M'$ and acquires (accordingly) united consciousness. In this fashion, commercial capital is set as distinct fraction engaged in the circuit form $C–C'$; while, industrial "productive" capitalists receive their economic consciousness from the circuit form $P\ldots P'$. Van der Pijl (1998: 52) aptly summarizes this train of thought:

> Looking over the shoulder of an imaginary entrepreneur engaged in one of these circuits, one can hypothesise a specific phenomenology. The perspective of the trader, which prioritises the profitable movement of goods and compares potential markets in terms of their capacity to absorb particular commodities; the *rentier* perspective of money capital, for which the money return is the sole decisive reference and which also, on account of its capacity to "totalise" and arbitrate competing productive and commercial ventures, redistributes capital between them; and finally, the productive capitalist, concentrated on securing the specific human and material inputs of the next, expanded round of production.

In this analytical scheme, the unity of the capitalist class is by no means secured, but is always based on the hegemonic presence of one particular fraction of capital. This hegemonic fraction imposes its own economic "logic" upon the others as a general pattern of economic life. The same fraction further enforces upon society forms of accumulation and political domination that pertain to it (based on a particular "historic bloc"). It is clear that we face here a historicist type of reasoning, which analyzes every capitalist fraction as an endogenously coherent and self-contained social "subject" corresponding to a particular institutional setting of capitalist society.

In this context, the neoliberal version of capitalism, having arisen in tandem with the rise of finance (financialization), is understood as the hegemonic era of the absentee money capitalist. It incarnates the victory of "money" over production, speculation over investment, and rent seeking over "wealthy" profit seeking. In other words, capitalist life is ruled by the parasitical logic of $M–M'$ and not by the "productive" pattern of $P\ldots P'$. Of course, this argument can be met in many different versions and analyses in the literature. Nevertheless, the final message is always the same: money capitalists (or the financial fraction of capital $M\ldots M'$) have confined the expansion of both productive industrial capital ($P\ldots P'$) and commercial capital ($C\ldots C'$).

The very same line of reasoning can be also met under a slightly different narrative in relation to the circuit of interest bearing capital.[8] In this case, industry or the productive version of capital is represented by the formula $M–C–M'$ instead of $P\ldots P'$, but the idea is pretty much the same; $M–C–M'$ is taken to describe a "standard" and "productive" form of capitalism in which the making of profits (the valorization of capital as a process of producing more value) is directly linked to the making of use values and is subservient to it. Money and use value need to travel on parallel trajectories, if capitalism is to be "healthy" and capable of delivering employment, social coherence, and stability. As a matter of fact, the rise of finance in the form $M–M''$ distorts this "natural" or "ideal" spirit of capitalism by deepening social inequalities, abolishing the social character of the state, and eventually leading into a deranging economic instability. Phenomena of this sort are thought to be the immediate consequences of the newly developed capacity of global finance to make money out of money ($M–M''$) avoiding the detour through the production of useful goods and services. According to this approach, finance is no longer tied to the production of use values, nor does it run on a parallel trajectory with the latter. Rather, finance circumvents the accumulation of use values in the search for profits in the sphere of (financial) circulation. Hence, what remains from the above circuit is the new formula $M–M''$, which crops up with the use value being left out and no longer being a mediating factor: the "productive" aspects of capitalism become repressed. The contemporary rise of finance denotes the domination of a particular fraction of the capitalist class (whose aim is counter-productive) as opposed to the industrial one. In this fashion, the intra-capitalist conflicts have been resolved contrary to the wishes of Veblen, Keynes, Schumpeter, Minsky, and Hilferding, in a setting that does not promote investment, employment, innovation, and industrial profitability.

This historicist line of reasoning radically departs from the spirit of Marx's analysis. In fact, it subordinates Marx's problematic to the approaches of Keynes and Veblen. As argued in Chapter 2, this analytical framework discards a crucial concept of the Marxian framework: the concept of social capital (Gesamtkapital).[9] In what follows, we shall briefly highlight two related critical points.

First, contrary to historicist reasoning,[10] individual capitals (capitalist firms) or capital fractions within a social formation, *are not* independent and self-conscious entities prior to their unity as a social class. They are transformed through capitalist competition (and not through the political influence of the state exercised from outside on the basis of the hegemonic historic bloc of a particular fraction of capitalist class) into elements of aggregate social capital. Through this mutual dependence, that is to say their constitution as social capital, the individual capitals or fractions of capital together acquire the status of a social class and function as an integrated social force that opposes, and dominates, labour. In contrast, then, to what is resolutely asserted in historicist approach, there is most definitely a concrete general class interest of social-national-capital, despite the potential for significant intra-capitalist struggles.

Second, the general circuit of industrial capital that Marx presents in the second volume of *Capital*, cannot be decomposed into partial self-conscious elements. Before the introduction of the more concrete analytical determinations of the third volume of *Capital*, Marx wants to indicate just two important points at the beginning of the second volume. On the one hand, he stresses that the valorization of capital presupposes circulation and financial transactions without being driven by them. On the other, he makes it clear that the presented circuit of "industrial" capital resembles the circuit of social capital as a whole and constitutes a *prototype* of the circuit of every single capital regardless of the fraction or the section to which it belongs.

We are going to elaborate on this last point. Marx writes in the second volume of *Capital*:

> Let us now consider the total movement, $M–C...P ... C'–M'$, [...]. Here capital appears as a value which goes through a sequence of connected and mutually determined transformations [...] Two of these phases belong in the circulation sphere, one to the sphere of production. [...] This total process is therefore a circuit. [...] The capital that assumes these forms in the course of its total circuit [...] is *industrial capital* – industrial here in the sense that it encompasses every branch of production that is pursued on a capitalist basis. [...] Money capital, commodity capital and productive capital thus do not denote independent varieties of capital, whose functions constitute the content of branches of business that are independent and separate from one another. They are simply particular functional forms of industrial capital, which takes on all three forms in turn.
>
> (Marx 1992: 132–133)

In this lengthy passage, quite contrary to the above-presented historicist reasoning, *Marx defines as "industrial" capital every form of individual capital, regardless of the sphere of production in which it is employed.* He further explains that in its circuit, each "industrial" capital constantly passes through the subsequent phases of money capital, productive capital, and commodity capital. In this sense, the historicist reading of Marx is rather arbitrary. *Every individual capital, whatever its origin, employs labor power, exploits it, and produces surplus-value.* Even if it functions in the financial sphere producing financial products and services, it subsequently passes through all stages attaining the form of money capital, commodity capital (in the form of the means of production and labor power before the production process and in the form of output after it), and productive capital (during the production process).

5 Introducing the notion of *Fictitious Capital*

Marx's *Capital* is a really tough piece. It is quite demanding for an uninformed reader. It is not just the unexpected conceptual encounters that one will have; it is also the numerous alternative interpretations, which have been put forward in the secondary literature. From this point of view, it is indeed an active text: it easily seduces even the most brilliant reader. And yet, at the same time, it resists trivial categorization; it escapes common interpretation; it carries something unique and irreducible. No matter how hard one tries, this piece of text will never match the shape of Ricardian thinking, Hegelian reasoning, Keynesian intentions, or Lacanian conceptualizations. So there is only one way out: to approach the text from the perspective of its uniqueness, trying to discover the new unprecedented idea that Marx implements through his writing.

In what follows, we shall focus on the concept of interest bearing capital which is a form of fictitious capital in the sense that it takes its value from the process of capitalization (securitization). Chapter 21 of the third volume of *Capital*, where the concept is introduced for the first time, has the title *Interest Bearing Capital*. The analysis of commercial capital has been finished and the book embarks upon the issue of finance. The circuit of interest bearing capital does not describe a particular fraction of capital but *is rather the most general and developed form of capital*. Therefore the real question of this part of the third volume is the role of finance in relation to individual capital when the latter is approached at the more concrete level of analysis. In the second paragraph of the same chapter we read:

> Money – here taken as the independent expression of a certain amount of value existing either actually as money or as commodities – may be converted into capital on the basis of capitalist production, and may thereby be transformed from a given value to a self-expanding, or increasing, value. It produces profit [...]. In this way, aside from its use-value as money, it acquires an additional use-value, namely that of serving as capital. Its use-value then consists precisely in the profit it produces when converted into capital. In this capacity of potential capital, as a means of producing profit, it becomes a commodity, but a commodity *sui generis*. Or, what amounts to the same, capital as capital becomes a commodity.
>
> (Marx 1991: 459–460, the trans. compared with the German original and slightly altered, see MEW 25: 350–351)

This passage indirectly warns the reader that proper understanding of the argumentation that follows presupposes the value-form analysis. Money is taken as the independent expression of value, and capital itself has become a commodity when seen in its most developed form. But most importantly: "the relations of capital assume their most externalised and most *fetish-like form* in interest-bearing capital" (Marx 1991: 515; translation corrected, see MEW 25: 404, emphasis added). Once again we encounter the terms: money, commodity, and fetishism. Therefore, the unraveling of Marx's reasoning in this part of Volume III passes necessarily through the argument of Volume I.

Marx's theory of capital is not an analysis of the psychological actions of the capitalist. It is not a response to the actions of a pre-existing subject. On the contrary, *it is the circuit of capital that imparts "consciousness" to the capitalist*. The power of capital is impersonal. In reality it is the power of money as such (Marx 1990: 165–1666). Proceeding to a more concrete level of analysis, Marx acknowledges in the third volume of *Capital*, that *the place of capital* may be occupied by two subjects. On the one hand, the *proprietor* or *money capitalist* (who possesses the property titles of the enterprise) and, on the other, the *functioning capitalist* (the manager). This means that a detailed description of capitalism cannot ignore the circulation of interest bearing capital. Marx's argumentation might be represented in Figure 3.2.

In the course of the lending process, the proprietor *A* (money capitalist) holds a *security* S, that is to say a written *promise* of payment (contingent in character) on the part of the functioning capitalist *B*. This promise certifies that A remains *owner* of the money capital *M*. He does not transfer his capital to *B*, but cedes to him the right to make use of it for a specified period. For simplicity reasons, we assume two general types of securities: bonds S_B and shares S_S. In the case of the former, the enterprise undertakes to return fixed and prearranged sums of money irrespective of the profitability of its own operations. In the latter case it secures loan capital by selling a part of its property, thereby committing itself to paying dividends proportional to its profits (given the future investment plans). If the company has entered the stock exchange and what is involved is share issue, then capitalist *B* corresponds to the managers and capitalist *A* to the legal owner.

Money taken as the independent expression of the value of commodities enables the active capitalist *B* to purchase the necessary means of production *Mp* and labor power *Lp* for organizing the productive process. As we discussed above, the latter takes place under a regime of specific relations of production (comprising a specific historical form of relations of exploitation) and in this way is transformed into a process for producing surplus-value. The money reserve that *B* now has at their disposal is the material expression of his social power to set in motion the productive process (economic ownership) and to control it (possession).

We shall return to the analysis of interest bearing capital in Chapters 7 and 8. For now, it suffices to draw a general outline of the basic consequences that are implied by this analysis.

First, the place of capital (the incarnation of the powers stemming from the structure of the relations of production) *is occupied both by the proprietor (money capitalist) and by the functioning capitalist*. In other words, the place of capital is occupied by agents that are both "internal" to the enterprise (managers) and "external" to it (security holders). Marx's general conception abolishes the

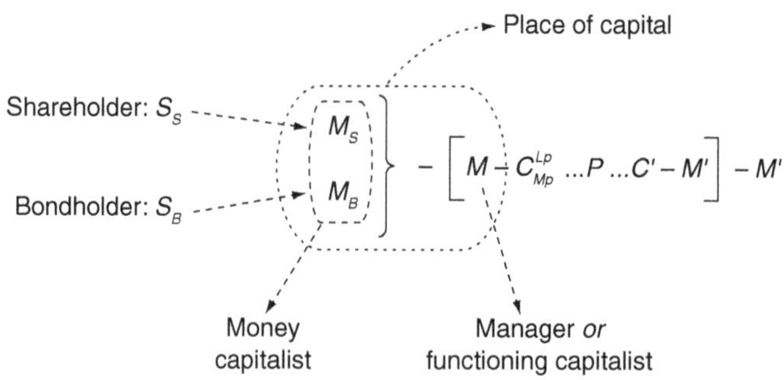

Figure 3.2 The place of capital.

basic distinction drawn by Keynes or Veblen, between the productive classes "within" the enterprise and the parasitical class of "external" rentiers. In his own words: "in the reproduction process, the functioning capitalist represents capital against the wage-labourers as the property of others, and the money capitalist participates in the exploitation of labour as represented by the functioning capitalist" (Marx 1991: 504). The *secondary* contradictions developed between the managers and the big investors certainly do exist, but they evidently pertain to a more concrete level of analysis.

Second, the pure form of ownership over capital (whether it is a question of money or productive capital) is financial security, corresponding, that is, to "imaginary money wealth" (ibid.: 609). The ownership title is a "paper duplicate" (ibid.), either of the money capital ceded in the case of the bond S_B, or of the "material" capital in the case of the share S_S. Nevertheless the *price* of security does not emerge either from the value of the money made available or from the value of the "real" capital. As already discussed in Chapter 1, the ownership titles are priced on the basis of the (future) income they will yield for the person owning them (capitalization in accordance with the current interest rate that embodies the risk), which, of course, is part of the surplus-value to be produced. In this sense they are *sui generis commodities* plotting a course that is their very own. Marx used the term "fictitious capital" to grasp this aspect of interest bearing capital (ibid.: 607–609, 597–598).

Third, the financial "mode of existence" of capitalist property – as a *promise* and at the same time a *forward-looking claim* for appropriation of the surplus-value that will be produced in future – makes the form of existence of capital itself a (financial) "derivative" in the sense that its valuation hinges on (derives from) the profit making capacity of the individual firm. Put briefly, capital appears in the economic experience as a "securitized" social relation. Stock and bonds, the two property vehicles in our general analytical frame, can be easily seen as primitive options.[11] Under the assumption of limited liability, the money capitalist buys the right to the earning capacity of the capitalist firm, while the maximum loss is equal to the acquisition price of the security. As we shall explain in Part III of the book, this may sound technical but in the Marxian analysis, it is not; it is a genuine result of a *reification* of a social relationship into a single commodity. Marx is very clear that the commodification of the relation of capital is associated with fetishism. In other words, the valuation of capital is based upon a particular representation of capitalist economy and this representation is effective in the organization of the circuit of capital. This outcome of Marx's problematic has totally passed unnoticed in Marxist discussions. And yet, it is the crucial one for the understanding of finance.

Fourth, as a straightforward outcome of the above point, "risk commodification" in the form of derivative products also lies at the heart of the circuit of capital. For those who are unfamiliar with the workings of modern finance, this point may not be so clear, but it will be properly developed in Part III of this book. The price of capital (as a security price) is based on a particular (ideological) interpretation of the anticipated results of capitalist exploitation that have not yet been materialized. It is a forward-looking process, which assesses and evaluates in advance, future events of the class struggle as *risks* (since the inner workings of an enterprise constitute a political terrain, the production of surplus-value, as a battlefield situation where resistance is being encountered, is never something that can be taken for granted). The rise of financial derivatives permits the replication (un-bundling and re-bundling) of security payoffs and hence the commodification of the "risks" associated with the ownership over capital.[12] At the same time, what can be commodified can also be priced, and this pricing is by no means socially neutral and arbitrary. It is based on a particular interpretation of capitalist reality, which calls forth behaviors and strategies that are required for the effective reproduction of capitalist power relations. This is exactly why Marx analyzes finance in the light of his theory of fetishism. We believe that the "secret" of financialization is to be found in the risk valuation aspect of modern finance, an aspect that is deeply rooted in the circuit of capital. From this point of view, finance can be also understood as a technology of power, which organizes capitalist power relations. Techniques of risk management, associated with the functioning of the "deregulated" money market, are indeed a critical point in the management of resistance from labor.

Fifth, the fundamental prerequisite of the developed version of finance is secondary trading, that is reliance on highly liquid money and capital markets. The pricing process, of both primitive securities and every single financial innovation (derivatives) in the light of the above reasoning, demands "continuous" financial values; and "continuous" pricing depends on the availability of funding liquidity. Although this effect has many consequences for the shape of the contemporary financial landscape (which we do not have the space to elaborate on here), we shall just mention the following one: "the smooth functioning of the financial system is predicated on the assumption that the option to trade can be exercised even under testing market conditions" (Borio 2007: 7; see also Persaud 2002; Dooley 2009). But this is precisely the fundamental contradiction of contemporary capitalism. The rise of finance makes capitalist exploitation more effective but heavily reliant on market liquidity. When the latter evaporates, the whole setting quickly becomes deranged. In other words, the demand for more discipline to the capitalist power relations makes the economic milieu more vulnerable and fragile. This is an unavoidable tradeoff, the root of the financial instability of our contemporary societies. Liquidity is endogenous to the system. At times of distress, the valuation of risk changes (for many reasons related to class struggle), the prices of assets used as collateral go down, market participants cut credit lines and/or raise margin requirements to defend themselves against counterparty risk, liquidity disappears when most needed, and practically the whole pricing process breaks down (see Borio 2007; Dooley 2009). This is a reading of what may be called Marx's "financial instability hypothesis": capitalist exploitation is destabilizing.

6 Finance, crisis, innovation, and the production of relative surplus-value

This book will revisit modern finance in line with the analytical framework described above. Of course, the argument developed so far does not exhaust the issue; it only sets a point of departure for further analysis. Explicitly or implicitly, Marx placed finance at the heart of capitalism, regardless of the historical phase of the latter. As will become clear in the following chapters, another comprehensive definition of capitalist economy could be "the economy of the promissory note," with all the analytical implications that stem from this thesis. In Marx's own words: "this social character of capital is mediated and completely realised only by the full development of the credit and banking system" (Marx 1991: 742).

One of the major consequences of the centrality of finance in capitalism is its crisis-prone character. In Chapter 32 of Volume III of *Capital*, Marx observed: "as long as the *social character of labour* appears as the *monetary existence* of the commodity and hence as a *thing* outside actual production, monetary crises, independent of real crises or as an intensification of them, are unavoidable" (Marx 1991: 649). As we know, financial crises are sometimes the prelude to, and sometimes the result of, a crisis of over-accumulation of capital. Sometimes, again, the financial crisis manifests itself independently of the broader economic conjuncture, that is to say it does not have any significant effect on the level of profitability and the level of employment of the factors of production in other sectors of the economy above and beyond the financial sphere or some specific parts of it. This, for example, is what happened in the case of the international financial crisis of 1987, when there was a collapse of share prices in stock exchanges, providing the international press with the opportunity to speak of a "return to 1929 and the Great Depression." But it is also what happened in the more than 124 crises in the banking system that were recorded between 1970 and 2007.

In Volume I of *Capital*, Marx further notes:

> the monetary crisis defined in the text as a particular phase of every general industrial and commercial crisis, must be clearly distinguished from the special sort of crisis, also called a monetary crisis, which may appear independently of the rest and only affects industry and commerce by its backwash. The pivot of these crises is to be found in money capital, and their immediate sphere of impact is therefore banking, the stock exchange and finance.
>
> (Marx 1990: 236)

It is thus evident that each specific financial crisis must be examined both in relation to its particular characteristics and in relation to its interaction with other spheres of economic activity and the wider economic conjuncture, before it becomes possible to draw conclusions as to its causes, its extent, and its consequences.

At the same time we must not forget that, in the context of the analysis of this chapter, financial intermediation is definitely a "productive" capitalist activity: *it produces surplus-value and exploits labor according to the established capitalist patterns*. This insight has also a series of important results for the understanding of finance. For instance, financial firms are also goverened by the two mechanisms of absolutely and relatively increasing the rate of surplus-value (i.e., surplus-value as a ratio of variable capital), namely: the production of absolute and relative surplus-value (see Marx 1990; Chapters 12 and 16).

This means that as in every other individual capital, innovations in financial firms are competition-driven by the realization of extra surplus-value. Competitive financial intermediaries always seek to introduce innovations to give themselves a comparative advantage, which secures them extra profits. This tendency, which is innate to the workings of capital, easily disseminates financial innovations throughout the economy, reducing the costs of the offered services. It makes financial innovation endogenous in the circuit of capital. Given the social correlations of power, technical change and financial innovation should be viewed as emerging from the tendencies determining the capitalist system as a whole, that is, from the trends regulating the expanded reproduction of social capital.

For instance, with regard to the process of relative surplus-value production,[13] Marx argued that technological innovation reduces the value of subsistence goods and therefore the value of a given wage basket (which itself is the result of class struggle). Thus, the same "real" wage costs less to the capitalist and augments the surplus-value produced. This is, indeed, a general analytical schema, which must be extended to finance as well. Innovation permits finance to reach different categories of households (even those which are struggling with precarious jobs) and reduces the amount of money that the capitalist has to pay for real wages, which secures the reproduction of labor power. Put simply, if a car is part of this basket, an average household can afford it with bank credit under lower wage payments. The same can be said with regard to children's education, family accommodation, health insurance, etc. Financial innovation reduces the value of the wage basket and therefore increases capitalist profits (of course this is just an aspect of the whole process of financial innovation).

In fact, this is exactly what we have particularly experienced as one of the aspects of the so-called financialization.[14] A much discussed development concerns the higher risk transfer to the household sector (see Borio 2007: 5–4). Household sector balance sheets have grown significantly (*not* just indebtedness). This means that *both* household debt *and* assets have been increased in relation to family incomes. In the light of the above analysis it is evident that financial innovation (in which subprime loans were just a minor moment) made room for relative money wage reductions. Recent trends in capitalism show that high indebtedness runs parallel to squeezed wages, declining income share, and increasing inequality.[15] *Nevertheless, in the spirit of Marx's analysis we argue for a different causality nexus than the one dominant in heterodox discussions. Increased indebtedness, based on competition-driven financial innovation, makes room for lower real wages and not vice versa.*[16] From a Marxian point of view, it is absolutely misleading to associate the contemporary rise of debt with workers' underconsumption or poor economic capitalist performance in Western societies.[17] As will become evident in the rest of this book, the rise of finance does not imply a weak but a strong and deeply established capitalism, when the latter is seen as system of class exploitation and capital valorization in the context of Marx's analysis.

Another mistake in contemporary discussions is that what has been increased is not indebtedness per se but reliance on balance sheet transactions in the household sector. We stress this because emphasis solely on debt hides other crucial sides of the very same process. Household financialization is based on the capitalization of both household costs and revenues. A household may borrow to buy a house property but this transaction adds an asset (house) and a liability (bank loan) to the family balance sheet. But above all, the same transaction is primarily based on the capitalization (securitization) of wage flows (wage relations), which appear as an asset in the household portfolio. This existence of the wage as a form of fictitious capital, was explicitly mentioned as a possibility by Marx in the third volume of *Capital*.[18]

In its own right, this development has four major consequences. First, a larger proportion of household wealth appears in the form of liquid assets (including home ownership), that is to say, in a form that is vulnerable to market risk. Second, at the ideological level it presents working class interests as identical with capitalist ones, since both capital owners and workers retain and increasingly perceive their wealth in the form of a liquid asset. Third, the overall financial system becomes more vulnerable and crisis-prone, and households become more affected by financial events.

But fourth, and most importantly, workers' households become more reliant on risk management for their social reproduction. This is the most important moment of financial innovation as a social process, because it is through this "risk management" channel that finance in general (not just household finance) shapes and disciplines social behavior under the norms of capital. In a precarious world risk management means both hedging and risk "exploitation." But one can "exploit" risk only in so far as one "plays good" with the rules of the game. From this point of view, finance can also be seen as a technology of power, which organizes the reproduction of power relations in capitalist society. Risk management does not tame the future but makes labor "hostage to its own fortune," that is to say, hostage to the demands of capital. The rest of the book will develop this general sketch.

Part II

Financial innovation, money, and capitalist exploitation

A short detour in the history of economic ideas

4 Derivatives as money?

1 Introduction: money, speculation, and derivatives

So far we have analyzed the social nature of money in capitalism in line with Marx's reasoning in his mature writings. We have not yet touched upon modern finance nor put forward our argument with regard to (financial) derivatives; we have not yet properly discussed financialization. Nevertheless, at least from the time of Hilferding's intervention at the start of the twentieth century and continuing until the present, there is a tendency in a small part of the literature to see derivatives as a money form. This chapter will focus on this issue and can be seen as a preliminary introduction to the workings of derivatives markets. And since the term derivatives brings to mind the activity of speculation, in this chapter we will rethink the interplay between money, speculation, finance and derivatives.

In the heterodox discussions there is a widely established perception: derivatives markets are just a Trojan horse for speculation, and the role of the latter is destabilizing. In this sense, the rise of derivatives is seen as a diversion from an ideal economic (industrial) version of capitalism. This insight runs contrary to the mainstream idea which, while it does not object the connection between speculation and derivatives, attaches a positive meaning to speculation: its role is stabilizing and enhances economic efficiency.[1] One does not have to mention the much cited intervention of Friedman (1953) or even to revisit earlier approaches like that of J. S. Mill (he emphasized the stabilizing role of middleman merchants without excluding the possibility of a crisis).[2] The notion of a stabilizing speculation was dominant even in pre-Smithian political economy.[3] The writings of Le Trosne, himself a follower of the Physiocrats, were among the first to clearly mention that speculative traders "play a kind of game of chance" which amounts to a zero sum game ("they stand to win as well as to lose," Le Trosne 1846: 958). He gives the following description:

> The whole art of the merchant consists in informing himself of the prices which exist in different places, in comparing them and knowing how to profit from the difference; a difference to which he has contributed nothing, and which his activities tend to efface. In fact, if an increase in value results

> from it [i.e., the merchant's activities] in the place of purchase, a lowering will result from it in the place of resale. The sum of prices remains therefore the same; the one rises only to the extent that the other falls. The merchant thus only studies the difference of prices in order to use it to his benefit; and if the causes of prices have changed during the interval of his activity, he can find himself to be losing instead of gaining. From this activity results therefore only an equalization of prices; an operation which is without doubt very useful.
>
> (Le Trosne 1846)

Once we introduce this insight into the analysis of finance, we arrive at the basic mainstream intuition about financial speculation: investors, who trade on superior information that has not been incorporated into the value of a security, will make a profit by bringing prices closer to their fundamental equilibrium levels. They receive a benefit for accomplishing a useful social operation. By and large, there are two ways of challenging this idea. The first comes from the Keynesian tradition and rejects the stabilizing role of speculation. In this fashion, the rise of finance and the overwhelming role of derivatives run against the development of the "real" economy. Nevertheless, there is another, less discussed and much less famous line of thinking. It sees financial speculation as innate to the development of capitalism, without accepting the mainstream line of reasoning. If capitalism is a system based on labor exploitation and financial speculation is a legitimate development within it, then the real question to be addressed concerns the nature of the linkage between speculation and capitalist exploitation. We believe that Hilferding's intervention is very important because it does address this question, unfortunately without properly answering it. This chapter uses his argument as point of reference.

Like Hilferding, we draw upon the very same theoretical resources: Marx's volumes of *Capital*. We see speculation as immanent in the workings of finance and finance as immanent in the workings of capital. This conclusion can easily be arrived at in the light of Hilferding's reasoning as well. Nevertheless, the big weakness of the latter's analysis has to do with the conception of money; he totally misses Marx's point. He does not understand that the commodity form of money is totally irrelevant to Marx's argument. Money is an expression of the value relationship and necessarily takes the form $M-C$. To continue, if derivatives are financial contracts that bear a price, then it is totally misleading to understand them as substitutes for money. They are commodities $C-M$ and the question to be asked is the following: *what do they commodify and what is the role of this commodification in the organization of capitalist exploitation*? Our response to this question will be developed in Part III of this book. Hilferding is unable to see the importance of this question although he underlines the economic significance of derivatives for the organization of capitalism; however, it is important that he addressed it.

2 A short note on Marx's conception of money

Marx's conception of money (and of the commodity) breaks with every possible notion that it is an autonomous entity whose existence is independent from the very existence of commodities. On this basis, Marx explicitly differentiated himself from both sides of the long-standing controversy between metallism (money possess a certain amount of value) and nominalism (money is a symbol of some kind). To put it simply, *for Marx value is not to be found in things, nor is it an imaginary relationship*. It appears in two distinct and polarized relationship-forms: money (which must be conceived under the formula $M-C$) and the commodity (which must be conceived under the formula $C-M$) as displaced results of the representational mechanisms of value.

Commodity and money are terms that are constituted as such by the relationship into which they are integrated: the value relationship. They cannot exist outside this relationship in an autonomous and self-contained manner; nor does this relationship have a prior existence. The relationship of value exists only in the components that comprise it. To use a different terminology, borrowed from the intervention of Althusser and Balibar (1997: 189–192), the value relationship retains the "effectivity of the structure over its elements" (money and value), where "the structure is immanent in its effects, a cause immanent in its effects, [...], is nothing outside its effects" (see also our discussion in Chapter 2).

Following this line of reasoning, the commodity $C-M$ is itself a relationship between a certain use value and the representation of the value of the latter as a price. This representation of value owes its existence to money, the form of value of commodities, which, as value, has the potential to be converted, immediately, into any use-value. Hence, the money form $M-C$ must be grasped in the following sense: *the commodity has been priced before entering into the exchange process (it has been produced to be value); it is always in a notional relation with money* (a relation which, of course, must be verified, or realized, in circulation, through its sale). This is the result of a specific social configuration of power relations. It is not given by the physical nature of the commodity but it is the striking result of the domination of capital. Money under the formula $M-C$ represents the carrier and the condensation of a relationship. *Money does not have any attributes external to the relationship of value*. It must be seen as $M-C$ because the commodity must be seen as $C-M$. Marx is quite clear in this regard:

> But so long as it is in circulation, it is always posited in a two-fold way, not only in that it exists as commodity with respect to money, but also in that it always exists as commodity with a price, exchange value measured in the measuring unit of exchange values.
>
> (Marx (1989: 483))

From this point of view, "*price* appeared as an *aspect of the commodity*" but at the same time "*money* appears as *the price outside the commodity*" (Marx 1993: 198). The not-by-itself-standing social nature of money can serve as a basis for critical appraisal of both neoclassical and Keynesian traditions of thought. On the one hand, neoclassical thinking has been haunted by the illusion that the structure of exchange can be put in motion without the money form (without the appearance of value and a general equivalent). Money is a useful ex-post invention to facilitate economic transactions minimizing costs involved in them.[4] This illusion is not able to provide microeconomic foundations for money in models of general equilibrium in which an attempt is made to "produce" money from an already operational exchange.[5] At the same time, the Keynesian tradition, emphasizing the credit-type social relations innate in money, dissociates the latter from the conditions of its existence (that is to say, as expression of the value relationship) linking it instead to the power of sovereign.[6]

If money is not perceived under the conditions of the relationship $M-C$, then the only alternative is to compromise analytically with different versions of functionalism.[7] In this chapter we shall argue that those who approach derivatives as new forms of money run this risk.

3 Capitalism, finance, and derivatives: the historical background to Hilferding's intervention

According to the mainstream financial history narrative, contracts similar to futures and options derivatives can be traced back to ancient societies (Markham 2002a: 4–5). However, the role of derivative-type contracts in pre-capitalist economies must not be overemphasized. The picture radically changes with the rise and establishment of capitalism; henceforth, the development of financial markets has always been associated with the spontaneous emergence of derivatives of different types. While we do not intend here to provide a comprehensive account of this unexplored relationship, it will be useful to comment on it briefly.

One can refer to many intriguing historical illustrations: primary forms of derivatives on sovereign debt can be found as early as 1390 in Venice; futures contracts were common on the Amsterdam Exchange by 1610, playing a crucial role in the famous Tulip Mania that arose around 1636; put options and "refusals" (call options) were being widely traded in London by the end of seventeenth century;[8] early forms of securitization in Geneva, no later than the mid eighteenth century, bolstered the indebtedness of the French monarchy (the coming of the French Revolution deranged the established credit lines, spreading financial panic in the banks of Geneva; see Hoffman *et al.* 2007: 150–151; see also Chapter 6); in 1821, and a broker from the London Stock Exchange complained that the trade in options was "now so frequent as to constitute the greater part of the business done in the House" (cited in Chancellor 2000: 97). In spite of all the relevant developments and episodes mentioned above, and despite the fact that at least from the beginnings of the nineteenth century derivative markets (and especially commodity exchanges) had been growing as an important feature of financial transactions, the discussions in political economy failed to touch even marginally upon the issue of risk trading.[9]

Undoubtedly, Hilferding was one of the exceptions to this long thread of theoretical ignorance. He writes at the beginning of the twentieth century when futures markets had been widely established in developed capitalist economies.[10] As we shall see below, his approach is focused on the futures market for tangible commodities, underestimating somehow the role of derivatives on financial securities. But even with this limitation, his embarking upon an analysis of derivatives remains an exceptional theoretical project, not only in the discussions of the period but also in political economy in general. He analyzes the development of the futures market as being of equal importance to the development of the stock exchange. He is able to watch closely both financial innovations and changes in the organization of finance. He lives in Berlin, which, as the capital of a newly unified Germany:

> grew rapidly as a commercial and financial centre, eclipsing Frankfurt as financial capital of the German Empire. [...] The growth of Berlin seemed to be a case of financial power following political power. Banks formerly headquartered in Frankfurt moved to Berlin, and the Reichsbank, the central bank of the German Empire, resided in Berlin.
>
> (Allen 2001: 62)

Hilferding fully realized that the development of the stock exchange, which captured the attention of the majority of interventions at the beginnings of the twentieth century – shifts which have been described as the transition to the cult of the common stock (see our analysis in Chapter 1) – was indeed parallel to another important development: that of the "commodity exchange" (that is to say, the development of organized derivative markets). This idea led him to emphasize the role of the standardized derivatives exchanges, especially on the futures markets for tangible commodities. He understood the economic significance that derivatives markets have for the organization of capitalism and made an effort to shed light on their workings by utilizing his Marxian analytical background.

Such an analytical project was less common in the discussions of political economy in the English-speaking world. Nevertheless, on the German theoretical scene there had been an ongoing debate on the role of the stock and commodity exchanges at least since the late 1880s:

> Debate in Germany over the nature and social impact of stock and commodity exchanges had first grown acrimonious in the wake of the major economic downturn of 1873–1879, which put an end to the boom times of the Empire's "founding era," as well as the rather spectacular charges of political manipulation and collusion levelled at Bismarck and the German financial elite by a range of conservative and socialist critics.
>
> (Lestition 2000: 289)

This debate – which opened the road for government legislation and committees of inquiry (Lestition ibid.: 290) – attracted the attention of famous scholars: even

Max Weber and Frederick Engels engaged in the relevant discussions.[11] The main issue which had dominated public discussions at the time was "whether it was possible or socially useful to regulate the kinds of 'speculation' that were carried on at the exchanges" (ibid.: 289). This type of question is relevant to contemporary debates with regard to policy responses.

Unlike Engels, Weber along with other social thinkers of the time was rather influenced by the intervention of Gustav Cohn, Professor of Public Policy at the University of Göttingen. Cohn had publicly opposed the set of alternatives offered by both the Social Democrats and Marxists:

> either to accept wholly the monopolistic power and fluctuating play of speculation of capitalists seeking profits, or to shift to its polar opposite – the collectivist vision of an expropriation of the power of private capital for the sake of general social welfare.
>
> (Ibid.: 299)

Contrary to both perspectives, the true alternative for Cohn was either to accept, on the one hand, the exchanges along with their innate tendency for speculation, not as a divergence but rather as "a necessary organ of the contemporary society rooted in private capital," or, on the other hand, to decide to "abolish the ownership of private capital entirely" (cited in Lestition 2000: 299). As we shall see below, this conception of speculation influenced Hilferding to some extent, determining his viewpoint on derivatives. In fact, speculation is understood by him not as a distortion of capitalism, but as the "most legitimate offspring of the basic capitalist spirit" (Hilferding 1981: 167). In this sense, the real dilemma is not between different regulated forms of capitalism but between capitalism and its negation.[12]

Regardless of how one appraises the final outcome of Hilferding's analysis, his attempt to incorporate the futures market in his general approach and analyze it using Marxian theoretical categories is quite exceptional in the tradition of political economy. Unlike theoretical interventions in the English-speaking world of the time, Hilferding was influenced by the German speaking debates and recognized the importance of commodity exchanges (derivatives) in the organization of capitalism. In other words, *the development of derivatives was seen as equally important as that of stock exchange*. Unfortunately, this part of his work has not been recognized.

4 Hilferding's theses on derivatives and speculation

Despite his weaknesses, Hilferding puts forward three important arguments with regard to the financial system and derivatives markets.[13] In what follows, we shall summarize the basic moments of Hilferding's viewpoint before discussing his conception of derivatives as a new form of money in the next section.

4.1 On the economic role of derivatives

As we have already mentioned, Hilferding fully understood that developments in stock exchanges are parallel to similar developments in commodity exchanges. From this point of view, derivatives are at the heart of the development of capitalism. The emergence of derivatives is always interlinked (to some extent) with the growth, development, and expansion of finance.

To use contemporary terminology, the model of the market that Hilferding had in mind was that of standardized futures contracts in tangible commodities wherein contracts are held until maturity (Hilferding 1981: 152). This is a rather simplified version of a futures market. Normally, in the latter, the majority of the positions held actually close prior to delivery. This is true for futures markets today as well as at the beginning of the twentieth century. We can think of it as follows. There is no reason to make the rather costly and inconvenient delivery: both counterparties net out their positions, realizing gains and losses, and if they still want to buy or sell the underlying commodity they go to the spot market. Clearing houses have always played an important role in offsetting opposite positions in the market (Markham 2002b: 105).

Hilferding is also completely aware of the "futures operations in the securities business," but he rather underestimates their economic role, arguing that "the futures business, while it facilitates the trade in securities, is not essential to it, and has no decisive influence upon prices" (Hilferding 1981: 152, 151). On the contrary, he believes that the case of commodities futures is quite different: they are essential to the commodity trade and price formation (ibid.). In this sense, he argues that commodity exchange procedures are similar to those on the stock exchange. In fact, this is probably the main real reason why he included a full chapter on futures derivatives in his book.

For Hilferding, the basic reason for the existence of futures markets on tangible commodities is to deal with price risk. His account of risk, however, is rather poor. In brief, he seems to consider risk as the "certainty that the profit which originates in production will actually be realized in circulation" (ibid.: 157). This general description implies risk in circulation. Nevertheless, despite this lack of clarity, Hilferding's analysis also allows for another type of risk: risk in production ("which results from a change in the conditions of production," ibid.: 158). This second type of risk describes unfortunate events that may occur during the production process while the first amounts to what we may call market risk. Hilferding argues that futures markets can "insure only against those fluctuations which arise in the course of circulation" (ibid.). Therefore he restricts his analysis by focusing on market risk. Nevertheless, this is not the most important aspect of risk in capitalism and, of course, derivatives in general deal with many different broad categories of risk.

Together with some other analytical shortcomings (which are not important enough to be mentioned here),[14] Hilferding's poor analysis of risk suggests that he was confused about the workings of derivatives markets. But this was a rather general problem. While the organized derivatives exchanges and sophisticated financial strategies were fully established at the beginning of the twentieth century,[15] the development of financial theory was relatively poor even in mainstream discussions. Bachelier's attempt (in his doctoral thesis) to introduce probability into the description of security price movements and to put forward an option pricing formula went unnoticed until the 1950s (when it was rediscovered by Samuelson in the library of the University of Paris). Irving Fisher's writings on financial theory embodied the slow progress in the field, and only dealt with elementary issues; they did not attract any serious attention before the 1930s.[16] The theoretical production at the beginning of the twentieth century is far behind the development of current financial theory, and the analysis of derivatives markets did not attract interest in academic discussions outside the German-speaking world.

Nevertheless, Hilferding not only understands the importance of the derivatives markets in the organization of capitalism but also sees very well the general economic gains resulting from the existence of futures markets along the lines of contemporary financial reasoning. For him, futures markets do not foretell the future accurately: "in reality, futures prices are purely speculative" (see in the passage below). But this is not the main issue with derivatives. Of course, many capitalists and "speculators" would be ready to pay a fortune for the "correct" spot prices in the future. Futures markets do not provide that sort of information. At the time of the economic decision, the capitalist is able to make an investment choice based on the quoted futures prices irrespective of how close the latter will be to the actual spot prices in the future. The capitalist is able to calculate the future profit abstracting from the market risk. They cannot know the exact spot price in the future, but the futures markets render that information redundant:

> In reality, *futures prices are purely speculative*. [...] The reason for wishing to know futures prices is that the processing industry must know the price of its raw materials when it has to make tenders. If the raw material season does not coincide with the time when the processing industry orders materials, it will need to know futures prices, especially in the case of commodities subject to sharp price fluctuations.
>
> (Hilferding 1981: 166; emphasis added)

In this sense, capitalists can smooth out their calculations on future profitability by focusing exclusively on how to achieve a more efficient exploitation of labor. There is only one institution that can make futures markets unnecessary: the monopoly combines. For Hilferding, business syndicates can use "their power to free themselves of this risk, either by maintaining stable prices, or by setting futures prices so high that in that way too they avoid all risk" (ibid.: 166). In this fashion, monopolistic combines can also be seen as *substitutes* for risk trading; their development "is eliminating the commodity exchanges" (ibid.: 163). This line of reasoning, possibly a reflection of the development of gigantic capitalist enterprises at the time of Hilferding, permits an unorthodox form of risk management. Hilferding's intervention invites us to reconsider the roots of the development of monopolies during this highly internationalized phase of capitalism (for a discussion of rise of monopolies in the beginning of twentieth century see Chapter 1).

4.2 Speculation and speculators: the innate spirit of capitalism

Probably one of the most revealing parts of *Finance Capital* is the conception of speculation. Quite contrary to what one might have expected of him, Hilferding sees a positive role in speculation activity in futures markets (from a capitalist point of view). More than that: he perceives speculators as a specific fraction of the capitalist class. This is based on a particular approach to speculation that must be highlighted.[17]

In Hilferding's reasoning, speculation is synonymous with something close to arbitrage. It is the search for "marginal profit" out of proper positions in the futures markets to take advantage of existing "price differences." For the class of speculators this type of economic activity amounts to a zero sum game:

> The futures trade is the most satisfactory form for all speculation, since every kind of speculation is a way of taking advantage of price differences which occur over periods of time. Speculation is not production, and since time represents a sheer loss to a speculator unless he is engaged in buying or selling, he must be able to exploit immediately all price differences, including those which will occur in the future. He must therefore be able to buy or sell at any moment, for any future moment of time, and this is precisely the essential characteristic of futures trading. [...] This sequence of purchase and sale transactions is purely speculative; its object is to reap a marginal profit. These are not commercial operations, but speculative dealings. The categories of purchase and sale do not have the function, in this case, of circulating commodities, or moving them from producers to consumers, but have taken on an imaginary character. Their object is the acquisition of a marginal point. The price of a commodity which a merchant sells on the exchange already includes the normal trading profit. [...] The exchange, however, buys and sells in a purely speculative fashion, and speculators make a marginal gain, not a profit. If one gains, another loses.
>
> (Hilferding 1981: 156, 154)

As we see, in Hilferding's reasoning, the activity of speculation pertains to its own terms and patterns, always winding up as a zero sum game. It has also a major result: it generates future prices and smoothes out market fluctuations by "creating smaller and more frequent oscillations" (ibid.: 156). This process is associated with "a specific class of capitalists, the speculators, [...] who assume the burden of these price fluctuations" (ibid.: 157). In Hilferding's argument, speculators comprise a distinct fraction of the capitalist class that receives a particular type of profit. The latter differs from industrial and commercial profit. As mentioned above, it is a form of a "marginal profit" which originates from properly structured arbitrage positions. Since "the profit of one speculator is the loss of another, [...] professional speculators only thrive when large number of outsiders participate in speculation and bear the losses. Speculation cannot flourish without the participation of the 'public'" (ibid.: 157, 158). This insight has three important consequences, which will be analyzed in brief.

First, Hilferding believes that speculators bear all the market risk, leaving industrialists and merchants focused solely on their productive activities.[18] This is wrong because futures markets transfer risk from one party to another but they do not eliminate it (on the contrary, sometimes they even create more). Every derivative contract requires two initial opposite positions (a short and a long one). Whatever the number and the size of the intermediating arbitrage or speculative bets, there will always be an initial and a final short and long position. Intermediaries cannot absorb all the traded risk. In fact, as we see below (in Section 5) the real function of derivatives markets is that they commodify different types of risk, letting them be bought and sold by counterparties with opposite risk profiles and appetites.

Second, Hilferding has linked the existence of speculators (as a fraction of the capitalist class) to marginal profit. But since, in his reasoning, the futures market is a zero sum game ("the profit of one speculator is the loss of another"), the total profit of the fraction of speculators must be equal to zero (at least as a tendency). Hilferding understands that it is contradictory to base the existence of speculators on a principle of no-total-profitability. That is why he argues that speculators thrive only when there is a large number of non-professional "outsiders" who finally bear the losses. In this sense, despite the fact that the total profit from speculation is zero, the capitalist faction of speculators as a whole ends up with a positive profit because the inexperienced "public" loses on a systematic basis (thus relieving industrial and commercial capitalists from the price risk, according to his argument). In fact, this amounts to income redistribution through the financial markets to the benefit of all fractions of the capitalist class, but especially to the speculators.

Third, the participation of the public adds to the instability of the markets. As we saw above, Hilferding believed that futures markets smooth out price fluctuations thus causing more frequent but smaller price changes. In this context there is hardly any room for crises. Nevertheless, "this does not prevent one speculative trend – for example, a 'bullish' trend – from becoming dominant for a time, and so long as this trend persists the price will be higher than the actual trading in goods would dictate" (ibid.: 159). Hilferding does not analyze the consequences of such a bullish trend in the market. His argument makes some room for the existence of crises; nevertheless, he mostly stresses derivatives' economic benefits, underestimating the instability that they might cause. He seems firmly convinced of the stabilizing role of speculation.[19]

Hilferding's point derives from this general outlook towards speculation in capitalism. In fact, he understands speculation as completely *rational* economic behavior in the context of the circuit of capital. Speculation is an activity of seeking a marginal profit; however:

> the pure margin business is actually the most complete expression of the fact that for the capitalist only exchange value is essential. *The margin business is indeed the most legitimate offspring of the basic capitalist spirit.* It is business-in-itself, from which the profane phenomenal form of value – the use value – has been abstracted. It is only natural that this economic thing-in-itself should appear as something transcendental to non-capitalist epistemologists who, in their anger, describe it as a swindle. *They do not see that behind the empirical reality of every capitalist transaction there stands the transcendental business-in-itself, which alone explains the empirical reality* [...]. Exchange value determines the whole of economic action, the aim of which is not the production or supply of use values, but the achievement of profit.
>
> (Hilferding 1981: 167–168; emphasis added)

For Hilferding, speculation appears irrational (a "swindle") only to those who are unable to grasp the real social nature of capitalism, which is not the production of use value but profit.[20] In capitalism, only exchange value is essential. As long as use value is abstracted, every profit seeking activity including speculation – every "business-in-itself" – is a legitimate reflection of the capitalist spirit. Those who cannot see this outcome – attempting to radically distinguish speculators from other capitalist business – are unable to comprehend the real nature of the capitalist mode of production. Speculation is not some sort of distortion of an ideal capitalist type; it is indeed "the most legitimate offspring of the basic capitalist spirit." That is exactly why Hilferding defines speculators as a fraction of the capitalist class.

4.3 The fundamental question with regard to capitalist exploitation

This last point about *speculation as an immanent characteristic of the capitalist relation* has many important analytical consequences. As we have argued above, Hilferding's overall intervention should be seen as a shift away from Marx's problematic;[21] however, his conclusion with regard to speculation brings to the fore an interesting question in line with the spirit of Marx's reasoning.

In Hilferding's analysis, finance capital is the fictitious form of the ownership over capital (the "pure" form of ownership, as he explicitly calls it) when this form is disposed of and controlled by the banking system. Finance capital is fictitious capital when the latter is, to a significant extent, taken over by the banking system, leading open markets to fade away (ibid.: 149, 225). This amounts to a particular form of institutional organization of the financial system. But quite independently to this institutional development, the investment and speculation in stock or commodity exchange is a "business-in-itself" detached from the sphere of production. For Hilferding, this is not a distortion of capitalism, but its highest development.

Hilferding also understands that before maturity, a futures contract can be seen as interest bearing capital ("a security for money which is temporarily idle";

ibid.; 154). He realizes that given the liquidity of futures markets, derivatives can easily become interest bearing securities attracting the capital of banks from alternative interest bearing investments (ibid.: 154). Finance capital encompasses derivatives contracts as well. This implies that they become *sui generis* commodities, a thesis which, as we shall see below, stands in contrast to his final conclusion according to which they are a form of money. Moreover, he points out that banks also support the liquidity of the market: they provide credit to speculators, allowing them to take on leveraged positions and make gains out of narrow price differentials. For Hilferding, this further stabilizes the trend of prices to the benefit of industrial capitalists.

Portfolios of gigantic banks concentrate on interest bearing securities whether they represent an ownership over capital or just the result of speculative positions in derivatives markets. The managers of these portfolios aim at higher values (or increased gains) and this must not be considered as a divergence from the true spirit of capitalism, but as the latter's very essence. Indeed, Hilferding devoted a significant part of his book to explaining how this new financial development is linked to the organization of surplus-value production (as a process of exploitation, of course). One could argue that his analysis has many limitations, mostly because the "monopoly structures" and the "predominance of banking intermediation" in the financial markets must not be taken for granted: they do not pertain to the social nature of the capital relation. Nevertheless, setting that aside, his intervention is indeed ingenious because it invites a new way of thinking about capitalism: *as a system of exploitation that is associated with an active portfolio management process*.[22] This is the real question involved in the project of finance capital. If balance sheet management is to be seen as speculation, then this speculation is not a distortion but a legitimate reflection of the purest spirit of capitalism.

This line of reasoning is also very important for the understanding of contemporary capitalism. Hilferding touches upon this without properly dealing with it. He seems to realize that the true challenge for the analysis of the modern and developed form of capitalism is to understand how this activity of speculation with regard to interest bearing titles (derivatives included) enhances and organizes the exploitation of labor. The analysis he sets forth is promising in this line but incomplete. Speculation as the real nature of portfolio management (the search for more value) is associated with the organization of capitalist production; it is not opposed to it and only marginally deranges it.

For Hilferding, the final result of banks' involvement in the futures markets is the gradual negation of these markets. The formation of "monopolistic combines" establishes fixed and stable long run prices. In the absence of price fluctuations, speculation (in Hilferding's definition) becomes totally redundant. There is also no need for a futures market since price risk has, to a significant extent, disappeared (ibid.: 163). Thus in the era of finance capital the "futures trade encourages a development, which is in any case a general trend, that culminates in the elimination of the futures trade itself" (ibid.: 163). "Monopoly capitalism" undermines derivatives markets. But, then, one could also argue the opposite:

the rise of international competition (decline of monopolies) brings derivatives markets to the fore. With this little twist, the argument of Hilferding still remains live in contemporary capitalism.

5 Derivatives as a new form of money?

5.1 Hilferding's point

Hilferding saw the development of commodity exchanges (futures markets) as equal in significance to the development of stock exchanges. Some of the insights of his reasoning have been described above; others fall outside the scope of the chapter.[23] Admittedly his analysis of derivatives proved insufficient for the understanding of their workings; but at least it is an approach that raises important issues, suggesting that the role of these markets must not be underestimated. In this regard, Hilferding's analysis remains crucial for discussions of contemporary economic developments.

In this section we shall make a more general point concerning Hilferding's argumentation. Regardless of the above-mentioned shortcomings in his reasoning, he attempts to approach derivatives from a general perspective, putting forward the thesis that they have become *a new form of money*.[24] In what follows, this point will be explained and assessed in the context of contemporary discussions. Conceiving derivatives as a form of money is exceptional at the time of his writings. Hilferding aims at the core logic of finance. In this regard, his intervention raises important issues even for the understanding of contemporary financial developments. Hilferding ended up arguing that the dominance of finance capital (i.e., the fictitious capital controlled by the gigantic banks) under the conditions of monopoly capitalism tends to eliminate derivatives markets. One of the reasons for this result is that monopolistic combines can be seen as particular institutional arrangements for dealing with risk in an internationalized economic environment (that of the beginning of the twentieth century).[25]

Attempting to generalize his approach, Hilferding comes to the following conclusion with regard to derivatives (this thesis looks at futures contracts in particular, but can be easily generalized):

> The distinctive feature of commodity exchange trading is that [...] *it makes the commodity, for everyone, a pure embodiment of exchange value, a mere bearer of price*. [...] In futures trading, therefore, *the commodity is simply an exchange value. It becomes a mere representative of money, whereas money is usually a representative of the value of a commodity*. The essential meaning of trade – the circulation of commodities – is lost, and along with it the characteristic of, and the contrast between, commodity and money.
>
> (Hilferding 1981: 153; emphasis added)

How are we to understand the above passage? According to Hilferding, derivatives markets provide a new manifestation of the commodity form as a pure exchange value without any reference to use value at all: the commodity as "a mere bearer of price." This is indeed a very mysterious abstract existence. In fact, the underlying commodity is not part of the derivatives markets. Instead of the commodity itself, derivatives markets encompass an abstract reflection of it, generating a duplicate appearance totally independent of any use value specification. Therefore, quite contrary to ordinary commodity spot markets where money represents the value of a commodity, in derivatives markets the futures contract becomes itself a "representative of money" and *thus exists as a monetary form in the sense that it now measures the value of the underlying commodity*. In this line of reasoning, derivatives become a new form of money.

This theoretical statement was not explicitly made by Hilferding, but our reformulation does not violate his theoretical problematic. According to the latter, money must necessarily be a commodity; gold's natural attributes secured its historical role as money. Hence, money measures something that already exists as the property of commodities: their value (see Hilferding 1981: 34–36). In the above passage it is clear that Hilferding believes that the independent existence of value can be equally represented by futures, since the latter represent money, which itself represented value in the first place. In other words, futures are a type of second-order representative of value and therefore necessarily play the role of money. This type of reasoning brings the status of derivatives close to that of credit money. In Hilferding's analysis, credit is a successful and convenient substitute for money: it performs the "work of money" by replicating its functions (ibid.: 82–83). For this argument, credit money is not money in a strict sense but it represents money. In exactly the same way, one could argue that futures are not money in the strict sense but a type of substitute for it. Futures, like credit, cannot be called money but they do retain a status of "moneyness."

From this point of view, Hilferding's argument can be reformulated in general terms as follows. For single commodities the "marketability and hence their convertibility into money at any time is assured because they have a world market" (ibid.: 153). The only problem is that unexpected price fluctuations make the ordinary money form rather insufficient as a reliable measure of value given the difference between the "short period of production as against the long circulation time resulting from continuous consumption" (ibid.: 152). The establishment of derivatives markets reinstates the missing stability by inventing a new form of monetary expression that is more stable in the role of the measure of value. Since the production process is a time-consuming procedure that extends internationally, derivatives markets enable the individual capitalist to assess the value terms of production inflows (means of production and labor power) and outflows (the final product) associated with the circuit of the individual capitalist enterprise $M-C-M'$ at every point of time and space. For instance, the capitalist is able to know, in the present, the future price of its distanced exports and imports. Now the capitalist can focus completely on the production of surplus-value. This information is the result of the futures contracts as mere bearers of price.

This line of reasoning establishes a new way of approaching derivatives markets. According to Hilferding, they set up a new measure of value in order to overcome price risk. This perspective opens up fertile ground for rethinking recent financial developments. It parts with explanations that associate derivatives with irrational behavior. Hilferding realized quite early the economic significance of derivatives markets for the organization of capitalism and attempted to deliver a proper theoretical explanation for their existence, unique in the discussions of his time.

5.2 Shortcomings in Hilferding's reasoning and prospects of a different analysis

Hilferding's reasoning foreshadowed to some extent more recent theoretical developments with regard to derivatives, in particular futures markets. Nevertheless, this part of his analytical contribution has remained largely untouched. As mentioned above, he was a pioneer in trying to analyze the development in derivatives markets through the categories of (Marxian) political economy. We have presented so far the problematic of his approach. In this section we shall address its shortcomings. This will help us clarify our point, which will be further developed in the following chapters and give us the opportunity to offer an introduction to the workings of futures markets (this is necessary for readers who are not familiar with contemporary finance). In brief, we believe that *derivatives do make a difference in economic life, especially in the contemporary landscape of capitalism, but as sui generis commodities and not as money (or 'representatives' of money).* To be sure, Hilferding was caught in the ambivalent position of seeing futures both as interest bearing securities (commodities) and money. However, the latter version is stronger in his thinking and the first was not elaborated.

Very simply, a futures contract is an agreement to buy or sell an underlying commodity at a certain time in the future for a certain price.[26] Both these details of the contract are specified and do change before maturity. The underlying commodity can be practically anything: a commodity, financial security or some abstract economic index. In fact, exchange rates and stock index futures constitute a great part of these markets today. Futures contracts are traded on organized exchanges in markets with very high liquidity. Just to give one example of the importance of all these markets, it is widely accepted that futures on the S&P 500 Index reflect market-wide price changes before component stocks.[27] When the very same type of contract is traded in the over-the-counter market (OTC), it is called a forward contract. We will not analyze the differences between these two types of contracts. For now it suffices to say that futures markets offer highly liquid standardized contracts that do not necessarily fit the specific needs of the investors; while if the latter go to the OTC market they can secure contracts tailor-made to their needs but with very low or even zero liquidity. As mentioned above, Hilferding focused his analysis on the futures markets for tangible commodities: commodity inputs and outputs of industries. The argument that will be developed in this section concerns any possible type of forward contract.

Let's assume that *K* is the delivery price of the underlying commodity as agreed in the contract at some point *T* before maturity; *S* is the market price on the delivery day, *q* is the quantity of the commodity to be delivered, and we are now in time *t* before delivery, as presented in Figure 4.1. This forward contract can be seen as a simple version of a swap agreement. The party to a forward contract that assumes a long position (i.e., wishes to buy the underlying commodity) in practice agrees to pay $K \cdot q$ amount of money in a specified future date and receive $S \cdot q$ (*S* is not known before *0*). That is, the investor will pay $K \cdot q$ (the price agreed in time *T*) in order to buy something that has value $S \cdot q$ (this is the amount of money that will be received if the commodity is sold as soon as it is acquired).

This type of transaction has two important consequences that were misunderstood by Hilferding. First, the prototype of every derivative agreement has the form of a swap between two money flows (not necessarily in the same currency denomination). *In order to understand the role of derivatives in the organization of capitalism we need to rethink the consequences of the possibility of swapping income flows from different origins on a massive scale worldwide.* We shall return to this type of question in Part III of this book (Chapter 8). Second, in our particular example the capitalist locks a price *K* for inputs or outputs far before maturity, enjoying obvious benefits from that (focusing on their main business activities). This fact was properly analyzed by Hilferding; nevertheless the risk hedging is not offered for free: there is always a cost to be assumed since the

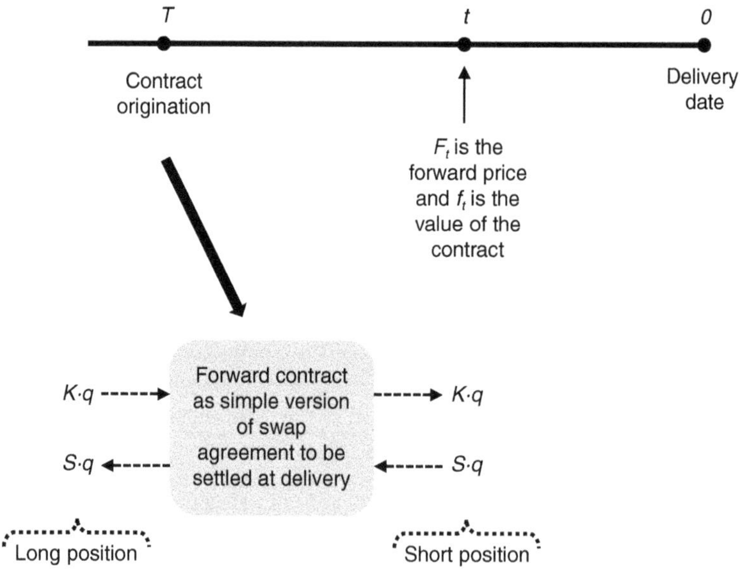

Figure 4.1 A simple forward contract.

exact level of S cannot be known before maturity. In other words, contrary to the belief of Hilferding, derivatives markets do not eliminate risk but, they provide a context to commodify and properly trade it. If so, how can we understand this outcome in our example?

For the party with the long position the contract has a value f throughout the period before maturity. Therefore, if F_t is the current forward price in time t, the value of the forward contract will be given by the following expression:

$$f_t = (F_t - K) \cdot e^{-rt} \quad (4.1)$$

where r is the interest rate (let's assume for simplicity that there is only one risk-free interest rate continuously compounded) and t is the remaining time to maturity. A simple way to understand the above expression is the following. If the forward price F in time t is higher than the initial forward price K when the contract was originated, the party with the long position gains because for the time being they appear to buy the underlying commodity cheaper. The cash difference $F-K$ at delivery can be discounted to the above expression. This discounted difference is equal to the value of the forward contract before settlement.[28] This makes the future contract a *sui generis* commodity.

In this regard, every capitalist who is involved in a long contract in the futures markets acquires a financial security with value given by the above expression. According to the pattern of prices, the value of the security can be positive or negative, indicating the respective gains or losses of the counterparties. In other words, risk hedging always has a cost. Hilferding (1981: 154) realizes that, given the liquidity of futures markets, derivatives can easily become interest bearing securities attracting the capital of banks away from alternative interest bearing investments. Nevertheless, he totally misses the point that this type of securitization is, in fact, a form of commodification of risk. In the ordinary case of interest bearing capital, the financial security represents the profit making capacity of the capitalist firm as estimated today. Its value is the result of the capitalization of future outcomes. In quite the same fashion, the forward contract represents the particular type of market risk and its value is the outcome of the capitalization of the future differential trend of prices as anticipated today.

This line of reasoning can be easily expanded to cover all other derivative contracts. The latter are, themselves, financial contracts that bear a money price. Hilferding was not able to clearly see this dimension because, as mentioned above, he erroneously thought that derivatives markets totally annihilate risk. In that case, derivatives might be considered as forms of money because they would bear a price without trading something. Nevertheless, derivatives markets do not eliminate risk. They commodify and trade it: risk is singled out of the underlying commodity, sliced up, and repackaged into a new commodity form which now acquires a price. Therefore derivatives markets transfer and price risk. Contrary to Hilferding's reasoning, derivatives contracts are not "mere bearers of price;" they are *sui generis* commodifications of risk. This development has important implications for the organization of capitalism. We shall return to these issues in Part III. In brief, derivatives markets are, to put it simply, organized in such a way that a net quantity of value emerges along with the isolation and packaging of a known concrete risk. This quantity is measured in money. As a result, because of the interposition of the notional exchange of the derivative with money, one particular and case-specific risk can be regarded as the same as any other. Hence, derivatives markets set up the dimension of abstract risk by making different concrete risks commensurable.[29] The form of abstract risk is risk measured in value, that is to say, money. Abstract risk is a mediating factor enabling different concrete risks to become social and commensurable to each other. In Part III, we shall discuss how this abstract risk is a crucial moment in the development of financialization and how the latter is inextricably linked to the organization of capitalist power relations.

6 Derivatives markets and money fetishism: Hilferding's approach as a bridge to contemporary discussion

6.1 Money fetishism

Hilferding's argument about derivatives and finance capital has implications which point beyond the limits of his own perspective and which cannot be fully developed within that framework. The basic problem with his approach is that he was not able to grasp the essence of Marxian value-form analysis and especially the crucial role of money. It will be interesting to elaborate on this last issue.

Some of Hilferding's theoretical shortcomings can be explained by his misunderstanding of Marx's conception of money. In brief, he understands money as a self-standing (social) "thing" in itself: *M*, and not as a value relation in the sense analyzed above: *M–C*. But, in plain terms, value is not in things, nor is it an imaginary relationship. Any possible divergence from this line of thought is necessarily dominated by what Marx himself called the fetishism of money.[30] There are two extreme alternatives in this respect: either the naturalization of money or the *super*naturalization of it.

On the one hand, we encounter approaches (and similar readings of Marx's text – like the one attempted by Hilferding himself), which consider money as just one more commodity (on the basis of its proper natural attributes). The process that distinguishes this commodity from the rest as a spontaneous result of the already established market relations in general is a *natural* one. In this sense money is nothing more than the means, which makes possible the expression of value that pre-exists in the commodities. This is the line of reasoning which unavoidably leads to the conflation of money with derivatives. Contrary to Marx's warnings (Marx 1990: 191) money is considered just as a particular standard of price but not as the necessary form of value. As a result, the basic message of Marx's value-form analysis has been utterly discarded.

This is pretty obvious in Hilferding's argumentation. If money is by definition gold, everything that represents or substitutes it necessarily plays the same role. There can be different ways of theorizing this type of relationship, but the bottom line is always the same. The independent existence of value as an attribute of commodities can be equally represented by futures, since the latter represent money, which represents value in the first place. In other words, futures are a type of second-order representative of value and therefore necessarily incarnate the role of money, signifying the standard of price.

6.2 Recent echoes of Hilferding's ideas

In an interesting essay,[31] Rotman (1987) underlines the fact that the financial landscape which emerged after the collapse of Bretton Woods gave birth to a re-specification of money into a rather new commodity version (totally detached this time from any gold underpinnings).

According to the author, this process presupposes two necessary steps. On the one hand, there was "the end of a 'grounding' of money signs in some natural thing imagined to have a pre-monetary worth," or alternatively, "the necessary absence of any intrinsic iconic value which supposedly precedes the money signs defined in relation to it" (ibid.: 96). This outcome can be seen as "the loss of transcendental origin" since gold was absolutely excluded from "the economic code" (ibid.). Nevertheless, this *de*commodification of money was accompanied by a simultaneous *re*commodification process of a different type: one without a value-specific origin. Modern money has become self-reflective: it acts as "a medium of exchange for itself, the basis for what it signifies" (ibid.: 92). In particular:

> As soon as the category of goods and commodities, with respect to which "money" acts as a posterior medium of exchange, contains *that* money itself as a commodity, the distinction between prior "things" and signs or tokens for these things disappears. [...] Money is always a sign, certainly when it is a medium, but also when it is a "thing," a commodity, being bought and sold. The duality here is an inherent feature of money used to buy and sell itself.
>
> (Rotman 1987: 95)

In plain terms, money may lose any possible linkage to any origin as a commodity with its own intrinsic value, but this very fact by no means implies that money altogether abandons the status of commodity. Its "capacity to act as a medium of exchange for itself" (ibid.: 92) makes it a self-reflective sign. Losing its gold standard origin "it signifies the possible relationships it can establish with futures states of itself" (ibid.). According to Rotman, in this new institutional configuration money becomes "xenomoney" and derivatives markets (financial futures/options in his reasoning) set forth an important intermediation in defining the value of money. Standardize derivatives markets make:

> present-day *traded* financial futures/options not only a new far-reaching monetary instrument, but also the means through which money – xenomoney – establishes itself as a sign able to signify its own future. [...] For

> what it signifies to be a market variable, and for it to be 'futured' in this sense as a continuous time-occupying sign, xenomoney, must be bought and sold in a market that monetises time; a market in which there exist financial instruments that, by commoditising the difference between the value of present money (spot rate) and its future value (forward rate), allow "money" to have a single time-bound identity.
>
> (Rotman 1987: 93, 92)

Rotman does not provide the details of this transformation, thus leaving important aspects of his reasoning unclear and rather confusing (he also underestimates the significance of OTC transactions; but this could not be easily predicted in the mid 1980s). He seems to believe that by waiving any possible claim on gold, modern money not only becomes self-referential but also faces a new type of problem: how to define and preserve its value. For him this puzzle is solved by the development of derivatives markets: by assigning today a future value in the exchange market. Of course, the contemporary development of financial derivatives renders this line of thought anachronistic, as it mostly reflects the tendencies of the earlier stage. But this is not the basic shortcoming. By approaching money as a self-standing and self-referential entity *M*, Rotman misses the social nature of its existence, namely the form $M–C$. In this respect, his thorough analysis suffers from a double misunderstanding. On the one hand, the commodification of the difference between spot and forward rate in the case of currency has to do with the "value" of money only to the extent that it commodifies exchange rate risk. It is this second part that is the crucial issue in futures markets. On the other hand, even this commodification of the difference between spot and forward rate is by no means a "monetization of time" as Rotman seems to believe. The establishment of forward prices and the commodification ($C–M$) of exchange rate risk do not create but *presuppose* the monetary form $M–C$. Standardized derivatives are not "far-reaching monetary instruments." They are in fact themselves based on the monetary form: isolation and rebundling of risk are accompanied by their expression in terms of monetary value. In other words the money form $M–C$ is the precondition of the whole process. We shall return to this fundamental issue in the following chapters.

Rotman's argument about derivatives seems to have been influenced by the discussions about off-shore Eurodollar markets that were attracting much interest in the beginning of 1980s (ibid.: 89–90). Eurodollars, i.e., dollars held outside US sovereignty, became a first example of "xenomoney" (i.e., dollars on foreign European soil). For Rotman this means money that has lost any possible connection with either precious metals or a traceable national origin.[32] In his problematic, the Eurodollar market is just one example of xenomoney, but his thinking seems to be heavily captured by the workings of this market.

In practice there have been several versions of Eurodollar banking intermediation.[33] Pure off-shore transactions were the archetypical form of this market. These are transactions that take place between residents outside the country of currency issuance (USA) and are subject to the law of another jurisdiction (see He and McCauley 2012: 35). A typical example from the 1970s would be the following: "a Middle East central bank deposits $10 million in a bank in London, which in turn lends the funds to a Brazilian oil importer" (ibid.). Over the long run, this off-shore intermediation among non-US residents has been the most important type of Eurodollar market transaction. However, another type of the latter, i.e., pure round-trip transactions, "grew to reach a rough balance with pure offshore intermediation by the mid-2000s" (ibid.: 37). In the second version, funds loop from the domestic economy back to it: "historically, pure Eurodollar round-trip would be better portrayed as linking New York and Caribbean centres, with banks in New York controlling assets and liabilities in their Caribbean branches" (ibid.: 36). This second type was not significant when Rotman wrote his essay; therefore we shall focus on pure off-shore transactions, which seem to be based on a money form totally detached from nation states that issue it.

The above point does not imply that xenomoney escapes national state control in general. Off-shore banking centers are subject to state regulations despite the fact that they intermediate transactions in different currencies. Indeed, it is the so-called *regulatory arbitrage* that drives the development of the market. This is quite obvious in the case of round-tripping types of transactions (see He and McCauley 2012: 40). Before the 2008 financial meltdown, US and Canadian banks were subject to minimum capital/asset ratios as well as capital/risk-weighted asset ratios. This was not the case for European banks (the implementation of Basel III changes this framework). The latter could borrow dollars from US money market funds and invest them in private asset-backed securities in the same market. Both sides of this transaction are US residents but the whole process is intermediated by the European banking sector. European banks could gear up their equity by thirty or forty times, "investing in assets with low risk weight, including well rated private mortgage-backed securities" (ibid.). In this sense, it is not that xenomoney becomes anonymous with respect to nation states; it is rather that contemporary finance plays a crucial role in the organization of neoliberal strategies to the benefit of capital.

The basic intuition of Rotman is met under a different theoretical grounding in the analysis of Bryan and Rafferty (2006, 2009), namely that: the "moneyness" of derivatives challenges the popular conception of money in many different respects. The authors counterpose to the widespread functionalist approach to money (both in its neoclassical and post-Keynesian versions; in this regard their analysis is indeed well-targeted), an essentialist critique: "with functionalist definitions of money, the focus is on the functions that money qua *money*, not what money is" (Bryan and Rafferty 2009: 2). But what is money? This point of the authors has, in fact, two interrelated facets. On the one hand, the "functionalist definition excludes monetary consideration of things" which may have "money attributes but do not exist so as to function as money" (ibid.: 4). In this sense, a "thing" does not have to concentrate all monetary attributes in order to play the role of money; it can partially intercept with what may be considered as the nature of money. But then how can we perceive the essence of money?

A possible way to decipher the authors' point is to consider money as the institution that delivers commensuration and equivalence (ibid.: 2, 4). In the line of reasoning:

> in their moneyness derivatives do not have a functionalist basis: derivatives exist as devices of risk-shifting; they do not exist *so as to be* money. They represent contractual devices of individual risk management, but, as an aggregate, as a *system of derivatives*, they commensurate different currencies, different interest rates, and a vast range of different asset types. Their money function, when we peel away what are essentially rhetorical debates about speculation vs hedging and transparency vs opacity, is to address the problem of monetary equivalence over time and space, but this function is incidental to the volumes of individual trades of risk-shifting.
>
> (Bryan and Rafferty 2009: 10)

This is the important moment in Bryan and Rafferty's argumentation. While single derivative instruments are not considered to be monetary units, derivatives as a system carry out a very crucial outcome: commensurability over time and space. From this point of view they acquire as a system, a status of moneyness. The difference of our approach will become clear in Part III.[34] In the context of the discussion of this chapter, we can think of derivatives as follows. If we reorganize the equation (4.1), we take:

$$F_t = f_t \cdot e^{rt} + K \qquad (4.2)$$

The precondition of having a forward price F_t is the existence of f_t, that is, the existence of a derivative contract as *sui generis* commodity with a price. From this point of view, in the absence of derivatives, there would not be forward prices. But this does not make them money. To recall Hilferding's alternative explanation, futures are interest bearing capital in the form of $C-M$. They bear a price and of course their existence makes F_t possible.

We shall repeat once more that money does not have any attributes external to the relationship of value. In plain words (to rephrase Marx's own argument), this means that even if someone takes a critical standpoint against the functionalist conception of money as a natural effect of commodity circulation (even if this effect is based on relationships of mutual "trust"), this does not necessarily put someone on "safe" ground. *There is always the opposite danger: of accepting the supernatural power of money that supposedly "creates" (commensurates) the movement of commodities.*[35] Money expresses commensurability (the value relation); it does not forge the latter.

7 Ideas for further research

We shall conclude this chapter by summing up ideas that require further development. While Hilferding argues as if futures are a new form of money, he also less decisively admits that they are *sui generis* commodities as forms of interest bearing capital. This latter insight is very important for understanding the role of derivatives in contemporary capitalism where the workings of financial markets are heavily based upon them.

But if derivatives are *sui generis* commodities, *what do they commodify*? And if they have a price, *what do they price*? Marx's analysis with regard to interest bearing capital will help us answer these questions. Hilferding's argument is very important because of the questions it posits despite the unsatisfactory nature of the answers it provides.

For Hilferding, given the "fictitious" character of derivatives, it is speculation that governs their marketplace. Speculation governs finance. This is not a distortion but a reflection of the true spirit of capitalism. Investors set up their portfolios comprising many different interest-bearing securities. Their interaction also "creates" new interest-bearing commodifications of existing risks. Investors search higher and guaranteed values. Part of their strategy is to take advantage of price discrepancies. If we follow Hilferding's line of reasoning within the Marxian tradition, then the crucial question is the following: *how can this active portfolio management process that dominates finance be associated with capitalist exploitation?* In the remaining chapters of the book we shall attempt to deal with this question, pointing out the significance of derivatives.

5 Finance, discipline, and social behavior

Tracing the terms of a problem that was never properly stated

with Paul Auerbach

1 A grotesque encounter (that did not happen): Hayek vs. Proudhon

The worst thing that can happen to a militant thinker who takes (or believes that they have taken) a radical standpoint is to find allies belonging to the wrong camp, the enemy camp. By and large, this was the unfortunate game that fate played with Proudhon. The latter demanded free credit as the solution to the inequalities of the capitalist system. One century later Hayek was to agree by proposing free banking. Of course, these two approaches are not as close as they seem to be. They are based on a different conception of the word "free." For Proudhon "free" meant unlimited, in terms of quantity, whereas for Hayek "free" signified the decentralized rationalization of credit issuance away from any possible government manipulation.[1]

We have already discussed the social ideas of Proudhon (see Chapter 1).[2] He did not have any serious problem with the institution of property itself but rather with the privileges that were derived from it: namely, property income received by rentiers. The key to social transformation was thus not to be found in revolutionary action but in a genuine reform of the financial system: *gratuitous credit* as a peaceful political project. Free credit would mean, in fact, negation of the artificial scarcity imposed upon money and therefore the abolition of every type of income received by absentee owners in the form of rent. In plain terms, free credit is priceless credit: debt without interest. Crucial to this project would be the replacement of the Bank of France by a *People's Bank*, which would obey different economic rules from those of a central clearing house without charging any interest. Schapiro (1945: 722) summarizes this argument as follows:

> A People's Bank (Banque du Peuple) was to be organized to take the place of the Bank of France. Unlike the latter, the former was to have no subscribed capital, no stockholders, no gold reserve. It was neither to pay nor to charge interest, except a nominal charge to cover overheads. All business transactions in the nation were to be centralized in the People's Bank, which was to be a bank of exchange and a market for all the products of the nation. It was to issue notes; based neither on specie nor on land but on actual

> business values. The chief function of the bank would be to universalize the bill of exchange by facilitating the exchange of goods between producers and consumers through exchange notes instead of money. [...] The dominating virtue of this scheme, according to Proudhon, was free credit in the form of exchange notes, universally accepted. With free credit a new economic order would arise, more free, more enterprising, more productive than capitalism. Private enterprise would remain, and competition, the vital force that animated all society, would continue to regulate market prices.

Schapiro (ibid.: 719) suggests that this standpoint met with the reaction of "great lower middle class of France, chiefly shopkeepers and artisans," against the major financial innovation of the time which gave rise to the big joint-stock enterprises and consolidated transportation facilities. True or not, such a critique of the financial system brings to mind echoes of a different theoretical and political tradition. It does not seem unreasonable to argue that this line of thought resembles to some extent the old fashioned British idea of free banking. Both approaches disapprove of traditional monopolistic central banking and give priority to the private creation of credit. In fact, the argument of free banking was not just a result of general free trade reasoning; it had its roots in, and was firmly associated with, the long-standing conservative attitude that distrusts "government management of paper currency" (Goodhart 1991: 19).[3] In this sense, the idea of free banking ran counter to the institution of Central Banks; but for quite different reasons. We shall not embark upon an exhaustive analysis of the arguments put forward by both sides. But we think that here we have touched upon a very important issue with regard to finance that we would like to emphasize.

Proudhon's conception of free banking aimed to eliminate the "price" of capital: in principle it was a project of the de-commodification of finance. Despite the practical difficulties of such a project, credit would flow in every possible direction without interest and therefore without a price. We shall have the chance to argue in the following chapters that while this idea was supported in a superficial manner by Proudhon, it presupposes a radical political agenda which cannot be found in his writings: a radical reorganization of social relations of power. This agenda was never properly addressed by Proudhon's narrow, theoretical and political reasoning: it is, in fact, a Marxian agenda. By contrast, by supporting free banking, Hayek wanted in the first place to eliminate every possibility of state interference with the valuation of capital. In fact, his thought regarding business cycles and monetary policy was from the beginning anchored around two central themes. The fundamental reason that:

> refers to all money at all times explains why changes in the relative supply of money are so much more disturbing than changes in any of the other circumstances that affect prices and production. [...] these facts make money a kind of loose joint in the otherwise self-steering mechanism of the market, a loose joint that can sufficiently interfere with the adjusting mechanism to cause recurrent misdirections of production unless these effects are

> anticipated and deliberately counteracted. *The reason for this is that money, unlike ordinary commodities, serves not by being used up but by being handed on.* [...] The interesting fact is that what I have called the monopoly of government of issuing money has not only deprived us of good money but has also deprived us of the only process by which we can find out what would be good money.
>
> (Hayek 1960: 325; 1979: 5)

The message of this passage is clear enough: government management of money disrupts the "achievement of the relative price relationships needed for intertemporal equilibrium in a production economy [...] in a setting of imperfect foresight" (White 1999: 111, 109). In other words, in a money economy, monetary policy must remain *neutral* so as not to derange the price signals that result from actual (intertemporal) relative prices. In his writings, Hayek was indeed ambivalent as to how to translate this condition of neutrality into a concrete policy agenda, but it is not so important for us to go into a detailed analysis of his ideas on monetary policy.[4] In his early theoretical argument about the business cycle (see Hayek 1931), Hayek seemed to take the Wicksellian standpoint, arguing that an unanticipated money injection temporarily reduces market interest rates below the established long-term price. This was a dangerous economic setting since it mispriced capital goods relative to consumer goods, deranging the proper relative prices (see White 1999: 114). While for many years Hayek flirted with the idea that a golden rule for monetary policy was to target a stable monetary circulation $M \cdot V$ over the global level (M stands for money and V for the velocity of circulation), he finally ended up (in his last work on monetary policy: *The Denationalisation of Money*) advocating that private firms should be allowed "to issue fiat-type monies chiefly on the grounds that a system of competitive issuers would more effectively achieve price-level stability than would a central bank" (White 1999: 117). For Hayek, free competition among different types of private money would lead rational economic agents sooner or later to choose stable-valued private fiat money over commodity money (ibid.). Stable-valued money was the different answer to the same problem; it was this answer that Hayek favored in 1970s.

The above claim of Hayek (in his late writings) sounds similar to Proudhon's political catchword. Nevertheless, Hayek's proposal runs contrary to Proudhon's. Monetary policy should not violate the price mechanism otherwise there would be a serious disruption in the organization of production: "successful calculations, or effective capital and cost accounting, would then become impossible" (Hayek 1978: 73). *Strictly speaking, while Proudhon was suggesting credit-without-price, Hayek was trying to come up with a policy rule that would give capital the proper price.* The solution was free credit issuance by private firms as the only way to secure good money: that is, money with stable value in relation to commodity money. This argument runs contrary to the existence of active central banking. Hayek became increasingly concerned with Keynesian-type polices and in particular "with the risks that the existence of a monopolistic

Central Bank provided to governments for excessive monetary expansion" (Goodhart 1991: 24). Nevertheless, as pointed out by Goodhart (ibid.), Hayek did see "a practical need for a Central Bank within the banking system as it existed in practice."[5] His primary fear was that the existence of a monopolistic issuer of money, even if this was necessary in periods of financial distress, would, in the end, be associated with non-neutral interventions.

We realize that these two extremely different approaches to finance touch upon a fundamental theme: *the issue of the valuation of capital*. As we shall discuss in Chapters 7 and 8, capital exists as a financial security. To use the established Marxian terminology, the pure form of capital is fictitious capital. For Proudhon, the problem of economic inequality originates from the very fact that capital has a price. Hayek, on the other hand, was worried mostly because monetary policy could easily misprice capital. This debate is a symptom of a latent cause: *the crucial role of the valuation of capital in the organization of the capitalist economy*. Strangely enough, it was Hayek's intervention that pointed to this issue. In what follows, we shall elaborate on this idea by revisiting the socialist calculation debate. Our reading will reveal a different aspect of this debate that is very important for the understanding of the role of finance.

2 Digression: on the background of the socialist calculation debate

We shall focus on the intervention of the two main participants in the debate: Hayek and Lange. The choice of these names is by no means accidental. Lange's intervention signifies the charm that mainstream neglect of finance exercised upon traditional Marxism. Hayek's engagement in the debate pushed his thinking to its limits, indicating the crucial role of finance in the organization of the capitalist economy. But first, we need to give a brief account of the background to the socialist calculation debate.

Long before the Bolshevik Revolution of 1917, the debate between the supporters of socialism and those of capitalism was interlinked with another theoretical dispute: between the labor ("objective") and the "subjective" theories of value. Nevertheless, this connection was not as straightforward as one might think: the defenders of socialism drew upon both theoretical traditions. In order to understand this we must bear in mind two different issues.

On the one hand, as we shall see below, the version of socialism established in these debates (at least during the first decades of the twentieth century) was a society with state ownership of the means of production.[6] If we assume that saving and borrowing take place only within the capitalist class (i.e., laborers do not save nor borrow), then this rather awkward version of socialism is close to a capitalism without capital markets, that is to say capitalism without finance.

On the other hand, traditional Marxism (though not Marx himself) argued that the labor theory of value is prior to every possible type of economic and social organization; market socialists (see below) put forward the very same idea with regard to the neoclassical theory of value. Both of these traditions argued for an *ontological primacy* of each theory of value over the institutional configuration of society. Taking that for granted, the above-mentioned model of socialism could, at least in principle, replicate the workings of capitalism because the equilibrium conditions could be specified and met without any reference to the price of capital. This was in fact the meeting point between the two different defenses of this type of socialism, with their common focus on static theories of value. They both underestimated the role of finance in capitalism and implicitly accepted that there can exist institutional conditions, which would enable the replication of capitalist economic efficiency in the absence of finance (that is, without any reference to the valuation of capital). In fact, the key issue in these discussions was not socialism, but capitalist finance.

2.1 Socialism and the labor theory of value: Mises vs. traditional Marxism

With few exceptions,[7] the Marxist tradition had adopted the viewpoint of the labor theory of value as labor expended (see Chapter 2). This set up a specific perspective on both socialism and capitalism. Without going through the details of numerous analytical interventions we shall summarize the basic idea, referring primarily to the argument of Hilferding (1949).[8] Traditional Marxism perceived capitalist social relations as extrinsic to labor itself; the latter thus retained ontological priority in the context of any type of social organization. From this point of view, traditional Marxism came to resemble a radical reading of classical political economy (Smith and Ricardo), having abandoned Marx's project of criticizing it, i.e., his *monetary* theory of value. Labor was understood as a transhistorical source of value pertaining to every possible social configuration, even to socialism itself. The only difference is that while in capitalism the value-creating character of labor remains hidden, in socialism it is openly manifested:

> The difference between socialism and capitalism, then, aside from whether private ownership of the means of production exists, is understood essentially as a matter of whether labor is recognized as that which constitutes and regulates society – and is consciously dealt with as such – or whether social regulation occurs nonconsciously.
>
> (Postone 2003: 60–61)

With the transhistorical ontology of this (classical) labor theory of value taken for granted, the elimination of markets for the means of production does not actually pose any significant problem for the organization of economic life: the price system is still viable thanks to labor time calculations.

Bearing this in mind, we can understand why, in 1920, Mises reacted primarily against the proponents of the (classical) labor theory of value, especially in the German-speaking world. According to his thinking, the latter offered a thorough validation of every kind of radical state interventionist social experiment against the free market. And the problem for him was not just Bolshevik Russia, but the very fact that these state intervention issues were gaining ground in Germany and Austria as well (see Hayek 1935a: 122). Therefore, the main theoretical enemies that appeared in the pages of Mises' paper were: Marx, Engels, Lenin, Trotsky, Kautsky, Neurath, and Bauer: the "fathers" of Marxism, the Bolshevik leaders, and the leading authors of German Social Democracy.

Mises' idea was simple. Following the established pattern in the literature, he equated socialism with the ownership of the means of production by the state. This was the dominant perspective on socialism, not only in heterodox discussions of the period but also in the debates in the years to come. Following the Austrian tradition of Böhm-Bawerk, he argued that any movement towards socialism would be a disaster. Why? Because "rational production becomes completely impossible" as soon as one gives up the conception of a freely established monetary price for the means of production (Mises 1935: 104). In other words:

> every step that takes us away from private ownership of the means of production and from the use of money also takes us away from rational economics. [...] Socialism is the abolition of rational economy. [...] There is only groping in the dark.
>
> (Ibid.)

From this point of view, finance (which coincides with capital markets in the absence of other forms of credit) is *sine qua non* for capitalism: the latter cannot function properly unless there is a price for capital.

According to Mises, economic rationality and efficiency is associated with the existence of a "price" for capital. This price is a valuable economic parameter for the making of efficient choices between alternative economic plans. For Mises, markets are not perfect. Monetary calculation, especially in the case of capital, "has its inconveniences and serious defects, but we have certainly nothing better to put in its place" (ibid.: 109). Economic life cannot afford to part with this type of imperfection – it cannot be conceived of in the absence of the capital market. It is meaningless to speak of prices in general (and economic action) when there are no indicators of expected profitability. The latter presupposes a market for capital and therefore finance. Hence, the crucial role of finance is not only to channel savings into investment; even more importantly, its role is to measure the efficiency of capital when the future is not known.[9]

2.2 Market socialists: the neoclassical theory of value as a defense of socialism

As we shall see below, Lange's intervention did not rely upon the labor theory of value but was rather heavily influenced by the so-called early market socialists. Before discussing his viewpoint in Section 3, we shall briefly mention two well- known forerunners: Friedrich von Wieser and Enrico Barone. Both wrote at the end of the nineteenth century. Neither of them was a socialist, and socialism was not their central analytical preoccupation. Their interventions were mostly critiques of the (classical) labor theory of value and not of the possibility of realizing a centrally-planned economy (Lavoie 1985: 83). While they followed different methodological approaches, they both came to the same conclusion. They believed that the newly founded subjective or marginalist theory of value had a validity that transcended and was independent of any established social regime. In this sense, they adopted the same analytical premise as their opponents: they also believed that their value theory retained ontological priority over any institutional organization, or type of society.

Accordingly, from their point of view, the neoclassical theory of value must not be seen as a bourgeois apologia; it is not an enemy but an ally of the revolution. In Wieser's worlds, the marginalist approach to value is so little "a weapon against socialism, that socialists could scarcely make use of a better witness in favour of it" (cited in Lavoie 1985: 82). Or to use Barone's formulations, "it is obvious how fantastic those doctrines are which imagine that production in the collectivist regime would be ordered in a manner substantially different from that of 'anarchist' production" (Barone 1935: 289). Although both authors made it clear that they did not write for or against socialism, they expressed serious doubts about the workability of a socialist system (Lavoie 1985: 83). They both put forward the idea that there exists a "formal similarity" (ibid.: 48) in the general logic of laws and choices that applies to either capitalism or socialism. This is the very same idea of similarity, coming from a different perspective this time, as the one we saw above with regard to the proponents of the labor theory of value.

This perspective sets forth the belief that socialism is just a peculiar form of capitalism governed by the same laws of production and value. The only difference comes from the different structure of ownership over capital. Such conceptions of capitalism and socialism fail to grasp the most important aspect of capitalist societies, namely the nature of social power relations. Of course, some might argue that the "collective" ownership of capital by itself amounts to a striking institutional shift in the organization of society. But does this shift challenge the nature of the capitalist relations of exploitation and political domination? The answer is definitely no. The Soviet Union (like other manifestations of actually-existing socialism) never ceased to be a class society. The ruling class was comprised of a layer of higher state and party officials on the one hand (who staffed both the political and the administrative-control mechanisms of the "planned" economy that secured the collective/state-capitalist appropriation of surplus-value), and on the other, the managers of the state enterprises.[10] The essential question with regard to socialism is not the (legal) status of the ownership of capital but the nature of workers' control over the social conditions of production and reproduction. We do not intend to elaborate further on this question here. But since the issue of the nature of capitalist power was left untouched in these discussions, the debate over capital as "collective property" was not actually concerned with the building of socialism *but indirectly touched upon the very role of capital markets and finance in capitalism.* From this point of view, *the main contributors in the socialist calculation debate were in fact discussing – in the name of central planning – the importance of finance for capitalism.* In what follows we shall revisit the debate from this viewpoint.

In this regard, the real achievement of the market socialists was to defend the neoclassical theory of value against the (classical) labor value version of it and *implicitly raise the issue of finance.* They unintentionally questioned the status that finance retains in the newly established neoclassical paradigm. And their initial answer underestimated this role; it rendered finance redundant and insignificant for the efficiency of capitalist production. After all, wasn't this the major outcome of the "formal similarity" position? If the neoclassical law of valuation is independent of the institutional framework of the society, then the regulation of the supply and the demand of savings throughout the economy can be organized by a central planner, at least in principle. As we shall see below, in this line of thought the role of finance is totally redundant and insignificant since the optimization conditions can be met without any reference to the price of capital. To use Barone's reasoning, the central planning board can simply replace Walrasian auctioneering in the financial markets (Barone 1935). In fact, this is the route followed by Lange.

3 Lange's challenge to the mainstream: the central planning board in the role of the Walrasian auctioneer

Lange entered the socialist calculation debate in 1936 without actually making any new theoretical contribution. He drew heavily upon the issue of "formal similarity" between socialism and capitalism from the perspective of market socialists: both presumed an ontological primacy of neoclassical value theory over capitalism and socialism. In this sense, the neoclassical theory of value becomes a weapon for socialists and aids in the configuration of the socialist regime. The conception that led Wieser and Barone "to doubt that socialism was impractical is extended by Lange to a practical analogy, which is used to show that socialism is as practicable as capitalism" (Lavoie 1985: 124). This point was raised against the Austrian critique. The challenge that Lange put forward against the neoclassical orthodoxy of the mid 1930s was simple but brilliant: *socialism can easily imitate the efficiency of market capitalism if the central planning board is able to supplant the Walrasian tâtonnment process.*[11]

As expected, the version of socialism defended by Lange was a form of economy with competitive markets for labor and consumption goods, but not for capital:

> in the socialist system as described we have a genuine market (in the institutional sense of the word) for consumers' goods and for the services of labour [...]. But there is no market for capital goods and productive resources outside of labour.
>
> (Lange 1936: 61)

With the assumption introduced in Section 2 above this is close to a version of capitalism without finance. In that case, the Walrasian trial-and-error process can be carried out even more efficiently by the central planning bureau than by a market process with private property; the bureau can replicate the role of finance in capitalism without giving up the optimization conditions associated with competitive capitalist markets:

> there is not the slightest reason why a trial and error procedure, similar to that in a competitive market, could not work in a socialist economy to determine the *accounting prices of capital goods and of the productive resources in public ownership*. Indeed, it seems that it would, or at least could, work much better in a socialist economy than it does in a competitive market. For the Central Planning Board has a much wider knowledge of what is going on in the whole economic system than any private entrepreneur can ever have; and, consequently, may be able to reach the right equilibrium prices by a much shorter series of successive trials than a competitive market actually does.
>
> (Lange 1936: 67; emphasis added)

We can briefly summarize Lange's argument as follows.[12] In an economy with no capital market, consumers are free to maximize their utility in the genuine markets for consumer goods. Nevertheless, capitalists, or rather managers of public firms, cannot be guided by the standard profit maximization rule since there is no market price for capital (as an index of profitability). They have no basis on which to estimate the different profitability prospects between alternative uses of a given amount of investment. According to Lange, this maximization condition can be replaced by two equivalent ones. This is the message of canonical textbook microeconomics. On the one hand, profit maximization leads to optimum output when marginal cost (MC) meets the price (p) of the product ($p=MC$). This is the first rule to be met by managers. According to neoclassical theory, marginal benefit (p) must not exceed or fall below marginal cost for the output to reach the optimum level. This rule can be satisfied without any calculation of profitability. On the other hand, the central planning bureau must also instruct the managers to choose a combination of factors that minimizes the average cost of production (ATC). In plain terms, this means that there are no profits above or below the normal level that would induce the producers to increase or decrease the level of production (or to induce inflow or outflow of capital from that particular branch of industry: the market is in equilibrium). Likewise, this condition can also be met without any knowledge of the profit rate and thus in the absence of capital markets.

The above argument has one important implication: the socialist economy of Lange can perfectly replicate the equilibrium position of neoclassical theory without any reference to the prices of capital and without any market for investment and saving. Capital markets and finance are redundant. In this respect, the result would be quite the same from a different theoretical perspective as in the case of the labor theory of value. In Lange's socialism there is an equivalent process of consumer utility maximization, while the profit maximization condition can be met by the two above-mentioned complementary rules imposed upon firm managers. The central planner will announce shadow prices to the managers and they will apply the profit maximization conditions to production accordingly. They will request resources upon these prices for the expansion of production. If the result is suboptimum (it does not clear the market) the central planner will take this into account in the new price announcement. For Lange, the function of prices is a "parametric" one:

> although the prices are a resultant of the behavior of all individuals on the market, each individual separately regards the actual market prices as given data to which he has to adjust himself. [...] Market prices are thus parameters determining the behaviour of the individual.
>
> (Lange 1936: 59)

This parametric function of prices does not change with socialism; it is only the forms of the "equations" that change (along with their "solution"). The only difference is that the role of the Walrasian auctioneer will be carried out by the planning bureau, presumably in a more efficient way than under capitalism. The equilibrium values of these parameters will be still determined by the "objective equilibrium conditions." As:

> Walras has so brilliantly shown this is done by a series of successive trials (*tâtonnements*). [...] Thus the accounting prices in a socialist economy can be determined by the same process of trial and error by which prices on a competitive market are determined.
>
> (Ibid.: 59, 66)

In the end, Lange's defense of socialism is weak. His conclusion is that the economy outlined in his model can become as efficient as capitalism. Since finance has no role to play in the neoclassical universe, its functioning can thus be replicated by the central planning board, leading to the very same outcome. Nevertheless, this is not much of a defense of socialism, since it functions merely as an indirect critique of the canonical neoclassical argument. However, there could be an alternative reading of Lange's point: since the capital market is insignificant in the organization of capitalism and the establishment of competitive equilibrium, then socialism as a regime of public ownership of the means of production can become a real economic alternative. Indeed, *the real contribution of the market socialist approach was not a genuine defense of socialism but a brilliant critique of mainstream thinking, which was unable to grasp the importance of capital markets and finance*. This challenge triggered a reaction from the Austrian economists. As we shall argue in the next section, Hayek's critique of the market socialists was also a way of emphasizing the central role of finance in capitalism, which in his view cannot be supplanted by any concentrated bureau or institution. It is this latent aspect of the debate that has passed unnoticed in the literature.

4 Hayek's contribution to the debate: why capitalism is unthinkable in the absence of finance

The engagement of the Austrians in the socialist calculation debate during the 1930s, gave them an opportunity to refine and publicize their viewpoint with regard to the nature of capitalism. In fact, as Kirzner (1992: 100) suggests, this debate was "important as a catalyst in the development and articulation of the modern Austrian view of the market." The Austrians, and Hayek in particular, critically distanced themselves from the established neoclassical orthodoxy of the era (the so-called model of perfect competition) while remaining strong proponents of the market system. In a sense, their response to the market socialists was an effort to defend the spirit of capitalism in the era of the "great transformation" (to use Polanyi's well-known expression; Polanyi 2001), in which significant state interference with the economy, in its different versions, was becoming a dominant paradigm of governance. In what follows, we shall focus solely on Hayek's contribution to the Austrian view of the debate. While Hayek continued to emphasize and develop his perspective throughout the post- Second World War period, the socialist calculation debate is important in that it revealed an aspect of his argumentation that remained, to a significant extent, hidden in his later interventions: the crucial role of finance.

At first Hayek continued in the spirit of Mises' argumentation. Nevertheless, the context of the discussion has changed: it is no longer the labor theory of value but rather the neoclassical value theory that is the fulcrum of debate. The proponents of socialism (in this debate) had adopted the "tools" of the enemy in order to make their own point. Hayek uses Lange's definition of socialism as his point of reference, admitting that, "it is essentially in this form that Marxism has been interpreted by the social-democratic parties on the Continent, and it is the form in which socialism is imagined by the greatest number of people" (Hayek 1935a: 18). His argument can be seen as a wider criticism not only of other "loose" ideas of socialism (ibid.: 20)[13] but also of the heart of the neoclassical static conception of equilibrium.

Hayek understands very well that market socialists draw upon the fallacies of the dominant neoclassical paradigm. In fact, it is the latter that is the real target of his critique. He fully grasps the fact that a thorough defense of an unstable capitalist system cannot be formulated on the basis of the standard neoclassical model of perfect competition and static equilibrium. The market system is not perfect but it is the only path to meaningful economic organization. In what follows, we shall reproduce the parts of his reasoning that we consider to be the most important. The central point in Hayek's argumentation is based upon a certain empiricist conception of knowledge: wherein knowledge cannot be aggregated and cannot be "produced" in the absence of capitalist competition. In an alternative formulation, the required knowledge of the existing "objective" production possibilities will not be available to anyone without competitive capital markets, even if one could collect and aggregate all the decentralized information spread throughout the economy, because it is only through the process of competition that this knowledge emerges. Hence, every negation of competition will lead to inferior results in terms of efficiency. No other economic regime can replicate or imitate the success of competitive free-market capitalism.[14]

For Hayek, "maximization" and "efficiency" are indeed the basic and proper economic aims but "the real economic problem which society faces [...] it is a problem of the utilization of knowledge not given to anyone in its totality" (Hayek 1945: 519–520). The issue involved with the concept of information or knowledge has two aspects. No economic regime, including a socialist one, ever reaches a static equilibrium. The character of every economic configuration is dynamic, rather than static. It is, indeed, characterized by genuine *dis*equilibrium: changes are frequent and unpredictable both in capitalism and socialism; and equilibrium is never actually attained. Therefore:

> all action will have to be based on anticipation of future events and the expectations on the part of different entrepreneurs will naturally differ. The decision to whom to entrust a given amount of resources will have to be made on the basis of individual promises of future return. Or, rather, *it will have to be made on the statement that a certain return is to be expected with a certain degree of probability. There will, of course, be no objective test of the magnitude of the risk.* But who is then to decide whether the risk is worth taking? The central authority will have no other grounds on which to decide but the past performance of the entrepreneur. But how are they to decide whether the risks he has run in the past were justified? And will its attitude towards risky undertakings be the same as if he risked his own property?
>
> (Hayek 1935b: 233–234)

According to Hayek, unlike the imaginary neoclassical universe, real life decisions are made upon the basis of expected unknown future incomes. We can attach "certain degrees of probability" to the latter, but in the end there is no "objective" measure of risk. This poses a much more difficult economic problem than the one usually acknowledged. It is one thing to address the difficulty the central planner has in collecting the immense amount of information needed in order to carry out the task of effective planning. However, there is also "another problem of even greater importance" (Hayek 1935b: 154), which is obviously more fundamental. The dispersed technical knowledge that the central planner is supposed to collect *does not even exist* in the first instance (ibid.: 210–211). It is of course "absurd" to assume that all this knowledge can be "concentrated in the heads of one or at best a very few people who actually formulate the equations to be worked out" (ibid.). But even if such a large amount of knowledge could be collected and implanted in a single mind the more fundamental problem that would be encountered is that "much of the knowledge that is actually utilized is by no means 'in existence' in this ready-made form" (ibid.). In other words, the market competitive process not only disseminates existing decentralized knowledge (the dispersal or communication of knowledge) but, more importantly, it contributes to its very production (the learning or discovery process).[15] Thus, *competition not only helps in communication, but actually generates in the first place much of the knowledge to be subsequently dispersed.* It is usually the dispersal-of-knowledge aspect of Hayek's reasoning that is emphasized in the secondary literature. Nevertheless, it is the second one (discovery) that is crucial in the understanding of the full message of the Austrian tradition (see Kirzner 1992: 139–140).

What are the implications of the above reasoning in the case of capitalism without a market for the factors of production? As we read in the above passage, future investment choices in any type of economy rely upon expectations of future circumstances. Such expectations encompass a certain anticipated return combined with a degree of confidence (probability) in its achievement. No economic action with regard to the future can be undertaken if there does not exist some estimation of risk. This estimation cannot be objectively known. It is thus open to change and revision. Yet market information is the only meaningful indication available to the entrepreneur, or anyone else, for deciding upon future economic events and embarking upon investment projects. The entrepreneur's subjective decisions concerning investment and risk-taking will thus be made taking into consideration existing prices for capital and risk, which, for all their defects, represent the best information available as a basis for decision-making.

In this fashion, market prices are *dis*equilibrium prices in the sense that, as signals or communicators, they are far from optimal operators. This conclusion also holds for prices of capital and for risk. Instead of informing economic actors of the "correct" path to follow, they offer incentives and disincentives that motivate them to explore and *discover for themselves* the true profitable alternatives. To put it simply, prices in competitive markets do not only spread information already discovered and given; *they motivate the very discovery process*. In their absence, this type of motivation will cease to exist. Therefore, even if someone manages to collect and concentrate all the existing information at any point in time it will be worthless because the negation of competition will significantly impoverish the real content of that information.[16]

This aspect of Hayek's argumentation was not so clear in his writings of the 1930s and 1940s. It is probable that he was not fully aware of the consequences of his problematic. Perhaps he hesitated for tactical reasons to attack thoroughly and directly the neoclassical orthodoxy. But Hayek did not fail entirely to emphasize it. The competitive market process is reliant on market data at any particular point of time in the sense that:

> *provisional results from the market process at each stage alone tell individuals what to look for*. Utilisation of knowledge widely dispersed in a society with extensive division of labour cannot rest on individuals knowing all the

> particular uses to which well-known things in their individual environment might be put. Prices direct their attention to what is worth finding out about market offers for various things and services. [...] We shall see that the fact that a high degree of coincidence of expectations is brought about by the systematic disappointment of some kind of expectations is of crucial importance for an understanding of the functioning of the market order. [...] Competition is essentially a process of the formation of opinion [...]. It creates the views people have about what is best and cheapest, and it is because of it that people know at least as much about possibilities and opportunities as they in fact do. [...] Yet this knowledge which is assumed to be given to begin with is one of the main points where it is only through the process of competition that the facts will be discovered.
>
> (Hayek 1948a: 95, 106; 1978: 181, 185)

In other words, markets do not only disseminate (imperfect) information, but they also (primarily) motivate economic actors to conform to specific economic behaviors. As Kirzner (1992: 160) summarizes:

> the importance of prices for coping with the Hayekian knowledge problem does not lie in the accuracy of the information which equilibrium prices convey concerning the actions of others who are similarly informed. Rather, its importance lies in the ability of disequilibrium prices to offer pure profit opportunities that can attract the notice of alert, profit-seeking entrepreneurs. Where market participants have failed to co-ordinate their activities because of dispersed knowledge, this expresses itself in an array of prices that suggests to alert entrepreneurs where they may win pure profits.

In plain terms, economic actors are living in a world of disequilibrium and uncertainty. The market system is the only tool they have to aid them in calculations about the unwritten future. Efficient economic calculation is unthinkable in the absence of disequilibrium prices of capital and of risk. It was this issue that was overlooked by the market socialists when they adopted the conception of perfect competition (Hayek 1948b: 188). In the absence of competitive markets the capitalist spirit of action will cease to exist. From this point of view any state interference with the market is a serious threat to the latter.

5 Keynes vs. Hayek: tracing the limits of radical Keynesianism

Keynes did not participate in the socialist calculation debate. Nevertheless, the spirit of his analysis was indirectly present in the discussions, even before the publication of the *General Theory*. The conflictual decade of the 1930s not only signified the end of the gold standard but also inaugurated an era of important controls over the international movement of capital. In the midst of a milieu of radical shifts in the social correlations of power favoring the working-class movement along with the crisis of the international financial markets, collective capitalists (states) broke with the economic settings of the liberal gold standard regime.[17] The new political agenda presupposed the drastic reshaping of the role of international finance. From this point of view, Keynesian proposals for financial reforms met with the spirit of Proudhon's claim, contrary to Hayek's beliefs. In fact, Keynesianism implicitly puts forward what was Hayek's ultimate nightmare: *the state's interference with the pricing of capital*. This radical aspect in Keynesian thinking was less observable in *General Theory*, but it did exist in Keynes' writings even before its publication. In what follows, we shall focus on a 1933 paper, published by Keynes in *The Yale Review*. This had initially been prepared for the Finley Lecture held at Dublin University College on 19 April of the same year.[18]

The ideological mood at the beginning of 1930, is eloquently described by Keynes as follows:

> There are still those who cling to the old ideas, but in no country of the world to-day can they be reckoned as a serious force. [...] The decadent international but individualistic capitalism, in the hands of which we found ourselves after the war, is not a success. It is not intelligent, it is not beautiful, it is not just, it is not virtuous; – and it doesn't deliver the goods. In short, we dislike it and we are beginning to despise it. But when we wonder what to put in its place, we are extremely perplexed.
>
> (Keynes 1933: 184–185, 183)

This text of 1933 is by no means an analytical treatise. Nevertheless, it has an ambitious target: the search of an alternative to the "decadent" and inefficient (according to Keynes' viewpoint) liberal and individualistic capitalism. Keynes seems to be interested in the preconditions that would allow for a form of welfare capitalism, although he was at the same time quite cautious about, and suspicious of, the existing social experiments towards this aim (with more obvious repulsion for the Stalinist model than Hitler's one).

Keynes sets forth his argument in the form of an apologetic historicism. His thinking is not against capitalism and he does not grasp capitalism as a system of organized exploitation. He rather limits his focus to the failures of the liberal version of capitalism, which dominated the first quarter of the twentieth century at least in the developed capitalist societies. According to his argument in the same paper, liberal ideas were useful in a different era throughout the nineteenth century. Economic liberalism was successful during colonialism (when the gap in the levels of capitalist development between the UK and the rest of the world was significant) and before the emergence of the joint-stock company, which changed the workings of finance by establishing the distinction between ownership and management. It was only in this past era that freedom in financial flows (in many cases parallel to migration flows) to underdeveloped economies significantly added to capitalist accumulation.

We shall not comment on the above line of reasoning (acknowledging, of course, its fundamental weaknesses). Nevertheless, we shall remark that in the latter there exists an implicit idea, which was to become a strategic belief for Keynes. The condition of existence of the welfare state, that is to say, the macroeconomic policies of supporting labor income and employment and of focusing on national economic development, could not be possible in a regime dominated by liberal international finance. This idea was clear enough in the paper of 1933. There are two fundamental points in Keynes' proposal.[19] On the one hand, absolute responsibility in designing and leading the domestic economy must fall exclusively on the state (state interventionism). On the other, the economic relations of a single country with the rest of the world with regard to the capital account must be politically regulated and controlled (national self-sufficiency). This was after all the essential viewpoint of Keynes' subsequent Bretton Woods proposal: international movement of capital should not disorganize the political autonomy of the rising interventionist welfare state.[20] As Keynes (1933: 180) noted: "advisable domestic policies might often be easier to compass, if the phenomenon known as 'the flight of capital' could be ruled out."

In the paper of 1933, Keynes' argument, briefly speaking, has two aspects.

The first one is well known to those who are familiar with Keynes' thinking. As further developed later in his *General Theory*, the target of economic growth could be better satisfied if capital ceased to be scarce. This would require a significant reduction in its "cost," that is, in the level of interest rate and financial yields. Such a regime would eliminate the class of rentiers (see also Chapters 1 and 7) who were seen as the parasitic owners of financial assets. Keynes thought this "euthanasia" project would be completed in the next thirty years.[21] With the benefit of hindsight, we can admit today that this was a rather ambitious estimation. Nevertheless, in the 1933 paper, Keynes acknowledged that the "euthanasia" of effortless investors would be "most unlikely to occur" under a "system by which the rate of interest finds a uniform level, after allowing for risk and the like, throughout the world under the operation of normal financial forces" (Keynes 1933: 185).

The second aspect of his analysis is far more important in the context of this chapter. It is this facet that has been underestimated in the literature. According to Keynes, the expansion of financial markets is a premise for the absolute generalization of the economic practices of "financial calculation," that is, of a procedure of quantification – and thus continuous assessment – of possible future economic outcomes:

> The nineteenth century carried to extravagant lengths the criterion of what one can call for short "the financial results," as a test of the advisability of any course of action sponsored by private or by collective action. The whole conduct of life was made into a sort of parody of an accountant's nightmare. Instead of using their vastly increased material and technical resources to build a wonder-city, they built slums; – and they thought it right and advisable to build slums because slums, on the test of private enterprise, "paid," whereas the wonder-city would, they thought, have been an act of foolish extravagance, which would, in the imbecile idiom of the financial fashion,

> have "mortgaged the future"; though how the construction today of great and glorious works can impoverish the future, no man can see until his mind is beset by false analogies from an irrelevant accountancy. [...] For the minds of this generation are still so be-clouded by bogus calculations that they distrust conclusions which should be obvious, out of a reliance on a system of financial accounting which casts doubt on whether such an operation will "pay." We have to remain poor because it does not "pay" to be rich. We have to live in hovels, not because we cannot build palaces, but because we cannot "afford" them. The same rule of self-destructive financial calculation governs every walk of life.
>
> (Keynes 1933: 186–187)

The message carried by the above passage is clear enough. For Keynes, the liberal version of capitalism is heavily associated with the domination of rules of financial "accounting" and "calculation" which are "self-destructive" in the sense that they misguide economic behavior. In other words, financial pricing misinterprets the dynamics of society leading to suboptimum economic outcomes. In this fashion, proper interference with finance will enhance economic efficiency, contrary to the argument of Hayek. Keynes understands the centrality of finance for the organization of the liberal form of capitalism, and, like Hayek, he seems to comprehend finance's part in disciplining and shaping social behavior. In fact his reasoning can be seen as an effort to realize possible ways of deranging this centrality of finance in the organization of the economy. He nevertheless fails to develop the theoretical terms, which would properly conceptualize how quantification of risk can be linked to the organization of the power of capital. As we shall discuss in the following section of this chapter, we need Marx's analytical context to address issues concerning this aspect of finance.

6 In the place of an epilogue: finance as trauma in the mainstream thinking

We shall now summarize the main findings of the above analysis. The debate between Lange and Hayek is indicative of the role of finance in capitalism. Keynes' considerations add to this line of reasoning. The above analysis does not reveal the social nature of finance, but it can be seen as a *practical gesture* that points to a real theoretical and political problem without providing the analytical means to properly grasp it. We shall try to address this problem and define the terms for an answer in the following chapters. The analysis of this chapter has more of the character of an introduction to the analytical difficulties in dealing with finance in capitalism.

Lange's defence of socialism, or at least the version of it that he considered to be appropriate, drew heavily upon the dominant neoclassical tradition. The neoclassical system emphasizes the static character of the economic equilibrium. The argument of Lange was that this static form of equilibrium can be easily replicated by the socialist economy. The version of socialism he chose to refer to as standard was really a type of capitalism without capital markets. In this regard, Lange managed implicitly to set forth two important points. First, he showed that a version of mainstream thinking that underestimates the role of capital markets can be easily utilized to defend the social paradigm of central planners. This was a strong provoking case against the mainstream discussions of the period. Second, the abolition of capital markets – and therefore of finance – could not only replicate the much advertised efficiency of capitalism but would also enhance economic stability. We must not forget that the debate takes place in the 1930s, when the consequences of the Great Depression were at the forefront of everyone's mind. Taming the financial instability of the capitalist system without sacrificing economic efficiency would seem an appealing alternative to the free-market system in a period when the latter was generating many unresolved contradictions.[22]

Hayek, along with the other Austrians, understood very well the message of these critiques, the most stimulating of which was undoubtedly that of the market socialists. In fact this challenge pushed their thinking to its limits. How could a mainstream liberal economist respond to a neoclassical defense of the state ownership of the means of production? There was one way out of this uncanny encounter: they had to differentiate their view of capitalism from the neoclassical ideal universe of perfect equilibrium. This departure was never clearly stated in the writings of Mises and Hayek (see Kirzner 1992: 111) and, of course, was never properly emphasized. Both writers were rather insecure in addressing the ultimate consequences of their argument. Nevertheless, the latter amounts to the strongest defense of the market system that one can articulate in the mainstream discussions. For when they defended the free market system, they not only responded to the proponents of socialism but also to everyone who had argued for strong state interference in the workings of the economy. It was not just socialism but every alternative "half-way house" that would negate the decentralized market system to some extent. Or to put it differently, it was not just Stalin as a central planner, but also Hitler as a fascist dictator and Roosevelt as a democratic "New Dealer" who were the objects of this critique. It was not just Lange and Lerner, but also Keynes and Kalecki, who were to be refuted.

In order to defend the market system, Hayek realized that he had to revise and partially criticize mainstream theory. Admittedly, the debate on socialist calculation triggered the process of elaboration and clarification of what is now described as Austrian thinking (Kirzner 1992). Against the challenge of the market socialists, Hayek actually highlighted the importance of the competitive market system primarily as a disequilibrium process. But since socialism, the debated concept, was perceived as a market system without capital markets, the debate implicitly touched upon the role of finance (under the simplifying assumption that only capitalists save and borrow). It was the role of finance in generating prices for risk that was obscured by the dominant neoclassical paradigm of perfect competition. From this point of view, Hayek's argument can be seen as a suggestion that capitalism is unthinkable in the absence of finance, that is, without a market for risk. This is so because the pure market system provides the motives for economic actors to *generate and discover* the knowledge ("alertness to and the discovery of as yet unknown information" Kirzner 1992: 104), which is, at the same time, to be dispersed and communicated to other parts of the economy.

In that sense, the real alternative to the market system is definitely not a process that can just collect decentralized knowledge, because even if this were possible it would deprive the economic system of the proper motives to achieve efficient targets: it would not stimulate discovery and economic action according to the norms of the capitalist system. Markets disseminate imperfect information but also motivate discovery and learning; they generate the information to be communicated. From our point of view, although the Austrians never put it that way, *this must be seen as a process of shaping economic behavior according to the spirit of capitalism.* For discovery and learning are simply the outcomes of an active engagement in proper economic actions. *The market system thus motivates a particular way of acting and it is only as a consequence of these actions that knowledge is discovered.* From this perspective, the real message of Hayek's response to market socialists – an argument that was never properly stated during the period of the debate – was that capitalism needs the capital market to organize proper business behavior and reproduce itself. With the establishment of central planning there will not be a "discovery process" on the part of managers, hence no proper capitalist behavior and therefore no efficiency in capitalist terms. In the end, every serious restriction of capital markets threatens the reproduction of the capitalist spirit.

In other words, Lange's provocative stance made Austrians implicitly touch upon the real issue with regard to finance. The unleashing of finance does not only channel savings to investment in a particular way, but it also sets up a particular form of organization of capitalist society. Hayek unintentionally touched upon this issue. Keynes' interventions also pointed at it, but neither of them managed to establish a proper analytical framework. As we shall argue in the following chapters, this is because neither of them had a proper theory of capital as social relation.

This result brings us to an unexpected twist. While Lange degraded socialism to a mere replication of capitalism's efficient achievements, Hayek implicitly realized the danger of undermining capitalist behavior and thus the nature of capitalist relations. *If we see economic behavior in capitalism as the outcome of the capitalist social relations of power, then Hayek's perspective renders capital markets central to the organization of capitalism as a system of exploitation. Finance has a crucial role in disciplining economic behavior according to the inner norms of the system.* At the same time, he also perceives every movement towards collective ownership of the means of production as a real threat to the logic of capitalist reproduction. In this sense, he implicitly ends up giving an unexpected endorsement to socialism that is much deeper and sophisticated than the superficial "defense" of Lange: every thorough state intervention in the markets, and in the capital market in particular, threatens to eliminate the capitalist spirit, making the existence of the system vulnerable in the context of the reproduction of its power relations.

This last point gives us the chance to revisit the socialist calculation debate, interpreting finance as *trauma* for mainstream discussions. We shall use the concepts of Lacanian psychoanalysis as an analogy in order to clarify our point.[23]

Of course, from a radical Marxian point of view, mainstream thinking in all its versions is just a theoretical ideology (using the Althusserian definition of the term; see Althusser and Balibar 1997): mainstream ideas misinterpret capitalist reality, but not in an arbitrary way. These systematic ideas are always interwoven with particular capitalist exploitation strategies stemming from reality itself. Mainstream theory systematizes ideas and perceptions that arise from, and are held in place by, social and economic power relations themselves (the "given" ideological representations of everyday "experience") without transforming their ideological content. Nevertheless, there is one more issue involved here. Mainstream economic reasoning always had the problem of thinking seriously about finance and properly incorporating it into theory, along with instability and crises. It seems that, as well as being a mystery, finance has also always been a *trauma* for the mainstream economic edifice.

Mainstream thinking offers an interpretation of the capitalist system by symbolizing capitalist reality in a particular way. It sets forth and reproduces practices containing particular symbols, ideas, concepts, questions, and visions that all together comprise what we may call the symbolic "misrecognition' of reality. Nevertheless, there is one element that persistently resists this symbolization in the context of mainstream analytical speculations: finance. It is not that mainstream thinking does not have theories of finance; it is that these theories are unable to incorporate the fundamental aspects of finance, its crisis-prone character and its key role in the organization of capitalist production, into orthodox neoclassical thinking. The recent financial meltdown is an eloquent indication of this fact. The pre-crisis confidence in the strength of the system was accompanied by a post-crisis unease that led to fatal economic policy mistakes. In order words, finance is the *real* of capitalism, a place that cannot be properly symbolized, and a factor that can never be completely absorbed into the mainstream ideological discourse. It will always be left over, unable to find its way to the established economic language, especially in the contemporary forms of capitalism.

To speak metaphorically, the above argument suggests that finance is a *trauma* for mainstream thinking. The socialist calculation debate manifests this fact very clearly. The response of Lange was a provocative act, perhaps not deeply significant but nevertheless an important focal point. It served to remind mainstream economists that their neglect of finance as an active and creative force in capitalist reproduction can be easily used as an argument for the negation of the market system. The reaction of the Austrians was a result of the existence of this trauma as if it was brought back into conscious memory. But since the unsymbolized real cannot intrude into reality without the breakdown of the capitalist apologia, the argument of the Austrians played the role of *fantasy* for mainstream thinking. It became the last defense against the traumatic encounter with the real; that is to say, with finance as manifestation of the exploitative and contradictory character of the system. This is the true contribution of the Austrian tradition to mainstream thinking. This tradition will always be mentioned as a defensive argument of last resort for the free-market system when the latter is in crisis, an imaginative context for capitalist apologia. It will always be the speculative border that cannot be crossed without serious consequences for the nature of an economic reasoning which purports to defend the capitalist system.

Part III

Rethinking finance

A Marxian analytical framework

6 Episodes in finance

1 Introduction

This chapter is really an introduction to Chapter 7, where we shall attempt to present and analyze the character of contemporary capitalism. Our emphasis will be on the issue of finance. Following Marx's analysis we shall attempt to associate finance (its content and recent developments) with the *logic of capital*. From this perspective, contemporary capitalism is not a parasitical deviation from a hypothetical ideal "productive" version that one should long for; finance is not dysfunctional, superfluous and annoying (although it may become so given the development of class struggle). Our argument will not defend the rise of finance, but it will attempt to clarify its key role in the organization of capitalism, arguing that the structure of our contemporary societies is a development stemming precisely from the innate nature of the capital relation.

Before embarking on our theoretical explanation, it would help the reader who is not used to the details of the world of finance if we presented some moments from the rich financial history of capitalism. The choice of these episodes is by no means arbitrary. On the one hand, the episodes describe several crucial aspects of our capitalist world, highlighting the historicity of the latter (of capitalist social formations and their international interconnections) and its connection with the organization and reproduction of capitalist relations (the causal regularities that act in every capitalist social formation, around which all types of historical contingence is being articulated). At the same time, these episodes suggest a different reading of the history of finance in capitalism. Therefore, these moments shape a first sketching of a theory and a history of capital and finance that have been waiting (for a long time, indeed) to be written, analyzed and properly discussed. This book has the ambition of being just a small step towards this unexplored line of thought.

Readers who are not familiar with financial engineering will have the chance to get an initial idea of the workings of finance, which are usually suppressed in the heterodox discussions. The message of this chapter is the prelude for the argument that we shall put forward in the following one.

2 Securitization in early capitalism: on the hidden side of events

It would be rather trivial to argue that capitalism presupposes finance for its own setting and reproduction. Nevertheless, as we have already argued, this formulation, which is not foreign even to mainstream thinking, can be met in a variety of different meanings, approaches, mechanisms, and causalities. Our point is that along with the quantitative aspect, finance also contains a *qualitative* one, which should not be left hidden and ignored.

A crucial moment in the financial system is the market for sovereign debt. This was always the case, even in times when borrowing against collateral by financial institutions was not as important as it is has become in the current financial landscape. Mainstream financial discussions accept that a certain level of sovereign debt is welcomed since it nurtures capital markets (see Hoffman *et al.* 2007; Ch. 1). This was a point also made by Marx (Marx 1990: 919, 920): "the public debt becomes one of the most powerful levers of primitive accumulation. [...] Along with the national debt there arose the international credit system, which often conceals one of the sources of primitive accumulation in this or that people."

In the eighteenth century, one of the convenient channels that French monarchs utilized in order to raise money was the issuance of life annuities (rente viagère).[1] The latter amounts to a particular type of bond security. It generates a regular income flow, which lasts until the death of the owner. In other words, life annuity itself is a form of derivative because its maturity is linked to the life period of the owner. This type of security quickly became an economic success. There is a simple explanation for that. On the one hand, the French absolutist state enjoyed the benefits of a liquid market for its sovereign liabilities while, on the other hand, the purchasers (typically wealthy fifty-year-old men) assured themselves a guaranteed income (through the reliability of the French monarchy) for life – "a great attraction in an era before there was any sort of private or public old-age pension" (Hoffman *et al.* 2007: 149). The price of life annuities was determined to satisfy both parties, usually returning 5 percent on the initial investment to the buyer, a stable but not extraordinary profit.

Soon, the same annuity securities appeared under a new derivative form, which gave the buyer the right to link the flow of interest payment not to his own life span but to the life span of some other third person. This feature made annuities even more attractive. There were several ways for an investor to take advantage of this arrangement. For example, a caring father could associate the payments with his daughter's life span, making her the recipient of a generous lifetime income. The payments would go on longer than the old father's remaining period of life. But the same arrangement also made room for a new profitable financial innovation because the buyer of the annuity could assign them to anyone they wished.

In the early 1770s, a number of rich Geneva bankers (who based their actions on statistical research methods which are systematic in terms of the standards of the period) started looking for young healthy girls (women used to live longer than men), usually at the age of ten, whose family condition implied very high life expectancy, and who had survived major diseases, especially smallpox (child mortality was extremely high in this period). The bankers bought life annuities from the French state in the name of these girls. In this manner, they achieved a very high expected maturity without giving away the ownership of the future flow of payments. In order to further eliminate the risks from an unexpected early death, the bankers created groups of thirty properly selected young girls and then purchased the same amount of life annuities from the French state, one for each girl (a primary form of risk diversification, one might say). Accordingly, they pooled together these securities, created new derived securitizations and sold them to other rich investors in Geneva. This early version of securitization became a big success mostly due to the good reputation of the bankers and trust in the French monarch. The financial intermediation had created a very appealing product which had taken into account the forecastable risks, "apparently" reduced the dangers that investors faced, increased return and liquidity, and gave rise to great intermediation profits for the bankers, which, in turn, satisfied the risk appetite of rich investors. Everything looked perfect, until something completely unexpected happened: the outbreak of the French Revolution.

There are many lessons to be drawn from this episode. We shall highlight two of them that are relevant to the priorities of this study.

2.1 On the nature of finance

It would be possible to isolate the "quantitative" aspect of this historical event, focusing the research on the instability and the implications to the economy caused by this innovative form of intermediation (we have here a clear example of a crisis which is practically linked to derivatives). Nevertheless, there is another crucial moment in the whole process, less apparent but far more important and strategic. Let's take a closer look at the preconditions of all these structured derivative transactions. For the latter to take place, there must exist a certain level of "knowledge" with regard not only to the creditworthiness of the French monarchy, but also to the living conditions of a significant part of the population. For instance, the innovation process presupposes a certain determination and categorization of the possible events (risks) that can cause a death, and a further assessment of these dangers along with their distribution to different parts of the population based on some statistical calculations. It is only in this context that the choice of the young girls can be properly made with the minimum of "risk" involved. It seems obvious that this process of financial innovation is closely related to a *particular representation of capitalist* reality, which is linked to established social perceptions and to dominant scientific ideas (these ideas are not of course independent from the relevant mechanisms of social control) with regard to the organization of life and the "training" of young people. We can easily understand that the generalization of this kind of financial practice would set up a stifling control context that would offer a brand new form of organization to the involved mechanisms of power.

Now imagine that the above line of reasoning pertains, in a professional and sophisticated manner, to the majority of capitalist firms, states, households, etc. worldwide. This "brave new world" of finance is not the result of the grotesque fantasy of a mind like Aldous Huxley's. On the contrary, it is quite close to the tendencies already existent within contemporary financial capitalism. Obviously, we encounter here an institutional configuration unstable and vulnerable to shocks. In the above episode, the securitization circuit came into crisis not as a result of some design flaw but because of a historical revolution: the French Revolution. The new French government fell behind on its interest payments and was soon paying the debtors in paper money, which had practically no international value:

> Not surprisingly, most of the Genevan bankers went bankrupt. So too did a number of investors, for in some of the investment pools, the bankers let the investors buy their shares on credit with only a small down payment in return for the investors' assuming the liability that the pool would remain solvent. In the end, nearly all the investors suffered, for when the banks failed, even investors who had not taken on any liability lost the annuity payments.
>
> (Hoffman *et al.* 2007: 151)

Nevertheless, the economic vulnerability of the system to unpredictable events is not the most important part of this story.

The theoretical sketch that we have tried to put forward does not solely approach the study of financial mechanisms (financialization) from the view point of their "productive" or "counter-productive" effects (finance as process of funding) – but situates the phenomenon of financialization in a whole series of its "positive" effects in the organization of capitalist reality, even if these effects seem marginal at first sight.[2] We believe that this second category of effects, that remain to some extent latent in the whole process, is the most decisive precondition for the circuit of capital and the reproduction of social power relations in general. In this regard, financialization is grasped as a complex technology for the organization of capitalist power, the main aspect of which is not income redistribution and economic instability, but the organization of capitalist power relations in line with a particular prototype. This process in motion encompasses different institutions, social procedures, analyses and reflections, calculations, tactics, and embedding patterns that allow for the exercise of this specific, albeit very complex, function that organizes the efficiency of capitalist power relations through the workings of financial markets. In the following chapter we shall attempt to theorize this process in the light of Marxian categories.

Derivatives are at the epicenter of contemporary finance (and of course in the episode we described). In the derivatives statistical data (as they are collected by the Bank for International Settlements: BIS), the size of derivatives markets is measured by the gross nominal or notional value of all deals concluded and not yet settled on the reporting date for several types of products (not all the products of the so-called structured finance). This is the notional amount outstanding. Figure 6.1 depicts the trend of this variable after 1998 for both OTC[3] and organized transactions (as it is quite clear, the first type of market overwhelms in the derivatives dealing). It is straightforward to realize that the expansion of the derivatives market is considerable and remarkably stable. The total size of both markets exceeds the 1,000 percent of world GDP or alternatively the 1,500 percent of the GDP of advanced capitalist economies.

Looking at Figure 6.1, one cannot escape from the following question: *how can the above trend be explained and what are its consequences for the organization of capitalist power and social life in general*? This question is closely related to another: Why hasn't economic and social research highlighted the importance of this trend? The majority of the researchers who embark upon the study of contemporary financial engineering, resort to speculation as the ultimate basis of their explanation. But then, how many times should the size of these markets overstep world GDP in order for us to realize that something else is going on?

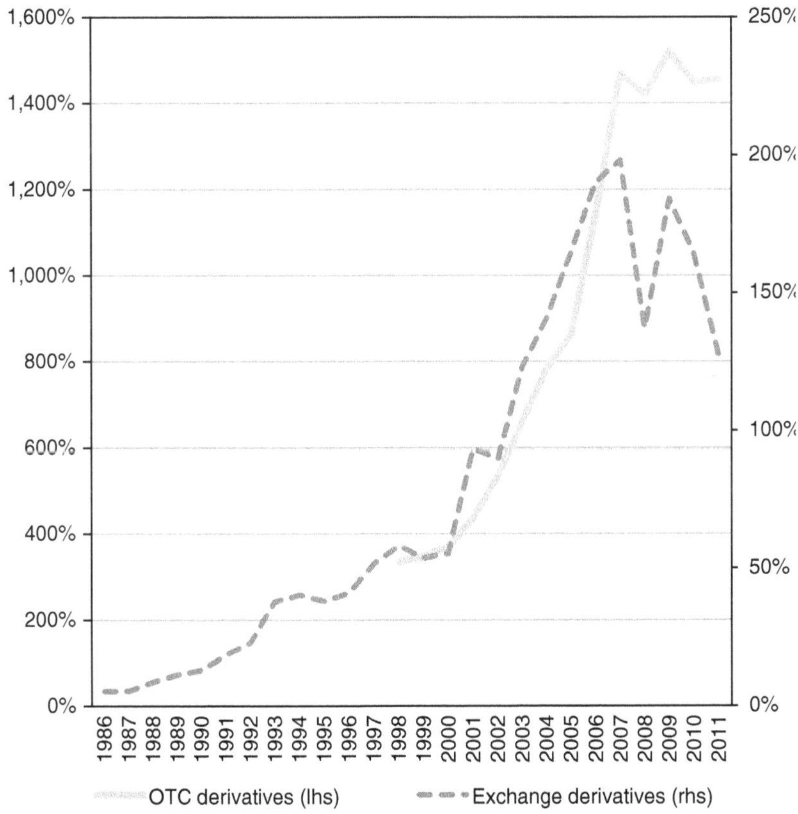

Figure 6.1 Notional amount outstanding of derivatives markets (OTC and exchange), as percentage of the GDP, advanced economies (source: BIS databases, IMF).

2.2 On the character of financial representation: finance and knowledge

There is another important lesson from the above story, which is present in the majority of financial crises throughout the history of capitalism, but most importantly in the recent ones. We shall briefly draw upon it in order to bring up some interesting issues with regard to the nature of finance.

The French Revolution was an unpredictable event. But there are numerous examples from financial crises that began when a well-defined financial mechanism came across events that were considered to be unthinkable. The LTCM (Long Term Capital Management) default along with the resulting mini crisis, subprime financial meltdown, and the euro crisis are just some recent examples. The trivial argument in discussions goes pretty much as follows. Reliance on past historical data is never a good guide for predicting the future of the system as a whole. Relationships that are valid in the past may not apply in the future; or, even if they apply, the "size" or the "nature" of the "sample" may not be "representative" enough to draw secure conclusions. In fact, this is the regular case pertaining to almost every major financial innovation: *no historical data exist for new products, and yet it is the existence of these products that will define the future landscape of finance.* Extrapolating from the performance of similar products is not a substitute and can easily underestimate significant involved risks. In other words, past data are also poor indicators of future trends because they may not apply to an evolving financial system that follows its own unique path. To give just one example, the same argument applied to macro stress tests (that is, to studies that test the macro stability of a financial system) is reproduced by a recent BIS research report. In the latter, Borio *et al.* (2012: 11) argue that macro stress test:

> reliance on past data also means that these models are not well suited to capturing innovations or changes in market structure. And yet, innovations – be they financial, such as structured credit products, or "real," such as the invention of railways – are often at the centre of the build-up of financial imbalances and the following distress.

Recent events seem to justify these critical ideas. If we return to our initial example, the outbreak of the French Revolution could not be forecast, but the benchmark case with regard to financial instability is a more modest one: systemic breakdowns are derived by normal size shocks (and not by extraordinary historical incidents). These "shocks" *cannot be predicted* because they do not fit into the representation of capitalist reality that is interlinked to the design of the involved financial instruments. As we discussed in the previous section, financial innovation is associated with a certain process of knowledge which is necessary to organize the pricing aspect of the whole set of financial products. Without this type of knowledge, the risks that define monarchy finances (the so-called dynamics of sovereign debt) and the living conditions of the young population of Geneva could not be specified and assessed, and, therefore, no financial product could be originated, since no one could come up with any meaningful estimation of the prices. In other words, the "actual' financial dangers that threaten the whole system cannot be easily identified because their significance cannot be captured by the dominant interpretation that the financial system utilizes in order to support the innovation.

This was quite obvious in the case of the US economy before the financial meltdown.[4] There was a strong growth of credit and an increase in the asset prices. Against this background, leverage measured in market prices was underestimated; the quality of assets used as collateral by the "shadow banking" sector to raise funds seemed especially good; risk premiums and price volatilities were exceptionally low. In plain terms, the system underpriced significant risks, supporting an aggressive risk taking, and seemed most solid precisely when it was fragile. Some might question the ability of finance to foretell the future, but this is the wrong debate to be launched.

According to mainstream thinking, financial markets reveal and disseminate significant information with regard to economic data. Nevertheless, "information" is not neutral and cannot exist outside a particular interpretation context. Therefore the functioning of financial markets is interwoven with a certain framework of "knowledge" (even if this is an ideological one). The latter is important despite its inability to foretell the future. It is quite obvious that the results of the class struggle are unique and unpredictable, but the knowledge innate in the process of finance is necessary to support the role of finance as a technology of power that organizes capitalist power relations. To put it differently, *finance is not so much about forecasting the future but about disciplining the present, even if this passes through the estimation of future outcomes.*

This message, which sets up in its own right a radically different research agenda for finance, is implied many times in mainstream economic writings. For instance, in the very same BIS report that questions the ability of macro stress testing to stand outside the established financial context of representation, it is explicitly suggested that stress tests are valuable in establishing a common reference point after the crisis, in the setting up of a new representation context (Borio *et al.* 2012). In other words, from the mainstream point of view the real issue when we have the outbreak of a financial crisis is not the economic implications, but the establishment of a new interpretation context that does not endanger the role of finance in organizing and reproducing social power relations along the lines indicated in this section.

3 The bankruptcy of Barings Bank: an introduction to the commodification of risk

Derivative markets capture the interest of the (unfamiliar) public only during the so-called dramatic events of financial crises. There are some striking examples, which have been addressed many times in finance textbooks. In this section, we shall discuss the default of Barings Bank in the mid 1990s. Our choice is not based on the publicity it has attracted (not to mention the relevant movie); nor do we consider this event as the most important among other dramatic events. We shall use it in order to present the workings of options markets and illustrate our thesis that derivatives are *sui generis* commodifications of risk.

The background is pretty much known:

> Barings plc, the oldest merchant banking group in the United Kingdom (established in 1761) was placed in "administration" by the High Court in London on 26 February 1995, and was taken over by ING, a diversified Dutch bank. Barings Futures (Singapore) (BFS), a subsidiary of Barings plc, suffered losses from large unhedged positions in futures contracts and options – exceeding the entire equity capital of the firm (estimated at US$860 million at the time). The final total loss was US$1.47 billion. Nick Leeson, general manager of BFS, was responsible for the subsidiary's trading strategies and losses. The fact that a relatively junior trader bankrupted a household name in banking attracted world-wide attention.
>
> (Steinherr 2000: 68)

Of course, while it is indeed difficult for someone to reasonably explain Leeson's futures and options investment strategies, it was not a personal mistake that drove the whole process of default.

For the moment, we shall focus on Leeson's options strategy. An option is a financial contract similar to a future, which was explained in Chapter 4. The difference is that the option gives the holder the right (and not the obligation) to buy or sell the underlying asset at a future date. The holder has not been committed to some action since they do not have to exercise this right. This right costs something, and therefore, unlike futures, the purchase of an option requires an up-front payment. There are briefly two basic types of options: rights to buy are named call options (or simply calls) while rights to sell are called put options (or simply puts).[5] Leeson had taken a substantial exposure by writing (selling) call and put options with the same strike price. According to the market jargon, when someone sells they take a "short" position in the market and when they buy they take a "long" position. The underlying index was Nikkei 225. This combination of short puts and calls is not complex and is known as a straddle position. The pay-off of writing a single straddle is depicted in Figure 6.2.

Line *AEC* shows the profit for the short call. With this contract Leeson sells someone else the right to buy the underlying index at a pre-specified date in the future (expiration date) and at an agreed exercise price *K*. At the maturity day, the other party will not exercise this right if the spot price *S* is lower than *K* (it is totally unreasonable to buy something at a higher price than the spot price). In that case, Leeson's gain would be the up-front premium *c* (equal to *OA* in the figure) he had received when he issued the call. On the other hand, if the spot price is higher than the strike price *K*, Leeson's counterparty will exercise the option buying the underlying index. In that case, Leeson will face losses equal to: $c-(S-K)$, given by the line *EC*. In quite the same way, it is easy to show that

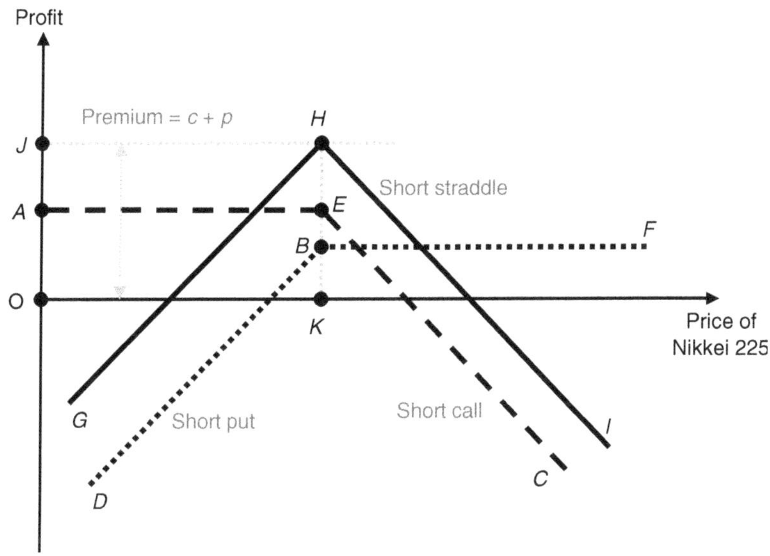

Figure 6.2 A short straddle.

Leeson's profit from the short put will be given by line *DBF*: for spot prices higher than *K* the counterparty will not exercise the put option, selling something at a lower price than the existing one. We get the final profit from the short straddle position if we add the two option profit lines (line *GHI*).

The important question follows: What is the economic nature of a short straddle options strategy? This position is appropriate for an investor who expects the spot price of the underlying asset in the future to be close to the strike price, that is, if the investor anticipates low price volatility. In other words, if the spot price in the future stays close to *K*, the investor will end up with a profit near to the premiums they received for issuing the straddle: $OJ=c+p$. It goes without saying that high volatility can easily be translated into huge losses. In this sense, Leeson's option strategy can be described as volatility trading. He expected the volatility of Nikkei 225 to remain low therefore taking a short position. Issuing a significant amount of naked puts and calls and anticipating stability in the market, he earned substantial amount of premiums (reporting them as profits) while exposing his firm to considerable risk when markets moved in an unexpected pattern. If we ignore for the moment the reasons for this bet, it is very important to understand the straddle as *mere commodification not of the Nikkei 225 index but of its price volatility*. Volatility is part of the risks attached to this abstract index. With the above strategy, which is quite trivial in options markets, this volatility risk can be singled out, isolated, repackaged, and traded separately from the index itself. It receives a price that is a more precise quantitative assessment of this part of the risk involved in the underlying asset. A higher straddle premium means higher (anticipated) "price" for volatility. There is one point that must be emphasized (we shall return to it in the following chapters). This price is measured in money terms, that is, despite individual estimations, it receives an objective measurement as an established value form. This is the driving idea for analyzing contemporary financial innovations linking them to fetishism as analyzed by Marx in *Capital*.

It is quite obvious that derivatives in the above sense are not money; neither do they play the role of money. They (along with the investment strategies they support) are *sui generis* commodifications of risk involved in the economic assets. On their basis, parts of risk can be re-bundled and priced. What is important from the perspective of political economy is to think about the consequences of this process, given the development and the size of derivatives markets.

Leeson's strategy was aggressive, risky, poorly planned, without analytical support and totally uncovered. Nevertheless, the point of this section is irrelevant to the conditions that led to the bankruptcy. The Kobe earthquake, in January 1995, precipitated a decline of 11 percent in the Nikkei 225, an increase in volatility that was catastrophic for Baring's subsidiary in Singapore. Leeson's nervous effort to deal with the events (building up an outstanding long position in the futures market of the same index in order to push price back to old levels) multiplied the problems and further elevated the size of the exposure.

One of the big lessons is that "even experienced and large institutions fail to have appropriate risk management or [...] control systems" (Steinherr 2000: 73). In this sense, "given the leverage of derivative products, a single trader can bankrupt a large financial institution" (ibid.). The organizational issues are thus the most important, and of course it is not accidental that they appeared at the period of transformation of the basic banking model way from "traditional emphasis on market-making and client business" into the new phase of "trading focus into high-margin areas, especially derivatives, proprietary trading and arbitrage" (ibid.: 73). Nevertheless, we believe that the most important feature of the above discussion is not financial fragility. In the case of Barings Bank "positions were unwound quickly and without undue stress because they were exchange-traded so that margins covered counterparty risk. [...] Had positions been of an OTC type, liquidation would have proven complicated" (ibid.: 74). The key issue concerns the *pricing of risk in terms of money*. We shall argue in the next chapters that this development is absolutely crucial to the contemporary organization of capitalist power.

4 The subprime crisis: the contingency of financial meltdown in the framework of neoliberal regulation

4.1 The neoliberal model for the regulation of financing

Present-day developments in the financing process date from the beginning of the 1980s and have their origins in the abolition of the restrictions that had been imposed on banks, on the international movement of capital, and on the mode of operation of stock exchanges after the crisis of 1929 (particularly in London and the USA). In other words, they have their origins in the emergence of what is called the *neoliberal framework for regulation* of the financial sphere. We say regulation and we do not use the usual term "deregulation" because in the neoliberal model there is no abolition of regulation or (in the final analysis) of the guarantees provided by the collective capitalist (the state) for such functioning of the financial system. The post-war Keynesian regulation (Bretton Woods) was merely replaced by a different kind of regulation that is compatible with the functions required by the neoliberal model of the financial system. A new comprehensive framework of rules and regulations is in full operation today. One example is the functioning of central banks as technical centers for underwriting the operations of the money markets and the credit system (carried out through a broad mesh of regulations, rules, and hierarchies), wherein the procedure for decision-making takes place beyond the boundaries of democratic legitimacy, in itself comprising a major systemic reform. Another example is the function of Basel I, II, and III as systems for regulating the behavior of banks that are under the control of the central bank, etc.

The basic characteristic of the regulatory framework for the financial sphere – which is a structural characteristic and core component of the neoliberal model – is the development of extra-bank (i.e., non-traditional) financing of the public debt and enterprises by the international markets. The enterprises, at first large internationally active ones but with subsequent extension to medium-sized companies of suitable creditworthiness, finance their activities mostly through non-traditional sources of credit. They issue short-term commercial paper, sometimes using the stock exchange, sometimes resorting to a variety of non-bank financial arrangements entered into for this purpose: including insurance funds, mutual funds, hedge funds, insurance companies, and a whole constellation of special forms of capital. It is not only business companies that subsequently acquire access to non-bank financing and risk-management facilities but also those seeking housing loans, student loans, loans for the purchase of a car, credit cards, and loans taken out by municipalities, etc.

This financing model presupposes securitization of debt and international mobility of capital, that is to say *the bringing into existence of an international space of multiple investment spheres for individual and isolated capitals, a space whose functioning makes these prerequisites into expanded consequences*. The financial markets have developed into a complex multi-dimensional system. They are not just money markets, bond markets, share markets, currency markets, and commodity markets. They also include derivatives markets and markets in every other kind of security. As a result, an *international of capital* has come into existence that is permanently on the lookout for secure profits and self-valorization of money. Reliable returns meaning that risk management (that is to say the probability of the expected return not being achieved) is the basic concern in an international market where multiple divergent forces are determining returns. It is a complex technique that prides itself on being a thorough science.

The functioning of the financial system and the means by which it is activated (for example the various forms of security) do not comprise merely vehicles for speculative investments. They are, in a much greater sense, components of a mechanism that makes a decisive contribution to the mobility of individual capitals, establishing the conditions for their competition. The system thus functions as a key link in the reproduction of overall social capital. *Exposing individual capitals to international competition for financing of their activities makes it possible for there to be rapid reward of profitable, and punishment of insufficiently profitable, investments.* This function has contributed, and continues to contribute, to the transformation of banking activity because of the change in the correlation of forces between banks and the money market. More specifically, and as always in relation to our subject, the process of liberalization of the financial system had significant consequences for the functioning of the banks, which may be summarized as follows:

1 Bonds and shares are both securities. But, in order for them to be able to act as sources of finance for individuals or insurance funds or other non-traditional banking institutions, businesses or private citizens (for example with housing loans, etc.), *other forms of securitization of debt must be developed.* Securitization of debt has become an important process. It has contributed both to the emergence of the contemporary credit system and to its current crisis.

2 The various non-bank financial schemes in operation in the international capital markets are not afflicted with the regulative restrictions that apply to banks, and are able to lend money at low rates of interest. This has had consequences for the functioning and the structure of the banking system. The new arrangements have squeezed bank profits and changed the composition of their workload, i.e., led to an increase in loans to households, and loans to cover consumer and housing expenditures, and a reduction in loans to businesses. Consequently, with the gradual reform of the system, the banks were led into increased securitization as a means of expanding their turnover. They turned to securing commission from financial facilitation as a source of profit.

   When a person (bank) takes out a loan, they are required to secure a certain amount of capital so that there will be some guarantee (collateral) in the event of the inability to meet their obligations. But this diminishes their prospects of lending money themselves because they are obliged to tie up a certain amount of capital. If this person sells the loan (that is to say issues a security whose holder receives the cash flow from the loan) first, they are not required to tie up capital, and second, they are able to withhold a proportion of the cash flow *as commission* for issuing the security and so to find a different source of profit, which is directly dependent on the extension of credit that is thereby achieved, that is to say the number of loans that are issued. This nevertheless entails some restrictions. First, in general the expansion of credit contributes to a rise in property values; second, the increase in interest rates affects the value of existing securities in the event of conversion into cash or in the event that they are used as collateral for the purpose of obtaining cash. This poses potential dangers of disturbance to the credit system, leading the monetary authorities to carefully consider whether they should raise interest rates. Low interest rates, by contrast, facilitate the expansion of credit under some conditions beyond the limits set by the requirements of capitalist production. As for the form taken by household finance, it should be borne in mind that competition between individual capitals is conducted through profitable investments exploiting innovations and seeking out unexploited regions, or regions that can provide an advantage by comparison with other individual capitals. Banks are not exempt from this rule. Intensified competition in lending to households, in so far as such loans have now come to account for a significant proportion of bank profit, is the basis for the issuance of subprimes and other equivalent types of loan, and the basis for effective exploitation of this type of loan within the overall process of securitization.

3 Liberalization has led to the excessive expansion of certain banks involved in international transactions which – though for some they represent outmoded practice – are very important *nodal points*, not only from the viewpoint of scale of transactions and obligations but also from that of the links they maintain within the overall context of the international financial system.

4 Moreover, given the development of over-the-counter (OTC) markets, of various off-shore companies, the development of special purpose vehicles (SPVs), of different money markets, bonds, securities, swaps, etc., or in other words the development, in general, of international activities utilizing a complex network of financial transactions and money flows that mostly evade all supervision and/or oversight, the system has become more intricate and complex. At the same time, the development of new forms of finance (linked to derivatives) has resulted in complex models of pricing and credit risk assessment that depend on parameters for which, in all likelihood, no data exists. To the extent that information does exist it, is likely to be extremely vulnerable to small changes (to say nothing of its inability to incorporate or measure potential risks and uncertainties created by the complexity of this network of relationships within the capitalist process of production and reproduction). Moreover, in contrast to the ideologies of abolishing the role of the intermediaries, what is conspicuous in the current crisis is the emergence of new intermediaries and a network of multiple interlinkages entirely lacking in transparency.

Finally, the emergence and consolidation of the neoliberal model did not take place from one day to the next. It did not appear as a comprehensive ready-made model but as a process of gradual elaboration taking into account failures, successes, and the changing environment. It did not automatically gain ground in all countries. It appears to have begun to be propagated, though still sometimes in a desultory fashion, following its rise to supremacy in the US and the UK. For reasons that have to do both with the history of its emergence and with the mode of articulation of international networking, the USA (and to a lesser extent the UK) have been the centers of the international financial sphere, from which tools, innovations, organizational forms, etc. have been propagated to the rest of the international system. Thus one element at the core of the model is this complex articulation of relations whereby Wall Street (along with other financial centers in the USA) and the City of London have functioned as a center for the dissemination of new regulations and forms of organization of the financial system.

4.2 Comments on different interpretations of the subprime crisis

There are interpretations of the subprime crisis that situate it at each of, or all of, the points in the chain of securitization. By and large, they all understand causality as synonymous with moral responsibility: "It is their fault." But the moralistic attribution of responsibility to subjects or extraneous factors is likely to hinder comprehension of the crisis as that which is engendered by the model of economic regulation itself.

Wrong explanation A: Subprime loans as the cause of the crisis

The commonest explanation focuses on the issuing of subprime loans. These are loans that are generally made available to borrowers who do not fulfill some of the formal requirements for taking out a conventional loan.[6] They were made available to the poorer layers of US society and to minorities, which therefore means that from the viewpoint of the credit system (which bears the greatest credit risk) they also required higher interest rates to counterbalance the risk. But they were also made to borrowers from other income strata who were deeply in debt, as well as those who used this form of borrowing for buying and selling houses. Finally, they represented an opportunity for borrowing for the purpose of rescheduling loans. There are also other categories of loans with similar characteristics.

It seems tautological, given that the crisis began with securities on subprime loans, to consider that the issuing of this type of loan is responsible for the emergence of the crisis. Even if we assume that this line or reasoning is correct, however, it cannot explain why such a crisis did not emerge between 1998 and 2001, when (once more) there was an increase in delays in paying installments and, therefore, similar problems with the securities issued on the basis of them. The reasoning is nevertheless fallacious. Not because it is not true, *but because it obscures the factors that operated in such a way as to nurture the crisis and then trigger it.* Why were subprime loans issued? And why were there borrowers who took them out?

The latter question seems to be easier to answer. First, home ownership and the availability of cheap loans to make it possible was a significant factor in securing consent to the neoliberal agenda not only in the USA, but also in other developed countries. In the course of development of the conditions for crisis, US president, in 2002, announced the (neo-conservative oriented) *Homeownership Challenge*, according to which the possession of one's own home was at the heart of the American dream. He then took steps to implement the program, whose aim was to increase the proportion of homeowners, particularly among minorities (Afro-Americans and Hispanics – those categories of the population among whom four years later one could observe the highest levels of inability to pay off loans and also the highest levels of home foreclosures), that is to say to groups mostly excluded from the traditional credit system. To carry out this program, which "could be implemented only by the state," many organizations responded by offering new types of housing loans so as to increase the options available to borrowers (evidently including the various categories of subprime, which took off spectacularly after 2002). Second, through the availability of loans, tax breaks and credit facilities (made possible by the existence of the home as an asset, see Chapter 3 on this issue), *the significance of the house itself changed*: It was also converted – even when seen as a "roof over one's head" – into a basis for bolstering one's income and was seen as an entry ticket to the facilities provided by the credit system (a genuine entry to the asset side of households' balance sheets).

Thus, in a context of stagnating real wages and the withdrawal of the state from a whole range of social services formerly provided "free of charge," the potential for increasing one's disposable income offered by entry into the credit system (particularly if the mortgage each year increases in value with the increase in land prices) is an important element not only of individual strategies but also of relief from the pressures being exerted by the system. There are other points that could be cited (for example the fact that, depending on the location of the house, one might have access to "more reputable" schools than those in the area of one's current residence), but what has been said is nevertheless enough to show that the development of the subprime market was set in motion by profounder elements in the neoliberal model and that today's crisis marks the limits of incorporation of social needs through the neoliberal model. In other words, the management of aggregate demand via borrowing, and the expansion of credit as a means of counteracting and making room for constraints on wages, has not been proved an effective management mechanism.

As for the first part of the hypothesis, that the issuing of subprimes is simply part of the speculative activity of the bankers who issued them, it is worth stressing that to understand the deeper significance of financial crises it is not useful to make very general references to "speculation" in the sphere of finance. Speculation as the reason for the issuing of subprimes is linked to another more elaborated explanation for the appearance of the crisis: the originate and distribute (O&D) model for the functioning of banks that has become predominant as banking practice. This is another way of defining the securitization process.

Wrong explanation B: The securitization process or the O&D model as the cause of the crisis

The issuing of subprimes is a product of securitization. Given that banks simply originated the loan and distributed the risk by selling the securities to others while retaining a commission for that service (O&D), they did not have sufficient incentives to examine the quality of the credit underlying the loan they had issued, as they would have had if they had kept the loan on their own balance sheet without being able to transfer it. Because their profitability depended on the volume of securities they issued, they had every incentive to extend credit without examining the risks too closely.

Of course, not all subprime loans are securitized. Securitization covered 28 percent of such loans in 1995, but this figure began to fall from 1998, only recovering from 2001 onward. In 2001, 50 percent of the value of subprime loans was issued due to securitization. This percentage gradually rose to 60 percent in 2003 and to between 75 percent and 80 percent from 2004 to 2006. But this is not the important figure when attempting to assess the validity of the above argument.

The relaxation of the regulations and conditions for the issuing of credit, with easy acceptance of collateral in periods of rapid growth of credit in a context of cyclical economic upturn, is a general phenomenon and is not particularly new. In the specific case we are examining, in a context of record low interest rates, low inflation, and stable growth in the developed economies, it appears as a natural consequence of the conditions of functioning of credit. Note that the relaxing of requirements for issuing credit, above and beyond questions of incentives, does not involve only the initial issuers of the loans (the banks that securitize the loans) but also involves security holders due to the general squeeze on all types of return (in relation to the risk-free securities: a clampdown on credit spreads).

One line of explanation for the credit crisis considers securitization of loans to be the cause of the crisis. The transfer of risk outside the portfolio of the lender agency is said to provide this agency with incentives to downgrade the quality of the issued loan. This explanation necessarily has as its supplement a second cause, which is faulty assessment of the credit risk by market participants and the credit rating agencies. Otherwise one cannot explain why securities, linked to low quality loans, were bought on a massive scale (unless one evokes the ignorance of "naïve" investors). Nevertheless, persisting with the logic of "mistakes," one cannot explain how many holders of capital (most of them banks with research departments and immediate access to a plethora of data) internationally made the very same "mistake" in their purchase of securities. For instance, the exchange of written reports between analysts in the international organizations and the central banks, which has been in public circulation since 2004 at the latest, made it clear that the methods of pricing and credit evaluation of CDO (Collateralized Debt Obligation) departments are "unsound," because they do not take into account a variety of factors.

Here, we are concerned with the intermingling of practices that *are always socially over-determined* (and it is on such relations that the elaboration of the specific mechanisms is based) such as those of the rating agencies, the lending and securitization mechanisms, etc. No manager of capital can easily say: "I know that the CDOs are high-risk and not easily sold and for that reason I inform you that this year you will be content with 3 percent profit. Don't look at others who are earning 9 percent profit because your money is at risk." In 2001, the manager would have received the answer: "introduce suitable differentiation into your portfolio, take security measures or risk insurance and throw in some money and we'll see." In 2005, the same cautious manager would have been told that they were a fool because others had earned a lot of money by retaining a larger proportion of their portfolio in CDOs. Faced with the demand for guaranteed securities and high profits, in the climate that prevailed after 2001, we can imagine the answer of the bank directors when they find out that they can make money from issuing securities and expanding borrowing, and by falling in with the responses of the remaining parties in the securitization chain.

But the pursuit of profit on a global scale has never been the privilege of a few. It is the outcome of arrangements imposed by (and making possible the elaboration of) the neoliberal model and also comprising a prerequisite for it. One consequence of neoliberalism is that a borrower who has lost their house, because of a sudden increase in installment payments owing to the expiry of the period of grace and insufficiency of their income, may simultaneously be a participant in the mutual fund that financed the mortgage-based securities and sought the issuance of the subprimes (looking for greater profitability), as well as being holder of a truncated portion of their own pension betting on the fall in value of the securities in which their insurance fund was investing. Their life (takes the form of a balance sheet and) is thus divided up in the same way as the portfolio whose fate is determined by good and bad moments for the markets. As was mentioned in Chapter 3, and will become more clear in the following part of the book, the rise of finance has generalized the "balance sheet form" throughout the economy: *not just the liability side, but the asset one as well.* It is exactly the implications of this fact that have passed unnoticed in the analyses of social sciences.

Wrong explanation C: The "bubble" in housing prices and low interest rates

In the United States, a sharp increase in house prices is to be observed between 2000 and 2006, with some areas showing a greater rise than others. For example in Los Angeles and Miami, a price rise of more than 160 percent is to be noted in a period of six years, while in Detroit the corresponding figure is 10 percent. On the basis of this increase in prices, construction activity starts to grow after 2002, leading to a record high level of housing supply in 2006 and probably playing an important role in the falling off in the increase of price rises in 2006 (which in turn had an effect on the servicing of debt). Above and beyond the fact that this period saw the expiry of the period of grace on a great proportion of loan contracts or low-repayment-rate subprimes that had been taken out previously, we have at the same time a hike in borrowing costs with concomitant difficulties in servicing debts, and simultaneous incapacitation of the chain of loans for buying a house, which one could later reschedule on more favorable terms because its value would have risen. Nevertheless the average increase in housing prices is considerably smaller, in fact many times smaller, than what was observed in other countries. The reasons for the increase in prices are not traceable only to the expansion of credit. They should also be sought in what was said earlier about the importance of owning one's own home and in the fact that following the dot.com meltdown, the purchase of a house seemed like the next risk-free refuge for investments. Another important factor was, of course, the record low interest rates after 2001 and the squeeze on various high-risk premiums (overall assessment of risk, that is to say).

There is, nevertheless, a big difference between recognizing the importance of the factor of low interest rates and regarding it as *the* reason for the increase in house prices. Much more so when it takes the form of a proposal that the FED (Federal Reserve System) should increase interest rates so as to bring a halt to the bubble in the housing market. For a start, after 2004, when the FED increased interest rates, a doubling in the proportion of subprime loans can be observed (from 335 billion in 2003 to 540 billion in 2004 and 600 billion in 2006). In general after 2004 and the gradual increase in interest rates, the categories of loans being made available included non-conventional variable-interest-rate loans, that is to say the loans through the medium of which the crisis made its appearance. Even worse, the monetarist-leaning proposal demanding an increase in interest rates large enough to be capable of curbing the rise in house prices (that is to say quite a significant rise), amounted, indeed, to a proposal that the economy should be led into a recession in 2001 so as to avoid the recession of 2008.

4.3 Financialization as precarious regulation

References to a general characteristic (speculation) or to the imperfections of the functioning of the financial system (O&D, faulty risk assessment, conflict of interests, asymmetric information between the parties to a contract, etc.) sheds little light on the two ends of the chain in the crisis process. *Nevertheless, the ends of the chain are the most important because they show up the contradictions in the neoliberal model that have nurtured, and then triggered, the crisis.* The rise in house prices, the issuing of subprimes, securitization, evaluation of securities, the relationship between SPVs and the money markets ... none of these are real causes. They are forms of appearance and vehicles for unfolding of the elements and relationships that comprise the neoliberal model, that is to say the particular form of organization of capitalist social formations after 1980.

Having already described the basic elements and the relationships that make up the core of the neoliberal model system we will confine ourselves here to drawing certain summary conclusions.

First, the squeeze on wages and the flexibilization of work relations, that is to say reduction in the bargaining power of workers against capital, are a success story of neoliberalism but *at the same time* represent one of the conditions for the nurturing and triggering of the crisis. The basic element in the equation is an accumulation of contradictory demands from the financial system. Increasing inequality in income distribution, reduction in the share accruing to wages, new types of commodification of human needs, and increasing discipline to the norms of the system pose problems for the management of aggregate demand in the interests of the smooth functioning of expanded reproduction and capitalist accumulation, as well as problems in organizing consensus to the model. *In other words, the conditions for increase in class domination of capital appear simultaneously as conditions undermining its sustainability.*

Second, the process by which the money markets acquiring "depth," that is to say the process of translating into capital every possible available sum of money that can be deposited in the various separate spheres of the financial system, is also a crucial element for the international dimension of the financial system as well as for mobilizing the entirety of the capitalist mode of production for the purpose of increasing profitability and accumulation. Thus, for example, it is regarded as a condition for the financial sphere acquiring "depth" that insurance systems be privatized or, in any case, that flexible criteria for their management be developed to enable participation in the international financial system. It represents success for the model that it enriches the markets with numerous players and mobilizes every sum of capital that cannot be directly invested in the production process so that it participates in the "club" of demands on future profit. Without the broader non-bank financing, there would be no securing of this type of mobility of capital and related broader funding potentialities. At the same time, however, this "depth" means ever greater pressures for risk-free profit and thus for the issuing of securities so that unexplored markets can be subordinated to the world of credit (with the consequent downplaying of risk and massive runs when secure profit is jeopardized).

Third, in parallel with depth goes its international character. This is a constitutive element of the model and its success, in so far as the economic world in its entirety is transformed into a "profit chart." The international character, together with market depth and generalization of risk management techniques and tools (such as CDS: credit default swaps) for ensuring security against risk, make for greater spread of risk: *a little risk for many (and so no great risk for any one party) and none for the system as a whole.* But the same elements (market depth and the international character in combination with the demand for security of yields), when the first doubts appeared in relation to the housing credit securities, functioned not as factors for hedging risk but for planetary proliferation of risk and distress. It is worth noting that the "wisdom of the markets," an important element in constructing the core of the neoliberal model, presupposes market valuation of every security (market-to-market value). It is exactly this that has caused the lack of trust between the players because the fall in value of the securities spoilt the balance sheets of the institutions maintaining them and protracted the uncertainty.

5 The EMS crisis of 1992–1993[7]

Monetary unions have two basic moments in their general design (this line of reasoning will become clearer in Part IV of the book). They are economic unions made up by different social formations, with different institutional settings and growth patterns. Nevertheless, all participants share a common strategic target: emphasis on fiscal austerity and competitiveness (exposure to international competition). This is a policy mix that favors the upper classes of society and is against the interests of labor. At the same time, this *sui generis* form of symbiosis hinges upon the workings of financial markets.

In this section we shall revisit the well-known 1992–1993 crisis of the Exchange Rate Mechanism (ERM) of the European Monetary System (EMS). The EMS system was the forerunner of the Euro area (EA) and its crisis to some extent set the ground of the subsequent institutional framework. From this point of view, the 1992–1993 crisis of EMS was an event in the long European movement towards economic and political integration.

At the beginning of the 1990s, the EMS was surrounded by solid optimism and widely considered as "the most ambitious experiment in the international monetary and exchange rate cooperation of the post-Bretton Woods era" (Buiter *et al.* 1998: 1). Its crisis in 1992–1993, which came just two years before the Mexican currency and financial crisis, led to a series of academic and political debates followed by numerous research outputs. These discussions were consigned to oblivion as part of the unpleasant past of the European Monetary Union (EMU) project and only revisited in order to draw lessons for the feasibility of the fixed exchange rate system in the region of East Asia. Here we shall reconsider the crisis of 1992–1993, trying to make a general point about the workings of contemporary financial markets. The lesson to be drawn can also help the understanding of the contemporary crisis of the EA.

The process of European unification[8] was more or less explicitly dominated from its very beginning by a pronounced aversion to exchange rate fluctuations. The financial turmoil in the decade of 1970s, and the unsuccessful attempts to establish a stable exchange rate system, brought the EMS to life at the end of 1978. After a short period of negotiations, this plan attained Community-wide consensus. In brief, there were three main features of the EMS.[9] First, according to the ERM, each European Economic Community (EEC) country committed itself to limit the fluctuation of its exchange rate within a band of ±2.25 percent around its bilateral central parity against other members of the ERM (the same limit was ±6 percent for Italy, Spain, the UK, and Portugal which had not joined the ERM from the start). Second, a new European Currency Unit (ECU) – a weighted basket of the ERM currencies according to each country's economic importance – was the new means of settlement among EEC central banks. Third, extensive financing mechanisms were created to ensure that each member state had the necessary resources to meet temporary difficulties in financing balance of payments deficits and defend bilateral exchange rate parities.

While the run-up to the crisis was in place from the beginning of 1992, speculative attacks intensified after the summer of the same year. In September, the British pound and the Italian lira left the EMS and depreciated. Other "weak" currencies (such as the Spanish peseta, the Portuguese escudo, and the Irish pound) devalued without exiting the ERM. The credibility of the ERM was irrevocably wounded. Market attacks continued in waves for the whole of the next year, but not with the same intensity. Financial markets were wavering between periods of tension and relaxation, triggering state interventions and parity realignments. The last act of ERM was to be written in the August of 1993, when the whole setting came under systemic pressure once more. The drastic reorganization of ERM rules was decided in an emergency meeting, which took place in Brussels on 1 August 1993. From this day, currency rates were allowed to fluctuate by 15 percent on either side of the central parity. The new commitment was not far away from a free float.

This silent breakup of the ERM did not negate the common target for a European unification. It rather made quite clear to all sides that the project would be non-functional in the absence of a common currency and proper institutional arrangements to safeguard it from a similar wave of speculative attacks. The new more flexible system, which lasted until the decision to lock the exchange rates in 1999 and replace them by the euro, was not utilized for implementation of demand-side expansionary policies. On the contrary, European states remained loyal to austerity-type policies and used the wider bands only as protection against speculation in order to recalibrate markets' expectations to the stability of the system.

5.1 Financial markets and monetary unions: a general sketching

Speculative attacks in foreign exchange (FX) markets were at the heart of the EMS 1992–1993 crisis. It is useful to reconsider the workings of modern finance and the way it fits into the events. Derivatives did play a crucial role since they were the proper vehicles for the bets in the FX market. Of course, they were not the cause: "if they had not existed, speculators would have used cash and incurred higher costs so that their gains would have been a bit smaller, but still substantial" (Steinherr 2000: 62).

The so-called uncovered interest parity (UIP) condition from international finance is the benchmark idea. It is quite simple. In an economic region, similar assets with the same maturity must have similar yields regardless the currency denomination. Therefore, interest rate differentials on similar assets cannot be consistent with the assumption of equal yields unless there is an expected currency realignment over the period.[10] The following equation can help us clarify the point:

$$r - r_f = S^e - S \tag{6.1}$$

r is the domestic interest rate for a single country (say Italy) while r_f is the interest rate on a similar asset in another (foreign) country of the union (say

Germany). S is the logarithm of the current exchange rate of the domestic currency in terms of the foreign currency (say price of lira in units of marks) and S^e is the logarithm of the expected price of the same exchange rate at the time of asset maturity.[11] Note that the expected price is usually reflected in the forward and futures exchange rate market. In that case, since all variables in the equation are given at every moment, the relevant condition is named covered interest parity. Our focus is now the exchange rate parities within a system of fixed currency parities, therefore we shall use the uncovered parity condition.

The message of the above equation is straightforward: interest rate differentials $(r-r_f)$ measure the expected (probable) shift in the exchange market (appreciation or depreciation: S^e-S). If market participants believe in the credibility of the pegged exchange rate between the two countries, then $S^e-S=0$, which means that there would be a tendency towards negligible interest rate differentials: $r-r_f=0$. Otherwise, a relative higher domestic interest rate $(r-r_f>0)$ is a signal of an expected exchange rate depreciation in the near future $(S^e-S>0)$.[12]

We can understand this as follows. If the interest rate in Italy is 15 percent and in Germany is 10 percent, then the Italian lira is expected to depreciate against the German mark by approximately 5 percent. Put simply, as the Italian lira depreciates, higher domestic yields will not make a stronger investment case as opposed to Germany for the same kind of assets. But uncovered interest parity has also another implication when read inversely: if market participants expect a depreciation of the domestic currency in the near future, an exchange rate peg can only be sustained by a rise in domestic interest rate r (or, alternatively, by a fall in r_f; nevertheless, this interest rate is out of the control of domestic authorities in the country with the weak currency). In practice this presupposes a policy mix of higher short-term borrowing costs, fiscal austerity, and intervention in foreign exchange markets (the maintenance of the proper amount of international reserves and credit lines with other central banks). It also presupposes loss in the control of monetary policy since it is subdued to the exchange rate peg. This result is in line with the general rule of international macroeconomics, the so-called "policy trilemma."[13] According to the latter, for an economy that allows free movement of capital across its borders, exchange rate stability can only be satisfied if monetary policy is the "variable" to be adjusted. Practically, this implies loss of traditional monetary policy tools.

The gradual liberalization of the European financial markets during the 1980s increased cross-border capital flows. Less competitive economies with higher growth prospects and interest rate yields, like Spain and Italy, experienced significant capital inflows. There were two basic reasons for this development (or alternatively, two sets of financial strategies).[14] The first is *portfolio diversification*. International investors and hedge fund managers could include assets in their portfolios from a bigger range of choices now encompassing the countries of the so-called European "periphery." The second reason concerns the profit opportunities from intra-ERM yield differentials in the context of fixed exchange rates. In plain terms, investors could exploit different interest rates between EMS economies betting on exchange rate stability. While there are many different ways to implement a bet like that, we can understand it as a simple case of a *carry trade*. The latter, which is a widely established investment practice in contemporary exchange rate markets, involves borrowing in a currency with low interest rate and simultaneously investing in another currency with higher interest rate.[15] If market participants anticipate a credible ERM, then the condition of uncovered interest parity does not hold: interest rate differentials can persist in the absence of exchange rate realignment. An investment in Italian assets will have higher expected returns than a similar investment in German assets, and this difference will not be offset by exchange rate depreciation since EMS economies are determined to defend the pegged ERM system.

It goes without saying that the functioning of financial markets is much more complex than that. Nevertheless, the above-mentioned two sets of strategies capture two fundamental tendencies.

5.2 Unpredictable events (class struggle) and the defence of the currency peg

From the viewpoint of a country with a weak currency (tendency to depreciate), defending the exchange rate peg is theoretically possible, but it comes with a social cost since it is premised upon a policy mix of austerity and higher borrowing costs (for both private and public sectors). Within limits, this policy mix is rather welcomed by the capitalist power since it disciplines state governance in lines with the neoliberal strategy. In the first place, this was after all the basic incentive for European economies to join the ERM. Nevertheless, the safe "limits" of austerity can easily be challenged by unpredicted events due either to internal class conflicts or to international conjuncture. Mainstream economic theory categorizes these two sets of unexpected events as "shocks" external to the economic systems in order to statistically model them. This is a rather misleading definition: it mystifies the real economic and political roots.

As a result there is a certain threshold beyond which a pegged exchange rate loses its "credibility" because defending it comes at a really high cost. For instance, a sustained rise in domestic interest rates in order to defend a weak currency can threaten the viability of the banking sector and can easily deteriorate aggregate demand and investment activity. This development in its own right may easily derange public finances. At the same time, a speculative attack in the absence of capital controls can only be met by resort to significant amounts of foreign exchange. In practice, this access to foreign exchange is hardly ever possible. But even under the ERM facility, which enabled inter-central bank credit lines (the so-called VSTFF), the strong currency country would be unwilling to provide unlimited credit since this would accordingly cause: first, losses for the central bank in the face of a possible exchange rate realignment; and second, a probable liquidity inflow to the economy which would endanger the anti-inflationary policy framework.

In other words, there is a certain trade-off between the "credibility" of a fixed exchange rate system and its inherent "sustainability" or "flexibility" in dealing with unfavorable developments. The commitment to defend the peg therefore cannot be considered as unconditional. In this sense, the policy costs it imposes both upon the 'center' and the 'periphery' of the EMS is the necessary condition for a possible speculative attack: speculators being aware of these "costs" can bet against the peg.

This is why the ERM left some room for adjustments through implicit escape clauses. In fact it was a fixed exchange rate system with *a limited option for realignment.* The flexibility of the peg is well verified by the data. For instance, between 1979 and 1985 the cumulative devaluation of the Italian lira and the French franc against the ECU turned out to be 20.25 percent and 9.25 percent respectively; while, the cumulative revaluation of German mark against ECU was 22.25 percent.[16] The real question involved is how to make room for possible realignments without sacrificing the credibility of the system along with its disciplining austerity character. In practice, this is a difficult equation to solve. Governments must devalue without signaling to the market that inflationary anti-austerity policies have been adopted. But this is not an easy and manageable target to meet.

5.3 Strategic sequential trading in the context of political economy

Financial players well aware of the above trade-off can set up their trading strategies. There are two extreme opposite types of bet: for and against exchange rate stability. We can rewrite the uncovered interest parity as follows (ΔS^e is the domestic currency depreciation):

$$r - \Delta S^e = r_f$$

This equation has the form of a currency swap. An interest rate payment $r - \Delta S^e$ on some principal amount in Italian liras can be exchanged against r_f cash flows in terms of German marks on a relevant principal. If financial investors speculate on the increase of exchange rate stability, then obviously $\Delta S^e = 0$. In that case interest rate differentials (due to different patterns of growth) can persist and the uncovered interest parity condition is clearly violated. Carry trade practices can generate a significant amount of profits. Practically speaking, someone can borrow in marks, immediately buy liras in the spot exchange market and invest in Italian assets, earning the positive difference of $r - r_f$. For short period investments, betting against the exchange rate parity is not a risky strategy as long as the currency pegs are stable, whereas potential gains are significant. This type of bet can be implemented in many alternative ways. In the case of EMS:

> to hedge against fluctuations of the returns (in dollars) on long positions in high-yielding currencies, such as lira, corporate investors and portfolio managers sold D-marks forward against the dollar, expecting to be able to sell liras and purchase the necessary D-marks on maturity, at a future spot price below the one implied by uncovered interest parity.
>
> (Buiter *et al.* 1998: 69)

For monetary unions, where the exchange rate stability is guaranteed by the common currency, the above line of reasoning has as major outcome: the development of persistent financial account imbalances. We shall come back to this issue in Part IV of the book. In that case the swap type of transactions hold for longer period of time. The average "peripheral" economy facing higher growth and profitability prospects than the average "core" economy ($r>r_f$) will steadily attract net capital inflows from abroad (while what is expected is convergence in the country-specific risk assessment by the market). In general, the investment strategy of borrowing in the "core" economy and investing in the "peripheral" economy can be considered as a swap agreement. Its value for the holder will be given by the difference between the long position in the periphery asset (say B) and the short position in the core economy asset (say B_f): $V=B-B_f$. As long as the union is not in crisis, this value will be always positive triggering capital inflows to the peripheral economy and outflows from the central economy (that is to say, financial account imbalances). By and large, this is how we should understand the build-up of current account imbalances in the case of Euro area (we shall return to this issue in Part IV). As long as there are (expected) growth rate differentials, V will be positive and current account positions will mirror financial account transactions.

But what if private sector investors anticipate a devaluation or loss of faith on the credibility of the fixed exchange rate system?

Let's take the example of the British pound, which joined the ERM in October 1990.[17] The UK had inflation three times higher than Germany, much higher interest rates, double digit public deficits, and most importantly a financial system full of home mortgages, the great majority of which had floating rather than fixed interest rate conditions. It is obvious that interest rate differentials suggested a forthcoming devaluation of sterling. The structure of the bet was now reversed. Anticipating some realignment in the near future, exchange market speculators borrowed in British sterling and invested in German marks or other strong currencies. This line of transactions is identical to selling the weak currency (sterling) and buying the strong one (D-mark) in order to take advantage of the coming devaluation in the short run. As we mentioned above, this profit seeking incentive could only be countered if the British government decided to raise short-term interest rates. Given the economic data, the UK government's position was vulnerable because the economic and social costs of defending the peg would be extremely high. Higher short-term interest rates could put the economy into a recession, threaten the stability of the banking sector, increase the debt burden to households, deteriorate public finance, and curtail demand. Private sector investors were well aware of all these events and came up with proper strategies (shorting the pound) to take advantage of government's predictable behavior.

In the case of our example, this is exactly what happened after the summer of 1992. We shall not go through these events. But on September 16, the so-called "Black Wednesday," a group of speculators, based on the shape of the UK economy and a series of other events in the context of EMS (which had wounded its credibility), launched an (uncoordinated) attack to force the withdrawal of the British sterling from the ERM. They anticipated that the British government would not be in a position to defend the peg. The pattern of events is pretty much known:

> in the morning the Bank of England raised the minimum lending rate from 10 percent to 12 percent. A few hours later, a new increase to 15 percent was announced but never implemented. Sterling closed below its ERM floor in London. In the evening, the Bank of England announced the "temporary" withdrawal of sterling from the ERM. A few days later, on September19, return to ERM was postponed indefinitely.
>
> (Buiter *et al.* 1998: 59)

The day after the crash, the Bank of England brought its interest rate back to 10 percent, validating ex post the expectations of the market and justifying the speculative attacks.

This strategic sequential type of trading is just one example of how financial markets work. Investors try to anticipate the pattern of events several steps ahead, thus forcing the counterparty into an "error." Their move hinges upon the analysis of the economic and political conjuncture and of relevant past moves and behaviors. It looks like a game of chess.[18] Nevertheless, *this strategic game was crucial for the organization of the EMS as a system that disciplines government policies to neoliberal austerity*. It may sound contradictory, but without the threat of "speculative" attacks the rules of the EMS could not be implemented and reproduced. In fact, markets take into account the likelihood of a negative development (trying to make profit out of that) and impose the terms on governments for dealing with it. Governments, being aware of the workings of the markets, organize their policies as a precautionary means of avoiding negative attacks. Governments address the dilemma "austerity or economic instability" to society and win consensus to the austerity agenda. This means that *markets attacks in line with the interests of capital are by and large the crucial moments in organizing consensus on austerity agenda*. They are two sides of the same coin.

The above setting is not of course shielded against crises and unfavorable developments. *But even crises are extreme moments within the very same disciplining mechanism*. What followed the September crisis of the ERM was not the breakup of the ERM system, but the quest for a tighter fiscal policy in the economies affected by the exchange rate crisis. Highly illustrative is the case of Italy, which experienced an attack similar to the one against sterling. The first serious tensions for the Italian lira appeared in the summer of 1992. The ongoing outflow of reserves reinforced consensus to further austerity and wage reductions. At the end of July:

> employers, unions, and the government signed a historic agreement on income policy, disinflation, and labor costs, which reformed the system of

> industrial relations, abolishing what was left of the *scala mobile*, that is, the automatic indexation of wages and salaries.
>
> (Buiter *et al.* 1998: 55)

After the severe attacks of September, Italy too took further steps:

> toward an ambitious project of economic reform, which hinged on containment of the budget deficit, privatizations of state enterprise, and stabilization of lira. The emergency budget for 1993, approved by the cabinet on October 1 and presented to the Parliament three weeks later, involved spending cuts (including a freezing of salaries in the public sector) and tax increases for 1993 amounting to 5.8 percent of GDP.
>
> (Ibid.: 61)

From this point of view, financial markets do not make states fade away but they are in line with a particular form of state governance: one which tends to dissolve the welfare side.

7 Fictitious capital and finance

An introduction to Marx's analysis (in the third volume of *Capital*)

1 Introduction

In a recent special report on financial risk in *The Economist*, it was argued that "the idea that markets can be left to police themselves turned out to be the world's most expensive mistake."[1] This statement reflects the stalemate of mainstream theory in the wake of the 2008 financial meltdown. At the same time, it suggests the limits of the critical character of all heterodox approaches. In plain terms, if mainstream thinking points to the instability and uneven distribution of income, which are associated with the workings of modern finance, then what is left for economic heterodoxy?

Of course, as we have already mentioned in Chapter 5, finance will always remain a trauma for mainstream theory. This means that the real content of finance cannot be properly grasped by the mainstream research problematic in any way whatsoever. On the other hand, heterodox analyses will continue to emphasize the unstable and unequal economic results that are brought about by the rise of finance. From their point of view, when finance exceeds some limits, it becomes irrational and dysfunctional.

In this chapter we establish the underpinnings of a different line of reasoning. To do so we return to Marx's analysis in the third volume of *Capital*. We think that the effect of finance must be captured in the light of the concept of fictitious capital, which in Marx's reasoning is associated with the process of fetishism. In other words, *fetishism lies at the heart of finance*. This conceptual setting, already dominant in Marx's writings, opens up a new radical ground (problematic) in the analysis of finance. It does not downplay the instability and inequality that necessarily accompanies new developments. But most importantly, it gives finance a crucial role to play in the organization of capitalist power relations. This role is not apparent at first glance, nor is it systematized by other heterodox approaches. Our analytical argument will be developed by both this chapter and Chapter 8.

2 Some preliminary demarcations

2.1 Specters of Keynes and Veblen

We shall shortly look at Marx's analytical problematic of finance. For the moment, however, we want to focus on what we see as the kernel of the Keynes–Veblen framework. This can be expressed in the following Figure 7.1.[2]

In the "material world" (of the so-called "real" economy), the quantity of capital can only be measured/interpreted in terms of heterogeneous capital goods (or, so as not to dissatisfy the proponents of the (classical) labor theory of value, we may add: material capital can only be measured in terms of labor time units). This capital produces income streams in the future measured also in "material" (or labor value) terms. In Figure 7.1, this process is depicted by transformation step 1. This "material" world also has its unique duplicate: the world of values (i.e., prices). As long as we are in the latter, future income streams in price terms (profits) are translated by step 3 into present capital value. This step presupposes a proper capitalization based on some rate of interest. Economic variables in this second world are all expressed in value terms: namely in money. These two co-existing universes are connected by step 2, in which future material incomes are matched to the corresponding prices.

It is not very difficult to summarize Keynes' and Veblen's common problematic in light of the above descriptions (based on our reasoning in Chapter 1). The spontaneous tendency of capitalism is to make the dimension of values totally autonomous (detached) from the dimension of the "real" economy. This outcome is also associated with the rise of the absentee owner who receives a parasitic rent. From this point of view, the dimension of values is self-standing, self-reinforcing, and systematically represses the world of material quantities. This theoretical speculation has always been very strong in the relevant discussions and can be found in different forms and under different conditions. In the Keynesian analysis, it is the demand prices of capital goods (as capitalized

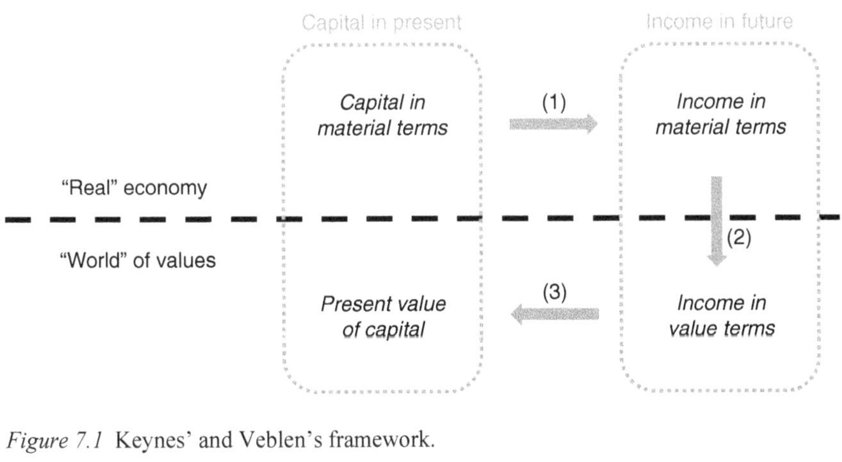

Figure 7.1 Keynes' and Veblen's framework.

expectations of future incomes) that drive supply prices (the "material" supply of capital). Since stage 2 in Figure 7.1 is loose, the absence of proper state intervention will always have (as a result) economic instability and underemployment of "material" resources.[3] Completely in line with this theory, Veblen would argue that the domination of capitalization and finance leads to absolute dissociation between the two above-mentioned levels. This shift radically transforms business life, embedding in it an economic spirit that deprives society of the fullest development of its productive capacities. In this sense, the rise of finance makes capitalism dysfunctional. It comes with the dominance of the parasitical absentee owner (Veblen) or rentier (Keynes) and sabotages the "real" creation of use values.

We shall give a further example, one that does not come from the field of heterodox economics. That is why it is more representative of what tends to become dominant within the social movements. In a recent pamphlet, which was inspired by the Occupy Movement, Noam Chomsky made the following point:

> Before the 1970s, banks were banks. They did what they were supposed to do in a state capitalist economy: they took unused funds from your bank account, for example, and transferred them to some potentially useful purpose like helping some family to buy a home or send a kid to college, or whatever it might be. That changed dramatically in the 1970s. Until then, there were no financial crises. It was a period of enormous growth – the highest growth in American history, maybe in economic history – sustained growth through the 1950s and 1960s. And it was egalitarian. [...] When the 1970s came along there were sudden and sharp changes: de-industrialization, off-shoring of production, and shifting to financial institutions, which grew enormously. [...] The developments that took place during the 1970s set off a vicious cycle. It led to concentration of wealth increasingly in the hands of the financial sector. This doesn't benefit the economy – it probably harms it and the society – but it did lead to tremendous concentration of wealth, substantially there.
>
> (Chomsky 2012: 28)

This rather long passage summarizes very well the spirit of the above-mentioned analysis; it is also a very neat formulation of a narrative that tends to dominate heterodox theory and politics. The ideal capitalism of the 1950s and 1960s was based on control of finance. The unleashing of the latter after 1970s harmed the "real" economy ("de-industrialization" and "off-shoring") and society to the benefit of the financial sector, which is totally detached from production. This theoretical schema can only be analytically justified in the light of Figure 7.1: namely, the domination of the dimension of values over the "real" economy.

2.2 Heterodox (Marxist) discussions on financialization: a brief summary

Financial engineering remains a mystery for the majority of heterodox analyses. The train of reasoning may be slightly different in each case, but the general problematic remains the same: finance in our contemporary societies has become dysfunctional (purely speculative) to a proper accumulation of capital. And of course, there is an important straightforward corollary: if financialization is a distortion, the causes of recent extraordinary financial innovation cannot be attached to the general dynamics of capitalist production.

Finance is usually approached in terms of quantity. Its rise has, therefore, the character of a monodimensional extension: over-indebtedness and/or over-spending. From this point of view, a relevant definition of financialization is the one offered by Ingham (2008: 169): "the increasing dominance of financial practices and the fusion of business enterprise with 'financial engineering.'" Finance is considered as something extraneous to business enterprise that can only contaminate the latter. Therefore the rise of finance is connected with the growth of something (debt, speculation etc.), which further penetrates and distorts different domains of the economy. This idea, based on "curious processualism" (the expression belongs to Martin (2009: 116–117)), is characteristic of a significant part of the discussions. But if the rise of finance is not a permanent tendency within capitalism, what explains its sudden ascendance? In brief, there are two general answers to this question. The following comments attempt to sketch the outline of the literature debates and not to provide a thorough account of them.

The first one has already been analyzed. It is the train of thought that draws upon Keynes' and Veblen's approaches. The rise of finance is linked to the hegemony of the absentee owner. This is rather the outcome of a conflict between the productive and the parasitic parts of the society, to the benefit of the second. The victory of the one sets the basic pattern of capitalist development as pertaining to its own agendas, targets, and economic priorities. Thus, it is not just a simple victory. It is a hegemonic predominance along with the rise of a new historic bloc (to use Gramsci's famous term), which amounts to a particular institutional setting of the society. The very same message can be arrived at via different types of reasoning. For instance, as we argued in Chapter 2, Hilferding's approach sees finance as a predatory social process and can be easily placed within the same categorization.[4]

The second school understands financialization as a mere byproduct of capitalism's inability to absorb the final product. This type of explanation can be found in two alternative versions. Both are revivals or sophisticated reformulations of the old underconsumptionist ideas and related debates.[5]

In a nutshell, the classical underconsumption theories, as they were developed by Sismonde de Sismondi and Robert Malthus, can be reduced to the following propositions. Within the capitalist economy there is an inherent tendency towards economic crises of generalized overproduction, due to the inability of effective demand to keep pace with production. When supply exceeds aggregate demand there is no endogenous dynamic tendency towards full employment equilibrium, because demand has priority over supply; it is demand that triggers and regulates production and not the opposite, as assumed by Say's Law. This general insight can be used as the departure for two different interpretations of contemporary capitalism. Many recent approaches to financialization explicitly or implicitly draw upon them.

On the one hand, the Malthusian argument attributes crises (and unemployment) first and foremost to over-saving by capitalists. This is equal to saying that underconsumption results from high capitalist profitability: if wages are relatively low compared to the level of profits, which are mostly saved, then the potential productive output cannot be absorbed unless there is an equal increase in final consumption. Capitalists encounter a prospective lack of investment outlets and capital becomes excessive and surplus. Following this line of thought, one can see finance as an unstable remedy, which, moreover, favors capitalist over-savers. Surplus capital can be recycled to low paid workers in the form of debt and/or stagnate in speculation. This is an undoubted benefit for the capitalist class as a whole because it solves the problem of surplus capital. The only shortcoming is that financial recycling cannot be considered as a permanent solution. Different versions of this idea can be found in Husson (2012), Resnick and Wolff (2010), and Mohun (2012). Of course, all these authors do not share exactly the same reasoning. Nevertheless, they do link financialization or related crises to a reading of Marx in line with the Malthusian version of underconsumption (capitalist over-saving due to high profitability in relation to wages).[6]

On the other hand, the alternative approach of Sismondi offers "low profitability" as an explanation of the same underconsumptionist problem. Output cannot be absorbed and profits cannot be realized because demand is insufficient due to low wages. Poor profitability makes capital stagnant and surplus since it can be channeled to production only in a declining pattern. In the absence of other welfare solutions to boost demand, financial recycling can become a crucial intermediation in decongesting the build-up of surplus capital. The argument is pretty much the same as the previous one. Finance and credit bubbles are the most favorable way for capital to curtail repression in output expansion and profitability without incurring major costs. In this sense, financialization is the unstable result of underconsumption based on poor capital profitability. Some authors, without abandoning the spirit of this reasoning, connect low profitability not just with low wage incomes (demand) but also with the high value of the already invested constant capital (overcapacity). In this sense demand always falls behind productive capacity. This explanation is just another facet of the very same idea. As profit falls there will still be some investment, which adds to the overall amount of capital and its productive capacity to exceed demand. This type of reasoning emphasizes the over-investment of capital relative to realized profitability. It describes one more channel of the downward pressure on the profit rate: it is not just the numerator (decrease in realized profit) of the ratio that counts but also the denominator (the increase in the amount of constant capital: overcapacity relative to poor demand). Many contemporary approaches can be included in this theoretical tradition where a long-term crisis of profitability is followed by a "growing reliance on credit bubbles to sustain economic expansion" (Callinicos 2010: 50). We can mention the following interventions: Callinicos (2010), Brenner (2002), Harvey (2010), Foster and Magdoff (2009), McNally (2009), Kliman (2012), and Lazzarato (2012).[7]

The proposed categorization of this section does not fully reflect the analytical wealth of all the relevant approaches. It is a general sketching that helps us to advance our point. Neither does it exhaust all current viewpoints about financialization. For instance, Arrighi (1999) sees the modern neoliberal organization of capitalism as a subversion of the hegemonic position of the USA, in a similar cyclical pattern to that experienced in the past by Genoa, Holland, and Britain. Faced with a setback in commodity markets, with profit opportunities for its capitals beginning to decline, a hegemonic power switches to financialization: financial capital flows elsewhere in search of profits (Krippner (2005) elaborates on this idea).

Our reading of Marx radically departs from all the above insights. To some extent, this must have become clear to those who have been reading the book from the start. Our point will be further clarified in the following chapters. Capital and finance are not just quantities that can be extended through space and time. They are social processes, which overlap with each other in many different ways. But primarily, finance is the everyday mask of capital: *it is capital's form of existence*. The rise of finance has followed the dynamics of capital on the background of class struggles from the very beginning of capitalism. This summarizes Marx's own major analytical contribution, which has been left unacknowledged in the relevant discussions and debates. Changes in the trend of the profit rate may have consequences for the development of finance, but these consequences cannot be one-directional and straightforward; nor do they transform the character of finance. Finance, in its modern sophisticated version, is something much more than accumulated liabilities and increased indebtedness. It presupposes a great amount of investment in mainstream research and financial innovation and it is based on major institutional developments, economic strategies, and state regulations within capitalist socictics, which *all* have their own unique history, institutional pace, and temporality. In this sense, *the history of finance can by no means be reduced to a mere reflection of the historical pattern of the profit rate. The authors, who see finance as so "flexible" that it can nicely and immediately fill the gaps caused by underconsumption if and when they arise, fail, in fact, to understand the true nature of finance in capitalism*. The fact that developments in finance are not contemporaneous and symmetrical with the trend in profit rate[8] is the true Achilles heel of all the above-mentioned Marxist traditions.

There are some striking exceptions in the heterodox analyses. We refer to the interventions of Bryan and Rafferty (2006; 2009), Martin (2002; 2007, 2009), and Bryan *et al.* (2009). Our argumentation has much in common with the latter. It is also influenced and motivated by them. Some differences have already been addressed; others will become clear in the following chapters (see also Sotiropoulos and Lapatsioras 2012 and 2014).[9]

2.3 Specters of Marx

Let's return to Figure 7.1. The critical step for the Keynesian type of reasoning is step 2: the meeting point between the "real" economy and the "world" of nominal values (or alternatively, where the labor theory of value meets the capitalization (pricing) of capital). This step generates expectations (E_t) of future income flows (D_{t+1}, D_{t+2}, D_{t+3}, ...) that will return to the owner of capital. In the elementary case of a common stock (D now stands for dividends), and if we accept, for reasons of simplicity, constant expected return equal to R[10] (which of course embodies the assessment of the overall involved risk), then the expected future income flow can be capitalized (priced) according to the following expression:[11]

$$P_t = E_t\left[\sum_{i=t}^{\infty} \frac{D_{t+i}}{(1+R)^i}\right] = \sum_{i=t}^{\infty} \frac{E_t[D_{t+i}]}{(1+R)^i} = \frac{E_t[D_{t+1}]}{(1+R)} + \frac{E_t[D_{t+2}]}{(1+R)^2} + \dots \qquad (7.1)$$

The message of the above (trivial in financial textbooks) mathematical expression is straightforward. Capitalization translates into a financial security with price P_t the expected value of a future income stream. In fact this is a process of securitization. By and large, it captures the workings of the financial sphere (the dimension of values): it is a permanent capitalization on the basis of existing "information" about future events in order to price different types of financial assets. Capitalization is captured by step 2 in the above-mentioned Figure 7.1. The liquidity of these markets indicates the ever-lasting process of present value assessment.

Nevertheless, from a Marxian point of view there are two fundamental misconceptions in Figure 7.1. Both concern step 2, which, interrelates the two distinct levels. On the one hand, *the true materiality of capitalism regards the complex articulation of social power relations, which organize and reproduce capitalist exploitation.* The material and technical specification of the means of

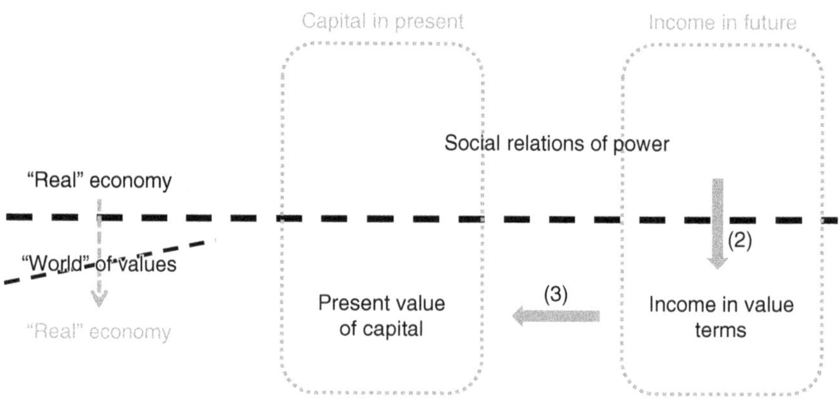

Figure 7.2 Marx's framework.

production is irrelevant from this point of view. In Figure 7.2, the social nature of the upper level has been changed. The world of values is not something discrete from the "real" economy. As was implied in Part I of this book, capitalist relations necessarily exist under the commodity form; they are not visible as such in ordinary life. They exist in their results under particular phenomelogical conditions.[12] The pure form of capital takes the shape of a financial security as *sui generis* commodity. In this sense, *the dimension of values (prices) is as real as the capitalist power relations that are expressed through it. It is the form through which social power relations cannot but be represented.*

The process of valuation, which takes place in the lower levels of Figures 7.1 and 7.2, is associated with the appearance of capital and cannot thus be understood without the process of *fetishism*. This is the key point that allows the understanding of Marx's reasoning and clarifies the differences from other mainstream and heterodox interpretations of the same process.

The appearance of capital under the commodity form (reification) is a *representation* of capitalist reality, comprising images, ideas, and perceptions which do not originate arbitrarily in our minds (i.e., in the mind of every economic agent) but arise from, and are held in place by, social and economic relations themselves (Montag 2003: 62). In other words, fetishism is not a subjective phenomenon based on illusions and superstitious beliefs. It refers to a socially functioning (mis)interpretation of economic reality. In this sense, the latter is made by objects (commodities), which are always already given in the form of a representation (Balibar 1995: 67). Therefore, step 2 carries out an intermediation, which is absolutely crucial to the organization of capitalist power. It *translates* into quantitative data (we mean the magnitudes of $E_t[D_{t+i}]$ and R) the dynamics of social power relations. This process can only be properly perceived on the basis of the Marxian concept of fetishism. Here fetishism does not simply mean the mystification of capitalist reality but also the embeddedness of social behaviors and strategies proper to the reproduction of class exploitation. This standpoint sets forth a radical new groundwork for the analysis of the financial system and is in line with Marx's argumentation in *Capital*. Marxist discussions so far have failed to highlight this aspect of Marx's reasoning. In the rest of this chapter we shall try to further explain Marx's point.

3 The place of Marx in debates about finance: a first demarcation

Before embarking upon Marx's argument, we can use the above preliminary notes in order to further clarify the uniqueness of his problematic. We shall attempt a brief presentation of the major issues in financial theory, namely the significance and the theoretical status of the question posited by both mainstream and heterodox economics: *how information is reflected in prices and how economic agents react to this*. We shall argue that, while the majority of economic debates concentrate on this question and accept its underlying terms, the Marxian argument challenges the empiricist basis of its formulation. This shift must be seen as opening a whole new analytical problematic for understanding finance and its place in the social configuration of capitalist society. It is this point that has been totally missing from relevant discussions leading to a common misinterpretation of Marx's viewpoint.

3.1 Discussions on EMH: the backbone of mainstream financial theory and practice

The Efficient Market Hypothesis (EMH) is a benchmark in debates on modern finance. This hypothesis has a central role in shaping contemporary financial markets and mainstream financial theory. There have been many pages written on EMH and many more devoted to its empirical testing.[13] As mentioned by Shiller (2000: 171–172), "the literature on the evidence for this theory is well developed and includes work of the highest quality." Nevertheless, the conclusions of the empirical research are divided and as a whole favor neither full acceptance of the EMH nor its total rejection.

For those who come from a background in political economy or social theory it is not difficult to understand this result. In fact, despite the sheer volume of empirical research, EMH is a theoretical argument that cannot be rejected; this point is made by Campbell *et al.* (2007: 24). Even well-established empirical testing (something that cannot always be taken for granted) usually assumes an equilibrium model that defines normal asset returns. If the evidence runs against efficiency, this could mean either that the market is inefficient or that the accepted equilibrium model is incorrect and must be replaced by a more accurate one that does not contradict the spirit of EMH. In the rest of this section we shall focus on what we take to be the core theoretical issue of EMH.

At its "most general level, the theory of efficient capital markets is just the theory of competitive equilibrium applied to asset markets" (LeRoy 1989: 1583). This idea resembles the Ricardian idea of comparative advantage:

> except that comparative advantage is conferred by differences in information held by investors, rather than differences in productivity among producers. [...] It is only differences in information – information that it is not "fully reflected" in prices – that confer comparative advantage, and that therefore can form the basis for profitable trading rules.
>
> (Ibid.: 1583–1584)

As a result, efficient markets based on agents' interaction must generate fair asset prices in a double sense: these must be prices that are close to economic fundamentals and that leave no room for "free lunch." Any other outcome would not be acceptable in the mainstream economic context of efficiency.

We can understand this theoretical statement as follows. At any point in time there is some fundamental information with regard to the underlying entities of financial securities (capitalist firms, capitalist states, etc.). This information concerns their present economic conditions (based on events that have already occurred) and their future prospects (based on events which are expected to take place in the future). If this information is not publicly available to all market participants in the sense that it has not been discounted in the market prices, then those who have the comparative information advantage at their disposal will act *rationally* to exploit market mispricing to their own benefit. Nevertheless, what is "generally known" is not very far from actual fundamentals (in other words, the amount of information which is publicly known is extensive); hence the profit-seeking behavior of rational investors will almost instantaneously incorporate the missing information into financial asset prices, thus eliminating the (relative) informational advantage. At the limit of this speculation, financial prices are always correct *given* what is actually known about economic fundamental: "in an efficient market at any point in time the actual price of a security will be a good estimate of its intrinsic value" (Fama 1965: 56). They cannot predict the future with absolute certainty, but at least they reflect what can be possibly known today about fundamentals.

Note that this line of reasoning does not rule out discrepancies between actual prices and intrinsic values based on economic fundamentals. In efficient markets the action of rational profit-seeking agents will make these discrepancies not systematic but *random* in character. Any systematic discrepancy would be a comparative advantage to someone and thus quickly lead to price corrections towards intrinsic values. It is not difficult to see why *the idea of market efficiency was, from the very beginning, linked to the random walk hypothesis*. The feature of "instantaneous adjustment" implies that:

> successive price changes in individual securities will be independent. A market where successive price changes in individual securities are independent is, by definition, a random walk market. Most simply the theory of random walks implies that a series of stock price changes has no memory – the past history of the series cannot be used to predict the future in any meaningful way. The future path of the price level of a security is no more predictable than the path of a series of cumulated random numbers.
>
> (Fama 1965: 56)

The conception of randomness originates from probability analysis and has also been used extensively in natural and physical sciences. In financial markets this condition is met under the rational behavior assumption, which neutralizes prices discrepancies as mentioned above. The basic intuition of the random walk is very old. Gerolamo Gardano (1501–1576), the famous Italian Renaissance mathematician whose love for gambling led him to formulate the first elements of probability theory, wrote in his 1565 manuscript (entitled *The Book of Games of Chance*):

> The most fundamental principle of all in gambling is simply equal conditions, e.g., of opponents, of bystanders, of money, of situation, of the dice box, and of the die itself. To the extent to which you depart from that

equality, if it is your opponent's favour, you are a fool, and if in your own, you are unjust.

(Cited in Campbell *et al.* 2007: 30)

The point of this argument is not to compare finance to gambling, but on the contrary, to a *fair* interplay between participants without any strategic advantage over each other. This is the essential idea of the so-called martingale stochastic process given by the following expression:[14]

$$E_t[P_{t+1}|P_t, P_{t-1}, \ldots] = P_t \Rightarrow E_t[P_{t+1} - P_t|\Phi_t] = 0 \tag{7.2}$$

In the above expression P_t represents cumulative winnings with respect to a sequence of information set Φ_t (which for simplicity contains all past values). This formula captures the meaning of a fair game, since it says that the expected incremental winning at any time is zero conditioned on the history of the game. If this formula is applied to financial markets, then its message fits nicely into the above analysis. In an efficient market:

> it should not be possible to profit by trading on the information contained in the asset's price history; hence the conditional expectation of future price changes, conditional on the price history, cannot be either positive or negative [...] and therefore must be zero.
>
> (Campbell *et al.* 2007: 30–1)

In this sense, the market can deliver no-free-lunch only when the best forecast of tomorrow's price is today's price: past data cannot be a good guide for successful investment action.

However interesting it would be, we don't have the space here to embark on a detailed analysis of the numerous mainstream debates on the issue of the random walk. As mentioned many times in the literature, this line of thought results in an uncomfortable corollary when it is pushed to its limits: if the market efficiently reflected fundamentals or instantaneously adjusted prices to them there would be no incentive for someone to act rationally. Why do financial investors care about costly information gathering, which will be soon incorporated in prices? In fact:

> if the purchased information makes profitable trades possible, security markets cannot be informationally efficient, while if it does, agents are irrationally wasting their money. [...] In an efficient capital market, agents should have no investment goals other than to diversify to the maximum extent possible so as to minimize idiosyncratic risk, and to hold the amount of risk appropriate to their risk tolerance.
>
> (LeRoy 1989: 1615, 1584)

This was the point to be emphasized by the seminal intervention of Grossman and Stiglitz (1976, 1980). Prices cannot perfectly reflect all the available information because otherwise it would not make sense for someone to spend real money on its costly acquisition without getting any compensation. Hence, either the random walk hypothesis does not hold or it would *ir*rationalize economic agents to the point of total passivity.

A random walker would understand this paradox from the very beginning and thus make room for some non-instantaneous adjustment. Of course, there are many other problems with the martingale model. The most important, with respect to economic reasoning, is to be found in the difficulty it has in accounting for risk. In plain terms, it cannot allow for risk aversion (the fact that there is some trade-off between expected return and assumed risk), which is the cornerstone of financial theory. The Capital Asset Pricing Model (CAPM) was an attempt to generalize the random walk thesis in order to include risk- averse behavior (with very poor empirical results).[15]

Nevertheless, we must emphasize another point that is dominant among both followers and critics of this idea. Our argument is summarized in Figure 7.3.

There are four key concepts involved in the above-mentioned discussion about EMH: (1) the nature of competitive equilibrium in markets (in the Ricardian sense of comparative advantage theory); (2) the conception of the economic rationality of agents along with the way they form expectations; (3) the random walk hypothesis (in the martingale form, as described above); and, (4) the latent conception of information in an economic world, which is supposed to be transparent. Point (1) is not challenged. Most critiques rejected point (3) and along with it they put forward different versions of economic rationality in point (2). For instance, this is clear in LeRoy's (1989: 1616) conclusion, which welcomes behavioral finance:

> The most fundamental insight of market efficiency – the reminder that asset prices reflect the interaction of self-interested agents – will remain. However, the contention that no successful trading can be based on publicly available information may have to go; it is this strict version of market efficiency that produces the empirical implications that the evidence contradicts. [...] Regrettably, it appears as if it is the assumptions of rationality and rational expectations that require reformation. [...] The recent literature on cognitive psychology provides a promising avenue for future research.

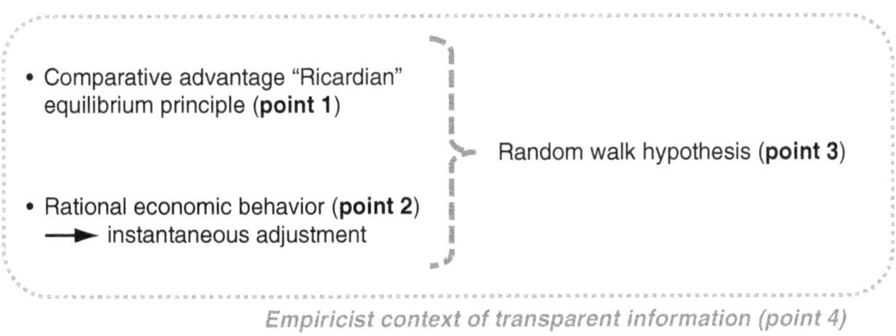

Figure 7.3 The mainstream scheme of market efficiency.

Premise (4), the empiricist conception of information and knowledge, has never been actually contested by any school of thought. It has never been explicitly addressed, even by the most severe critics, and yet *it is this presumption that holds together the whole analytical edifice*. Below we shall challenge this analytical precondition in the light of the Marxian analysis.

3.2 Behavioral departures

Rejection of the "instantaneous adjustment" thesis along with the random walk hypothesis is identical to throwing away the idea that prices reflect economic fundamentals. This development leaves room for many different research programs which, focusing on financial instability, challenge the idea of randomness. To do so, they usually come up with different versions of rationality reshaping point (2). Since many of these versions draw upon psychological assumptions, they are usually perceived by mainstream economists as research programs that argue for economic irrationality. Nevertheless, this is not the case. Both the mainstream approaches to economic behavior and the alternative versions which challenge it, attempt to put forward particular models of economic rationality (different versions of economic anthropology). In what follows we will emphasize that even the most critical Keynesian insights do not challenge the empiricist conception of information suggested by point (4).

We shall start with Herbert Simon. Decades before the success of so-called behavioral finance, he had argued that individuals are characterized by "this type of goal-oriented but cognitively restricted behavior" described as Bounded Rationality. The economic agent "has become a pragmatic information processor with limited aspirations to achieving efficiency or optimality" (Foley 2004: 92). Individuals confront a complex social reality without the luxury of having "unlimited time and brain power to devote to decision making" (Fox 2009: 179). They have no other choice than to use heuristic shortcuts and useful rules of thumb. They behave rationally in a bounded way. Society is transparent to them but they cannot deal with the enormous amount of information they face.

The existence of heuristic rules of behavior, common to all or to a significant number of economic agents, runs against the random walk hypothesis because it can be associated with pre-specified patterns in pricing. An investor may discover and take advantage of the latter. In this sense, the absence of randomness is identical to mispricing fundamentals. Individual judgments about future and uncertain events are based on heuristic rules that sometimes lead to severe and systematic errors. This line of thought was the leading idea of the intervention of the well-known behavioral psychologists Tversky and Kahneman. In their seminal 1974 paper on judgment under uncertainty, they put forward the following argument:

> Many decisions are based on beliefs concerning the likelihood of uncertain events [...]. These beliefs are usually expressed in statements such as "I think that...," "chances are...," "It is unlikely that...," etc. Occasionally,

> beliefs concerning uncertain events are expressed in numerical form as odds or subjective probabilities. What determines such beliefs? How do people assess the probability of an uncertain event or the value of an uncertain quantity? [...] people rely on a limited number of heuristic principles which reduce the complex tasks of assessing probabilities and predicting values to simpler judgmental operations. In general, these heuristics are quite useful, but sometimes they lead to severe and systematic errors.
>
> (Tversky 2004: 203)

Economic researchers who were dissatisfied with the empirical evidence of the EMH turned to this type of argumentation. For instance, Shiller (2012) along with Akerlof (see Akerlof and Shiller 2009) end up flirting with the Keynesian concept of animal spirits. They use the latter in the above context of a psychological theory of human nature to deal with the complexity of contemporary capitalism. They argue that investment actions:

> must be influenced by the social milieu and by the psychology of other. [...] Fluctuations in animal spirits that are shared by large numbers of people are [...] social phenomena, the result of epidemic social contagion, which makes these fluctuations very hard to comprehend and predict. [...] There is no escaping the role of animal spirits in driving prices and financial activity.
>
> (Shiller 2012: 172–173)

As we have already discussed in Chapter 1, the extreme version of the behavioral type of critique of mainstream finance came very early in the interventions of Keynes and Veblen. Paul Davidson (2002: 174; emphasis added) provides a lucid summary of it:

> The classical efficient market hypothesis is in direct contrast to Keynes's belief that a freely flexible market price system can generate *psychological beliefs* creating volatility in market evaluations of financial assets which can then violently depress the real economy. [...] The widespread acceptance of the efficient market hypothesis has driven Keynes's *psychological liquidity preference approach* to the formation of spot market evaluations from most academic discussions of financial market performance.

This is what remains common to all the above arguments, which challenge the EMH in the light of the reasoning we developed in Chapter 1. Finance has become complex and can only guide investment action through the pattern of second-order-observation (or other heuristic rules). Hence, the linkage between financial prices and fundamentals becomes loose and arbitrary, heavily based on psychological factors. When the market is left to itself, speculation (second-order-observation) becomes the dominant practice, leading to a deranged financial instability and sub-optimal resource utilization. Trends in prices are potential sources of capital gains without any direct relation to underlying real investments and production capacity.[16] In the context of Figure 7.3, points (2) and (3) are disputed; nevertheless, points (1) and (4) remain intact.

3.3 Society is a complex setting of non-transparent social relations: the origin of Marx's framework

Every systematic approach to Marx's theory of finance in relation to the above-mentioned analytical debates must begin by fully challenging presumption (4) (see Figure 7.3). Every other alternative would just squeeze Marx into an inferior position within the presented context. In other words, Marx's problematic challenges the only element that was implicitly adopted by all interventions discussed so far. He thus breaks new ground in a radical rupture with the dominant empiricist framework.[17]

The common idea in the above discussions concerns the concept of information. The capitalist world is thought of as transparent and the financial process as a relationship between a given object (the capitalist reality) and a given rational subject (the market participant). At this general level the status of the object (discontinuous or continuous capitalist reality, mobile or fixed, fundamentally uncertain or not) and of the subject (rational, psychological etc.) is not very important. Full knowledge of economic fundamentals presupposes gathering full information, which is not given to any individual. The world is transparent. Information is already there. But its distribution is uneven, asymmetrical, and more importantly its acquisition is extremely costly. Random walkers accept that all existing information is by and large incorporated in prices, allowing for some delay due to the adjustment process. In this sense, future prices are truly unpredictable. Individuals face prices that closely embody all relevant existing information. They do not "know" everything, but this is not the point. They take action on the basis of prices that incorporate all available knowledge. The world is transparent to investors through the signals given by prices; it is as if investors know everything (or almost everything) when they take decisions. However, as already mentioned, this is not a commonplace in discussions. Given the complexity of the world or given the structural uncertainty that governs future trends, it is argued by the critiques that economic agents resort to shortcut psychological rules to guide their economic actions. This results in the loosening of the connection between information and pricing. Information about fundamentals is out there, the true knowledge of society already exists, but this knowledge cannot easily be embodied in asset prices, giving rise to unstable financial results.

In Marx's universe, the notion of information is vague. *Capitalist reality is not transparent.* It is formed as a complex setting of social power relations, which are not revealed in everyday experience as such. *These power relations exist in the form of a particular representation.* The latter mystifies their social nature, calling forth proper norms of individual behavior that are accepted (lived) by economic agents as the truth of their reality. From this point of view, information and pricing are already immersed in the context of capitalist ideology. Certainly, prices may be perfect, imperfect, or totally misleading with regard to information about fundamentals. *But economic fundamentals themselves along with their reflection in prices (economic models) are already defined within the inescapable field of capitalist ideology*. Financial prices reflect, efficiently or not, the ideological setting of capitalist society. In this way, their role might be very active in the organization of capitalist exploitation.

We believe that this approach to finance is dominant in Marx's theoretical system and we shall elaborate upon it. As has already been mentioned, our analysis is inspired by the writings of Althusser (and his followers). The latter theorized the Marxian understanding of the emergence of socially necessary misrecognitions (socially necessary in the sense that they underwrite those practices that reproduce capitalist relations of production) and integrated it into a broader theory of ideology (and so of ideological state apparatuses).[18] The starting point must be a view of ideology as a totality of social practices, which are openly reproduced, taught and implemented in ideological institutions or tacitly linked to the state and operating in such a way as to reproduce the social capitalist order. The main element is not that ideology is associated with various forms of indirect coercion but that the ideas in which it is codified are *organic*, i.e., they contribute to the reproduction of capitalist relations. They thus not only become "acceptable" to members of society, but are experienced by them as expressions of the truth of social life. In this sense they are the foundations of a necessary relation between subjects and the conditions of their existence.

The most important element in this approach is the link between ideology and the subject (and their subordination), which Marx conceptualizes in a way that is entirely different from anything in previous philosophical traditions and, of course, in the form of a total rupture with the above-mentioned empiricist context. Capitalist society is not transparent and the organic representations that are linked to it are not external to the existence of individuals. As it emerges from Marx's analysis, reality is not only the "thing," the "entity," the real "sensible thing," but also the illusion, the "supersensible thing."[19] These constitute the necessary components of reality, even though they amount to a misapprehension of it and a naturalized projection of historical constructs. Just as real are the non-transparent and ideologically coerced behaviors, which emerge from this reality. In this way, Marx's theory transcends the classical distinction between the society and the individual-subject, revealing that *there are no subjects outside of society but rather practices which constitute subjective identities on the basis of historical elements*. The subject does not constitute the world, as asserted by idealism, but the world gives birth to the subjectivity of the individual.

4 The concept of fictitious capital in Marx's analysis

4.1 The theoretical argument

When Marx introduces the circuit of interest bearing capital: $M-[M-C-M']-M''$ and the role of the money capitalist in the third volume of *Capital*, he does not speak of a specific fraction of capital but he analyzes the more concrete form of the circuit of capital itself (see Chapter 3).[20] The circuit of interest bearing capital cannot be thoroughly grasped without reference to the concept of fictitious capital. In other words, *the pure appearance form of capital is necessarily the fictitious form*. The latter can only be understood in the context of the Marxian theory of fetishism. This is how we should understand Marx's analysis in the third volume of *Capital*.

As we have already discussed, interest bearing capital is fictitious capital; that is to say, it is a financial security priced on the basis of the income it is expected to yield in the future. Interest bearing capital is the concrete form of capital in the shape of a *sui generis* commodity. The process of capitalization also maintains a central role in the works of other heterodox thinkers, such as Keynes and Veblen, who wrote many years after Marx.[21] From our point of view, Marx's major theoretical contribution to the analysis of finance is the association of capitalization with *fetishism*. On the basis of the analysis that accompanied Figure 7.2, it is easy to understand that the pure (and most developed) form of appearance of capital is its fictitious form.[22] It is "fictitious," not in the sense of imaginary detachment from real conditions of production, as is usually suggested, but *"fictitious" in the sense that it reifies the capitalist production relations*. Surprisingly enough, a great many of the Marxist analyses of the third volume of *Capital* have failed to pay due attention to this fact. Nevertheless, Marx's message is clear and indisputable:

> Capital appears as a mysterious and self-creating source of interest, of its own increase. The *thing* is now already capital simply as a thing; the result of the overall reproduction process appears as a property devolving on a thing in itself [...]. In interest bearing capital, therefore, this automatic fetish is elaborated into its pure form, self-valorizing value, money breeding money, and in this form it no longer bears any marks of its origin. The social relation is consummated in the relationship of a thing, money, to itself [...] which is how the production of surplus-value by capital appears here. [...] In this capacity of potential capital, as a means of producing profit, it becomes a commodity, but a commodity *sui generis*. Or, what amounts to the same, capital as capital becomes a commodity.
>
> (Marx 1991: 516, 459–60)

Marx's formulations leave no room for ambiguities. They should be read in light of his elaborations on the issue of commodity fetishism in part 1 of the first volume of *Capital* (Marx 1990).[23] To sum up, capitalist exploitation appears as a "thing," as a *sui generis* commodity, as a financial security. As we analyzed it above, this appearance is a *representation* of the capitalist reality comprising ideas, perceptions, and theoretical schemes which do not originate in agents' minds but arise from, and are held in place by, social and economic relations (Montag 2003: 62). In other words, fetishism is not a subjective phenomenon based on illusions and superstitious beliefs. It refers to an economic reality mediated by objects (commodities), which are always already given in the form of a representation (Balibar 1995: 67).

Marx introduces the concept of fictitious capital, and speaks of fetishism, when he gives an account of the social nature of financial markets. He wants to underline the fact that capital assets are the *reified* forms of the appearance of the social relation of capital, and so their valuation is associated with a particular *organic* representation of capitalist relations. They are objectified perceptions, which obscure the class nature of capitalist societies and call forth the proper mode of behavior required for the effective reproduction of capitalist power relations. It is in this spirit that we articulate our main suggestion: that financial markets have an active role to play in the organization of social power relations. The so-called dysfunctionalities that are attached to them comprise unavoidable moments within a power technology that shapes and organizes different forms of class exploitation. In other words, *capitalization has to do with valuation as a result of a particular representation on the basis of risk and the way this valuation reinforces and strengthens the implementation of the "laws" of capital.* This is the fundamental lesson to be addressed by Marx's text.

If security *S* as a *sui generis* commodity is a reification of the capital relation, its valuation (that is, its very existence as an exchange value) necessarily relies on a particular representation and a quantification of the sociopolitical and economic conditions of capitalist production. Quite independently of the efficiency of the markets in disseminating information about fundamentals, these fundamentals have already been shaped under the conditions of capitalist ideological norms. The multiple economic-technical-political "events" (that is, every event of capital valorization and resistance to it) that might either emerge within the capitalist enterprise or concern it are, in this way, converted into "objective perceptions" and quantitative signs within capital markets. And since the latter tend to encompass different aspects of daily life, the above security *S* does not have to be property over capital. The financial system provides a representation and quantifications of different power and social relations in general.[24]

We shall repeat that this framework must not be confused with debates regarding the EMH. In these debates the point of tension is about the effectiveness of information gathering: Are market participants capable of grasping the essential part of observed reality, and properly assessing fundamentals, or does the latter remain buried in an impenetrably complex economic universe? Yet, both sides share the same perspective about the nature of the relationship between the observing subject (the market participant) and the observed object (capitalist reality). The former is presented as *external* to the latter, and the latter is apprehended as totally transparent. Hence, the disagreement concerns the ability of market participants to gather useful information and the way in which this affects their decision making. Marx's argument of fetishism breaks with this empiricist problematic. In his perspective, the observing subject is always already *captured within* and *dominated by* the "supersensible" but *objective* forms of appearance of the existing complex of capitalist power relations quite irrelevant from the quality of available information.[25] Regardless of the status of their observations, regardless of the status of the information gathered, regardless of the way one assesses it, this is how the observing agents *are constituted and motivated*, thus becoming part of capitalist objectivity alongside observed social relations and in a proper relation to them.[26]

We shall try to further clarify our point with the illustration that follows. It is based on a trivial example from the theory of corporate finance, namely: the market for corporate control.

4.2 An illustration[27]

The general framework of the Marxian argument has a number of less visible, but more fundamental, implications for the analysis and comprehension of present-day capitalism. Financial markets contribute to the intensification of competition and the mobility of individual capitals (strengthening the tendency towards the establishment of a uniform rate of profit). This process in itself secures more favorable conditions for the valorization (labor exploitation) of individual capitals. It also channels savings into investments (with the latter having the causal priority). But, most importantly, the analysis outlined in the preceding sections suggests that finance (especially in its neoliberal commoditized version) becomes a site for the evaluation and monitoring of the effectiveness of individual capitals. This process does not rely on the quality of gathered information.

Finance originates an overseeing process of the effectiveness of individual capitals. It is actually a type of supervision of the circuit of capital. Economic "fundamentals" do not have an objective status prior to their "knowledge." They always exist in the form of a particular interpretation of capitalist reality. In other words, fundamentals are already defined within the domain of fetishism. From this non-empiricist point of view, the distinction between "fundamentals" and related "information" ceases to be so clear. We shall not elaborate on this issue here. To illustrate our point we shall take into consideration two different, but extreme, cases in financial markets of the kind that can be found in non-Marxian debates (in the knowledge that these examples are just simplifications).

In the ideal case of market efficiency, security prices issued by a capitalist firm capture the dynamic of exploitation as it is expressed in economic fundamentals. Firms that fail to create a set of conditions favorable to exploitation will soon find market confidence evaporating. This will be translated into a reduction in the value of the firm's liabilities. In the mainstream argumentation this correction is necessary to compensate capitalist investors (money capitalists) for the increased "risk," which is in turn due to the decline of the economic prospects of the firm. In this context, the term "risk" is not a well- defined term. For the moment, we shall accept a first naïve definition that can be found in Hilferding's approach. According to this, risk can be seen as a "degree of certainty" (Hilferding 1981: 157), or alternatively the "degree of confidence" (if we borrow a similar term from Nitzan's and Bichler's analysis; 2009: 208), that capitalists have in their own prediction about future profitability.

But what if the asset prices of this particular firm have become totally detached from fundamentals? Of course there will be important consequences at the concrete level of analysis, but from a strategic point of view the result will not be radically different, since the markets have not ceased to oversee the firm within the above-mentioned framework of fetishistic representations. The firm price is not fixed, and the valuation can be easily changed. Whatever the pricing result, *permanent market overseeing means permanent interpretation of capitalist dynamics under certain ideological criteria that reinforce particular exploitation strategies*. Quite independently (at an abstract level of analysis) of the market's informational efficiency, this process embeds certain behavioral criteria and puts pressure on individual capitals (enterprises) for more intensive and more effective exploitation of labor, for greater profitability. This pressure is transmitted practically by means of a variety of different channels.

To give one example, when a big company is dependent on the financial markets for its funding, every suspicion of inadequate valorization (even if it is totally unreasonable) increases the cost of funding (increased risk), reduces the possibility that funding will be available and depresses share and bond prices. Confronted with such a climate, the forces of labor within the highly conflicting environment of the enterprise face the dilemma of deciding whether to accept the employers' unfavorable terms, implying loss of their own bargaining position, or whether to contribute through their "inflexible" militant stance to the likelihood of the enterprise being required to close (the transfer of capital to other spheres of production and/or other countries) or to be taken over. The latter option is equally unfavorable to workers since it will be accompanied by a violent restructuring of working conditions. Evidently, the dilemma is not only hypothetical but is formulated preemptively: *accept the "laws of capital" or live with more insecurity and unemployment*. This dilemma is immanent in the nature of fictitious capital and its implementation does not rely so much on the quality of information or the efficiency of the market.

This pressure affects the whole organization of the production process, the specific form of the collective worker, and the income correlation between capital and labor. It ultimately necessitates the total reconstruction of capitalist production, more layoffs and weaker wage demands on part of the workers. The restructuring of the enterprise means, above all, the restructuring of a set of social relations with a view to increasing the rate of exploitation. It is thus a process that presupposes, on the one hand, the increasing power of the capitalist class over the production process itself, and, on the other, the liquidation of all inadequately valorized capital (downsizing and liquidating enterprises) and thus economizing on the utilization of constant capital (which is assured by takeovers). Hence, "market discipline" must be conceived as synonymous with "capital discipline."

5 Epilogue: towards a political economy of risk and a new understanding of financialization

The Marxian argument presented so far (with regard to finance) should not be restricted to the analysis of individual capitals (capitalist firms). It can easily be generalized to all market participants. One might think that the case of sovereign borrowers is not so different in the end: by and large, modern finance secures the reproduction of the neoliberal form of capitalist power. The mechanism resembles the case of individual capitals. As well as providing a particular form of funding, financial markets secure and reinforce the neoliberal hegemony, that is, the uninterrupted implementation of the neoliberal political agenda.

Let's think this process through to its limits. Dilemmas similar to those faced by the workers in an individual firm are faced by sovereign borrowers. They ought to be careful and not diverge from the fiscal discipline imposed by the neoliberal agenda, otherwise they may put themselves in the uncomfortable position of losing the "trust" of markets and turn to the "bad" IMF (or to its European relevant: the ESM). On the basis of this "material" blackmailing, the most significant social consensus in the logic of capital is usually organized. If the class struggle triggers radical political events such as the blocking of privatizations and/or the central government being compelled to run budget deficits, markets will re-price risk so as to signal their lack of confidence in raising the borrowing cost (lowering the price of outstanding debt). This may work as a correction back to the neoliberal agenda or precipitate default. When things become marginal, a default is not unwelcomed by the capitalist power because it restores, in a violent way indeed, the neoliberal strategy of the capitalist state.

Contemporary capitalism (the term "neoliberalism" is too restrictive to capture all its aspects) amounts to a *re*composition or *re*shaping of the relations between capitalist states (as uneven links in the context of the global imperialist chain),[28] individual capitals (which are constituted as such only in relation to a particular national social capital)[29], and "liberalized" financial markets. This recomposition presupposes a proper reforming of all components involved, in a way that secures the reproduction of the dominant (neoliberal) capitalist paradigm. From this point of view, contemporary capitalism comprises a historical specific form of organization of capitalist power on a social-wide scale, wherein governmentality through financial markets acquires a crucial role. The way we read Marx's argument in the third volume of *Capital* opens up a new problematic of approaching modern finance. We shall elaborate on this issue in the next chapter.

8 Financialization as a technology of power

Incorporating risk into the Marxian framework

1 Introduction to the dimension of risk

We shall pick up the thread of our argument from where we left it in the epilogue to the previous chapter. Marx's analysis in the third volume of *Capital* is incomplete in the sense that he did not have the chance to finish, edit, and publish his manuscript. More than that, the manuscript itself is far from having the form of a final and revised version. With the analysis of the previous chapter we have reached the apparent limits of Marx's text on the nature of finance. These limits are related to the content of fictitious capital as a key analytical concept. Nevertheless, these limits must not be seen as explicit and unsurpassable constraints; they, are at the same time, implicit outlines of a particular theoretical problematic which defines the horizon of all possible questions to be raised with regard to finance. Therefore, the analytical problem for us is: how can we further develop Marx's line of argument? Or, to put it differently, how can we develop his conceptual system without abandoning his unique problematic? In fact, this is what we shall attempt to do in this chapter.

We have argued that fictitious capital (interest bearing capital) is the concrete form of existence of every individual capital. This is a decisive point in the understanding of Marx's agenda. It means that at the more concrete (complex) level of analysis, the circuit of capital is properly given only as: $M-[M-C-M']-M''$ or $M-M''$. This formula amounts to a commodification of the capitalist relationship which now takes the form of a *sui generis* commodity (security) that bears a price: $C-M$. This is in fact the critique Marx makes of Proudhon. When discussing finance, Marx repeats over and over again that "capital as capital becomes a commodity" (Marx 1991: 460; MEW 23: 451). Fictitious capital is thus linked to fetishism, the process of the reification of capitalist social relations. Those who fail to comprehend this aspect of Marx's argumentation also miss the crucial issue involved: the representations associated with the pricing of financial instruments are *active* components of the organization of capitalist power.

This is the solution to the fundamental problem that was addressed by Hilferding (as we discussed in Chapter 4). In other words, the big secret of finance is that the valuation process does not have to do with some competitive determination of the security price alone;[1] it also plays an active part in the reproduction of capitalist power relations in their specific mode of operation. This, in fact, is the message of Marx's argument about fetishism when applied to finance. The reification of social relations and their transformation into financial products *make them given as objects of experience that are always already-quantifiable in the context of a misrepresentation which is combined at the same time with the norm of behavior they call forth* (see Balibar (1995: 66) for this understanding of fetishism). Everyday financial calculations and estimations (an outcome of the complex practices of market agents and institutions immersed in the world of financial commodities and backed up by cutting edge financial research) thus deform and misrepresent capitalist class reality, imposing upon market participants a particular kind of consciousness and a certain specific strategic behavior.

We shall now attempt to develop this argument by addressing the issue of the *risk*, which is heavily involved in the financial process. We have already mentioned that the process of capitalization continuously commodifies claims on future expected income streams, whether they accrue from surplus-value, taxation, or wages (see also Chapter 3). Such commodification means that the class struggle and its results become quantified. This quantification is based on a prior representation of capitalist reality: several singular social events are spontaneously interpreted and then converted into quantitative signs (the prices of commodities). These events, once properly defined in the dominant language of finance, frame the *dimension of risk*. Hence, both the concept of fictitious capital and the practice of capitalization that lie at the heart of Marx's analysis presuppose a certain determination of risk.

The value of a financial security – the value of capital – does not follow but rather precedes the production process. It exists, not because the surplus-value (or any other flow of income) has been produced and realized in corresponding markets, but because financial markets are in some degree "confident" that this will happen (we have already used this formulation as a first definition of risk in previous chapters). The fictitious commodification $C-M$ of the capital relation is based on estimations regarding future outcomes and, accordingly, it presupposes a certain conception of risk.

This is what we shall try to do in this chapter: bring risk into the discussion. Risk is a term that dominates mainstream and heterodox discussions on finance. Yet, its analytical content remains vague and unclear. We intend to reorganize Marx's framework in order to understand contemporary financial developments focusing on the concept of risk. By referring to risk we do not embrace the mainstream perspective. We place risk in a very different context. In neoclassical reasoning, events capable of happening are taken for granted; they are considered as products of a transparent world comprising the economic reality (information=knowledge). Other heterodox approaches do not challenge the empiricist basis of this speculation but rather express concerns about its internal constraints. Marx's framework breaks with this empiricist framework: *The dimension of risk is created by particular fetishistic representations of the events-outcomes of class struggle*. In the following sections we shall elaborate on this issue.

2 The invisible aspect of financial markets: normalization on the basis of risk

2.1 Calculation of risk lies at the heart of mainstream financial theory

In his famous best seller Malkiel (2011: 197) makes the following statement about the conception of risk in mainstream discussions:

> Risk is a most slippery and elusive concept. It's hard for investors – let alone economists – to agree on a precise definition. The American Heritage Dictionary defines risk as "the possibility of suffering harm or loss." [...] Once academics accepted the idea that risk for investors is related to the chance of disappointment in achieving expected security returns, a natural measure suggested itself – the probable dispersion of future returns. Thus, financial risk has generally been defined as the variance or standard deviation of returns.

This passage is indicative of the mainstream conceptualization of risk. Risk is regarded as the confidence – in terms of probabilistic chance – of achieving a future price and, thus, the statistical variance of the price can become a "self-suggested" measure of it. Securities with an expected high variance of returns are considered to be more risky than those with lower variance. This line of reasoning has a very important consequence, which has not been systematized in mainstream discussions. Let's assume that we have two financial securities: A is a UK sovereign bond and B is a share of a US listed firm. We also assume that the price of B is expected to be twice as volatile than A. In that case, the mainstream argumentation suggests a relation that takes the form (V is variance; j holds only for subjective estimations of the hypothetical individual j):

$$V_B^j = 2 \cdot V_A^j \tag{8.1}$$

or, in general:

$$x \cdot V_A^j = y \cdot V_B^j \tag{8.2}$$

The above line of reasoning implicitly attempts to define risk in terms of a basis common to all financial assets. In addition to the fact that this formula cannot be extended to all categories of risk, it is also insufficient for commensurability between different concrete risks. There are two reasons for this.

First, this formula is not a value form expression since neither side (V_A or V_B) expresses the value of the other, while the anticipated variance does not measure risk in a universal way equally accepted by all market participants. Every market participant j forms their subjective expectations with regard to the variance and comes up with estimations of the form:

$$x \cdot V_A^j = y \cdot V_B^j = z \cdot V_C^j = \ldots \tag{8.3}$$

These estimations are not "homogeneous" for all participants.[2] Mainstream analysis can by no means suggest how these variances can be measured on a common ground without simplistic ad hoc assumptions (like those of the CAPM; see below). One can offer many different explanations of the process of expectations formation (here, mainstream imagination is very narrow) but in the end the result will be always the same: risk cannot become commensurable on a subjective basis.

At the same time, as long as we talk about security prices, statistical variance (even at the subjective level) cannot be used as a measure of different concrete risks. The price of every security is based on a particular assessment that always concerns a wide group of risks. In this sense, the previous formulas cannot be extended even potentially to different "single" or 'sub-groupings' of risks. This suggests further limitations to the possibility of commensuration. At this stage, the mainstream conception of risk implicitly addresses the issue of commensurability by establishing variance as a measure of "total" risk; it does not, however, explain how traditional financial markets can directly measure different heterogeneous risks in a meaningful and objective way.

This insight became the groundwork for the development of modern portfolio theory after World War II. Modern finance is based entirely on this theoretical paradigm, which was developed a couple of decades before the rise of neoliberalism. The heterodox approaches that continue to link financialization to the trends in profitability in the 1980s and 1990s, completely fail to understand that *the rise of finance is not an economic byproduct of a single reason but a tendency that was already in motion long before the coming to power of Reagan and Thatcher*.

In the mainstream paradigm there are two principle ideas: risk-averse investors and portfolio diversification. It would not make any sense for mainstream investment practice if the idea of risk was detached from the level of financial returns. Rational investors, who want high returns and guaranteed outcomes, are risk averse: they request a higher return to compensate for a higher risk. Given thus the risk-averse hypothesis, and the conception of risk in terms of volatility, it is rather straightforward to argue that investors can reduce their total portfolio risk with diversification. Why? Because if someone puts together risky assets of different types in the same portfolio, then it can be easily argued that the total portfolio risk is reduced: the lower the asset covariance of the financial returns, the less risky the total portfolio (since total variance will be lower). In general this reflects a practical financial device established long before the coming of modern portfolio theory. The idea is simple: "because company fortunes don't always move completely in parallel, investment in a diversified portfolio of stocks is likely to be less risky than investment in one or two single securities" (Malkiel 2011: 205). For instance, no one would put in the same portfolio the shares of a car manufacturer and those of its tire supplier: covariance would be close to perfect since the returns would move in parallel. An unfortunate event in the first would equally hit the profitability of the second. Markowitz's (1952) main point was that given the above-mentioned conceptualization of risk, investors would hold a mean-variance efficient portfolio, in the sense that they would choose a portfolio with the highest expected return for a given level of risk (variance).

In this context, risk has not become commensurable although it is treated as such. In other words, it is only on the basis of commensurability that Markowitz's diversification strategy can make sense (variance as an objective measure common to all). The statistical concept of covariance captures the indirect outcome of adding different groupings of risk to the same portfolio. There will be invisible multifaceted interaction between different single risks that will result in lower overall portfolio risk. This is the implicit message of Markowitz's intervention: unrestricted financial markets make possible a certain indirect treatment of single risks.

The famous Capital Asset Pricing Model (CAPM) was just a simplified step forward from Markowitz's initial insights. In the mid 1960s, Sharpe (1964) and Lintner (1965) developed the economy-wide implications of the above framework based on the very restrictive assumption of homogeneous expectations. In brief, this assumption erases the letter j from the above expression of variances, imposing de facto commensuration of the different risk groups involved in the determination of the financial return. The homogeneity condition translates subjective expectations of return and variance into objective ones (generally shared by all participants). In this fashion, the expected return and variance of the next period is regarded as exogenous and can be used to determine current asset prices as those prices that simply induce agents to bear existing risk willingly (LeRoy 1989: 1604). In the absence of market frictions (the beloved assumption of mainstream pricing models), if all investors hold optimally mean-variance efficient portfolios, then the portfolio of all invested wealth, the market portfolio so to speak, will be itself a mean-variance efficient portfolio. The risk of every portfolio can therefore be measured in relation to the market as a whole: the latter serves as a point of reference.[3]

2.2 *The real function of financial markets: normalization on the basis of risk*

The concept of risk as analyzed by mainstream financial theory totally misrepresents what really takes place in financial markets. This is due to the adopted empiricist context. In this section we shall elaborate on issues that have already been developed in the previous chapter. Our point is that the significance of Marx's intervention can be summarized as a break with the empiricist problematic,[4] which dominates debates on finance.

Identifying risk as volatility conceals what participants in financial markets *actually* do. Let's consider for the moment one aspect of the latter: numerous well equipped research departments of different financial institutions try to estimate the future trends of financial prices for securities all over the world. They collect information about economic "fundamentals" as the latter are determined according to their models. This information is, of course, defined on a statistical basis, in terms of conditional probabilities concerning future outcomes. As Luhmann (2003) aptly puts it, financial calculations presuppose an "adaptation to chance." However, in the context of mainstream analysis, the fundamentals themselves are already fetish images of capitalist reality. They are ideological concepts that set out a certain representation of the dynamics of capital that is necessary for the reproduction of capitalist exploitation strategies. In this sense, whatever the "efficiency" of markets in dispersing information, that is, in incorporating new information in prices, the pricing process itself is based on a organic *mis*representation of capitalist reality (as a complex configuration of power relations). Anticipation of "mean price" and "statistical variance" (as a rough expression of risk) for every financial asset takes places within this fetish context. All these issues have already been developed previously in Chapter 7. Markets may misjudge the "efficiency" of an economic agent, they may overlook fundamental information in their pricing, but *the interpretation criteria they follow disciplines agents to the norms of the logic of capital regardless of the pricing accuracy*. This is a critical point, which stems from the genuine analytical content of the concept of fictitious capital in the Marxian framework. The argument is illustrated in Figure 8.1.

In the light of the above argument, we understand risk as the dimension that contains potential social events capable of happening in the future, along with an estimation of the chance of their realization. These events are defined under the norms and problematic of capitalist ideology. Economic agents believe that the given "information" of capitalist reality constitutes a transparent interpretation of this reality. However, their lived experience, along with the way they theorize and systematize it in mainstream analytical models, is marked by the themes of bourgeois ideology. The latter provides a certain knowledge of the world, which

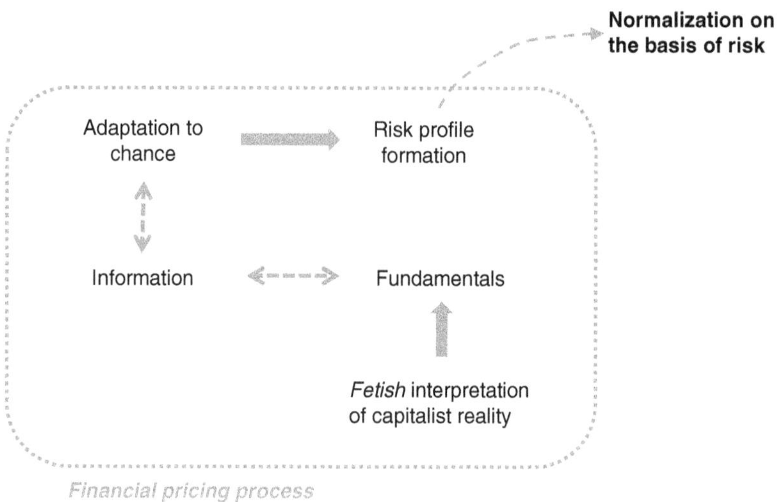

Figure 8.1 Normalization on the basis of risk.

makes agents spontaneously "recognize" themselves in particular roles. Nevertheless this recognition is at the same time a systemic misrecognition of the class and power nature of capitalist economies.[5] Thus, risk is the set of all possible ideas, images, and estimations of future events in the context of capitalist ideology. *Risk is the way capitalist agents perceive the future from an ideological point of view. Risk is the anticipation of future trends (usually expressed in probabilistic terms) on the basis of the fetish mystification of capitalist reality.*

We can understand that without this intermediation of risk, it is absolutely impossible for capitalization to take place. In fact, capitalization as a pricing process presupposes a mode of representing, identifying, arranging, and ordering certain social events of *perceived* reality, which are first "distinguished" and then objectified as risks. In other words, capitalization is not possible unless there is some specification of risk, that is to say, unless specific events are objectified, accessed and estimated as risks. We shall call this process adaptation to chance (see Figure 8.1).

The pricing process relies on the dimension of risk. Nevertheless, the latter takes a particular shape when embedded in financial markets. Its real nature must be emphasized. In order to price securities of different types, financial markets do indeed become the terrain upon which every market participant acquires a risk profile, which serves as a basis for pricing any contingent claim against them. They are fields within which risk profiles are actually shaped. Financial markets thus *normalize market participants on the basis of risk*: the markets identify, disperse and distribute risks to market participants (see Figure 8.1).

The designation of risk comprises two concurrent moments.[6] While all market participants are exposed to risk, the same risk categories (concrete risk events) do not apply to all of them. At the same time, and this is the important moment, even those who face the same concrete risks do not suffer the same (estimated) possibilities for the realization of these risks. In other worlds, *the ideological anticipation of the future, when decentralized in the case of individual participants, takes the form of a risk-profile formation: possible events combined with a necessary indication of their chance of realization.* This is why we call this process "adaptation to chance." Financial pricing is necessarily associated with adaptation to chance. Each market participant, that is to say, is distinguished both by the concrete risks they run and the probability of risk to which they are exposed. A concrete risk is accessible only in so far as it is differentially distributed in a market population, because its chance of realization is not the same for all individuals associated with it.

But now we reach the most important consequence. This process of risk-profile formation, which lies at the heart of everyday financial activity (quite irrelevant to the information efficiency of the markets), can at the same time be interpreted as a process that *normalizes through a specific individualization.* It is predicated on the assumption "that all the individuals who compose a population are on the same footing: each person is a factor of risk, each person is exposed to risk" (Ewald 1991: 203). This does not mean that everyone causes or suffers the same concrete risks or that they are exposed to the same probability of these concrete risks. By attributing risk profiles to market participants, financial markets distinguish one participant from another and so individualize them in terms of risk. But the individuality conferred no longer correlates with an "abstract, invariant norm" (ibid.); quite the contrary, it is an individuality relative to that of other members of the market population.

Nor must we forget that participants in the financial markets are associated in the first place with different social power relations. It is evident that what we encounter here is a complex market "population" constructed out of a variety of social power relationships, which, of course, are not capable by themselves of guaranteeing order and organization. How, then, is this market population "governed" or "regulated?" A detour through Foucault's later writings may prove helpful in dealing with this particular problem because what we are faced with is the configuration of a specific *technology of power* which, unlike the multitude of different social power relations (disciplines, in Foucault's theoretical discourse), is applied to the agents comprising the market "population," superimposing upon them a different mode of normalization. We will attempt to clarify our point by referring to Foucault's conceptual framework. We nevertheless stress that there are considerable differences between the point we are trying to make and Foucault's theoretical preoccupations and objectives.

3 A necessary detour: the Foucauldian concept of governmentality

3.1 Foucault's approach to the issue of the regulation of a disciplinary society

After the mid 1970s, Foucault gradually refocused his research priorities on the issue of the organization of society as a whole. In this sense, he indirectly touched upon the question of the capitalist state, a theoretical theme that was at the heart of the analytical debates of the left during the period. In what follows we shall present the central idea of this particular phase of his intervention. We shall approach his text as "Althusserians"; in brief, we shall read Foucault the way Balibar (1997) read him. We shall explain Foucault's argument about governmentality and bio-politics (see Foucault 2003, 2007) and try to "implant" it as an abstract idea in the analysis of finance. What interests us in Foucault's insights is not a desire to reproduce his reasoning as to how governmentality precedes the capitalist state in the organization of bio-politics.[7] Foucault touches upon the issue of "order" and "cohesion" and this is exactly the aspect of his work that we would like to discuss: if a population is comprised of a multiplicity of disciplines (power relations), how can we apprehend its order, cohesion, regulation, and organization?

In his seminar given on 17 March 1976, Foucault provided a general sketch of his future research agenda. According to his argument, in the eighteenth and nineteenth centuries, societies experienced the emergence of disciplinary powers (social relations of power), whose institutional configuration was open to change but whose social footing was indisputable. Society was based on a disciplinary technique that "centers on the body, produces individualizing effects, and manipulates the body as a source of forces that have to be rendered both useful and docile" (Foucault 2003: 249). This is the idea that is central in his previous studies and approaches to the structure of power; it is posed not in terms of alienation, imposition, or external domination, but rather of a productive shaping of bodies. Nevertheless, Foucault seems to understand that capitalist reality cannot be fully captured if someone relies solely on the analysis of disciplinary mechanisms. There is something more involved in the reproduction of capitalism on a mass scale as a population of docile bodies. We shall quote Foucault's own lucid formulations:

> After the anatomo-politics of the human body established in the course of the eighteenth century, we have, at the end of that century, the emergence of something that is no longer an anatomo-politics of the human body, but what I would call a "biopolitics" of the human race. [...] Now I think we see something new emerging [...]: *a new technology of power, but this time it is not disciplinary*. This technology of power does not exclude the former, does not exclude disciplinary technology, but it does dovetail into it, integrate it, modify it to some extent, and above all, use it by sort of infiltrating it, embedding itself in existing disciplinary techniques. [...] Unlike discipline, which is addressed to bodies, the new nondisciplinary power is applied not to man-as-body but to the living man, to man as-living-being; ultimately, if you like, to man-as-species. To be more specific, I would say that discipline tries to rule a multiplicity of men to the extent that their multiplicity can and must be dissolved into individual bodies that can be kept under surveillance, trained, used, and, if need be, punished. And that the new technology that is being established is addressed to a multiplicity of men, not to the extent that they are nothing more than their individual bodies, but to the extent that they form, on the contrary, a global mass that is affected by overall processes characteristic of birth, death, production, illness, and so on.
>
> (Foucault 2003: 242–243, emphasis added)

To put it schematically, Foucault poses and answers the following questions: if subjects are the productive result of social power relations (or, alternatively, the meeting point of different disciplines), what secures the organization and reproduction of a heterogeneous social whole which is evidently not an outcome of a single discipline? Why do societies need state governance or "top-bottom" regulation (which cannot be seen as the straightforward projection of the institutional outline of disciplinary mechanisms)? No one working within Foucault's analytical paradigm could ignore this type of question. Indeed, it indicates his radical differentiation from the Hegelian conception of the social whole: these questions can only be posited if the social whole is not seen as homogeneous and contemporaneous with its component parts and levels.[8] The social totality (even in the case that it is superficially approached as a sum of disciplined bodies) does not have a center, a heart, a universal spirit: if one cuts through it with a "knife" they will not discover any essence. To reformulate this in an Althusserian manner: the "essential section" is just impossible (Althusser and Balibar 1997: 104–105). If you cut through the social whole, the only finding will be its acentric complexity. This point of Foucault's intervention is properly developed by Balibar (1997).

The population governmentality research project attempts to grasp what is left unexplained by the analysis of the disciplines: namely, the nature of their articulation and their organization into a single reproducible social setting. From this point of view, Foucault surprisingly encounters the specter that he was explicitly striving to avoid: Marx's theoretical system. As Balibar (1997) indicates, with the agenda of governmentality and biopower, Foucault is gradually (or partially) transformed into a theoretician of the articulation of social practices and obviously, to that extent, approaches Althusser's reading of Marx.

Our aim is not to go into a detailed discussion of Foucault's late research project, nor to comment on the way it was adopted and incorporated into subsequent sociological and philosophical discussions. We shall argue that the abstract outline of governmentality as a particular technology of power, which co-exists but does not coincide with the different social power relations,[9] can be extended to the analysis of financial markets. In other words, the concept of "governmentality" or "non-disciplinary regulation" may prove useful for clarifying our point about financial markets, with the same question being posed with regard to them: how can we apprehend their order and organization when we know that different power relations are dispersed and exercised within them? We suggest that modern finance can be approached as a technology of power in line with Foucault's general insights. There are three key abstract elements that characterize this process of regulation:

1 *It has a heterogeneous population as its target*: Regulation is not centered upon the individuality of the agents (we conceive the latter as result of social power relations) but on a population comprising of heterogeneous agencies. Although, this is not so clear in Foucault's reasoning, we see this technology of power as one that organizes the effectivity of power relations and secures their reproduction. The governmentality of the population and the disciplines do not exist at the same level. They are not mutually exclusive and can be articulated with each other (Foucault 2003: 250). Following this line of thought, we can argue that financial governmentality also has the market population as its target and that it does not exclude multifaceted social relations of power, but (to use Foucault's formulations from the above passage) rather "dovetails" into them, integrating them, "modifying" them to some extent, and above all, using them by "infiltrating" them and embedding itself in them (Foucault 2003: 242).
2 *It deals with collective phenomena*: The latter have their "economic and political effects, and [...] they become pertinent only at the mass level"; they are

also phenomena which are "aleatory and unpredictable when taken in themselves" (ibid.: 246). Finally, they are serial phenomena that occur, and have to be studied, over a certain period of time (ibid.). For instance, from the "population" of listed capitalist firms in US stock exchanges some percentage of them is expected to go bankrupt over a certain period of time. A certain number of mortgages are also expected to fall behind. Events that may seem manageable from an individual point of view become collective phenomena when seen from the perspective of the market (population) as a whole.

3 *Collective phenomena are grasped in statistical terms*: This is probably the most important point with regard to the governmentality of a population and is a direct result of the above point. Foucault makes it clear enough:

> the mechanisms introduced by biopolitics include forecasts, statistical estimates, and overall measures. And their purpose is not to modify any given phenomenon as such, or to modify a given individual insofar as he is an individual, but, essentially, to intervene at the level at which these general phenomena are determined, to intervene at the level of their generality.
>
> (Ibid.: 246)

In the next section we shall apply to finance the abstract notion of governmentality, without this implying that we embrace the totality of Foucault's analysis. The reader must bear in mind that our following analysis is restricted to the domain of finance. Foucault's theoretical scheme is inadequate to describe society as a whole, mostly because it fails to understand the centrality of the capitalist state.[10]

3.2 Reloading Foucault in the Marxian context of finance

According to Foucault, social power relations are defined on the basis of particular ends. This describes a "normal" situation while every deviation from it is automatically considered as an abnormal development, which has failed to conform to the norm. Disciplinary normalization consists first of all in positing an abstract model:

> an optimal model that is constructed in terms of a certain result, and the operation of disciplinary normalization consists in trying to get people, movements, and actions to conform to this model, the normal being precisely that which can conform to this norm, and the abnormal which is incapable of conforming to the norm. In other words, *it is not the normal and the abnormal that is fundamental and primary in disciplinary normalization, it is the norm.*
>
> (Foucault 2007: 85, emphasis added)

As is schematically indicated in Figure 8.2, the normal-abnormal distinction is *the result of the norm*, which is set according to the aims of a particular relation of power. For instance,[11] in the case of a capitalist firm, the general rule is to (exploit labor so as to) maximize profit. In principle, we have a clear target and a series of deviations from it since not every firm achieves the same level of profitability ("efficiency" in exploitation) and some of them may even default. One can come up with many different examples. This idea is captured in Figure 8.2.

At the same time, this type of normalization intersects with the regulatory one. Now, the given distinction between normal/abnormal is seen as a collective phenomenon that acquires a statistical form. The version of statistical theory used (more or less sophisticated) is not so important at this stage of analysis. In the case of financial markets, this is the type of normalization that individualizes on the basis of risk, as mentioned in the above analysis. Deviations are seen as potential risks and, from the viewpoint of finance, risk is defined and distributed accordingly to different participants.

We consider the above scheme to be useful for comprehending the functioning of the financial sphere. The type of normalization on the basis of risk coexists with the type of normalization that pertains to (economic) power relations but at a different level. The former is based on and reinforces the latter. From this point of view, finance can be approached as a regulatory technology of power. It is a form of governmentality over the market "population." In line with Foucault's insight, we may argue that normalization on the basis of risk dovetails with disciplinary normalization, integrates social power relations and uses them by infiltrating them to some extent. We are now able to express more concretely our argument that financialization is indeed a power technology, a type of "governmentality" over complex financial markets. It is superimposed on existing economic power relations (which shape different market participants) with a view to organizing their functioning and their reproduction.

What is strikingly missing from Foucault's analysis is a proper materialist theory of ideology and the capitalist state; these are two issues that he obviously

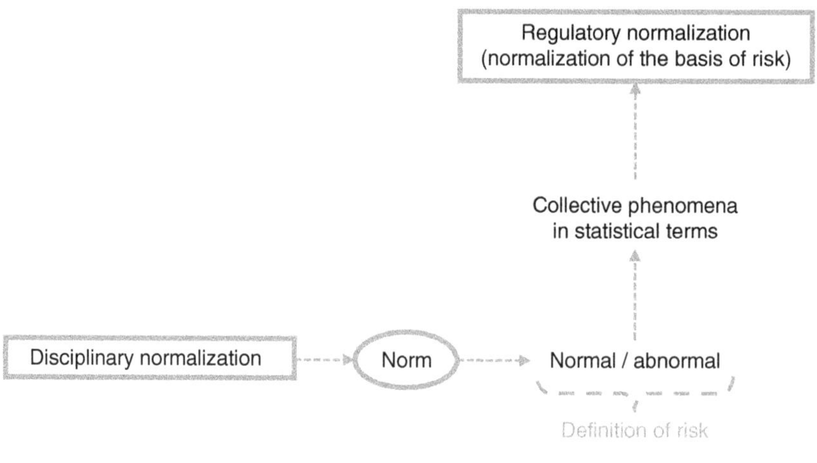

Figure 8.2 Two types of norm.

underestimated or unexplainably avoided in the course of his academic research. In his reasoning, every technology of power presupposes a system of knowledge, which contains rules of truth common to all (see Balibar 1997, Deleuze 1986). But how transparent is reality for those who receive this type of knowledge? Is the way agents conceive of the norm (let's say profit maximization as in our example) the same as what is *actually* taking place within the limits of every discipline (capitalist exploitation)? That's why Foucault's analysis of regulatory normalization is illuminating but it cannot easily be extended to capture exactly what is actually going on in the organization and reproduction of power relations on a collective basis, not to mention the state and the ideologies that are necessarily connected with it (nationalism, in the form of "the national interest," or in the more aggressive versions, of national superiority and "historic destiny" etc.).[12] To put it differently, Foucault's analytical reasoning cannot always avoid the fallacy of empiricism.

In the context of financial markets, power relations are not transparent to the eye. In this sense, the "norm" and the distinction between "normal and abnormal," which is the basis for the definition of risk (see Figure 8.2), express the "truth" as felt by economic agents. It is a truth, which, however, constitutes a sum of ideological representations of capitalist reality that are associated by a particular type of misrecognition. In this sense, the generalization of the dimension of risk (of thinking and acting in terms of risk) and the respective normalization of the market participants are already constructed upon the phenomenon of fetishism. We have already elaborated these issues.

From this point of view, modern finance (financialization) is not only about intensive quantitative assessment and information gathering. The valuation process carried out by financial markets is not neutral but fetishistic in character, i.e., it shapes a *particular* representation on the basis of risk that reinforces and strengthens the implementation of the tendencies innate in capital. In a pointed formulation, Martin (2009: 109, emphasis added) stresses that:

> financialization, a moment in the genealogy of capital, does extend and refine accumulation, but it also elaborates mutual indebtedness as a more general feature of human sociality from labor to lived experience. More than a shift from one axis to another, it is the way that capital speaks its social relations. *Risk becomes not simply a form of calculation, a way of knowing, but also invites a kind of being.*

We believe that this is exactly what is at stake with financialization: *it is a way of perceiving-representing reality from the viewpoint of risk, shaping a particular kind of being that facilitates the expanded reproduction of social capital.* We have already noted that the process of capitalization presupposes some designation of risk. This designation is a structural part of the representation carried out by the financial sphere. In order to "observe" the capitalist reality, financial markets presuppose a particular normalization on the basis of risk: within these markets, concrete risks are dispersed and identified as necessary moments of a particular representation which emanates from, and hammers out, the "living experience" of market participants, shaping and guiding their strategies.

In order to describe the workings of contemporary finance, we have borrowed a concept from Foucault's writings: that of governmentality as regulatory normalization. Of course it is not merely a matter of borrowing a word. Our intent is to fully "expropriate" the concept and properly utilize it in the framework of the Marxian analysis of political economy. This conceptual loan helps us understand how financialization has so far been developed as a technology of power, to be superimposed on other social power relations for the purpose of organizing them and reinforcing them in strength and effectiveness. This argumentation draws upon Marx's framework of financial assets as reifications of capitalist power relations. Our idea of normalization on the basis of risk illustrates this connection.

For instance, a capitalist firm that goes to the markets to raise funds acquires a risk profile, which depends to a significant extent on its ability to pursue effective exploitation strategies in a competitive economic environment. Of course, the visible norm or target involved here is not capitalist exploitation as such but its basic result: profitability. In quite the same manner, a capitalist state as sovereign borrower acquires a risk profile that captures its ability to organize neoliberal hegemony by avoiding undesirable (from the perspective of capitalist power) class events. These risks are respectively defined as normal/abnormal distinctions, which are, in the first place, the result of an organic ideological interpretation of capitalist reality. The risk profile of a wage earner depends heavily on his or her docility in the face of the reality of labor relations. It seems reasonable to argue then, that normalization on the basis of risk *does not impose disciplinary roles but rather tests and reinforces compliance with them*. In this fashion, normalization on the basis of risk is innate in the workings of financial markets and amounts to a specific technology of power imposed upon market participants for the purposes of organizing the workings of capitalist social power relations, to make their functioning more efficient and well-targeted.

Now we are able to draw an abstract diagram of power technology involved in the workings of modern finance. If a market participant is captured in a world of risk, "trapped" within social practices, which individualize them as bearers of a risk profile, then they are necessarily constrained to deal with this by resort to appropriate *risk-management* attitudes and strategic action. The latter comprises two interconnected moments:

1 On the one hand, given one's risk profile, proper insurance or hedging against risk must be implemented.
2 On the other, one can improve one's position by "exploiting" risk, that is to say implementing actions that will foster efficiency in achieving particular targets (efficiently complying to norms) as defined by social power relations.

Taken together, these two moments provide the outline for a complex technology of power. The latter embraces an ensemble of different social institutions, reflections, analytical discourses, and tactics. A general overview of the agents involved in contemporary financial markets might give an idea of what we mean by this: banks with sophisticated research departments, hedge funds, rating agencies, newspapers, think tanks etc. In this sense, not only does risk calculation (along with the resultant pricing of the various types of securities) imply "power" over the future (the aspect of hedging) but also, and above all, it implies *control* over the present.[13] Attaching a risk profile to an agent (a capitalist firm, a state, or a wage earner etc.) means accessing and measuring their ability to conform in a docile manner to roles within a complex world that is underwritten by power relations. Risk calculation involves systemic evaluation on the part of every market participant of the efficiency with which particular targets (norms), as defined by social power relations, have been achieved. Every market participant *lives* risk as their reality and becomes caught up in a perpetual effort to improve their profile as a competent risk-taker, in this sense conforming to what is required by the "laws" of capitalism. It must not be forgotten that the key issue in our reasoning is not the "correctness" of the market valuations but the existence of these valuations per se based upon particular interpretative criteria in line with the ruling ideology.

Our argument about finance is not yet complete. On the contrary, it has reached its most important step. This is because there is still a crucial problem to be solved: the implementation of financialization as a form of governmentality over markets is incomplete in the absence of *commensurability* between the different concrete risks. In what follows we shall argue that (financial) derivatives are necessary in modern finance as effective answers to the problem of risk commensurability. This development is undoubtedly the foundation of financialization.

4 A short introduction to the brave new world of finance

Before we discuss the commensurability of risk, we shall introduce derivatives with the help of a simple illustration. The reader has already obtained a preliminary idea of these from Chapters 4 and 6. This section sheds light on another facet of derivatives markets.

We shall agree with the claim of mainstream financial theory that one of the most significant institutional innovations in contemporary societies has been the development of derivatives. Of course it is wrong to exaggerate like many mainstream economists, and argue that the development of derivatives markets is a "fundamental revolution whose significance is comparable to the Industrial Revolution" (Steinherr 2000: 25). Nevertheless, we must place derivatives at the heart of the contemporary organization of the circuit of capital.

We shall describe the essential parts of modern risk management with the help of the following simple example.[14] Suppose that agent A buys a financial security S. The latter is associated with many different concrete economic risks, which play an active role in the determination of its value. For simplicity's sake, let us say that these different risks come down to two general categories: *interest rate risk* and *default risk*. Note that while the price of S depends on these two risk categories, they cannot be traded separately. To manage risk, *A* engages in the following balance sheet actions (see Table 8.1). In a first step, *A* enters into a contract commitment with a person (agent *B*) who owns a US Treasury Bond. They agree to "swap" (exchange) their assets. The former transfers to the latter the security *S* along with all the payments on it and receives a long term bond of the same maturity along with the payments that the US treasury makes on it (we shall not bother too much with the details of this transaction in the context of this example; let's suppose that the two securities have the same value).[15] Agent *B* is now bearing the default risk on the initial security *S*. Table 8.1 depicts the equivalent structure of portfolios after the above-mentioned agreement.

Step 2, in Table 8.1, depicts what will happen if agent *A* gets rid of interest rate risk. They find a holder of a US Treasury Bill (agent *C*) with the reverse risk appetite and make a similar agreement. They accordingly "swap" (exchange) their assets along with the corresponding payments (rolled over at maturity).

This is what the capitalist world looked like at the time of Keynes and Veblen: that is, a time long before (financial) derivatives dominated finance. Derivatives contracts (mostly in the organized exchanges; see Chapter 4) were not absent at the beginning of the twentieth century, but for a number of reasons their role was marginal to the organization of finance. Hence, the main characteristic of risk management (which was very important for individual capitals in a period of increasing internationalization of capital) was that *it was all done on the balance sheet*: the majority of the transactions were executed in the cash market. Portfolio diversification was the most significant risk management strategy. The typical characteristic of diversification is that it could not be clearly separated from other balance sheet objectives (Steinherr 2000: 17). The unprecedented internationalization of capital flows made this practice of diversification dominant in the movement of capital worldwide, even before the beginning of twentieth century. As a matter of fact, "in the late nineteenth century, the major creditors [...] held internationally diversified asset portfolios in a way that no group of countries does today" (Obstfeld and Taylor 2004: 57).[16]

Experiencing this reality, Veblen explained the ascendancy of finance in his time as result of the dominance of the absentee owner upon "real" wealth production. This dominance sabotaged the institution of industry to the benefit of security holders and financial brokers. The world of finance was presented as completely detached from capitalist production. In Veblen's perspective, capital has become an intangible commodity, property is a fleeting moment, and the

Table 8.1

	Agent A		*Agent B*		*Agent C*	
	Assets	*Liabilities*	*Assets*	*Liabilities*	*Assets*	*Liabilities*
	Security *S*		Treasury Bond		Treasury Bill	
Step 1	Treasury Bond		Security *S*			
Step 2	Treasury Bill				Security *S*	

capitalized prices of ownership titles involved in the above portfolios of the three agents hardly bear any meaningful relation to the dynamics of capitalist production. Finance cannot capture the trends of real life. Keynes developed his reasoning along the same lines (the analysis we have put forward comes into sharp contrast with these considerations).

The rise of the derivatives markets largely separated risk management from other balance sheet objectives. This is a major development that makes risk commodification possible. Derivatives are now the key instrument for risk management in general. To continue with our previous example, instead of exchanging their ownership titles, the three persons in the illustration are able to incur "similar" risk exposures by exchanging and netting out the flow of payments on these titles. In other words, they can enter into consecutive derivatives contracts. Table 8.2 is equivalent to Table 8.1.

A still holds title to security *S*, but has swapped the cash flows on it for the cash flows on a sequence of Treasury Bills. This type of agreement generates a Credit Default Swap (CDS) and a trivial Interest Rate Swap (IRS). Agent *A* is the one funding the security issuer, but now agents *B* and *C* bear the isolated credit risk and interest rate risk respectively: "If the bond defaults, then person B is responsible for the loss." If short-term interest rates rise above security yields, then person *C* is the one who will make a loss. "No matter what happens, Person A gets the return on a riskless Treasury bill. Market convention treats Person A as the 'buyer' of a credit default swap, and the 'buyer' of an interest rate swap" (Merhling 2010: 192). Of course, as recent experience has proven, all these settlements cease to have any meaning in a systemic event that encompasses the financial system as a whole. But this belongs to another discussion.

A first introduction to derivatives occurred in Chapter 6. Derivatives are so called because they are based on (or "derived" from) an underlying commodity or asset(s) (or abstract performance index). This is the trivial textbook definition. The problem with this type of definition is that it cannot distinguish decisively between derivatives and ordinary financial securities. In general, the latter are financial contracts, which are also "derived" from an underlying earnings potential (in the form of an income stream to be materialized in the future). Moreover, to give a trivial example from the textbooks of finance, stocks or bonds can be seen as primitive options since under the regime of limited liability the maximum loss is the known acquisition price of security. To be sure, the crucial issue with

Table 8.2

	Person A		*Person B*		*Person C*	
	Assets	*Liabilities*	*Assets*	*Liabilities*	*Assets*	*Liabilities*
	Security *S*		Treasury Bond		Treasury Bill	
Step 1	CD Swap			CD Swap		
Step 2	IR Swap					IR Swap

derivatives – especially with financial derivatives – is that concrete risks (default and interest rate risks in our illustration) can be singled out, sliced up, traded, and transferred to another party without giving up the ownership of the underlying commodity. The illustration in Tables 8.1 and 8.2 (along with the examples already presented in Chapters 4 and 6) is indicative of this process of risk "repackaging" (and, therefore, of risk commodification). Of course, default and interest rate risks can also be seen as groupings of other concrete risk components. Risk management on the basis of derivatives comes up with ways to commodify and price component risks as well.

It is, however, theoretically more fruitful to continue regarding them as derived forms for they actually pertain to a bundle – and usually a complex one – of straightforward basic operations in spot markets. This is also obvious in the examples used so far in this book. CDS and IRS are the outcome of the "condensation" of a bundle of spot market transactions into a single financial instrument. Otherwise we could not pass from Table 8.1 to Table 8.2. Only in this way can different specific risks be isolated and repackaged.

Let's recall the structure of a future: a standardized obligation to buy or sell the underlying asset in the future. A three-month forward purchase of foreign exchange is equivalent to borrowing for three months in the domestic currency, buying the foreign currency in the spot market, and investing this amount for three months in a foreign-currency denominated asset. In both cases no initial capital is required and all prices are known at the time of contracting (Steinherr 2000: 18).[17] In other words, the future contract has been replicated by an alternative self-financing strategy. If these two equivalent strategies have different pay-offs then profit-seeking intermediaries will make a riskless profit by making a proper arbitrage bet. In general, by figuring out replicate portfolios and imposing the no-arbitrage condition (the so-called law of one price) we can price even the most complex derivative instruments.

In quite the same manner, a trivial swap agreement between two income flows, like the one presented above, can be seen as a simultaneous long (buy) and a short (write) position on hypothetical assets with the same cash flow structure. It is in this sense that financial derivatives are reducible to appropriate equivalent (replicate) portfolios of assets and liabilities. The main theoretical contribution of Black, Scholes, and Merton, who laid the groundwork for the development of derivatives markets by solving the mystery of options pricing, comes down to this finding: they realized for the first time that options can be priced by finding the proper replicating portfolios of other securities that have the same future pay-offs (their proof was based on a particular paradigm of mathematics: continuous time stochastic processes). Using the no-free-lunch principle, they managed to calculate the price of options.[18] "This method of pricing options has since been used to price literally hundreds of other types of derivative securities, some considerably more complex than a simple option" (Campbell *et al.* 2007: 339). It goes without saying that unfettered and "unregulated" financial transactions are the necessary precondition for the effective pricing of different derivatives (risks) because otherwise there would be no replicate portfolios. In other words, the dominance of derivatives develops in tandem with the (gradual) abandoning of every possible market restriction.

The most important consequence of the above pricing principle with regard to derivatives is that, besides the law-of-one-price (the no-arbitrage principle), it only presupposes minor agents' rationality: agents must only prefer "more to less," having thus a motive to exploit arbitrage opportunities (Campbell *et al.*: ibid.). Therefore:

> the pricing formula for any derivative security that can be priced in this fashion must be identical for *all* preferences that do not admit arbitrage. In particular, the pricing formula must be the same regardless of agents' risk tolerances, so that an economy composed of risk-neutral investors must yield the same prices as an economy composed of risk-averse investors.
>
> (Ibid.)

This analytical result is used to defend the generality of derivatives pricing.

The centrality of the no-arbitrage principle has been emphasized by MacKenzie (2003, 2004), in his analytical framework of performativity. For him, and following closely the reasoning of Callon (1998), economics performs the economy in the sense that it is the (mainstream) economic theory embedded in financial markets that brings economic life into being. The mainstream conceptualization of arbitrage is thus "the key terrain" in which to investigate the principle of performativity (MacKenzie 2004). MacKenzie is right in highlighting this aspect of mainstream analysis. Nevertheless, the no-arbitrage principle is not the only important principle for the pricing process of derivatives and of course it cannot explain the connection between competitive behavior in the market and the organization of capitalist exploitation strategies in general. The no-arbitrage principle is indicative of the demand of the markets to be unfettered, so as to commodify risk and set forth the particular technology of power involved in finance. Having taken the analysis thus far, we are now close to concluding our argument. There is only one final point missing: the one that links risk commodification to the workings of finance as a technology of power.

5 Why are derivatives the necessary precondition of modern finance if the latter is to be seen as a technology of power?

In other words, why is financialization incomplete in the absence of derivatives? In this section we will show why it is in derivatives that the fundamental precondition of the contemporary organization of capitalism is found.

In the theoretical context developed by Veblen (and Keynes), all these new financial developments appear as a further disengagement from capitalist production: as new means for profit seeking to the benefit of the absentee owner and the institutions that secure his dominance (financial intermediaries). For instance, adopting this standpoint, Wigan argued that derivatives implement "a second level of abstraction from the underlying" industrial conditions, and "in so doing, derivatives propel the further abstraction of ownership from its 'real economic' basis and lend ownership a truly universal character" (Wigan 2009: 166, 167). In Keynesian terminology, derivatives add to the opacity of financial transactions, strengthening the motive for "second-order-observation" and raising economic instability. For other heterodox approaches, like the one offered by Norfield (2012: 104), derivatives are seen as the byproduct of the inability of capitalism in major capitalist powers to overcome weak profitability: " 'financial innovation' was an easier way to make money than productive investment," and, therefore, "derivatives helped postpone the crisis by adding fuel to a speculative boom, but they made the crisis worse" (ibid. 129).

In this fashion, derivatives are understood as a form of further detachment from capitalist production, and since the latter is a process of exploitation (according to Marxian framework), all these approaches implicitly come to the very same point: the development of derivatives is associated with "less" exploitation since the archetypal productive sector of the economy is being suppressed. It is clear that our standpoint runs counter to this line of reasoning. Finance sets forth a particular way of organizing capitalist reality and derivatives are the necessary intermediate moment. Let's see why.

Financial markets normalize economic actors on the basis of risk. Different risk profiles are associated with different identified concrete risks when combined with different probabilities of realization. Nevertheless, *if we drop the naive hypothesis of homogeneous subjective expectations, then the process of normalization can have as many versions as the number of individual expectations about future outcomes.* In other words, if financial markets set up a particular technology of power, and if normalization on the basis of risk (risk- profile formation) is the basic prerequisite of this, how can the *universality* of risk estimations be achieved? Or alternatively, if there is no guarantee that all these significantly different types of concrete risks can ever be compared with each other in terms of a common objective measure, how can the above-mentioned targets of financialization as a power technology be satisfied?

It is evident that in order to associate *normalization on the basis of risk* with the *organization of social power relations*, different types of risk, along with the subjective probabilities attached to them, need to become (1) *singular*, (2) *mono-dimensional*, and (3) *measured in an objective way*. We can understand this as follows. While every (capitalist) power relation has a singular target (norm), the deviations from it (risks as *ab*normal trends; see Figure 8.2) are multiple and heterogeneous in character and possibility (given the ideological dimension of risk). For instance, what is worse for an exporting capitalist enterprise (questioning its capacity to produce profits): a workers' strike or an exchange rate appreciation that leads to the same profit loss? What is worse for a capitalist state: public deficits and debt surging due to tax reductions for capital and the rich, or due to the financing of social benefits? "Efficiency" as defined in the context of social power relations (disciplines) is mono-dimensional and singular by definition. It establishes the undisputable norm. The same cannot be said about risk assessment: now, we have different categories (abnormal deviations) and different "subjective" viewpoints upon them (always dominated by capitalist ideology). Hence, *the process of normalization on the basis of risk will not result in a singular and coherent representation of a class struggle reality in the absence of commensurability between different concrete risks*. Without the latter, financialization will not be able to become a technology of power.[19]

This is where (financial) derivatives finally come into the picture. Derivatives markets shape the dimension of abstract risk, imposing commensurability upon different concrete risks and establishing an objective measurement for them. This idea can be found in a different analytical context in the analysis of LiPuma and Lee (2004). The multi-dimensionality and multi-subjectivity of the dimension of risk are overcome and thus reduced to a single objective level. The process of financialization (as described above) is indeed incomplete in the absence of derivatives. They are thus not the "wild beast" of speculation but the fundamental prerequisite for the contemporary organization of social power relations.

6 Derivatives and the dimension of abstract risk: the closure of our argument

We shall highlight once more the practical consequence of the rise of derivatives: as a system they tend to establish a single and socially validated measure of different categories of risk. With derivatives, risk is measured in money in an autonomous manner. It is not so much what economic agents believe, but *what the market suggests*. We shall argue that this amounts to a major change in contemporary capitalist economies.[20]

It has become clear to the reader that with derivatives (and especially with financial derivatives), concrete risks can be singled out and transferred to another party without giving up ownership of the underlying commodity. While financial assets can also be seen as embodiments of risks, it is only with the rise of derivatives that these risks can be priced and traded independently of the security itself. Hence, the fundamental assertion of mainstream financial theory, namely that derivatives markets consolidate the commodification of specific-concrete risks, is therefore worth taking seriously. This rather "practical" indication brings to mind a whole series of theoretical speculations surrounding Marx's value-form analysis in the first volume of *Capital*.[21] The question now is the following: How can the "commodification of risk" be understood in Marxian categories? How can we extend Marx's value-form analysis in the case of derivatives markets?[22]

We shall begin with a simple illustration: a trivial fixed-for-floating rate swap. We believe that the swap is a core form that typifies all financial derivatives (see our analysis in Chapter 4). As we explained in Chapter 4, future and forward contracts can be replicated by a swap agreement. An option is almost the same but with the addition of a right. In general, a swap is an agreement between two parties to exchange cash flows in the future (under particular conditions, of course). This is the case of the interest rate swap that was utilized in the context of Table 8.2. Let's assume that security A is a sovereign bond of a developed capitalist country (let's say Greece) yielding fixed income R_A, while B is a loan to a US capitalist firm with floating interest rate R_B (both rates are defined on some principal). At an abstract level, the swap embodies within itself the well-known equation between two money income streams (because it is the two income streams that are "exchanged"):

$$x \cdot R_A = y \cdot R_B \tag{8.4}$$

In this equation, it is not the exchange values of two commodities that are being equated but two different money income streams, that is to say: two different parts of the security. It should, moreover, be mentioned that the above exchange relation does not comprise a value expression in the Marxian sense of the term, because neither of the two income streams expresses its value in the other. The value expression of each income stream has been established as it is already measured in money terms. From this point of view, it is rather misleading to argue, like Bryan and Rafferty (2009: 10), that derivatives, "as an aggregate" system, "commensurate different currencies, different interest rates, and a vast range of different asset types." This type of commensuration has already been settled by their monetary expression. On the other hand, there is another type of commensuration set up by derivatives: commensuration of different concrete risks, to the extent that derivatives markets commodify and price them: make them appear in the form $C-M$. However, before we examine this issue, let's continue with our illustration.

Income streams R_A (in euros) and R_B (in dollars) are commensurable as money expressions. What are the social preconditions for their quantitative confrontation in the ratio of x/y? The money streams of A and B can be made comparable and exchangeable *only when the social terms of capitalist exploitation in the case of B, and capitalist governance in the case of A, can be uniformly represented and thus compared (under the same perspective)*. The above equation (within the swap) rests on this fundamental presupposition: it is capable of representing and making commensurate a series of class conflicts (already identified as risks), which are involved in capitalist valorization in general. Or alternatively, the above income stream equation is possible on the basis of organizing the objective representation – and so the commensuration – of a universe of concrete risks (as already identified class events) which determine the dynamics of capital valorization and the reproduction of capitalist power. In this sense, the qualitative institutional difference signified by the emergence of derivatives is that there now exists a *more* integrated, sophisticated, normalized, and accessible way of representing events pertaining to the circuit of capital and the organization of class power in general. The result is that concrete risks, along with the attached probabilities, tend to become objectively assessed: they acquire a status independent of any subjective estimation. Merton, a well-known guru of the workings of the derivatives markets, has described as follows the new financial developments:

> With the vast array of financial instruments and quantitative models for estimating exposures to risk, there is now a greater opportunity to eliminate risk exposures of the firm on a more targeted and efficient basis by hedging specific, non-value-enhancing risks. The cost is that the user of hedging techniques must have *a more precise, quantitative assessment* of the firm's business risks than the user of equity capital. In turn, greater need for precision places greater demands on the use and accuracy of mathematical models that measure exposures.
>
> (Merton 1994: 459–460, emphasis added)

Financialization and derivatives markets have made possible the thorough "scrutiny" of financial assets by establishing a *universal way* of interpreting and understanding reality from the viewpoint of risk. Given that standardized or tailor-made derivatives incorporate some of the concrete (known) risks, derivatives can be understood as commodifications of risks $C-M$. As a consequence, every risk traded in derivatives markets can be approached from either of two perspectives: it can be seen either as *concrete* or as *abstract*.

As we have mentioned many times already, derivatives should not be understood as money.[23] Derivatives themselves are, by virtue of their own constitution, always measured in money terms already. Even the swap in our example of a financial agreement, will undergo value changes according to the changes in the social circumstances related to the two underlying assets. For instance, an unexpected unfavorable fiscal deterioration of the sovereign borrower in our illustration will be accompanied by a change in the value that the swap itself bears. In this sense, we approach derivatives as implements that are useful for a particular form of organization and representation of the circuit of capital, totally in line with the fetishist character immanent in the existence of such representation. They participate in and complement a universe of partial representations (such as those involved in different types of portfolios) as (reified) duplicates of capital and other social relations. They represent, monitor, and control the terms and the reproduction trajectories of the capitalist relation.

At the same time, we already know from Marx's value-form analysis that the commensurability of different, contingent, concrete risks presupposes a self-sown *abstraction* from their concrete character and their subsequent transformation into singular, and therefore quantitatively comparable, risks. What is required is a redefinition of the actual concrete risks that are involved in the constitution of risk profiles. The condition of existence and the possibility of self-sown abstraction (along with its modalities) are provided through the money form. From this point of view, "the distinction between concrete and abstract risk does not imply the existence of two types of risk, but two inescapable dimensions of risk implicated in the construction and circulation of derivatives" (LiPuma and Lee 2004: 149).

Abstract risk is the mediating dimension of any concrete risk, enabling thus all different concrete risks to become social. Under these social conditions the plurality of heterogeneous types of risk tends to be reduced to a single level because markets are developed in which different risks are commodified and exchanged with each other: $x{\cdot}IRS=y{\cdot}CDS=z{\cdot}[FX\ \text{future}]=\ldots$. The derivatives markets are, to put it simply, organized in such a way that a net quantity of value emerges along with the isolation and packaging of a known concrete risk. This quantity is measured in money. As a result, because of the interposition of the notional exchange of the derivative with money, one particular and case-specific risk can be regarded as the same as any other. Abstract risk is the concrete and specific risk actually involved in a particular situation when seen in the light of the formation, organization, and measurement of risk as risk in the framework of the expanded reproduction of capitalist power, that is measured in monetary terms.[24] The form of abstract risk is risk measured in value, that is to say, money.[25]

7 Epilogue: the dynamics of contemporary capitalism

This chapter's argument has analyzed developments in contemporary capitalism in the light of Marx's categories. It does not see the rise of finance as a distortion. Quite the contrary, it relates financialization to the dynamics of the capital relation. Financialization is seen as a particular technology of power, developed within the context of the financial world. Our framework converges to some extent with those of the notable works of Bryan, Rafferty and Martin.[26]

This social nature of finance is completely misunderstood in heterodox discussions, which are dominated by the spirits of Veblen and Keynes, or even Proudhon and Ricardo. Even authors like Graeber (2011: 372), who attempt to challenge somehow the established heterodox analytical consensus, fail to see money and finance as something more than a political contention between creditors and debtors. It is, once more, the quantitative aspect of finance that is stressed and emphasized (we shall return to this issue in the final chapter of this book).

On the other hand, there is the critical demand from within the mainstream domain to "democratize finance." Shiller, in a recent book, draws upon an old idea of Akerlof, arguing that "business communities can be caste-like if there is a suitable culture and there are leaders who encourage exclusionary behavior" (Shiller 2012: 232). Advanced finance can thus become a tool for the financial elite, which wishes and manages to preserve its status against the outsiders, i.e., those who do not belong to the financial community and therefore cannot outcompete the financial-caste businesses. Here we see a different connection between economic power and finance than the one envisaged by Keynes and Veblen. The rise of advanced finance is a neutral tool, which favors financial interests (the absentee owner) only when it is misused. In other words:

> it is not the financial tools themselves that create the caste structure, though their mechanisms are part of the equilibrium. The same financial tools can also, if suitably designed and democratized, become a means to break free from the grip of any caste equilibrium. Truly democratic finance can enable one to escape outcast status.
>
> (Shiller 2012)

This demand for the democratization of finance should rely "more on effective institutions of risk management," that is to say, "under financial capitalism many of our best protections, and inspirations, come not directly from government but from our own private financial arrangements" (ibid.: 235).

Our approach differs from these critical arguments both within and without mainstream theory. The latter see finance as a tool that distorts the ideal spirit of capitalism to the benefit of financial elites. The only difference concerns the nature of the tool: whether it is neutral or inextricably interlinked to these financial elites. In our viewpoint advanced finance is a development absolutely in line with the social nature of capitalism, at least as it is described by Marx. It is not a simple tool, but a technology of power, which facilitates and organizes the reproduction of capitalist power relations. If, for reasons of simplicity, we had to see finance as a tool, *it would be a very useful tool in the hands of capital.* Contemporary advanced finance is just one crucial facet of advanced capitalism. There are important political implications to be derived from this reasoning that must be part of a future research project.

We have now reached the end of Part III of the book. Part IV will deal with more concrete issues of the recent economic conjuncture, focusing on the crisis of Euro area. The latter is a *sui generis* monetary union. While most of its contradictions concern the workings of contemporary finance, this aspect is usually underestimated or suppressed in relevant discussions, especially in the heterodox field. Our studies of the crisis of the Euro area are not just an effort to apply elements of the Marxian reasoning developed so far in this book to a concrete example. They are also an attempt to trace the limits and the contradictions of financialization. From this point of view, the practical message of the analysis can be extended to grasp worldwide developments.

Part IV

The crisis of the Euro area

9 Towards a political economy of monetary unions

Revisiting the crisis of the Euro area

1 Introduction

The common European currency had a long history before its actual inauguration (the so-called "quest for exchange rate stability in Europe"; see Buiter *et al.* 1998: 3). It has already completed its first phase, which was "unkindly" stopped by the financial meltdown in 2008. Of course, the latter did not cause the crisis; it just exposed the accumulated contradictions of the first phase. The problems that soon appeared in the banking and public sector have little to do with the "toxicity" of the CDOs. To put it in the most general terms, *capitalism internationally went into a phase of the re-pricing of risk*, with everything entailed by that process (that is to say new arrangements for pricing financial instruments). Re-pricing means re-interpretation and the latter is not just a "false" explanation of the economic problems but is a suitable viewpoint for the very organization of the interests of capital along the same neoliberal lines.

The stylized facts of the first phase of Euro area (EA) have been widely discussed during the last three years, not always in an illuminating or coherent way. Cross-country differentials in growth and inflation, persistent current account (or financial account) imbalances, real effective rate appreciation (mostly for countries with current account deficits), and the setting up of a leveraged and highly integrated banking system were the most striking developments. For those who have followed the past debates about the crisis of the Exchange Rate Mechanism (ERM) of the European Monetary System (EMS), all these events may give a feeling of vertigo; nevertheless, both the protagonists and the stage (the institutional framework) are different this time, although we have not seen the final act yet. Given the character and the long history of the project of the euro and given its nature as a mechanism for organizing the interests of capitalists, anticipating its demise is not a safe bet. We shall return to this question in the next chapter as well.

It is absolutely impossible to exhaust the issue of the EMU (European Monetary Union) in a single chapter. Therefore, in what follows we shall try to provide the outline of our own explanation of the euro project and its contradictions. From this point of view, this chapter can also be read as an introduction to a Marxian political economy of monetary unions. As will become clear below, we place financial account imbalances at the heart of our story, arguing that the euro project is a favorable strategic setting for European collective capitalists. This explains our decision to include a chapter on this subject in a book about finance. This also highlights the difference of our perspective from both the official narrative and other heterodox approaches.

2 The discontinuity in mainstream reasoning

There is a basic theoretical rule in the practice of psychoanalysis (at least in its Lacanian version): it is in the discontinuity of the discourse that the latent "cause" must be hidden. This principle suitably applies to the shift in the official interpretation of capitalist development in the Euro area (EA). This section will point out the discontinuity manifested within the official discourse and discuss its cause. The argument will be developed on the basis of our general thesis about finance.

Persistent current account imbalances and differentials between countries in growth and inflation were developments that were being monitored and emphasized before the start of the financial crisis in 2008. What changed strikingly was the attitude in the mainstream and official narrative. Before 2008, current account imbalances where celebrated as the basic mechanism for accommodating growth differentials in the environment of the common currency. In other words, imbalances were approached as evidence that the economic experiment of the common currency was actually delivering. They were "good" imbalances. Suddenly, this interpretation was quickly replaced by another one, which placed the roots of the crisis in the "imprudent" and "reckless" domestic behavior and policies both of private (firms and households) and public sectors. Post-crisis official explanation relies on the idea of "bad" imbalances.[1]

It may sound strange, but underneath the apparent discontinuity there lies an implicit continuity. Both pre- and post-crisis explanations were there to serve the long-term interests of the strategies of capital across the EA. The root of the change must be sought in the change of the economic conditions of class struggle. New political agendas created the demand for new theoretical lines.

In the pre-crisis period, Blanchard and Giavazzi (2002) established the groundwork for the discussion.[2] In the context of neoclassical general equilibrium theory, current account imbalances mirror net saving positions (net financial flows) originated by the catching-up process. They are "good" and welcomed. Their persistent character is explained by the reallocation of capital flows in such a way as to accommodate different growth prospects between member states with different GDP per capita levels. The fast growing economies in the "periphery" can rely on external savings to undertake additional domestic investment projects while they increase their own consumption (thus reducing national savings). This is not a big problem, since the resulting deterioration in current account positions would be gradually offset by higher future income levels (the outcome of the catching-up process). Using panel data for several groupings of OECD (Organisation for Economic Co-operation and

Development) and EU countries since 1975, Blanchard and Giavazzi showed that current account positions have become increasingly related to the level of output per capita of countries both within OECD as a whole and within the EU itself (although this tendency is stronger within the EU). They concluded: "the channel appears to be primarily through a decrease in saving (typically private saving) rather than through an increase in investment" (Blanchard and Giavazzi 2002: 148). This line of reasoning was the benchmark in the relevant discussions. Current account imbalances were grasped as the sign of efficient capital allocation (within the EA), which promotes economic convergence.

In post-crisis mainstream writings there is a tendency towards the gradual decomposition of the above argument. Eichengreen (2010) summarized the alternative explanation, suggesting that imbalances finally proved to be "bad." In his account, economic convergence is conditional not only on the gap in per capital incomes but also on the *quality* of domestic institutions. This idea summarizes the theoretical problematic that governs the post-crisis official discourse. Imbalances were driven mostly by "domestic distortions" such as irrational asset booms, reckless borrowing and lending, and lack of fiscal discipline. Eichengreen, in particular, attempts to justify the point that the level of corruption is more significant for the explanation of intra-European imbalances than growth differentials. For him the whole process of imbalances was based on a disguised institutional malfunctioning.[3] This type of interpretation dominates official discussions and is also very close to the dependency idea to be found in many heterodox approaches, namely that the euro damaged less-competitive economies of the "periphery," causing "underdevelopment" and "destruction" of their "productive base."

The point of the shift is clear. To put it simply, if current account imbalances are seen as the result of optimal capital allocation in the context of the common currency (with a close linkage in goods and financial markets), then how should one defend austerity policies in the post-crisis era? Why not maintain the very same net savings channels that were established before the collapse of Lehman Brothers instead of attacking labor? In that case, the rational response to the crisis would be the preservation of financial imbalances. The optimal allocation idea runs contrary to the economic justification of austerity. Since the collective capitalists throughout the EA (and all over the globe) embarked upon the agenda of austerity in order to secure the interests of capital, they need to present current account imbalances as some kind of economic misapplication and malfunctioning. This line of reasoning sets forth a particular causality in accordance with the balance of payments identity (for simplicity reasons, in what follows we shall assume that current account balance CA is identical to trade balance):[4]

$$Y-(C+I+G)\equiv CA\equiv S_H+S_F+PB \tag{9.1}$$

Let's focus on the right side of the identity. S_H is the net savings[5] of households, S_F is the net savings of firms and PB is the public budget, which is in turn the net savings of the public sector. Net savings are equal to net capital outflows, which increase residents' holdings of foreign liabilities. It is obvious that if net savings become negative, this amounts to net capital inflows from abroad. The post-crisis official narrative argues that when an economy faces current account deficits (or reductions in its surpluses) then the reason must be one of the following: private sector *dis*-saving, public sector *dis*-saving, or both. In this fashion, national "imprudence" and "institutional malfunctioning" are offered as the main explanation of any problems in economic development. This is a highly moralistic kind of reasoning, suggesting that these economies are "profligate," "reckless," "incontinent" and live "beyond their means." This is the result of a particular reading of the causality in the above identity. Negative *CA* is seen as an aggregate consumption that exceeds the productive capacities of the economy ($C+I+G>Y$). This can be due to either of two alternative reasons. Either over-borrowing from abroad boosts domestic demand at levels that overtake productive capacity *Y*; or, alternatively, it masks the structural gaps in competiveness and productivity. Therefore the suggested cure for the rebalancing of negative current account positions is domestic deflationary policies (an asymmetric response in the context of EMU). This in turn means the curbing of wages and public spending (public benefits) and privatization of public goods (fiscal consolidations). Imbalances are "bad," or at least sub-optimal, on the part of deficit countries, and therefore attacking the interests of labor must be the proper economic response. The resulting policy mix must reflect the neoliberal agenda. Recession is seen as the proper way to bring profligate countries back to the path of economic virtue. This logic is described by Figure 9.1.

Here we have to mention that this type of interpretation does not solely pertain to mainstream thinking. Many different approaches from the left, while rejecting the futile moralist basis of the mainstream, end up underwriting the very same type of causality. They put emphasis on the institutional malfunctioning of the EA in the context of the classical dependency schema. In this way, the EA project serves the national economic interests of the most competitive countries of the "center," such that dissaving is the only way left for the "weak" countries of the "periphery" to fill the gap in competiveness. We find here the revival of the old problematic of dependency, which declares the priority of the international factor over the internal dynamics of the class struggle.[6]

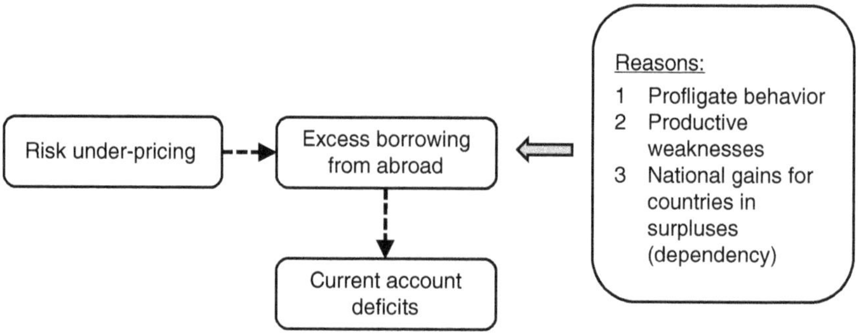

Figure 9.1 The misinterpretation of the EA crisis.

We do not have space here to elaborate on the interventions that adhere to the problematic of dependency. According to this perspective, the main contradiction of the EA is one between nations (rejecting the priority of the class struggle). The capitalism of the "center" is perceived as being responsible for the plight of the peoples of the "periphery." The "number one enemy" of the latter, therefore, is not the power structures of the "periphery" but the capitalism of the "center." This is a strange enemy since it cannot be overthrown directly but only indirectly struck at through a "national course" that can effect delinkage from the bonds of dependency. This political agenda, which in fact subsumes the social movement to the margins of a new strategy of capitalist power, brings to the fore variations of the old idea of Arghiri Emmanuel (1972) about unequal exchange. The analytical premises are (implicitly or explicitly) still the same: a common rate of profit throughout the EA and higher productivity gains of labor in the "center" than in the "periphery." Of course, as we shall see in Section 4, and try to explain in Section 3, these assumptions neither fit the empirical evidence nor provide a thorough explanation of the symbiosis within the EA. But primarily, they fail to grasp the nature of the economic policies that are being implemented in the midst of the recession.

3 Towards a Marxian political economy of a monetary union

3.1 Back to the issue of money: currency unions, transaction costs, and the search for good money practices

There are many different aspects involved in the formation of a monetary union. In this section we shall narrow down our study to the case of the European Monetary Union (EMU) and focus on the aspect that we consider to be the most important: the one that drove the whole project of the common market and, finally, the common currency. The next chapter will add more determinations to the picture.

There is no doubt that the Optimum Currency Area (OCA) paradigm – a trivial section in the international macroeconomics textbooks, which was initially associated with the names Mundell, McKinnon and Kenenof (see Goodhart 1998) – was at the heart of the discussions about the adoption of a common European currency. To what extent it actually influenced the thinking of those involved in the preparation of the treaties remains an open question (see Wyplosz 2006). Nevertheless, this is not the main issue here. The point is that the OCA paradigm offers the necessary theoretical basis for mainstream discussions for every monetary union and thus for the European one. Goodhart (1998) summarizes the basic idea, tracing its roots in the mainstream theoretical foundations of money. The latter can only be understood as a genuine invention that reduces transactions costs, which would be faced by market participants in its absence. This is also the reason for any innovation introduced in the monetary system. Money is the direct product of the commodity exchange, which exists prior to and independent of it. This idea:

> has led numerous economists to construct models showing how the private sector could evolve towards a monetary economy as a function of a search for cost minimisation procedures within a private sector system, within which government does not necessarily enter at all.
>
> (Goodhart 1998: 409–410, 419–420)

The OCA can be seen, accordingly, as a natural extension of this analytical idea into the spatial domain:

> if the origin of money is to be seen in terms of private sector market evolution, whose function is to minimize transaction costs, then the evolution of a number of separate currencies in differing geographical areas should, analogously, be analysed in terms of private sector market evolution, whose function would have been to minimize some set of (micro-level) transaction and (macro-level) adjustment costs. [. . .] Those costs depend in part on market imperfections, whereby there is imperfect flexibility (either spatial, i.e., migration, or in (nominal) wages) in labour markets. The standard litany of factors affecting OCAs then follows, such as size, openness, labour market flexibility, concentration or diversity of production, nature of and specificity of shocks (whether symmetric or asymmetric), etc.
>
> (Goodhart 1998: 409, 419–420)

Put simply, it is the elimination of transaction costs that drives the whole process (see also Buiter *et al.* 1998). There must be a divorce between state interference with money (expansionary policies) and currency areas since "there is no reason why currency domains need to be co-incident and co-terminous with sovereign states" (Goodhart 1998: 420).

The framework just described brings to the fore the specter of Hayek (see Chapter 5). For mainstream arguments, the non-innocent interference of sovereign states in their monopoly over money is a common distortion of general equilibrium. This prerogative must be abolished and then the workings of the OCA will secure optimum private and public economic transactions. This was, after all, the declared reason for abandoning national monetary policy at least from the mid 1980s:

> an asymmetric system where the low-inflation country sets the pace of system-wide monetary policy was suddenly seen as an opportunity for monetary and fiscal authorities in inflation-prone countries to make an explicit and publicly verifiable commitment to contain and overcome the forces making for domestic inflation and loss of international competitiveness.
>
> (Buiter *et al.* 1998: 27)

Yet, the question remains open: How is the putative "good money" agenda of OCA linked to the interests of capital? How can the above-mentioned overcoming of the "forces making for loss of international competitiveness" be grasped? While there are different aspects to our answer, the following section will deal with the issue pertaining to private sector (individual capitals).

3.2 An outline of the strategy of the euro

Present-day neoliberal capitalism has proved to be a nightmare for both the proponents of protectionism and those who comprehend international trade as a "rob thy neighbor" type of game.[7] The same is true for the architecture of the EA, or for the case of every monetary union between economies with different levels of development and productivity.

Contemporary capitalism favors the free movement of capital and commodities worldwide. Developed and developing social formations have by and large willingly adopted this agenda. Critiques of the latter (explicitly or implicitly drawing upon the problematic of dependency) analyze the whole process in terms of economic "plundering" or "unequal exchange." More competitive individual capitals will gradually displace less competitive ones and likewise more competitive economies will do the same, pushing less competitive ones to the point of disintegration. The result of this line of reasoning may appear in different forms in the literature but the general idea is always the same. The group of more competitive economies forms the "center" of the economic world. The "center" is homogeneous and symmetrical (different levels of productivity converge and there is close interlinkage between the different economic sectors). On the other hand, the rest of the economic world comprises the less-developed "periphery," which evolves in a heterogeneous and asymmetrical fashion.

Anyone who travels around the so-called European "periphery" will realize how strong these opinions are in political and academic discussions. The EA is seen as the backyard of a competitive "center" (itself dominated by Germany). It is usually argued that the latter has improved its exporting capacity within the EA by leaving the less-competitive economies of the "periphery" in a state of "underdevelopment," which has undermined their "productive base." The persistent current account imbalances, which are a measure of trade imbalances, are thought to be the immediate result.

We have criticized the above approach extensively in the context of international political economy, showing how inadequate it is to the description of contemporary developments (see Milios and Sotiropoulos 2009, 2010, 2011). The general idea is simple. The global market is not just the area for international transactions but is also the economic and social framework for international capitalist competition, by means of which international market prices are formed. The global market and the formation of international prices do not, however, lead to the formation of a general rate of profit for the uniform "global economy" (that is to say, in Marxian terms, the creation of international production prices) because international competition has its own modalities and patterns. International competition is not a mere generalization of nationally-based competition. The necessarily national composition of capitals (as parts of national *social capital*) *modifies* the functioning of capitalist competition in the global market and so preserves and reproduces international differences in the productivity of labor, growth prospects, and national rates of profit. In this sense, international competition does not eliminate as a tendency the circuit of capital in the less competitive countries, but rather serves as a condition for its "modernization" and restructuring. *International competition does not put capital into danger. Quite the contrary, it is a condition for its reproduction.*

To understand contemporary developments in the organization of capitalism it is therefore necessary to free ourselves from every "mercantilist" influence so as to develop a persuasive interpretation of why developed and developing social formations are attracted – despite the reality of uneven development as it impinges on them – *to a strategy of exposure to international (economic) competition.*

In all of the texts dating from the period of his theoretical "maturity" (in the sense that Althusser assigned to this term),[8] Marx never ceased to believe that competition is an analytical determination *which is inscribed in the capital relation itself.* It is, in other words, a form of appearance of capitalist exploitation and a condition for the constitution of capital as a social force.[9] But for Marx, capitalist development is, at the same time, a question of the balance of class forces and it depends on the form of capitalist hegemony and on the terrain of a specific social formation. How can these two observations help us to understand the agenda of the EMU?

To answer this question, we must first investigate another equally fundamental question that has repeatedly been posed in the relevant discussions: Why should a social formation with a lower level of productivity "want" to enter into an economic and monetary union with more developed social formations? The answer is complex, but is to be sought in the Marxist argument according to which, for the developed capitalist countries, the strategy of exposure to international competition (promoted on a variety of bases and with various divergences, depending on the corresponding national vested interests) is the strategy *par excellence* of capital.

The key prerequisite for unimpeded capital accumulation is the existence of favorable social conditions for the valorization of capital, and capitalist competition is to be included among such conditions.[10] A country that is not organically integrated into global markets and inserts significant barriers and controls of different kinds into the relations between its individual capitals and the global market, will not be able to achieve both high rates of capital accumulation and the deepening of the power of the capitalist class over the working classes. This means that if a capitalist country has entered into the phase of developed or developing capitalism, the route of exposure to international competition is the most appropriate strategy for organizing bourgeois power: *as a model for the continuing reorganization of labor and the elimination of non-competitive individual capitals to the benefit of overall social capital.*

For a number of specific historical and social reasons which have to do both with the organization of capitalist power (in the developed European states) and the specific imperialist conditions of the post-war period, a variety of European state entities set in operation the plan for the single market (at least from the early 1970s) led mostly by the intention to secure exchange rate stability.[11] The plan in question gradually came to embody a long-term strategy for the management of European capitalisms, predicated of course on the introduction of a single currency. The crisis of the EMS (European Monetary System) in 1992–1993 made it clear that economic unification (the single market) could not become a reality without monetary unification. Nevertheless, the implicit message of the very same event was that every variant of monetary unification would ultimately have difficulty avoiding imbalances between the different member countries.

It is by no means hard to understand that the plan for the single market should not be achievable in a regime of flexible and floating exchange rates. In all likelihood, a devaluation of its national currency by one member would induce the other member states to resort to various forms of protectionism as a defensive response. And from that point onwards, the greater the instability of exchange rates, the more powerful would be the pressure for the introduction of protectionist practices, with the result that the goal of economic unification would remain a perennial delusion. At the same time, as is emphasized by Buiter *et al.* (1998), a devaluation "would undermine hard-earned anti-inflationary gains," in other words, it would undermine the exposure to international competition, while at the same time it "would represent a relaxation of the external constraint on domestic fiscal policy." We realize, thus, that the fear of hostile devaluations was not the major reason for the adoption of the common currency. The most important fears were linked to the relaxation of the disciplining policies with regard both to the circuit of capital and the organization of state governance.

Moreover, the likely growth of commerce within the European community would elevate the derivatives markets into the sole mechanism for offsetting the risks posed by the exchange rates (in the absence of a common currency). It would, however, be entirely impossible to imagine a single market being constructed on the basis of over-extended and jittery derivatives markets. The crisis of 1992–1993 also proved that fixed exchange rates would be a vulnerable setting to accommodate different growth patterns within the EMU. A common currency, along with the fundamental arrangements of central banking and the interbank payment system, would be the necessary next step.[12] No country could therefore support the plan for a single market and at the same time resist the introduction of the single currency: the result would be the cancellation of the strategy of exposure to international competition.[13]

Member countries accordingly relinquished the exercise of an autonomous monetary policy. It is in any case well known that the liberalization of capital movement in conjunction with fixed exchange rates (or alternatively the abandonment of the national currency) necessarily amounts to loss of control over monetary policy.[14] The procedure in question represents a certain way of dealing with what has come to be called the "trilemma" of economic policy and amounts to an extremely aggressive capitalist strategy. In particular, the "needs" of labor are sacrificed to satisfaction of the demand for capital mobility (i.e., capitalist competition) and exchange rate stability. Indeed, the celebrated or notorious Delors Report, which takes for granted and regards as "natural" the specific power plan of the single market, saw monetary union as something self-evident and inevitable. In reality, the institutional framework of the EMU is interpretable as a systematic solution to the policy trilemma.

This is an economic environment that crushes traditional welfare-state policies, imposing the harshest demands of capital over labor. Given capitalist profitability, it is the increase in productivity in relation to the real income of labor (the "terms" of labor) that is the *variable that is called upon to bear the burden of adjustment* to new capitalist conditions and, in particular, to the environment of the EMU. From this viewpoint too, the age of contemporary neoliberalism resembles the period of the gold standard.[15] What does this mean? It means that pressures from the functioning of the EMU are focused on the core of capitalist exploitation and create the preconditions for the continual restructuring of labor. The EMU puts into effect an extreme variant of the strategy of exposure to international competition, which can continue to exist only through the continual "adjustment" of labor. It follows from this that the *EMU strategy is a specific mode of organization for capitalist power.*

To sum up our point, in the analysis above we argued that the strategy of the euro corresponds to a mechanism for continuously exerting pressure for the reorganization of labor in the various member countries. This is the deciphered message of the OCA paradigm. In this respect, working people are being systematically attacked both at the "center" and at the "periphery" of the EA. The logic of dependency is a poor explanation for the developments and equally a poor guide for policy action. The mechanism of the EA is an ideal diagram for the organization of capitalist power in line with the tendency of "exposure to international competition," which is innate in the logic of capital. It goes without saying that in practice the adaptation of this mechanism cannot be perfect, nor could it ever be. It is a strategy that is always combined with contradictions stemming from the class struggle.

4 An alternative description of the first phase of European symbiosis: *stylized facts*

The official explanation for the current economic predicament of the euro is heavily based on the supposed existence of two interlinked conditions in the deficit countries: reckless borrowing and low competitiveness due to relatively high wages. Of course, this is an interpretation that favors austerity type policies; and austerity benefits capital. So it is a convenient interpretation for a particular configuration of power.

It takes two to tango: for reckless borrowing, a reckless lending is required; therefore, reckless finance (see Figure 9.1). However, finance cannot be reckless for such a long period (covering the first phase of the Euro area). Finance may aggravate existing contradictions, making contemporary economies vulnerable.

But also, finance is a particular technology of power that provides a setting for the organization of capitalist exploitation. At the same time, competitiveness is a condition attached to the relation of capital. It is not so easy to be grasped and measured. A common measure of competitiveness contains a standard set of price and cost indicators, namely the real effective exchange rate (REER) based on labor costs and international relative prices. But the relation of the trends in REER to the social dynamics of competitiveness remains imprecise.

We mentioned above that the global market is not just the area for international transactions, but the economic and social framework for international capitalist competition, by means of which international market prices are formed. If we assume that tradable goods are close substitutes (in reality this is not true, but at this level of analysis it is a reasonable assumption), then prices cannot diverge beyond certain narrow limits. When economic borders are open and capitalist firms are exposed to international competition, a general loss in competitiveness would be expressed in a reduced corporate profitability, declining productivity, lower growth rates, and higher unemployment growth in relation to inflation. In plain terms, it would be a disease with obvious symptoms. Neither of these symptoms can be observed for the countries of the European "periphery" during the first phase of the EA. In the period 1995 to 2008, Greece experienced a *real* increase of the GDP amounting to 61.0 percent, Spain 56.0 percent and Ireland 124.1 percent, quite contrary to what happened to the more developed European economies. The GDP growth over the same time period was 19.5 percent for Germany, 17.8 percent for Italy and 30.8 percent for France.[16] Moreover, as we can see in Figure 9.2, higher growth in the "periphery" was associated with higher profitability and both were linked with deterioration in current account positions as a general tendency. If current account deficits are taken as an indication of loss in competiveness, then how can their positive correlation with growth and profitability be explained? It is obvious that another interpretation must be offered.

It can be safely argued, therefore, that the exposure to international competition that was effected through integration into the single currency imposed significant labor restructuring to the benefit of capital while simultaneously securing for the (less competitive) countries of the "periphery," satisfactory rates of growth, profitability, and capitalist development. We will not attempt to go into a detailed description of the economic data, but we must highlight one major consequence of all of these: the convergence in country-specific risk assessment between different social formations in the EA.

We shall accept (bearing in mind the restrictions of such a simplification) that the valuation of sovereign debt is closely related to the overall country-specific risk assessment.[17] In plain terms, this means that falling long-term yields, or rising secondary market asset prices, reflect the expected returns on existing and new investment in the debtor country relative to the corresponding expected returns on alternative investments abroad. The improvement in the country-specific risk is therefore the result of *both* a country's idiosyncratic growth and

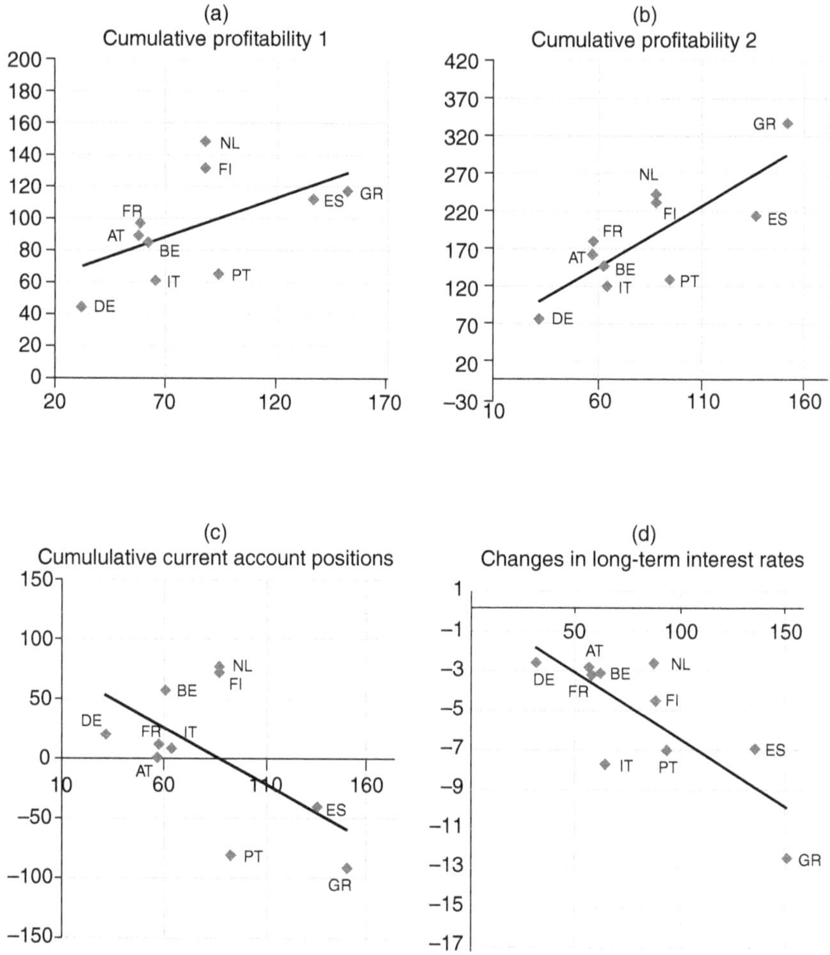

Figure 9.2 Cumulative growth, profitability, and current account positions (percent of GDP) for EA countries, 1995–2007 (cumulative growth on the horizontal axis) (source: AMECO database, our calculations).[18]

profitability prospects, and their relation to the growth and profitability prospects (mostly) in other countries of the monetary union (since we are talking about a monetary union, where exchange rate risk has been practically eliminated). In this sense, the country-specific risk was not mispriced by the financial markets, as suggested by official explanations. The advanced capitalist economies of the EA have suffered economic slack by contrast with the higher rates of growth and profitability that were experienced by the less advanced European capitalisms. By and large, these differential growth and profitability prospects in the context of the EMU (see Figure 9.2) were the driving force behind the convergence in the country-specific risk assessment. Of course, there are institutional reasons which have added to this trend (attached to the workings of the European Central Bank),[19] but this fall in interest rate spreads (see Figure 9.2, chart d) cannot be explained solely on the basis of institutional shifts. The key point in understanding this fall is the very fact that the EA is not a single economy but *a monetary union, which has been proceeding at a dual speed.* In other words, it is an economic region, with the same currency, which comprises social formations with different growth prospects.

It is thus not unreasonable to argue that this reduction in interest rate spreads (on the back of different growth patterns in the context of the EMU) attracted large capital inflows and supported large increases in credit and asset prices.[20] It goes without saying that this process boosted domestic demand in the "periphery" through various channels.[21] At the same time, EA economies with their different growth prospects were without exception incorporated into the same monetary policy regime, that is to say the regime of uniform nominal interest rate imposed by the European Central Bank (ECB) against the collateral of sovereign debt. If the ECB did not distinguish between the country-specific risks of different member states, why would markets bother to do so? These interest rates were considerably lower for the countries of the "periphery" than they had been prior to the introduction of the single currency. This fact, in conjunction with the higher rates of inflation prevailing in these countries, was translated into even lower real interest borrowing rates for the local banking sector. These are the conditions that laid the groundwork for the explosion of (private and public) domestic borrowing.[22]

Figure 9.3 depicts the results of these trends. In the light of the above comments, the difference between growth rates and the long-term interest rates captures to some extent the way markets perceive, in terms of risk (improvement in country creditworthiness), the growth prospects in the EA. This difference was constantly increasing for Greece and Spain during the first phase of the EA (1994–2007) while it remained at negative levels for Germany, despite a low interest rate in absolute terms. On this basis, *current account deficits are neither the result of imprudent borrowing nor the outcome of economic weaknesses. They reflect the significant capital inflows and the domestic credit surging in the countries with better relative growth prospects.* Both these factors boosted domestic demand, resulting in a deteriorating trade balance and upward pressure on the real exchange rate. In the case of Spain and Greece, the increasing REER reflected the persistent deficits in current accounts or surpluses in financial accounts (net capital inflow). Germany experienced quite the opposite effect.

This line of argument places current account imbalances in the context of the EA as a result of a particular mode of symbiosis, one that pertains to a *sui generis* monetary union. The current account deficit, in other words, *cannot be seen* as the immediate outcome of a corresponding deficit in competitiveness, if the latter is to be understood as a social relationship. Nor can it be approached as the outcome of reckless borrowing in the context of "unreasonable" low interest

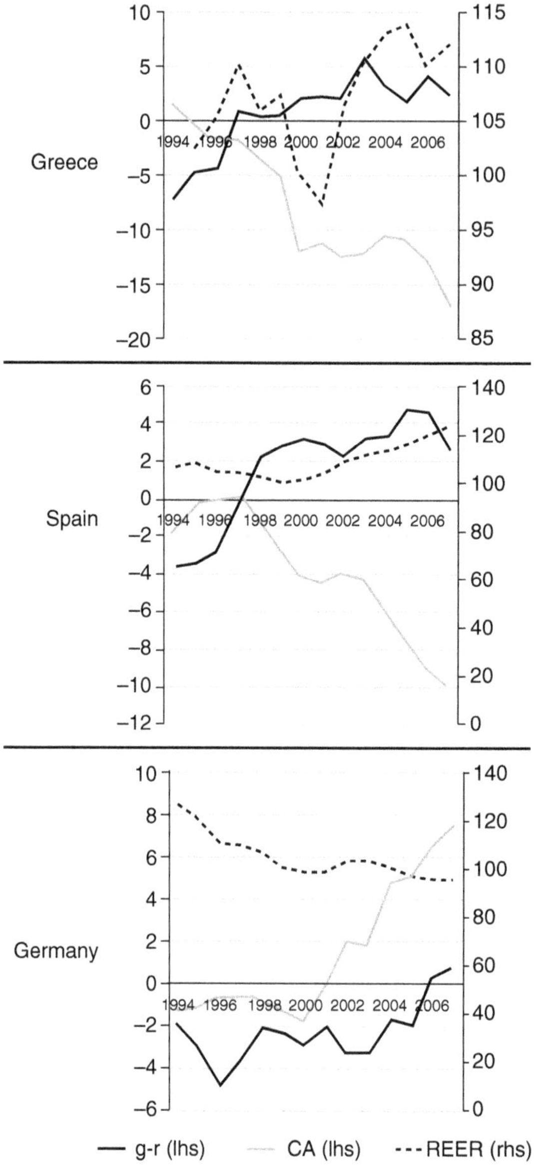

Figure 9.3 Rethinking current account imbalances (g is growth, r is the nominal long term interest rate, CA is the current account balance as percentage of GDP, and REER is the real effective exchange rate) (source: AMECO database, our calculations).

rates (market mispricing). From this point of view, current account imbalances are not "good" or "bad": they are the result of the development of class struggle in the context of the specificity of symbiosis within EMU. This has a very basic conclusion: current account imbalances must be primarily understood as financial account imbalances. The next section deals with exactly this remark and its associated contradictions.

5 Financial account imbalances and the strategic dilemma of the euro

The strategy of the EA is a mechanism for continuously exerting pressure for the reorganization of labor in the various member countries. The plan for the common currency, and its institutional setting, obviously generates strategic benefits for the collective capitalists of every country that participates in it. Nevertheless, its implementation is not free of contradictions and impediments.

We have seen that the mechanism of the euro was based on a specific form of symbiosis between countries with different growth prospects that triggered persistent financial account imbalances. We also argued that there is no clear association between competitiveness and financial account (or the corresponding trade account) imbalances. According to the balance of payments identity, a persistent trade deficit in a fast growing ("peripheral") country reflects negative net savings, i.e., excess domestic capital formation (private and public) over national savings (private and public). Nevertheless, we believe that the mainstream analytical utility maximization framework, associated with the general equilibrium model, provides a poor explanation of the tendencies, mostly because of the difficulty in modeling the intertemporal choices of economic "agents" (households, firms, and governments) on solid and meaningful ground.[23] As discussed above, a more fruitful way to think about the general persistence in net saving imbalances in the case of the EA, is to emphasize capitalist profitability and the way it is translated into financial prices. In other words, *financial account positions are associated with the dynamics of capital and the way it is reflected in the pricing of risk*. Relatively higher anticipated future income streams on capital, in the context of the common currency, is the basic reason for net capital flows and the associated changes in real exchange rates and relative prices. Practically speaking, this means that *imbalances do not mirror changes in competitiveness, but rather the economic developments of a particular form of economic symbiosis*.[24] There are two facets of this process that must be highlighted.

Persistent net capital inflow (negative net savings) in a growing country boosts domestic demand and indebtedness. A rise in domestic demand aligns productive firms with the domestic market and increases the economic weight of the non-tradable sector and services. Relative upward pressures on the real exchange rate are the immediate outcome: neither do they indicate poor economic performance, nor are they associated with low profitability and increases in unemployment (at least in the case under discussion). At the same time, surging domestic demand in the less competitive European economies of the "periphery" functions as a mild form of protection for domestic individual capitals.[25] This can be approached from two different angles:

1 For a less developed capitalist economy, access to international markets can indeed be a way for implementing the strategy of exposure to international competition and for potentially translating this into high(er) levels of growth (and an increase in productivity levels). Nevertheless, it is a process based on a basic presupposition: the less competitive countries (of the "periphery") must be in a position to impose uninterruptedly a drastic restructuring of labor. This restructuring passes through the liquidation of less efficient individual capitals and the creation of new, more competitive, ones. The dynamics of capitalist competition promotes labor restructuring and new antagonistic forms of exploitation, but is inevitably a process fraught with delays and resistances due to the development of class struggle. In this respect, financial account imbalances accompanied by a boost in domestic demand work as a protective buffer to the pressures of international competition, mitigating the "costs" of participating in the euro. In other words, financial account imbalances offer an adjustment factor: they are equivalent to an 'economic surplus,' which functions as a mild form of protectionism.[26]
2 At the same time, *an unsustainable pattern in financial account imbalances turns the above-mentioned buffer into an "impediment" in the strategy of the euro.* Strong domestic demand, and the extension of indebtedness, may offset to some extent the pressures for the continual restructuring of labor and undermine exposure to international competition. So this is not welcomed by the collective capitalists, who regard it as a very dangerous trade-off. This explains the European consensus at the highest level of the EU bureaucracy, for control of both wage inflation and the creation of financial liabilities. In this way, policy makers attempt to exert indirect control over the build-up of financial account imbalances and domestic demand, so as to secure the effective functioning of the mechanism of the euro as a project aimed at the reorganization of labor. Of course, these trends cannot be easily controlled at a bureaucratic level: the dynamics of capital are not dictated by state governance alone.

We are thus confronted with what could be called *the strategic dilemma of the euro.* Persistent financial account imbalances, and the corresponding rise in indebtedness, are at the same time *an adjustment buffer of* and *an active contradiction to the project of the euro.* On the one hand, they contribute to the necessary social consensus (relieving the pressures imposed upon labor) in the particular capitalist strategy of capital. On the other, they form an unwelcome pattern of symbiosis, both as a mere contradiction of the euro mechanism and as an economic setting which is particularly vulnerable to unexpected and unforeseen economic events. *This is a general point with regard to modern finance. It can discipline (as a power technology) but it can also accommodate imbalances.*

The latter may easily work contrary to the discipline prospect and to the overall stability of the system. The case of the EA is a good illustration.

The long-term dilemma of the euro is more strategic than appears at first sight. Given the neoliberal spirit of the EA, it constitutes a point of departure for dealing with imbalances, by means of economic recession and income deflation. This is a very aggressive strategy on the part of the European ruling classes, but it is the only one that can reinforce the dynamics of capital without jeopardizing the neoliberal agenda of the euro.

In brief, the European strategy for dealing with the crisis has as its main objective the further embedding of the neoliberal agenda. It will always stay one step back from the "real" needs of the time so as to lead states into the path of conservative transformation by "exposing" them to the pressure of markets. This strategy has its own rationality, which is not obvious at first glance. It sees the crisis as an opportunity for a historical shift of the correlations of forces to the benefit of capitalist power, subjecting European societies to the conditions of the unfettered functioning of markets. We shall elaborate on this issue in the following chapter.

10 European governance and its contradictions

1 Introduction

During the period immediately after the recent financial meltdown, European officials were caught up in an unexplained optimism. Nevertheless, the developments that followed the collapse of Lehman Brothers struck at the heart of the euro. From this point onwards we all became witnesses of the most grotesque course of events. Strong beliefs about the past collapsed completely and were converted into their opposites: the economic miracles suddenly became the "PIGS" of today; giant European financial companies became zombie institutes, non-existent in the absence of the ECB's efforts and pivotal interventions; the powerful European Monetary Union (EMU) became as strong as its weakest over-indebted link; the putative solidarity between different member states suddenly vanished; the bail-out of the financial intermediaries entrapped public finances.

Ten years ago, reference to the "welfare character" of European sovereign states (as opposed to other parts of the capitalist world) was regarded to be rather trivial. Nowadays, this sounds like a bad joke. Austerity has become Europe's second name and contagion is no longer a theoretical outcome: it is happening here and now. In fact, *contagion* and *austerity* are interlinked to each other in a dangerous vortex which, strangely enough, ends in a "rational" outcome: *it uncompromisingly secures the interests of capital throughout Europe*. In this chapter we shall deal with the dynamics of this vortex, pointing out its scope along with its vulnerabilities.

The analysis of the previous chapter makes it clear that the euro is not just a currency; it is a mechanism. The introduction of the euro has established a particular form of symbiosis among different capitalist economies. We need to understand the euro in systemic terms: this mechanism amounts to a particular organization of exploitation strategies and forms of capitalist power. The interests of labor and the capitalist states (collective capitalists) do not share the same aims and targets. It is, therefore, meaningless to criticize the putative irrationality of the policies implemented by collective capitalists; it is necessary, rather, to unmask their innate class logic. The current system of capitalist power may be violent and brutal, but it is by no means irrational.

In what follows, we shall focus on the ongoing sovereign debt crisis so as to try to present the vulnerabilities of the euro-symbiosis and the rationale of the European responses to the crisis. The basic idea is that these responses have as their primary preoccupation the deepening of the neoliberal organization of capitalist power; in other words, they should not be seen as strategies against the crisis but as *strategies against the resistance of labor*. By referring to European strategies as a whole, we do not mean to underestimate the existing secondary contradictions between the different participating social formations in the project of the euro. These contradictions have remained (so far) within the margins of a single hegemonic agenda, which, at least after 2010, sets as its priority economic recession as a means to proceed with the neoliberal reforms (with some minor financial regulations).

2 A general sketch of economic policy in contemporary capitalism[1]

It is rather common in relevant discussions to look for parallels between state finance and the structure of enterprise finance. States have balance sheets, which contain assets and liabilities. Tax revenues (direct and indirect) can be considered as the most important "asset" pertaining to states. At the same time, states also issue liabilities with different maturities and different terms (domestic or external debt). Nevertheless, the parallelism is rather loose since sovereign states do not *actually* default: despite the superficial similarities, debt holders do not have the status of legal owner, and most importantly there is no such thing as bankruptcy and liquidation of states in the case of a financial mismanagement. This is the fundamental asymmetry between state finance and corporate finance. Capitalist states organize and reproduce the economic and political dominance of capital.[2] Financial markets neither endanger nor sabotage this role. Indeed, they contribute to a particular form of its reproduction: the neoliberal one. In what follows we shall briefly explain this point.

Mainstream approaches present two general points which praise the advantages of global financial markets.[3] On the one hand, financial markets channel the world's savings into their most productive uses. In the case of sovereign states, this means that countries with little capital can borrow from abroad to finance investment in infrastructure without changing the domestic rates of saving or "disrupting" economic activity by "printing" money. On the other hand, the role of international capital markets is to discipline policy makers. According to the argument: every irrational behavior will generate capital outflows and render crises more likely; therefore financial openness provides motives against administrative mismanagement or fiscal 'imprudence.'

The above perspective, which predominates in the academic research, takes the standard model of intertemporal household utility maximization as a point of departure.[4] But to try to equate capitalist economies with poor and rich households – which face different types of future income streams and therefore are engaged in financial transactions in order to smooth their streams of real consumption according to their tastes – is very slippery ground. Trends in global capitalism do not verify this analogy. The so-called financial liberalization imposed some discipline at the cost of making the system vulnerable to crises. At the same time, capital does not always flow "downhill," that is from richer to poorer economies (as expected by the theory). The landscape of global finance is much more complex than that.[5] The general equilibrium idea can hardly fit the complexity of global capitalism.

Nevertheless, this not the major issue with regard to the neoclassical scheme. In the latter there is the demand side (state borrowing), the supply side (private savings) and an interest rate, which, as equilibrating factor, brings about a nice balance between the two. Fiscal imprudence will supposedly raise the cost of funding, thus making policy makers more cautious about their actions. However, this type of reasoning fails to grasp the main issue with regard to contemporary finance. *Put simply, every specification of "supply," "demand" and "interest rate" presupposes a pricing context, which is based upon a certain representation of reality.* This pricing process is not as straightforward as is implied by mainstream thinking, since there is an interconnection between the valuation of these three economic variables (supply, demand, and interest rate).

Both the demand and the supply side consist of economic entities with balance sheets. Sovereign borrowers' liabilities coincide with lenders' assets. In Marxian terminology, both assets and liabilities are fictitious commodities that capitalize future income streams. This means that their value is the result of discounting upon contingent future events. Present values are only possible on the basis of estimations of an unknown future; but the latter presupposes particular representations of capitalist reality. In other words, the fictitious character of balance sheets renders these representations active elements in the organization of the pricing process. If we define risk as the established dominant interpretation of future economic circumstances, then finance is unthinkable in the absence of risk assessment and specification.[6]

The sovereign balance sheet is based on several income inflows (revenues) and outflows (expenditures). These two sides are parts of a wider capitalist strategy established by the state. The most important issue here is the capitalized fictitious values of these inflows and outflows or, alternatively, *the very fact that in the era of financialization these flows are treated as fictitious securities*. This capitalization is the result of a particular interpretation of economic activity by the markets. In fact, financial markets establish a particular way of perceiving and assessing the nature of state policies along with their funding mode. For instance, the fiscal risks that may arise out of a reduction in taxes to the benefit of capitalists (a reduction of income inflow) will *not* be priced the same as either an equal increase in education expenditure (an increase of an income outflow) or an equal decrease in the taxation of wage earners. In other words, these risks will be priced differently according to their social nature since the functioning of the financial markets is dominated by the neoliberal ideological interpretation of reality. The loss of income from privatizations, the loss of income from tax reductions for the rich, the loss of income from tax reductions for the poor, and the increase in the expenditure for providing public goods such as education and public healthcare, will therefore lead to different balance sheet conditions and different debt dynamics, mostly due to the way they are priced. The international financial markets do not only reallocate the savings worldwide, but primarily set forth a particular representation of the capitalist reality. Accordingly, sovereign assets and liabilities are priced on the basis of this "prejudiced" narrative. The equilibrium identity between assets and liabilities is the outcome of a particular perspective of the capitalist reality and does not precede it.

This is how markets discipline states. The representations generated by the markets are not neutral; on the contrary, they define economic "fundamentals" in such a way that it is easier for the neoliberal hegemony to be established and reproduced. Different policy actions receive different valuations and bring about different debt dynamics. This means that in terms of pricing, economic alternatives to neoliberalism are presented to a significant extent as unattractive and inefficient. This functioning of markets creates conditions so that capitalist economies fit safely into the neoliberal "corset." It does not amount to new forms of dependency and it certainly does not denote the withering away of sovereign states. States have assets and liabilities, but they are not economic entities like capitalist firms. They cannot be owned by their creditors and therefore cannot go bankrupt. The financialization of their activities merely indicates the embedding of a particular form of capitalist state power, of class governance, undoubtedly more authoritarian, crude, and violent. From this point of view, neoliberalism can be defined as a historically specific form of organization of capitalist power in which "governmentality" through markets plays a crucial role. *The real target of neoclassical theory is not fiscal prudence in general, but a particular form of fiscal prudence: a prudence appealing to the interest of capitalists.*

The above context substantially disorganizes every serious attempt at an alternative economic policy, not to mention any attempt at a radical shift in the organization of economic life. In other words, governments are "motivated" to act as genuine guarantors of the core interests of capital, securing the consensus to neoliberal strategies. Every alternative economic policy plan will immediately bring about a *re*-pricing of the balance sheet income flows thus changing the debt dynamics and restraining the alternatives of the governments. *With this argument, we do not want to understate the need and the realism of alternative economic policies; we just suggest that these policies can be implemented only in so far as social movements and political powers exist that push the state policies in different directions.* To put this differently, we stress the strategic role of markets in an attempt to uncover the real message behind the neoliberal strategy. Of course, there is always room for resistance and political solutions that diverge from the neoliberal objective.

3 The Euro area as a *sui generis* monetary union

A single currency area is not identical with a zone of fixed exchange rates. One usual mistake in the relevant discussions is the following: many scholars seem to think that Euro area (EA) states just peg their national currencies to the euro as if the latter was a mere foreign currency. This assumption usually leads to the most grotesque explanations. Nevertheless, the euro *is* the national currency of every member state of the EA (and of course it is more than that; see the analysis of the previous Chapter 9). It is a national currency of a peculiar kind. It is a currency without traditional central banking. And this is a major change, at least for the bigger economies of the EA (such as Spain or Italy). In what follows, we shall explain the logic of this unique situation. In particular we shall explain why:

- The EMU, by imposing more discipline to the neoliberal project, has become more vulnerable to crises (elevated sovereign default risk); and,
- The emphasis on "moral hazard" is so crucial for the neoliberal agenda in the context of the EMU.

3.1 More discipline in exchange for more instability: the dangerous trade-off in the case of the euro

In the usual nation-state setting, a single national fiscal authority stands behind a single national central bank. In plain terms, this means that:

> the combined fiscal-financial-monetary resources of the fiscal authority and the central bank must be sufficient to provide the central bank with the resources it requires to fulfill its role as lender of last resort and market maker of last resort and to meet its macroeconomic stability objectives.
>
> (Buiter 2008: 9)

As we know, this is not the case with the EMU: there is no solid and uniform fiscal authority behind the European Central Bank (ECB). Member states issue debt in a currency that they do not control in terms of central banking (they are not able to "print" euros or any other type of currency, at least not for a considerably long period of time).[7] In this context, governments will not always have the necessary liquidity to pay off bondholders. Financial stability can be thus safeguarded only through fiscal discipline, i.e., through preserving fiscal policies within the neoliberal corset.

As mentioned above, this should not be taken as a real sacrifice on the part of sovereign states. On the contrary, it is considered as a welcome condition for the organization of neoliberal strategies, because *the disintegration of the welfare aspect of the state is now the only route to financial stability*. Nevertheless, this institutional arrangement comes with a serious cost, a danger that the old discussions, with regard to the Eurozone, strikingly underestimated. The economies of the EA have voluntarily subjected themselves to an elevated default risk.[8] Let's focus for the moment on this particular question.

When a government with a large amount of foreign-currency denominated sovereign liabilities faces a change in the "mood" of the markets[9] – that is, a re-pricing of risks associated with its assets and liabilities, possibly expressed as a sudden freezing of the inflow of capital (a liquidity crisis, let's say) – it will experience an explosion of debt servicing costs on the foreign currency, and the derailment of its budget balance. This is bad news for debt sustainability (and financial stability). The government must immediately tighten fiscal policy in the midst of a recession (an economic recession is likely to be the result of such risk revaluation since the terms of state borrowing reflect the terms of private borrowing), communicating to the markets its ability and willingness to continue servicing its foreign debt. The government has to convince the markets that it can secure a social consensus to the neoliberal corset; or, in other words, policy makers must ensure that they can impose fiscal prudence in the way markets dictate it, according to the mainstream line of reasoning (securing the interests of capital). Such policies, in the midst of a recession, are not unlikely to lead to a severe crisis. In the case of a monetary union like the EA, the significant financial interconnectedness of the member states raises fears of contagion, which is also reflected upon the distressed governments. As mentioned many times in the relevant literature, this is a vulnerable macroeconomic setting, prone to a self-reinforcing and self-fulfilling type of sovereign debt crisis.

For European citizens this story might well give a sense of *déjà-vu*. It bears a striking resemblance to their current condition. The example of a state with a large debt in a foreign denomination resembles (but it is not identical to) the fiscal conditions of the EA.

Things would not necessarily be this way if the economies of the EA had not abandoned their former national currencies. In this hypothetical case, a *moderate* exodus from the government bond market would cause a manageable devaluation in the exchange rate without undermining the liquidity conditions of the economy. Foreign investors would get rid of the sovereign debt but they could not take the national currency equivalent with them. Financial intermediaries with foreign debt would feel some pressure but the quantitative easing window (i.e., according to the contemporary expression, the printing of money) put forward by the central bank could alleviate the pressure, thus satisfying the liquidity preferences of the financial sector. But even in the extreme case of financial distress, the national central bank could simply "print" money (this is a notional electronic transaction), thereby lending directly to the government in order to prevent sovereign default. We have to note that this is one possibility among others and holds mostly for the larger economies. This possibility is not so strong in the case of smaller economies (like Greece, Ireland, and Portugal).

By adopting the euro as their new common currency, the participating countries (i.e., their ruling classes) have made a "dangerous" choice. They have voluntarily curtailed their capacity to deploy meaningful welfare policies, subjecting themselves at the same time to a high degree of sovereign default risk. This has turned out to be a risky trade-off. A moderate exodus from the sovereign debt market (i.e., a moderate risk re-pricing) now distorts the liquidity conditions in the economy and leaves the state with only one path: fiscal tightening, high interest rates, recession, debt un-sustainability, crisis, and default. Economies that face liquidity problems in their sovereign debt markets may not go all the way down this path (given the policy responses at a European level) but, in any case, recessionary policies are the only route suggested by the existing shape of the EA. If sovereign states are massively caught by the unfortunate spin of this vortex, *crisis is just the other way to implement the neoliberal strategies*, more unorthodoxly and violently this time. European states have voluntarily placed themselves in a predicament where markets can actually force them into default, but this is an issue within the European policy setting.

3.2 EMU and moral hazard: the triumph of neoliberalism

We have seen so far how the states of the EA have subjected themselves to a high degree of sovereign default risk. This was a development underestimated by the architects of the euro. On the other hand, a much more frequently discussed issue was the restriction of public debts. We shall not go through all the discussions that gave birth to the so-called Growth and Stability Pact. We shall just focus on its principal logic.

We have to stress once more that, as regards the disciplining of state policies to the neoliberal corset, the key issue is not the level of public debt or deficit, but the way markets interpret the connection of these fiscal variables with the other crucial parameters of debt dynamics (growth rate, interest rate, primary balance). Hence, the disciplining process contains two crucial moments: the whole configuration of debt dynamics *and* the pricing of involved risks by markets (which, of course, is based on a particular representation of reality given the institutional background). It was pretty obvious from the beginning that the context of the euro could possibly "confuse" market supervision, making room for potential fiscal expansion contrary to the dominant neoliberal spirit. There are several reasons for this, some more important than others. For one thing, European bank regulation put a zero capital charge on all EU sovereign debt, prefiguring the subsequent narrowing down of interest rate spreads. This means that commercial banks could borrow in the wholesale market at Euribor, and then buy European sovereign debt, gaining the spread as risk-free profit. The return on this carry trade was extraordinary, pushing the market to underestimate some of the risks involved in sovereign indebtedness. We could mention more examples.[10] For instance, the ECB lent cheap to the commercial banks, accepting sovereign bonds of different EA countries as collateral with the same quality. In other words, the ECB justified by its actions the negligible risk differentials.

But the basic issue was that markets, being aware of the financial interconnectedness within the EMU, felt sure that no country would be left to default since such an event would have wider economic implications for the EA. Indeed, until 2008, the markets put all sovereign debt pretty much on the same footing, narrowing down the spreads. Of course the difference in the interest rate spreads cannot be solely explained in terms of institutional reasons. As we argued in Chapter 9, long-term interest rate spreads also capture the overall country-specific risk: that is, the growth prospects within the particular institutional setting. In this sense, the convergence of the long-term interest rates of Greece and Germany reflects the growth differentials when the latter are considered within the context of the EA.

Nevertheless, this seems like a serious limitation to the disciplining mechanism of markets. To use market language, the context of the EMU also elevated the risk of moral hazard. Without some ad hoc regulation, there were not enough incentives either to prevent governments from issuing too much debt or to take the necessary measures to deal with it. This condition *could* be seen as giving some space for the implementation of welfare policies. Nevertheless, it did not. Markets might be unable to supervise the sovereign states "efficiently." It was the invention of the Growth and Stability Pact that was designated to solve the problem. This pact explicitly banned every type of bail-out and deprived the ECB of the right to buy sovereign debt on a regular basis. It made the euro an international currency without the backing of a traditional central bank. Moreover, it imposed an artificial ceiling on public debt and public budgets: Since financial stability was to be secured by fiscal tightening, and since the euro symbiosis would not let markets properly impose fiscal disciplining, there emerged the need on the part of capitalist power to politically impose ad hoc fiscal rules and forms of political supervision. Their key role was to supplement markets in their overseeing duty. If markets were unable to price sovereign risk in the EMU properly, then explicit political regulation would have been necessary to solve this problem by imposing appropriate rules. Nevertheless, when it comes to the relations between sovereign states the strict application of these rules cannot be taken for granted.

In any case, the structure of EMU (market supervision and the Stability Pact) did provide a context for the control of public finances and, aside from some minor violations, succeeded in tightening them in line with the demands of the neoliberal model. This is pretty obvious if we take a quick look at the dynamics of debt. Let d_t be the amount of sovereign debt at year t, pd_t the primary deficit for the same year (expenditure before interest payments minus revenues), g_t the nominal growth rate, i_t the implicit interest rate and, sf_t the stock-flow adjustment. All these variables are expressed as ratios of GDP. Then from the fiscal balance identity, we can easily receive the following equation:

$$d_t = pd_t + \left(\frac{1+i_t}{1+g_t}\right) \cdot d_{t-1} + sf_t \qquad (10.1)$$

The equation can be approximately rewritten as follows:

$$d_t - d_{t-1} = pd_t + (i_t - g_t) \cdot d_{t-1} + sf_t = pd_t + i_t \cdot d_{t-1} - g_t \cdot d_{t-1} + sf_t \qquad (10.2)$$

In brief, given the level of debt d_{t-1} the above expression measures the contributions to the debt dynamics of several factors: pd_t is the annual contribution of primary deficit (a positive primary deficit adds to the debt); $i_t d_{t-1}$ is the contribution of the interest payments (they add to debt); $-g_t d_{t-1}$ is the contribution of growth (higher growth means lower debt); sf_t is the contribution of the stock-flow adjustment. Figure 10.1 shows the cumulative changes of these variables for the first phase of the EA, namely the period 1995–2007 (we exclude Luxemburg from our sample).

Despite the post-crisis official viewpoint, the first period of the EA succeeded in controlling the dynamics of sovereign debt. Even in cases like Greece and Italy, which carried sovereign debt much higher than the arbitrary Maastricht threshold of 60 percent, the factors that contributed to the increase of debt in each case were (more than) counter-balanced by factors pushing in the opposite direction. For Belgium, another over-indebted case, the total contribution of the above factors was to decrease the debt. All these developments were steadily accompanied by

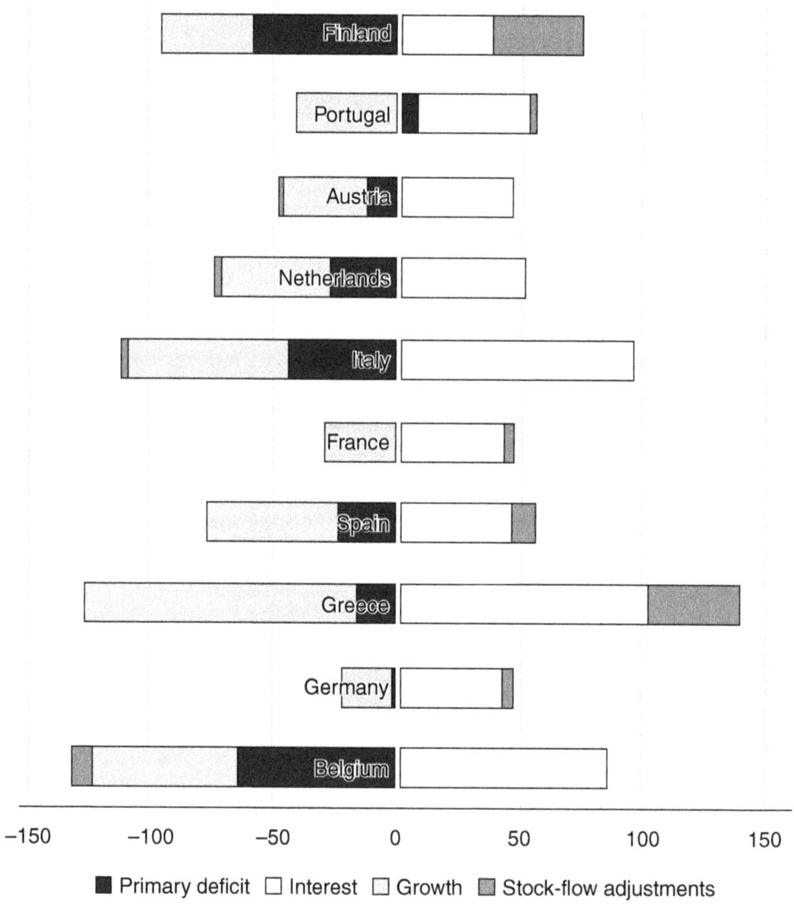

Figure 10.1 Cumulative contribution to debt for 1995–2007 (percent of GDP) source: AMECO database, our calculations.

the implementation of neoliberal policies that favored reductions in public expenditure and promoted tax relief for capitalists and wealthy households. From this point of view, the first phase of the EA was consistent with its own targets: disciplining state policies to the agenda of neoliberalism without putting debt on unsustainable track. Note that for the majority of cases, including the so-called extreme case of Greece, the contribution of the primary deficit was negative (for this particular period European states ran cumulative primary surpluses).

The official fears that the institutional setting of EMU might give rise to 'profligate' and 'imprudent' elements in the fiscal policies *were right but in the wrong direction*. The most interesting finding from Figure 10.1 is the following. For pretty much every country in our sample, positive and negative tendencies to debt dynamics were by and large balanced. This means that overall levels of sovereign debt were not significantly changed. It was mostly the contribution of growth that counterbalanced interest rate payments (in an environment of decreasing interest rates) and made room for neoliberal fiscal policies. In other words, *given the level of growth and the increasingly favorable milieu for interest payments, the debt did not decrease to the Maastricht levels because of neoliberal tax relief to the benefit of capital and wealthy individuals*. Greece is the most indicative example in this line. We shall deal with it in the next section. For Greece, strong growth, combined with the reduction in borrowing costs, left the sovereign debt ratio intact at the level of 100 percent for the whole period under examination. The major cause was the shortfall of revenues in relation to the expenditures, regardless the so-called inefficiencies in the state apparatus (which of course are not Greece's prerogative). Figure 10.2 shows that this result holds for the other EA countries as well.

Chart 10.2a suggests that the implicit interest rate, although more rigid than the nominal long term interest rate, hinges heavily upon capitalist growth.[12] This implies that the interest rate on existing debt is endogenous to growth and follows its trend. Higher growth in the context of the EMU was translated into lower overall borrowing costs. Chart 10.2b also has the expected shape: as a general rule, we see that the higher the growth contribution to the decline of debt, the higher the cumulative primary surpluses. *But this fact was not due to an increase in revenues*. Quite the contrary it is evident, from charts 10.2c and 10.2d that higher (cumulative) growth was accompanied by lower (cumulative) fiscal revenues and expenditure. This finding means that higher growth in the context of declining borrowing costs (in the frame of the EA) did not endanger the neoliberal principle of reduction in public spending ("less state") while it *did* give room for substantial tax relief to the benefit of capital and rich people, as is indicated by the lower levels of cumulative revenues. In fact, the EMU setting provided a strong basis for the materialization of the most offensive neoliberal agenda. *If there was any profligacy at all, this was due to the tax relief enjoyed by the top social strata*. From this point of view, those who analyze the recent fiscal crisis in the EA as the result of irrational binge are right, indeed, but for a different reason. There was a binge, but the working class was not invited. In that case the rules of savoir vivre were broken…

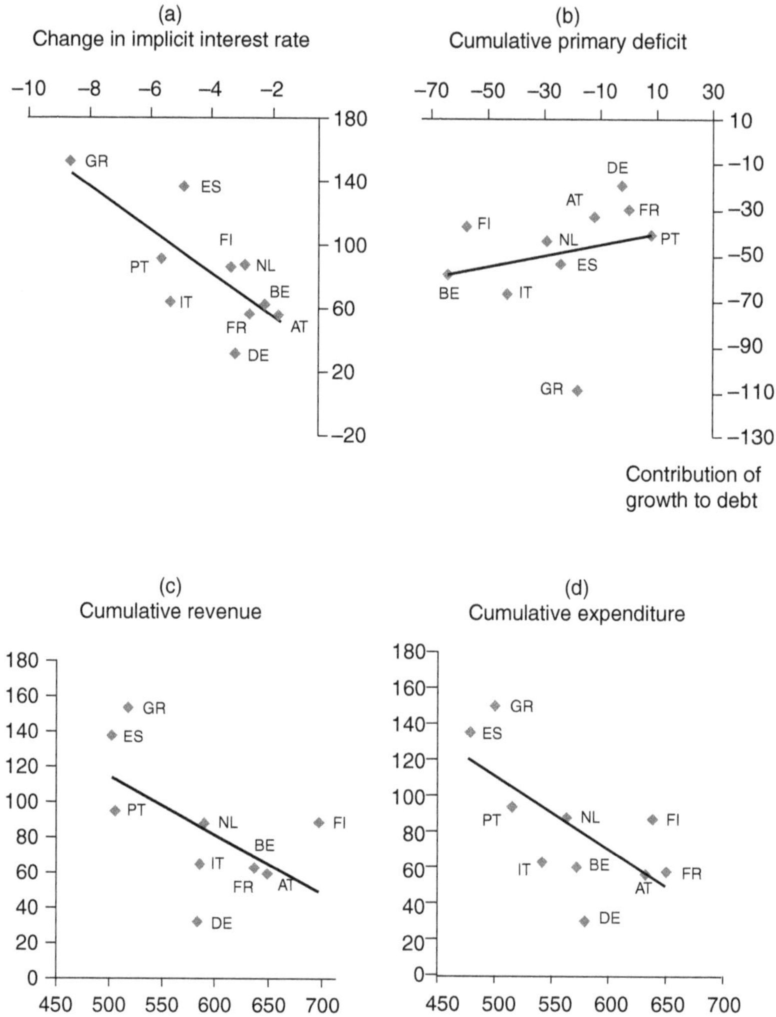

Figure 10.2 Factors contributing to increasing indebtedness in relation to growth (or growth contribution to debt, all variables are expressed as percentages of GDP), EA, cumulative changes for 1995–2007. Growth appears on the vertical axis (source: AMECO database, our calculations).[11]

3.3 A necessary digression: Greece as an extreme case of neoliberal governance

At the moment of writing, market scrutiny is falling heavily on Spain and Italy while growth forecasts about Germany are disappointing. The future of European capitalism seems insecure, especially under the current dominant austerity policies. But it is still Greece that is considered as a special case.

Greece fits nicely into the above line of argument. It is an extreme case of how an aggressive neoliberal agenda may lead to the development of severe economic and social contradictions. As we have seen, Greece's participation in the EA in the first few years after 2000 was accompanied by lower interest rate costs and higher than average growth rates. Nevertheless, the public debt ratio remained stable and gradually increased only after 2004. It is evident from equation 10.2, that we should focus on the trend of the primary balance, which bases itself on the relationship between revenues and primary expenditure (expenditure before interest payments). Figure 10.3 reveals the roots of the particular dynamics of sovereign debt.

The Greek fiscal condition is steadily improving until its adoption of the euro. Public revenue increases until 2000, but from this point it is stabilized at levels much lower than the European average. The trend of primary deficit, and therefore of sovereign debt, hinges upon this pattern of revenues since public expenditures are rather inelastic throughout this period (see Figure 10.6). Figure 10.4 sheds light on the revenues from direct taxes in Greece in relation to the European average. The difference is striking. For the whole period under examination, direct taxes in Greece are more than 4 percent of GDP lower in relation to EU27 and 3 percent in relation to EU12. The cause of this difference is quite obvious. The state was neither able nor willing to collect taxes from a particular part of the society: capitalist firms and wealthy families.

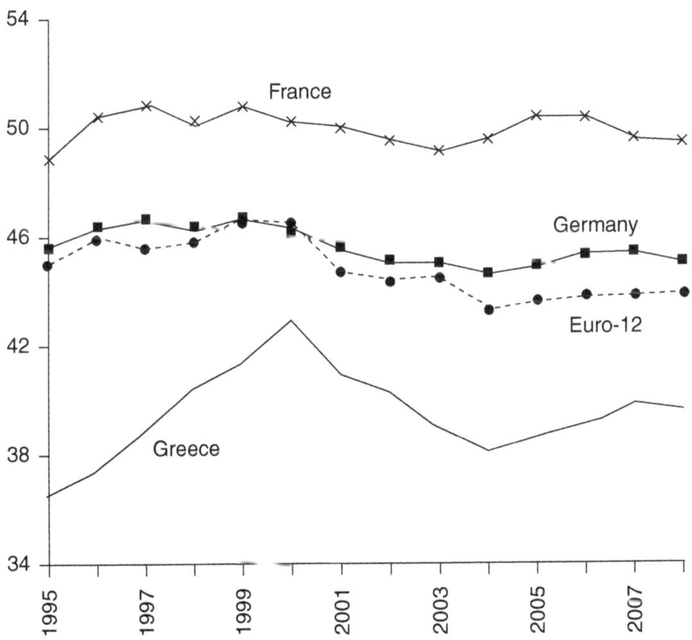

Figure 10.3 Total public revenues in Greece and the EU (percent of GDP), 1995–2008 (source: AMECO database).

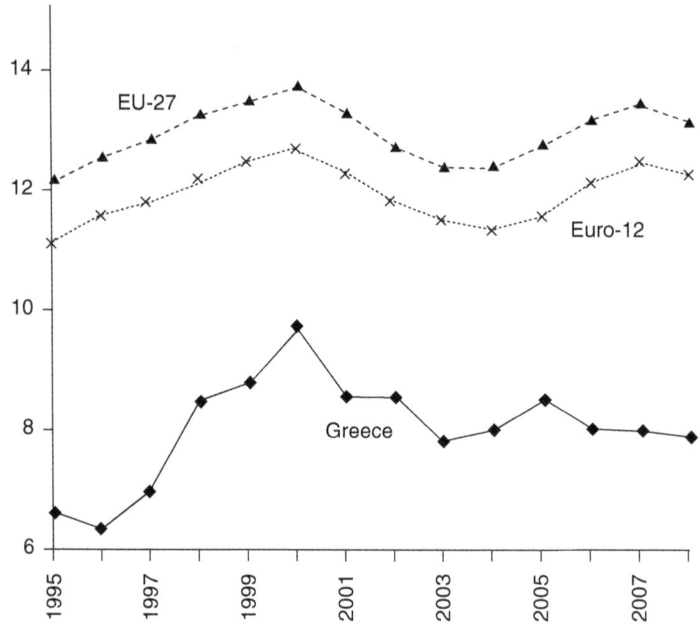

Figure 10.4 Direct income taxes in Greece and the EU (percent of GDP) (source: AMECO database).

We shall just put forward three comments to complete our argument.[13] First, even the head of the IMF (International Monetary Fund) points out in an interview that from 2010, while workers and pensioners paid the level of contribution which they were required to do, an unexplained tax immunity was applied for rich people.[14] Second, since 2007, OECD reports made it clear that it was the reduction of effective corporate tax coefficients that undermined fiscal conditions. Third, comparative studies of different European tax systems suggest that the problem with revenues is in fact a question of secondary income redistribution to the benefit of capitalist firms and high incomes.[15] Limitations of space do not allow us to analyze the influence of other components of public revenues. We shall give just a few examples. Indirect taxes were used as substitute for tax reductions for corporations. In the case of social security contributions, a significant quantity of public revenues were lost because many firms did not pay their contributions and because of the high levels of uninsured labor.

To understand the effect of the shortfall in revenue collection on the dynamics of public debt, it would be interesting to calculate the debt ratio under the hypothetical assumption that Greek governments had collected revenues at the level of EU27, EU12 or even Germany (as alternative scenarios). Some rough estimations can be found in Figure 10.5.[16] The latter depicts, in a very eloquent manner, the importance of low direct taxes and tax evasion by corporations and wealthy

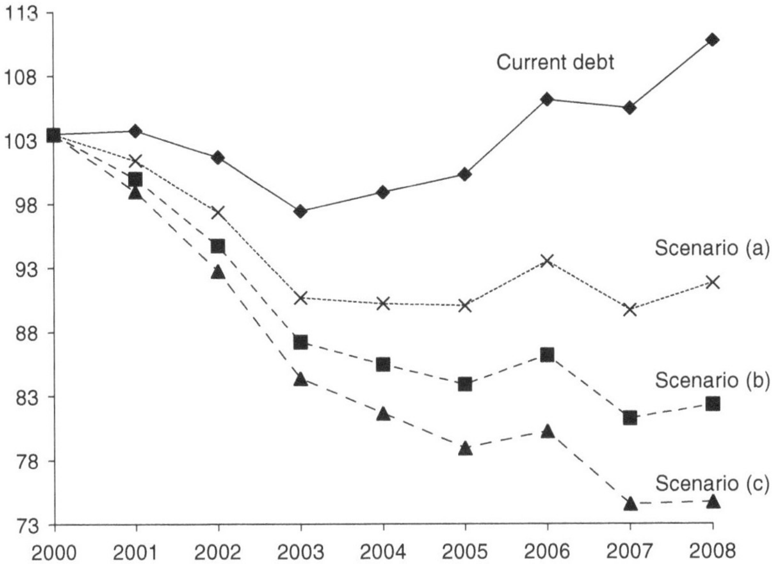

Figure 10.5 Alternative scenarios for the dynamics of Greek sovereign debt. The figure shoes the hypothetical trend of the debt (percent of GDP) if the level of income revenues (per cent of GDP) in Greece were the same as: (a) in Germany, (b) in Euro-12, (c) in EU-27 (source: AMECO database, our calculations).

households for the pattern of sovereign debt. The Greek economy met the implications of the 2008 financial crisis with levels of debt and fiscal deficits much higher than those that might exist if Greek governments *had not* done what they did in fact do. That is to say, if they *had not*: first, based the collection of taxes mostly on wage laborers and pensioners; second, supported extensive tax exemptions and reductions for the corporate sector, which experienced remarkable profitability (much higher than the European average, see Chapter 9); third, tolerated and facilitated tax exemptions through intra-corporate group transactions and off-shore firms; and finally, adhered to the neoliberal idea that the public sector should be reduced, and that the best way to accomplish and reinforce that was to load it with deficits (a strategy which has been applied with success in most of the developed capitalist countries).

The last question to be addressed is whether it was the extraordinary amount of public expenditure that led to the unsustainable debt path. Figure 10.6 suggests that the answer is negative. In the case of Greece, *the fundamental cause of relatively large increases in sovereign debt – despite the high growth rates and the exceptionally low borrowing costs – was not high expenditures in relation to revenues, but the shortfall of revenues in relation to expenditures*. This fact is evident regardless of the extravagances of the state apparatus or of the other things that the state apparatus did (and still does) to stimulate the performance of

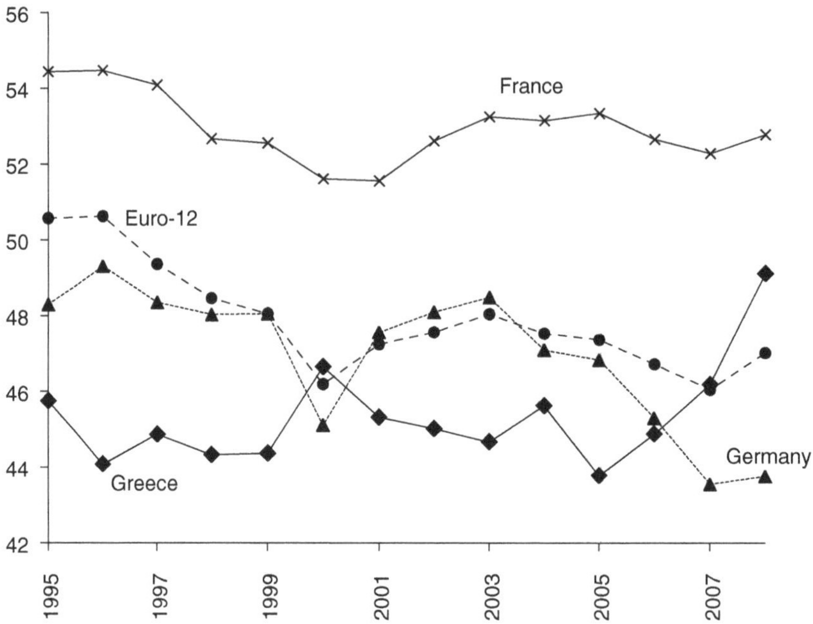

Figure 10.6 Public expenditure in Greece and the EU (percent of GDP) (source: AMECO database).

the private capitalist sector (construction sector, capital involved in heath care, etc.).

As is clear from Figure 10.6, public expenditure in Greece was lower than the EU or EA average levels for the whole period under examination (yet, close to these European averages: after 2001 differences stay between 2–3 percent; the pattern changes of course after 2008, mostly due to the crisis). However, primary expenditure is significantly lower than the corresponding European averages, see Figure 10.7 (interest expenditure was much higher than the rest of the EA and EU countries).

The reason for the increase in primary expenditure from 1995 to 2000 was *not* the increase in expenditure on social benefits (from 13.5 percent of GDP in 1995 they reached 14.8 percent in 2000), nor an increase in wages (the total wage expenditure was 10.1 percent of GDP in 1995 and 10.5 percent in 2000). Expenditure on social benefits and wages as percentages of GDP rose only marginally after 2000 (3 percent and 1 percent respectively for the whole period, up to the beginning of the crisis).

3.4 Moral hazard and market discipline

After the start of the 2008 crisis, European officials, along with participating governments, were faced with a very difficult puzzle: first, how to deal with the

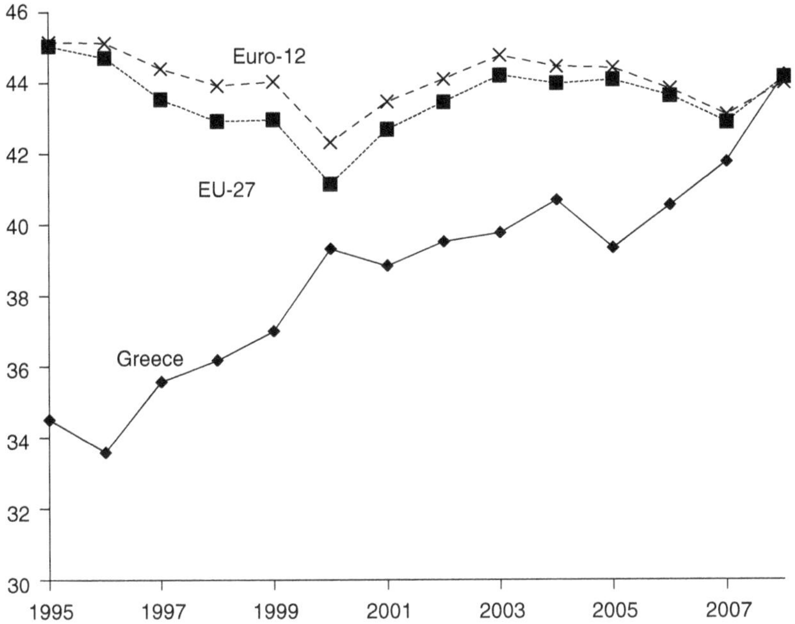

Figure 10.7 Primary expenditure in Greece and the EU (percent of GDP) (source: AMECO database).

enormous economic problems and contradictions without undermining the neoliberal context of the EMU; second, how to create proper policy mechanisms for intervening in the mess, turning the crisis into a chance for a further boosting of the neoliberal agenda; third, how to set up new rules to overcome the vulnerabilities of the past without negating the conservative edifice of the EMU; fourth, how to correct the problems while avoiding the "overcorrection" that would make room for the implementation of social welfare policies in the future; and finally, how to use the tremendous fire power of the ECB without turning it into a "traditional" central bank.

Within the scope of this book, it would be pointless to revisit the episodes of the EU summits or to speculate on what may happen in the near or far future. The European capitalist powers have jointly decided to exploit the current crisis so as to extend the neoliberal agenda. And since the EMU is not an integrated political union, in the light of the above reasoning: *the capitalist responses to the crisis have necessarily to be complementary to the functioning of the markets*. If not, the markets cannot play their disciplining role and the central authorities are unable to mandate the neoliberal reforms. In plain terms, interference with the market in the context of the EA would block or undermine the role of modern finance as a technology of power. Figure 10.8 illustrates this result and it must be read in contraposition to Figure 10.2.

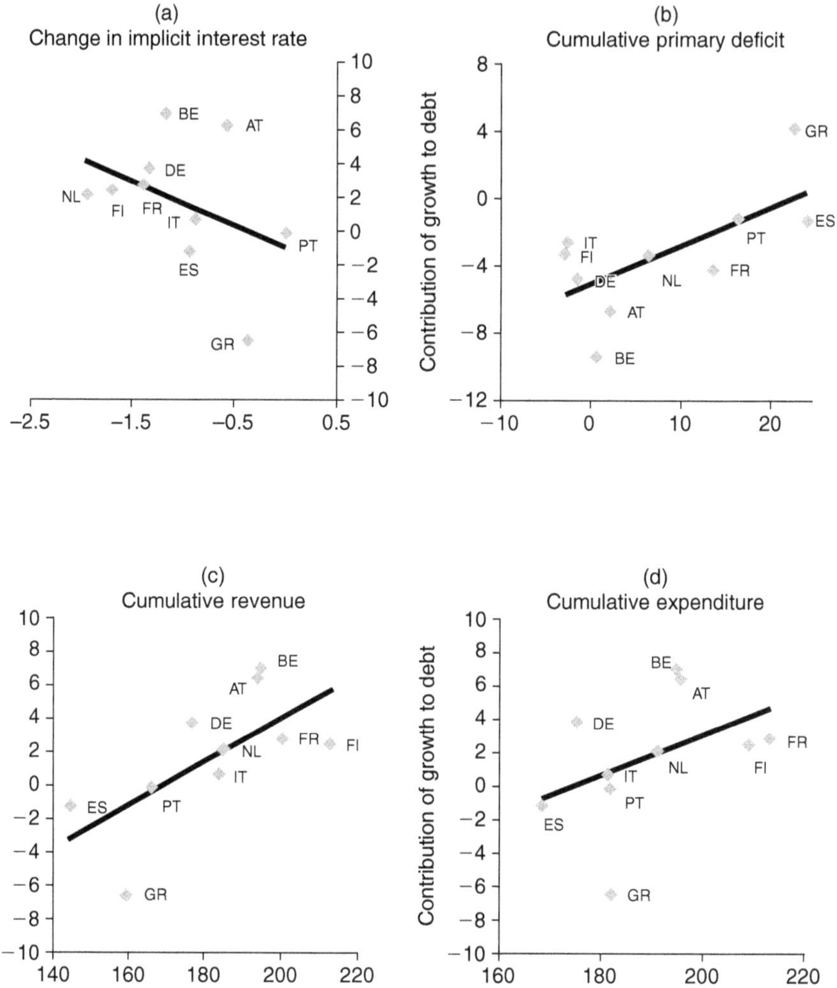

Figure 10.8 Factors contributing to increasing indebtedness in relation to growth (or growth contribution to debt, all variables are expressed as percentages of GDP), EA, cumulative changes for 2008–2011. Growth appears on the vertical axis (source: AMECO database, our calculations).[17]

Of course, the macroeconomic behavior of an economy is very likely to differ with respect to the underlying economic phase. Chart 10.8a does not imply any radical change in the endogeneity of the implicit interest rate, given of course the shift in the pricing of risk by markets (the implicit interest rate responds mildly to the perspective of the markets, since it concerns all the outstanding debt). The same holds for chart 10.8b. But the explanation for the latter is now very different during the recession years, since the contribution of (cumulative) growth is rather positively linked to (cumulative) revenue and expenditure in charts 10.8c and 10.8d. This is exactly the opposite of what held for the pre-crisis years. It justifies the principle of austerity in the context of the EA: the crisis (low growth) is by and large being used as a means to further neo-liberalize state governance. Given the inelastic parts of public expenditure and the lower tax incomes, recession is now approached and used as a tool for further reductions in total expenditure and further relative fiscal burdens to labor. This is the result of the above-mentioned type of governance: official responses complementary to the role of the markets. In other words, austerity has been rendered the major economic policy for developed European capitalist formations. Of course, all these observations describe general trends, which also depend on the results of class struggle.

The commentators, or analysts, who blithely criticize European leaders misunderstand this point. Not only do European officials always have a second and a third plan in reserve, their decisions must impel the neoliberal agenda without violating the functioning of the markets. Otherwise the crisis cannot be exploited as opportunity for capital. In simple terms, aggressive neoliberal measures and reforms would not be implemented in the participating countries if the ECB had worked as a fiscal agent from the beginning, if its intervention in the secondary sovereign debt markets had been deeper and more persistent, if the fire power of EFSF (European Financial Stability Facility) or ESM had been sufficient to deal with the core needs of the sovereigns, if LTROs (Long Term Refinancing Operations) and OMT (outright monetary transactions) were more decisive, if the current plan for Spain had been imposed on Ireland, if the plan for Cyprus were not insane, if.... *The grave character of the crisis might have been avoided but in a totally different direction: one ensuring some protection to the living standards and the labor rights of the working classes.* This would have been a different Europe, though: a Europe promoting less drastically the interests of capital.

In brief, the European strategy for dealing with the crisis has as its main target the further embedding of the neoliberal agenda. It will always stay one step back from the "real" needs of the time so as to lead states onto the path of conservative transformation by exposing them to the pressure of markets. This strategy has its own rationality, which is not completely obvious at first glance. It perceives the crisis as an opportunity for a historic shift in the correlations of forces to the benefit of capitalist power, subjecting European societies to the conditions of the unfettered functioning of markets. In Section 4, we shall discuss how all the already proposed plans fit nicely to this picture. Of course, the future of class struggle cannot be safely dictated...

4 Rethinking the EMU: a general outline and its workings

At this point we can sum up the arguments that we have analyzed and developed so far, in order to clarify our viewpoint. We shall attempt to put forward a general outline of a political economy of the EA (although the point can be easily extended to the analysis of every monetary union).

We have seen so far that the EMU is a *sui generis* monetary union: one without a central authority possessing the typical characteristics of a capitalist state. Two other points about the EMU are also worth mentioning. First, the EMU sets up a context of symbiosis that elevates default risk to secure austerity. Second, it must rely on the elimination of moral hazard as the only way to allow different capitalist formations to be governed according to the neoliberal agenda, thus aggressively promoting the interests of capital. Official responses must not block the functioning of financial markets, even during the crisis; *they must exist only with the status of complementarity to markets.* This has one important result, which we shall briefly elaborate on.

We can rewrite the balance of payments identity that we introduced in the previous chapter as follows (for simplicity reasons we assume that current account is equal to net exports NX):

$$NX=S-\Delta D \Rightarrow \Delta D=NI-F=\textit{net imports}-\textit{net capital inflow} \qquad (10.3)$$

In the above expression, D stands for the sovereign debt and S for the net savings (their negative value is equal to net capital inflow F in the economy). NI stands for the net imports (it is the negative value of NX). Let's think of this identity in the light of the argument developed so far. In general, we shall argue that causality in this identity is a structural one. It is defined by the dynamics of capitalist development and the way this development is reflected in market experience: in other words, by the way it is represented from the viewpoint of risk. This means that there are no straightforward functional relations. We shall introduce some simplifications in order to make our point clear. These are, of course, in line with the empirical evidence from the pre-crisis phase of tranquility.

During the pre-crisis period, we saw that changes in sovereign debt were usually unimportant. The price of ΔD depends on growth prospects within the EMU and the character of domestic economic policies. Countries with high debt and high growth prospects can easily accommodate tax relief for capital without deterioration in the debt dynamics. This was one of the basic results of the first face of the EA. Of course there can be different outcomes, but for reasons of simplicity we shall assume that $\Delta D=0$, an assumption which is close to the empirical evidence. At the same time, we have argued so far that financial account imbalances will necessarily be developed in a monetary union of countries with different growth levels. This is a condition that makes participation in a monetary union appealing to capitalist powers of both less- and more-developed capitalisms. However, this leaves just one adjustment variable in the above equation: net imports. This is our basic result. Ceteris paribus, net imports (or the trade balance in general) is the factor that is more likely to accommodate the financial flows of capital in the context of catching-up (growth and profit rate differentials). This is in line with our conclusion that trade imbalances and REER divergence were the results of the process of European symbiosis: it is a weakness that pertains to the whole setting and is linked to strong capitalist development in deficit countries.

This is a central contradiction, which is also in line with our argument in Chapter 9. High net imports are likely to be associated with a surge in domestic demand, inflation costs, and indebtedness. This is an indirect protection to individual domestic capitals. It runs contrary to (but it does not negate) the strategy of exposure to international competition that transfers restructuring pressures to individual capitals. In the case of a re-evaluation of financial risk that stops net capital inflows, it will lead to unsustainable patterns. The only viable route for coping with emerging imbalances without violating the neoliberal nature of the EU is austerity (an asymmetric response to curb domestic demand along with other European measures to mitigate the contradictions), which is supposed to improve both the current account and the pricing of the country's specific risk.

Given the financial interconnectedness and the above-mentioned vulnerability of the EMU, any risk re-pricing may easily lead to financial and sovereign debt crises. In other words, the EMU is a very favorable setting for capital but one that has an Achilles heel. By and large, this explains the contemporary predicament.

The argument is illustrated in Figure 10.9 (of course there are several limitations in this visual depiction). It describes a tendency which is dominant, but which also faces multiple countertendencies resulting from the aleatory development of class struggle in each social formation and the overall institutional shifts that this struggle dictates. In any case, it is a brief explanation of the basic trends that characterized the first phase of the EA and is also a good guide for future thinking. It must be read in the light of the argumentation that has been developed so far in this book.

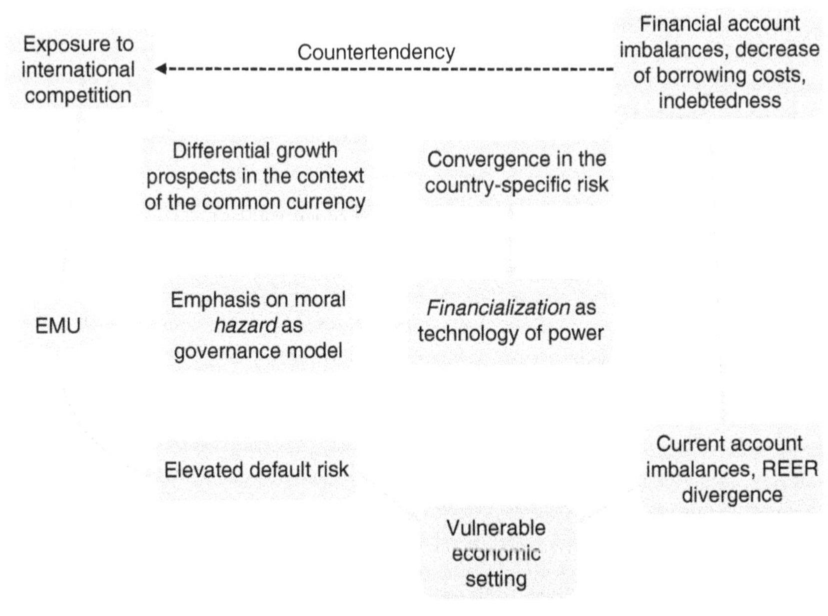

Figure 10.9 The political economy of EA: a summary of our argument.

5 Welcome to the desert of European capitalism

What would be a brief way to summarize our point about the current crisis of the EA? The causes must be sought in the contradictions of a particular form of European symbiosis and the lack of any European frame of crisis resolution. When the crisis arrives, the structure of financial account imbalances is not so important: a leveraged banking system can easily destroy public finances and an indebted sovereign can easily kill the banking system. From this point of view, monitoring just the state budgets under ad hoc political rules is, by and large, meaningless. The primarily asymmetric type of responses which have been implemented so far (the burden of adjustment falls heavily on the distressed economy) are in line with the neoliberal governance of the EMU (an emphasis on moral hazard) and they rather use the sovereign debt as a means to austerity (lower taxes for capital and privatizations) and devaluation of labor (better conditions for capitalist exploitation). In this sense, they are economic policies that are genuinely designed to miss their declared fiscal targets but retain as a strategic horizon the "sustainable" reorganization of economic and social life to the benefit of capital. This is the message of Figure 10.10. It depicts the changes of the last two years (the numbers for 2012 are estimations) in unit labor costs, sovereign debt, and unemployment for the economies of the EA. What is presented by the state and European officials as a story of success, is actually a story of disaster.

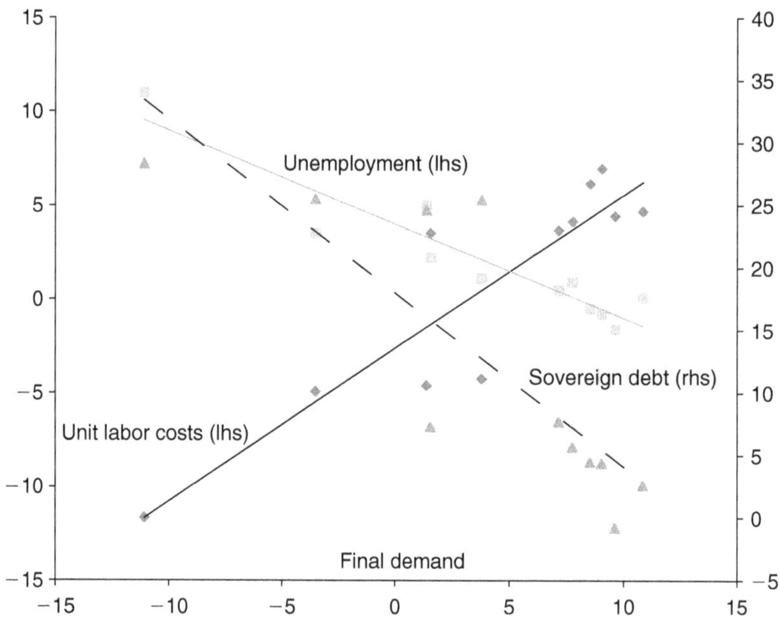

Figure 10.10 Changes in (nominal) unit labor costs, sovereign debt (percent of GDP) and unemployment in relation to final demand for 2010–2012, EA countries (source: AMECO database (data for 2012 are estimations)).

Economic recession (lower final demand) is used as a means for imposing favorable conditions of capital valorization (it reduces unit labor costs and REER, and boosts exports in relation to imports); but it increases debt and unemployment. At the same time, debt overhang is also used as means for fiscal consolidation and further neo-liberalization of the capitalist state. In a midst of a recession, a country with a current account deficit cannot put its sovereign debt on a sustainable track by solely relying on labor devaluation and fiscal consolidation because this is not enough to generate sovereign net savings and reduce borrowing costs. In that case, there are two possible trends.

On the one hand, there is econometric (and common sense) evidence[18] that a possible current account rebalancing based on asymmetric responses by a deficit country may take a relatively long period. This means a prolonged period of recession or poor economic growth, which will also be associated with a severe deterioration in the living conditions of the population, and the quality of the democracy. This is not so much a re-adjustment but a conservative social reshaping led by an authoritarian state interference. It is also very likely to have spillovers that will affect all EA economies at all social levels.

Another mainstream "solution" would be to return quickly to the pre-crisis differentials in growth and profitability, which would stabilize the net foreign liabilities in the deficit countries and invoke capital inflows. Given the highly uncertain economic environment and the lack of a crisis resolution frame (at a "federal" level), this is a highly unlikely option. The plan for a banking union along with interventions by the ECB, is an attempt to deal with these problems without violating the condition of moral hazard: to support intra-European financial flows and provide a policy framework for taming the crisis without jeopardizing the neoliberal character of the whole project. It is an aggressive plan for the European working classes, a promise for a gloomy political and economic future.

European governments, and the ECB, have been proved unwilling so far to do "the right thing in time" in order to decisively mitigate the consequences of the crisis. There are institutional limitations, but this is a poor excuse and it downplays the important room for policy actions that still exists even within the current context of the EMU. As we discussed above, it is a mistake to interpret this behavior as "irrational" or "short-sighted." Drastic intervention in the crisis would undermine the usage of debt overhang and economic recession as tools for the devaluation of labor. It would undermine the strategic rule of moral hazard as a governance model to the benefit of capital since it would create the real "hazard" of blocking austerity and neoliberal reforms. It is exactly this event that, from a class point of view, must be considered as irrational for capitalist power.

Without going into details, what we should expect in the near future is the application of the same rule: policy responses always one step behind the workings of markets. Despite its contradictions, this process can secure the final target of European capitalism: the formation of the "white Chinese worker" in the EU. Possible future plans and financial innovations (a banking union; debt restructurings, bay-backs and write-offs; redemption bonds, safe bonds, or even Euro bills etc.) will not be designed as solutions to the misery of the working people but will simply serve this single strategic scope. The real issue in the European crisis is not the contradiction between North and South, or that between debtors and creditors, but the fundamental contradiction in capitalism: the one between capital and labor.

What would be a possible way out? This is a political and not a technical question. In other words, there may be many different answers depending on the social correlations of powers. The radical left must have one strategic aim: to uncompromisingly defend the interests of labor. This means that it must resist the agenda of devaluation of labor against all its alternative versions whatsoever…

Conclusion

A theoretical and political project for the future

There is a very brief way – and indeed a provocative one – to summarize the basic message of this study. In his mature writings, Marx emphasizes something that is really missing from other heterodox approaches to capitalism: the *conception of value as a social relationship*. From the lengthy manuscript of *Grundrisse* to the first edition of *Capital* (which he edited himself) this conception of value is the starting point of every concrete attempt to analyze capitalism. It is a central theme, with important theoretical and political implications. It also means that what is really missing from the non-Marxian political economy is the understanding of capital as a social relationship. That's why in Marx's system the concepts of value, money, capital, ideology, finance, and class struggle are systemically interlinked to each other. By and large, this was exactly our research plan in this book.

Let's return to the issue of money.[1] As argued in Chapters 2 and 4, mainstream approaches understand money as a convenient medium of exchange, adopted to facilitate pre-existing commodity (market) relations. In this sense money is celebrated as a brilliant invention, which significantly reduces the costs involved in market transactions (the mainstream discussion of monetary unions is based exactly on this idea; see Chapter 9). It is indeed a powerful device, which can easily derange equilibrium conditions and therefore the ultimate target of policy makers (monetary policy) is to come up with meaningful ways to neutralize its economic role. On the other hand, contrary to this "metallist" approach, there is the "chartalist" theoretical tradition. It sees money as a fundamental debt relationship, as an IOU, which has an existence prior to market commodity relations. All different IOUs are integral parts of a structured hierarchical system on the basis of which we find the state. It is the sovereign power of the latter that originates money in the first place, by imposing a tax liability on every citizen.

The two above-mentioned schools of thought, despite their obvious differences, have something in common: they cannot theorize value as social relationship. In the case of the metallist tradition, the commodity is prior to money and the notion of value precedes and is totally external to the exchange. Chartalism somehow reverses the causal relation between commodity and money, but the latter as liability also remains external to the exchange value relation. This line of reasoning is different from Marx's context of value-form analysis. Commodity and money are terms that are constituted as such by the relationship into which they are integrated: the value relationship. They cannot exist outside this relationship in an autonomous and self-contained manner; nor does this relationship have a prior existence. The relationship of value exists only in the components that comprise it. As already underlined, this is a particular type of causality where the structure is immanent in its effects and is nothing outside them (this is indeed one of Althusser's major points in his reading of Marx).

The question that arises then is the following: why is this difference important in a study of finance? Why does Marx's framework of value-form analysis lead to a radically different understanding of contemporary capitalism? Our answer is simple. If money as debt (IOU) is defined prior to, and independent from, the value relationship in non-Marxian political economy, then we end up with radically different possible discourses about indebtedness and finance in capitalism. In this case, the creditor-debtor relationship becomes the most general social relation which gives rise to a particular form of human subjectivity: the indebted agent. Lazzarato (2012), in his latest intervention, reminds us that the roots of this argument are to be found in Nietzche's *Genealogy of Morality*, but they also characterize young Marx's "Comments on James Mill" in a period when he was under Feurbach's strong theoretical influence. In this way:

> the constitution of society and the domestication of man result [...] from the relation between creditor and debtor. Nietzche thus makes credit the paradigm of social relations by rejecting any explanation 'à l'anglaise,' that is, any explanation based on exchange or interest.
>
> (Lazzarato 2012: 39)

As we tried to show in the first part of this book, the non-Marxian heterodox approaches accept in their variety the existence of an asymmetrical creditor-debtor social relation, which either encompasses and subjugates (or distorts) all other economic activities or co-exists with them in an antagonistic and uncompromised manner.

Marx's argument differs in many crucial ways from the above scheme. Of course money has a "body" (matter) as liability (and this cannot be defined independently from the institutional context of a financial system) but, practically, *it owes its existence to the value relation*. It is out there in the first place as a representation of value, as the form of the value of commodities, which, as value, has the potential to be converted, immediately, into any use-value. In this sense, the money must be depicted by the formula $M–C$ and the commodity by $C–M$. The value cannot be determined separately from and prior to its forms. The commodity has been "scheduled" as a price before entering into the exchange process (it has been produced to be valued); it is always in a notional relationship with money.

In Marx's analysis, the value relation is an abstract expression (or embryonic form) of the capital relation where the money functions as an end in itself. From this point of view, debt as a social category is now subsumed to the logic of capital. This is an important analytical conception with many crucial implications for the understanding of capitalism. Capital's most concrete form in capitalist societies has always been an asset attached to a liability. Hence, debt is central and not just because its creation (quantity) is governed by the dynamics of capital (demand determined). At an abstract level (before introducing other debt relations), capital encompasses the debtor-creditor relation and takes the form of a financial security. Strangely enough, debt still remains the central issue in this Marxian discourse, but now the questions to be posed are different because we encounter a *reification process*: a social relationship (capital) which exists as a *sui generis* commodity (or financial security – an IOU). To put it simply, what is important with the IOU in the Marxian framework (and what is also significant for the interpretation of capitalism in its contemporary version) is to understand why this IOU circulates as a commodity at a price that is different from the principal amount written on the financial obligation. In other words, the secret of capitalist society lies in the fact that these IOUs have a price or, as Marx put it, that "capital as capital becomes a commodity." It is exactly this issue that has been entirely downplayed by the non-Marxian political economy (or even more so by the Marxist discussion as well).

That's why Marx uses the notion of interest bearing capital to describe the most concrete form of capital, the way that capital exists in reality. And, of course, the content of interest bearing capital (capital as financial security) invites the concept of fictitious capital as further clarification of the whole process. Here the use of the term "fictitious" must not confuse us. Capital exists as a commodity with a certain value. It exists as *C–M*. The pricing process is absolutely crucial because it mediates the commodification (securitization) of the capitalist exploitation process. The price of capital is not imaginary, aleatory or psychological: it is fictitious. It does not owe its existence to the "costs of production" and obviously is not equal to the "amount of money that changes hands" or to some principal value written on the IOU. It is an outcome of a particular representation of capitalist exploitation, which translates into quantitative signs the results of class struggle. From this point of view, the notion of fictitious capital can only be fully grasped in the context of Marx's materialist theory of fetishism and ideology. This also explains the puzzle of why Marx associated so closely and carefully his discussion on finance with the issue of fetishism (see our analysis in Part III of this book).

If the price of capital as IOU hinges upon a particular representation of capitalist reality (within the problematic of capitalist ideology), then the issue of the informational efficiency of markets ceases to be so central to the understanding of finance. The big secret of finance is that the valuation process does not have to do only with some competitive determination of the security price, but primarily plays an active part in the reproduction of capitalist power relations. The reification of social relations (and their transformation into financial products) makes them appear as objects of experience that are always-already-quantifiable in the context of an ideological misrepresentation, which is combined at the same time with the norm of behavior it calls forth. This is the key message of Marx's argument about fetishism and finance.

The next step is to extend the above notion of fictitious capital to different categories of indebtedness. The financial markets are sets of transactions that allow for commodifications of different power relations. The credit–debt relationship does not solely pertain to the workings of the capitalist firm but can also be applied to the case of sovereign governments, pension schemes, universities, households, etc. In this sense, financial markets seem to lose their uniformity as they encompass a "population" of heterogeneous agencies, which, of course, are themselves results of different power relations. Here is where risk and (our definition of) governmentality enter into the discussion. This complexity does not make finance fall apart, but on the contrary it means that finance, along with a certain way of funding, becomes a technology of power that efficiently secures the reproduction of capitalist power relations. In order to describe better this important dimension of finance we have borrowed a concept from Foucault's writings: that of governmentality. This is not merely a matter of borrowing a word. The idea is for the concept to be fully "expropriated" and properly utilized in the elaboration of the Marxian analysis of political economy. The conceptual loan helps us understand how financialization has so far been developed as a technology of power, to be superimposed on other social power relations for the purpose of organizing and reinforcing them in strength and effectiveness.

Risk is no longer a notion external to the logic of capital. Contrary to the majority of relevant social approaches, risk is not an extraneous threat. It is an ideological representation of the dynamics of capitalist exploitation and rule. It is innate in the workings of fictitious capital. The valuation of IOUs is based on risk in the sense that it relies on a prior representation of capitalist reality. It presupposes a mode of representing, identifying, arranging, and ordering certain social events of perceived reality, which are first "distinguished" (upon ideological criteria) and then objectified as risks. In other words, the valuation of IOUs (capitalization) is not possible unless there is some specification of risk, that is to say, unless specific events capable of happening are objectified, accessed, and estimated as risks. We called this process adaptation to chance. We shall not repeat all the steps of our reasoning. But we should emphasize two very important moments in this "adaptation to chance."

On the one hand, it is rather evident that financial markets normalize on the basis of risk by attributing risk profiles to different market participants. But this normalization process must not be seen as one that generates a universal form of subjectivity: that of the "indebted man" or the "entrepreneur of the self" (Foucault) – in any case, we are not talking here only about individuals. This normalization on the basis of risk is an integral part of the nature of finance as technology of power. It entraps individual participants in a world of risk. It dictates compliance to the social roles imposed by power relations. It secures the pattern of capitalist exploitation and the reproduction of capitalist rule. At the same time, it is not just linked to the rise of mutual indebtedness but primarily to the imposition of the balance sheet type of accounting upon every market participant. Risk is not only something to be hedged away but also to be exploited, diversified, and repackaged and traded. The basis for the latter is the commodification of both sides of the balance sheet: the securitization of debt obligations (the liability side of the balance sheet) is parallel to a similar securitization of income prospects (the asset side of the balance sheet). Nevertheless, the total structure of capitalist power has not been absorbed by finance. A complete analysis of capitalism, and its reproduction, exceeds the limits of finance and presupposes a proper theory of capitalist exploitation, capitalist competition (social capital), capitalist ideology (in the form of ideological state apparatus) and, of course, capitalist state.

On the other hand, our argument with regard to finance gives a totally different meaning to the rise of derivatives markets. Being commodifications of risk, they play a central role in the workings of finance as technology of power. They commensurate different categories of risk and, from this point of view, they stabilize the disciplining role of finance, representing in a uniform way different aspects of the circuit of capital (absolutely in line with the fetishist character immanent in the existence of such ideological representation). That's why we concluded that derivatives are not the wild beast of speculation but the necessary precondition of the organization of the domination of capital. The rise of derivatives does not imply "less" exploitation (in the sense of an increase in unproductive or speculative activities) but "more."

This type of reasoning derives directly from Marx's theoretical problematic in *Capital*. It offers a quite different explanation of contemporary capitalism (or financialization) from those that are usually found in mainstream or heterodox approaches. It provides the necessary background for future analytical projects and research agendas with regard to the nature of contemporary capitalism. It also implies a central political message. We would need another book to make our point explicit but we can use the few remaining lines in this epilogue to sketch our general idea.

First, the rise of finance is neither a threat to capital, nor does it indicate a weakness of the latter (its inability to secure proper accumulation patterns). Finance sets forth a particular technology of power (along with a particular mode of funding economic activities), which is completely in line with the nature of capitalist exploitation. Derivatives are integral parts of this process, to the extent that it differentiates and normalizes on the basis of risk, but also unifies (commensurates) into a single interpretation, partial economic activities and ideological representations of reality.

Second, while finance is not extraneous to capitalist power, it does not coincide with it. In other words, finance does not soak up capitalist relations and, of course, is not contemporaneous to their dynamics. The social geography of the latter does not overlap with the configuration of modern finance (despite its extending pattern). But more importantly, the social whole is a structured and complex totality, which cannot "rely" solely on this function of finance for its reproduction. For instance, the central role of the capitalist state and the ideologies attached to it play a crucial role in the organization of the class domination of capital.

Third, the fight against finance, the demand that finance should become a public good under democratic control, is a radical target in contemporary conditions as a means to derange the social nature of the financial landscape. It can also give rise to different approaches to economic and monetary policy. Nevertheless, it cannot by itself guarantee the overthrow of the capitalist regime, since it does not by itself challenge the heart of the capitalist power that is the capital relation and the bourgeois state. Resistance to finance is, practically, a process of de-normalization (de-individualization), which liberates people from the threat of risk, providing them with more space to breathe and organize their struggles against multiple capitalist power relations. But it does not eliminate or disintegrate the latter. In this sense, the fight against modern finance should be associated with a general anti-capitalist plan that, among other frontiers, must seek to take over and destroy the capitalist state…

Notes

1 The parasitic absentee owner in the Keynes–Veblen–Proudhon tradition

1 In this section we shall just provide a general outline without entering into a thorough discussion of classical political economy. For more on this issue, see Milios *et al.* (2002), Postone (2003), Heinrich (1999), and Arthur (2002).
2 Hence, the value of a commodity (as a characteristic or property of the "economic good") derives from labor and (quantitatively) is proportional to the labor time which has been expended on its production.
3

> As soon as land becomes private property, the landlord demands a share of almost all the produce which the labourer can either raise, or collect from it. His rent makes *the first deduction from the produce of the labour* which is employed upon land. [...] Profit, makes a *second deduction from the produce of the labour* which is employed upon land.
>
> (Smith 1981: I.viii.6 and 7, emphasis added)

4 As Smith has already pointed out, profit as such has nothing to do with the coordination and surveillance functions of production, carried out by the entrepreneur or company executive. Given this, one could also consider capital remuneration as rent, in the same way as land remuneration.
5 At this point, we need to make a necessary remark. We use the term "problematic" according to Althusser's definition. In brief, "problematic" designates "the particular unity of a theoretical formation and hence the location to be assigned to this specific difference" (Althusser 1969: 32). A problematic is not a particular theoretical argument but a more systemic term: a way of asking questions about the world, introducing new principles and establishing new research methods (see also Althusser and Balibar 1997).
6 Of course, in the case of land, "natural" scarcity in the same context of property relations adds to the outcome of scarcity, but it does not explain its "absolute" component.
7 See for instance Hayek (1931), Schumpeter (1994).
8 See Garegnani (1979), Eatwell (1983).
9 Cited in Chancellor (2000: 97). See also Chapter 4.
10 See Rubin (1989), Chancellor (2000: 98).
11 For a more complete description of these changes and related literature see Milios and Sotiropoulos (2009; Chapter 7).
12 For the notion of "monopoly" according to the analysis of Marx, see Milios and Sotiropoulos (2009; Chapter 6).
13 In 1927, John Moody, founder of the credit ratings agency, declared that "no one can examine the panorama of business and finance in America during the past half-dozen

years without realizing that we are living in a new era." In April of that year *Barron's*, the investment weekly, envisaged a "new era without depressions" (Chancellor 2000: 193). It is very funny to consider how this belief about the taming of the business cycle becomes 'common sense' before the outbreak of a severe crisis. In quite the same mood, Robert Lucas (a well-known professor at the University of Chicago and Nobel prize winner of 1995), in his presidential address at the annual meeting of the American Economic Association, declared that the "central problem of depression-prevention has been solved, for all practical purposes" (cited in Krugman 2008: 9).

14 "The excessive build up of inventory was believed to be the most common cause of the economic cycle" (Chancellor 2000: 193).

15 In fact, the unprecedented internationalization of capital flows had made the practice of diversification dominate the organization of the movement of capital worldwide, even before the start of twentieth century (see Obstfeld and Taylor 2004: 57).

16 We shall revisit these issues in the light of our reasoning in Chapters 7 and 8.

17 See Fox (2009: 16–18); for a general presentation of these two different views see Fama (1965).

18 It is well known that (the increase of) capitalist exploitation is *always* based on the production of both absolute and relative surplus-value. As Marx puts it:

> The prolongation of the working-day beyond the point at which the worker would have produced an exact equivalent for the value of his labour-power, and the appropriation of that surplus-labour by capital – this is the process which constitutes the production of absolute surplus-value [...] The production of absolute surplus-value turns exclusively on the length of the working-day; the production of relative surplus-value completely revolutionizes the technical processes of labour, and the groupings into which society is divided.
>
> (Marx 1990: 645).

And further: the "methods of producing relative surplus-value are, at the same time, methods of producing absolute surplus value" (Marx 1990: 646). However, the whole historical period of pre-industrial capitalism as well as the first period of the Industrial Revolution is characterized by a social relation of forces that renders production of absolute surplus-value the *dominant role* in capitalist expanded reproduction. As Marx describes it:

> After capital had taken centuries to extend the working day to its normal maximum limit, and then beyond this to the limit of the natural day of 12 hours, there followed, with the birth of large-scale industry in the last third of the 18th century, an avalanche of violent and unmeasured encroachments. Every boundary set by morality and nature, age and sex, day and night, was broken down. Even the ideas of day and night, which in the old statutes were of peasant simplicity, became so confused that an English judge, as late as 1860, needed the penetration of an interpreter to explain "judicially" what was day and what was night. Capital celebrated its orgies. As soon as the working-class, stunned at first by the noise and turmoil of the new system of production, had recovered its senses to some extent, it began to offer resistance, first of all in England, the native land of large-scale industry. For three decades, however, the concessions wrung from industry by the working class remained purely nominal.
>
> (Marx 1990: 389–90)
>
> Capital's drive towards a boundless and ruthless extension of the working-day is satisfied first in those industries which were first to be revolutionized by water-power, steam, and machinery, in those earliest creations of the modern mode of production, the spinning and weaving of cotton, wool, flax, and silk. The changed material mode of production, and the correspondingly changed social relations of

> the producers first gave rise to outrages without measure, and then called forth, in opposition to this, social control which legally limits, regulates, and makes uniform the working day and its pauses.
>
> (Marx 1990: 411–412)

For our full argument see Milios and Sotiropoulos (2009; Chapter 7).

19 Marx (1990: 437).

20 For more comments on this issue see Milios and Sotiropoulos (2009; Part II).

21 For instance, almost all the Marxist approaches of the period – and despite their severe debates – explicitly or implicitly shared the viewpoint that *Das Kapital* was no longer adequate for the description of capitalism. See Milios and Sotiropoulos (2009; Part I and Chapter 11).

22 We are referring here to *The Theory of Business Enterprise* (see Veblen 1958) and *Absentee Ownership* (see Veblen 1997).

23 A very interesting theoretical attempt to analyze contemporary capitalism using the logic of Veblen's approach is to be found in Nitzan and Bichler (2009).

24 In particular, "With the advance into the new era, into what is properly to be called recent times in business and industry, the capitalization of earning-capacity comes to be the standard practice in the conduct of business finance, and calls attention to itself as a dominant fact in the situation that has arisen. The value of any investment is measured by its capitalized earning-capacity, and the endeavors of any businesslike management therefore unavoidably center on net earnings" (Veblen 1997: 60).

25

> It is the ownership of materials and equipments that enables the capitalization to be made; but ownership does not of itself create a net product, and so it does not give rise to earnings, but only to the legal claim by the force of which the earnings go to the owners of the capitalized wealth. Production is a matter of workmanship, whereas earnings are a matter of business.
>
> (Veblen 1997: 61)

26 As we mentioned above, the conceptualization of profit as absolute rent has tended to become dominant in recent heterodox discussions.

27 The very same line of reasoning is reproduced in the famous argument of Chapter 12 of the *General Theory* (Keynes 1973). We shall return to Keynes' approach in the following section. See also Sotiropoulos (2011), Milios and Sotiropoulos (2009).

28 For the same conclusion see Dillard (1980) and Wray (1998).

29 In this sense, he imitates the hesitations of Ricardo: admitting that "everything is produced by labor" but not formulating that "profit is part of that expended labor."

30 For the nature of this debate see Harcourt (1972), Howard (1983).

31 We shall agree with Mattick (1980: 20) that Keynes' "theoretical revolt" against neoclassical analysis "may better be regarded as a partial return to classical theory [...] and this notwithstanding Keynes' own opposition to classical theory." This paradoxical conclusion is not baseless. Through this formulation Mattick highlights one of the key aspects of critique. In order to be critical of neoclassical dogma, he had to rethink (among other things) the way that income is distributed between social classes. This point of departure is therefore what links him to classical political economy. Smith's analysis (and to a lesser extent Ricardo's) focused attention on issues that have to do with the institutional determination of income distribution. The same issues come to the fore in post-Keynesian readings of Keynes (Garegnani 1979).

32 The radical interpretation of Keynes' point is given by the following passage:

> the attitude toward the rentier is not fully explained until the emphasis on the role of the active entrepreneur has been clearly indicated. Disappearance of the functionless rentier is incidental to the practical program which makes the entrepreneur the initiator of economic activity. Society has no particular stake in the

> inactive, nonfunctional rentier. On the other hand, anything that dampens the ardor of entrepreneurship is inimical to the welfare of society as a whole. In an economy in which enterprise is carried on largely with borrowed capital, the payment of interest to the rentier-capitalist acts as a brake to progress. A reduction in the cost of transferring purchasing power out of the hands of inactive rentiers into the possession of active entrepreneurs is obviously a stimulus to enterprise.
>
> (Dillard 1942: 68)

33 This is Keynes' famous illustration:

> or, to change the metaphor slightly, professional investment may be likened to those newspaper competitions in which the competitors have to pick out the six prettiest faces from a hundred photographs, the prize being awarded to the competitor whose choice most nearly corresponds to the average preferences of the competitors as a whole; so that each competitor has to pick, not those faces which he himself finds prettiest, but those which he thinks likeliest to catch the fancy of the other competitors, all of whom are looking at the problem from the same point of view. It is not a case of choosing those which, to the best of one's judgment, are really the prettiest, nor even those which average opinion genuinely thinks the prettiest. We have reached the third degree where we devote our intelligences to anticipating what average opinion expects the average opinion to be. And there are some, I believe, who practise the fourth, fifth and higher degrees.
>
> (Keynes 1973: 156)

34 Some useful remarks on this issue can be found in Jameson (2011: 45–46).

35 For an interesting presentation of Proudhon's ideas in the light of Keynesian thinking see Dillard (1942).

36 In what follows, we shall refer to the mail exchange between Bastiat and Proudhon, which took place as a mini debate in 1849–1850 (see Proudhon 1849–1850). Our references will mention the number of the letter and the paragraph.

37

> Is it possible, yes or no, to abolish Interest on Money, Rent of Land and Houses, the Product of Capital, by simplifying Taxation, on the one hand, and, on the other, by organizing a Bank of Circulation and Credit in the name and on the account of the people? This, in my opinion, is the way in which the question before us should be stated.
>
> (letter 7.§9)

See also Chapter 5.

38

> But the Capitalist lender not only is not deprived, since he recovers his Capital intact, but he receives more than his Capital, more than he contributes to the exchange; he receives in addition to his Capital an Interest which represents no positive product on his part. Now, a service which costs no Labor to him who renders it is a service which may become gratuitous: this you have already told us yourself.
>
> (letter 5.§30)
>
> Here, however, Capital never ceases to belong to him who lends it and who may demand the restoration whenever he chooses. So that the Capitalist does not exchange Capital for Capital, Product for Product: he gives up nothing, keeps all, does no work, and lives upon his rents, his Interest, and his Usury in greater luxury than one thousand, ten thousand, or even a hundred thousand laborers combined can enjoy by their production.
>
> (letter 11.§56).

39 For this connection see Dillard (1942: 69–70).

40 In 1792, Great Britain held a subordinate position in the financial system of Europe, the London money-market had yet to come into its own, and the movement of capital was still into and out of England. In 1815, though the fact was scarcely appreciated at the time, the situation had radically changed. Amsterdam had fallen; and London had not only taken its place as the predominant financial market of Europe, but was able to play the part in a way that dwarfed the earlier efforts of the Dutch city.

(Acworth 1925: 81–82)

41 This line of reasoning has no relation to Marx's argumentation. See Chapter 3 and also Milios and Sotiropoulos (2009; Chapter 9). The attempt is quite obvious in the contemporary analyses of workerism, to subordinate Marx's thought to that of Keynes and Veblen (for instance see Vercellone 2010, Fumagalli 2010, Marazzi 2010, Negri 2010).

42 See Hobsbawm (1999), Economakis and Sotiropoulos (2010).

43 We base our exposition in Rajan (2010) and Jensen (2001). The message of the mainstream approach to finance is central in all the relevant textbooks: see Brealey *et al.* (2011).

44 We shall return to the discussion on EMH in the Chapters 7 and 8.

45 For instance, see Lapatsioras *et al.* (2008).

2 Ricardian Marxism and finance as unproductive activity

1 The value of commodities is the very opposite of the coarse materiality of their substance, not an atom of matter enters into its composition. Turn and examine a single commodity, by itself, as we will, yet in so far as it remains an object of value, it seems impossible to grasp it. [...] *Value can only manifest itself in the social relation of commodity to commodity.*

(Marx 1990: 138–39, emphasis added)

2 "Equal value" implies value measured independently in terms of *quantity* of "labor expended" for the production of such commodities.

3 "It has become apparent in the course of our presentation that value, which appeared as an abstraction, is only possible as such an abstraction, as soon as money is posited" (Marx 1993: 776).

4 [A]s the dominant subject of this process [...] value requires above all an independent form by means of which its identity with itself may be asserted. *Only in the shape of money does it possess this form.* Money therefore forms the starting-point and the conclusion of every valorisation process.

(Marx 1990: 255)

5 Within the value relation and the expression of value immanent in it, the abstractedly general [i.e., value] does not constitute a property of the concrete, sensorily actual [i.e., of the monetary form] but on the contrary the sensorily actual is a simple form of appearance or specific form of realisation of the abstractedly general (...) *Only the sensorily concrete is valid as a form of appearance of the abstractedly general.*

(MEGA II, 5: 634, emphasis added)

6 It is worth mentioning here that Marx named his theoretical system "critique of political economy" (which is actually the title or subtitle of all his economic writings of the period 1857–1867) to underline his radical deviation from classical political economy and value theory.

7 From our point of view core interventions for this kind of Marxism are the ones by Althusser and his students.

8 We shall just offer two brief examples:

> Value as a specific form of appearance of labor in the commodity-producing society. (Value as historic, temporary appearance). During our above exposition we arrived at a puzzling, from first sight, conclusion: The value of a commodity is determined by labor, although it does not express itself in quantities of labor (measured in labor-time).
>
> (Duncker *et al.* 1930: 16)

and:

> Value is a reflection of the social relationships of the producer with the commodity-producing society. [...] The exchange value of a commodity is only revealed in exchange, however. It does not emerge from it. [...] Like each commodity separately, so the whole world of commodities has two poles: at the one pole is use-value, i.e., different commodities, at the other is values, i.e., money.
>
> (Pouliopoulos 2004: 11)

9 The question arises of what may be the possible causes of Marx's ambivalences towards classical political economy. Answering in a general way, one may say that the issue simply reflects the contradictions of Marx's break with Ricardian theory, contradictions that are immanent in every theoretical rupture of the kind. See also Althusser (1976).

10 Heinrich (1999) and Garnett (1995) are excellent examples of a contrasting, undogmatic stance, irrespective of the fact that they identify various types of ambiguity in *Capital*.

11 See Milios and Sotiropoulos (2009; Chapters 6 and 11), Milios and Sotiropoulos (2011).

12 Hilferding's argumentation heavily influenced the formation of the so-called classical approaches to imperialism (Luxemburg, Bukharin, Lenin...). With few exceptions, basically the vacillations of Lenin's writings and aspects of Bukharin's intervention, the latter shared a common belief: capitalism has undergone radical and structural transformations, with the result that Marx's analysis is no longer sufficient for a comprehensive description of it. In other words, the "latest phase of capitalist development" (whose scientific understanding Hilferding was attempting to arrive at) was explicitly or implicitly considered as obviously divergent from the capitalism described in *Das Kapital*. Nevertheless, this theoretical project has one fundamental premise: the abandonment of the theoretical category of *social capital* ("Gesamtkapital" in the German text), which plays a crucial role in the analysis of Marx. See also Milios and Sotiropoulos (2009; Chapters 1 and 3).

13 Embodied in the structural framework of social capital, the individual "capitalist is simply personified capital, functioning in the production process merely as the bearer of capital" (Marx 1991: 958). In this regard, the capitalist is not the subject of initiative and change but is subjected to the laws of evolution and change of social capital, imposed as incentives on their consciousness through competition (Marx 1990: 433).

14 The resulting decline in the average profit rate due to the "enormous inflation of fixed capital" (Hilferding 1981: 186) can only be overcome by the formation of capitalist monopolies. At the same time, "combination smoothes out the fluctuations of the business cycle and so assures a more stable rate of profit for the integrated firm" (ibid.: 196). The elimination of competition also serves the interests of banks: big enterprises can achieve maximum profits without endangering the borrowed capital that they have raised from the bank (ibid.: 191).

15 We do not have the space here to go through the details of this argument. For more see Milios and Sotiropoulos (2009). The notion of individual capital in Hilferding's analysis resembles more the Weberian conception of a profit-making organization ("Verband"; see Weber 1978: 48–62, 90–100).

16 We can interpret the vacillation in Hilferding's writings as follows. He adhered to the (classical) labor theory of value while at the same time he followed closely Marx's text, which, despite its contradictions, parts profoundly with the Ricardian reasoning. In this regard, Hilferding, without realizing it, reproduced in his writings different discourses about finance: a dominant one based on the Ricardian context and a subordinate one which is closer to Marx's problematic.

17 See Hoffman *et al.* (2007: 60–63).

18 For Morgan and Company, protection consisted in repeatedly defending foreign investors in the boisterous American market. For the Rothschilds it involved rescuing the Bank of England and persuading weak states like Spain and Brazil to resume their debt payments after a crisis. A reputation of this sort could, of course, generate extraordinary expectations: in a crisis, investors might expect a fabled intermediary to step in and solve the problem. And such expectations are still with us. When the investment bank Salomon Brothers was jolted in 1991 by a bidding scandal in the market for government debt, Warren E. Buffett took over as interim CEO to salvage the firm's reputation—a sign that such matters are still important, particularly after a crisis (Hoffman *et al.* 2007: 62).

19 This is Fine's own sketching (ibid.: 112) which obviously coincides with the general spirit of the institutionalist line of reasoning. It is institutionalist in the sense that, given the fundamental asymmetry in their nature, the unity of different fractions of capital into a single power against labor can be secured only under the hegemony of one of them. We shall return to this issue in the Chapter 3.

3 Is finance productive or "parasitic?"

1 As we discussed in Chapter 2, this line of thought is already clear in Hilferding. For instance, following Shaikh and Tonak (1994), Mohun (2006: 350) argues as follows:

> activities purely involving the sale of the output and the purchase of inputs (commercial activities), or the mobilizing of sums of money and credit to finance production (financial activities) are not part of production. For all that these activities employ large numbers of people in wage labour relationships, they are concerned with alterations of the form in which produced value exists, or with organizing precommitments and claims on future produced value. Because they circulate value rather than create it, they are unproductive.

2 The enterprise (i.e., the individual capital according to Marx's terminology), and not the isolated worker, is the actual producer. It is impossible to distinguish between "productive" and "non productive" workers within the enterprise. As Marx puts it (1990: 1039–1040):

> With the development of the *real subsumption of labour under capital* or the *specifically capitalist mode of production*, the *real lever* of the overall labour process is increasingly not the individual worker. Instead, *labour power socially combined* and the various competing labour powers which together form the entire production machine participate in very different ways in the immediate process of making commodities, or, more accurately in this context, creating the product.

3 For a general discussion of the financial intermediation see Goodhart (1989), Hoffman *et al.* (2007), Steinherr (2000), Borio (2007).

4 For a thorough discussion of Marx's "epistemological break" see Althusser (1976).

5 For instance, we can indicatively mention here the following interventions: Minsky (1993), Palloix (1977), O'Hara (2006), van der Pijl (1998), Duménil and Levy (2011), LiPuma and Lee (2004), Davisdon (2002). The following statement by Callinicos (2010: 30) is characteristic: "Marx distinguishes between three kinds of capital – productive, commercial and money-dealing capital. [...] Commercial and money-dealing

capitalists are able to secure a share of the surplus-value generated in production thanks to the economic functions they perform."

6 We do not find a single argument in the literature. What we see is a spectrum of converging approaches, which, by and large, share the same analytical line. In this section, we attempt to present the "average" outline of them by tracing their shared problematic.

7 For a first discussion of the issue of Marx's expositions and the difficulties it poses see Althusser (2006).

8 For a nice review of this perspective see Streeck (2009).

9 For a systematic elaboration of these issues see Milios and Sotiropoulos (2009) and Chapter 2.

10 As we mentioned in Chapter 2, the origin of this historicist or institutionalist approach in Marxist discussions can be traced to Hilferding's intervention.

11 This is indeed a core idea in the modern financial theory upon which the valuation models of derivatives are based (see Steinherr 2000: 18). We shall return to this issue in Part III.

12 See Part III, also Borio (2007), Steinherr (2000).

13

> The value of commodities stands in inverse ratio to the productivity of labour. So, too, does the value of labour-power, since it depends on the values of commodities. Relative surplus-value, however, is directly proportional to the productivity of labour. It rises and falls together with productivity. The value of money being assumed to be constant, an average social working day of 12 hours always produces the same new value, 6s., no matter how this sum may be apportioned between surplus- value and wages. But if, in consequence of increased productivity, there is a fall in the value of the means of subsistence, and the daily value of labour-power is thereby reduced from 5s. to 3, the surplus-value will increase from 1s. to 3. [...] Capital therefore has an immanent drive, and a constant tendency, towards increasing the productivity of labour, in order to cheapen commodities and, by cheapening commodities, to cheapen the worker himself.
>
> (Marx 1990: 436–437)

14 We shall return to these issues in Part III of the book.

15 For instance see, Borio (2007), Atkinson *et al.* (2011), Milanovic (2011), Stockhammer (2012), Onaran, Stockhammer and Grafl (2011).

16 We shall review heterodox approaches to financialization in Chapter 7.

17 It is, indeed, very difficult to imagine a different causality for a long period of time: if households face a continuous squeeze in incomes, the last thing they will do is to take more debt.

18

> The form of interest-bearing capital makes every definite and regular money revenue appear as the interest on a capital, whether it actually derives from a capital or not. [...] Let us take the national debt and wages as examples. [...] Moving from the capital of the national debt, where a negative quantity appears as capital – interest-bearing capital always being the mother of every insane form, so that debts, for example, can appear as commodities to the mind of the banker – we shall now consider labour-power. Here wages are conceived as interest, and hence labour-power as capital that yields this interest. [...] Here the absurdity of the capitalist's way of conceiving things reaches its climax, in so far as instead of deriving the valorization of capital from the exploitation of labour-power, they explain the productivity of labour power by declaring that labour-power itself is this mystical thing, interest-bearing capital.
>
> (Marx 1991: 595–596)

4 Derivatives as money?

1 On these issues see Bryan and Rafferty (2006: 198 199).
2 See for instance Mill (1976; IV.I.§5).
3 We would like to thank Richard Van den Berg for highlighting this point for us and making the translation from the French original text.
4 For a comprehensive discussion of the origins and the contemporary models of this theoretical idea see Goodhart (1989, 1998). For the same issue see Chapter 9.
5 See also Goodhart (1998), Itoh and Lapavitsas (1999: 233).
6 For a discussion on the origins of the Keynesian account for money see Wray (2004) and Lavoie (2011).
7 For a similar viewpoint see Bryan and Rafferty (2009).
8 See Markham (2002a: 265–266). "The first documented appearance of what are now called puts and calls occurred on the Amsterdam bourse during the tulip mania of the 1630s" (Allen 2001: 44–45).
9 Undoubtedly there are many possible explanations, but these issues fall beyond the scope of this chapter.
10 See Markham (2002a: 267–269), Markham (2002b: 93–94), Allen (2001: 40–55), Steinherr (2000).
11 For instance see Weber (2000). At the same time, in a paper published in 1880, Engels wrote:

> the German Empire is just as completely under the yoke of the Stock Exchange as was the French Empire in its day. It is the stockbrokers who prepare the projects which the Government has to carry out – for the profit of their pockets.
>
> (Engels 1989: 280)

We see that in this intervention, Engel reflects the problematic of Ricardian Marxism (see Chapter 2).
12 To what extent Hilferding was actually inspired by Cohn's perspective remains an open question to be addressed in future research. It is clear that Hilferding did not quote Cohn directly but only indirectly from the "Börsen-Enquete-Kommission" reports (the commission which was established in 1892 and focused on the commodity exchanges; with speculation being one of the main issues). In the chapter dealing with futures, Hilferding refers many times to these reports. The link between the approach to speculation in these reports and Hilferding's line of reasoning is another open question for future research.
13 For an analytical account of Hilferding's argumentation see Sotiropoulos (2012a, 2015).
14 See Sotiropoulos (2012a).
15 See Markham (2002b), Obstfeld and Taylor (2004).
16 In brief, Fisher puts forward the "first formal equilibrium model of an economy with both intertemporal exchange and production" (Rubinstein 2006: 55); and a rough version of the random walk hypothesis (Fox 2009: 13). His 1930 book, *The Theory of Interest: As Determined by Impatience to Spend Income and Opportunity to Invest It*, actually refines and restates his earlier theoretical outcomes.
17 We have to mention that the same idea about speculation was also applied by Hilferding to the analysis of the stock exchange (see Hilferding 1981: 134).
18 Once more, he repeats: "by reducing the circulation time for productive capitalists, and assuming the risks, speculators can have an effect upon production itself" (Hilferding 1981: 161). In this way, the "most important function" of futures markets is "the possibility of insuring oneself by unloading the losses due to price fluctuations upon the speculators" (ibid.: 159).
19 The analysis of this chapter is focused on this particular part of *Finance Capital*. In other parts of the book, Hilferding revisits the issue of speculation offering additional

grounding for the same line of thought. For instance, in Chapter 20, he argues that the "mass psychoses which speculation generated at the beginning of the capitalist era [...] came to an end in the crash of 1873. Since then, faith in the magical power of credit and the stock exchange has disappeared" (Hilferding 1981: 294). In this respect, losses from crises make the public wiser and as a result speculation becomes less destabilizing, at least in the period after the crisis of 1873. We see that the reasons offered to downplay the destabilizing role of speculation are much wider than those mentioned in the section of the book devoted to futures. It is obvious that this type of reasoning is unable to explain past and recent developments in capitalism.

20 From this point of view, he seems to agree with the reasoning of Weber and Cohn concerning the issue of speculation and how it is interlinked with the logic of capitalism (see Weber 2000: 309–310; Lestition 2000: 299).

21 See Chapter 2, Milios and Sotiropoulos (2009; Chapter 6).

22 The idea of finance capital is indeed a notion of banks controlling the capital titles, which exist as financial securities. In general this is a "portfolio management" type of reasoning, whatever the criteria of this management (and it is clear that for Hilferding, institutional criteria other than profit maximization may also be taken into account). In this section we suggest a reconsideration of Hilferding's viewpoint, which must also be read in the context of a broader understanding of *Finance Capital*.

23 For a detailed account of Hilferding's argumentation and its shortcomings see Sotiropoulos (2012a, 2015).

24 Bryan and Rafferty have recently put forward an influential argument about the same point. Their assumption is that derivatives serve as a new form of global money, playing "a role that is parallel to that played by gold in the nineteenth century": the role of "anchor to the financial system" (Bryan and Rafferty 2006: 133). Another approach that meets (to some extent) with the argumentation of Hilferding is the one offered by Rotman (1987). We shall comment on both in this chapter.

25 According to Hilferding, there were other important causes of the establishment of monopoly capitalism. Nevertheless, the existence of monopolistic combines obviated the need for risk management (see Section 2 above). For a general presentation of Hilferding's point with regard to the monopoly capitalism and a critique of it, see Milios and Sotiropoulos (2009, Chapter 9).

26 The workings of the futures and forward markets that will be analyzed in the section can be found in any relevant textbook. For instance, see Hull (2011).

27 See Durbin (2010: 86).

28 We shall not go through the preconditions of this type of valuation. In brief, the basic idea is that markets must be efficient in the sense that the no-arbitrage principle applies.

29 For the issue of abstract risk see LiPuma and Lee (2004), Sotiropoulos *et al.* (2012), Sotiropoulos and Lapatsioras (2012, 2014). For an interesting perspective on derivatives see also Bryan, Martin, and Rafferty (2009), and Martin (2007).

30 We shall follow here Marx's point as it is developed in the first part of the first volume of *Capital*. See also Balibar (1995: 58–59) and Milios and Sotiropoulos (2009; Chapter 5).

31 The overall message of this essay exceeds the scope of this chapter. We shall focus on the part of Rotman's argument only in so far as it relates to our discussion on derivatives and money.

32 Though it dispenses with the apparatus of signature, personal witness, and attachment to an original owner, paper money retains its domestic, national indexicality; it relies as a sign on its use within the borders and physical reality of the sovereign state whose central bank is the author of the promise it carries. In contrast, xenomoney is without history, ownerless, and without traceable national origin. If paper money insists on anonymity with respect to individual bearers but is

> edictally bound on the level of sovereignty, xenomoney anonymises itself with respect to individuals *and* nation states.
>
> (Rotman 1987: 90)

33 For an interesting discussion of the historical trends of this market see He and McCauley (2012). In what follows we shall draw heavily upon the information they provide.
34 In this line see also Sotiropoulos and Lapatsioras (2012, 2014).
35 See also Balibar (1995: 59).

5 Finance, discipline, and social behavior: tracing the terms of a problem that was never properly stated

1 See Chapter 1 and Hayek (1979).
2 For a nice summary of his argumentation see Schapiro (1945: 719–723).
3

> Central banks were generally set up initially in the eighteenth and nineteenth centuries to provide finance on beneficial, subsidized terms to the government of the day, and were often awarded in return with certain monopoly rights in note issuing. This combination led, all too easily, to circumstances in which the Central Bank's note would be made, at moments of crisis, inconvertible legal tender, in order to provide, in effect, the receipts from inflationary tax to the authorities. Distrust with paper currency sprang primarily from such occasions: e.g., John Law's Banque General in France in 1716, the suspension of convertibility in the United Kingdom of the Bank of England, 1797–1819, and the issue of assignats by the Caisse d' Escompte in 1790.
>
> (Goodhart 1991: 20)

4 For a systematic account see White (1999).
5

> It is not to be denied that, with the existing sort of division of responsibility between the issues of the basic money and those of a parasitic circulation based on it, central banks must, to prevent matters from getting completely out of hand, try deliberately to forestall developments they can only influence but not directly control. But the central banking system, which only 50 years ago was regarded as the crowning achievement of financial wisdom, has largely discredited itself.
>
> (Hayek 1978: 100)

6 This was indeed the dominant perspective, but not by any means the only one. Discussions within Marxist revolutionary circles in the period were rich in scope and content. The key issue was not the replication of the efficiency of capitalism, but the overcoming of the nature of capitalist political and economic domination. For this line of reasoning, the key problem with socialism is not the role of the central planning bureau but the structure of "soviets" as forms of workers' democratic control over the power and violence of capital, and of course the revolutionary destruction of the state. These issues remain beyond the aims of this chapter.
7 Clearly Rubin and his value form analysis was one of those (see Chapter 2; Milios *et al.* 2002).
8 We shall follow Postone's argument (see Postone 2003; ch. 2). Here, we refer to Hilferding's dispute with Böhm-Bawerk on the labor theory of value (see Hilferding 1949).
9 For a clear summary of Mises' argument see Lavoie (1985).
10 See Milios and Sotiropoulos (2009; Chapter 10).
11 In this sense, Lange simply repeated Taylor's earlier point (see Lange 1936: 56, 66; Lavoie 1985: 118–119). In 1929, Taylor offered a planning model in which the socialist central bureau could achieve a practical equilibrating solution using a trial and error method (thus resembling the Walrasian auctioning process).

12 See Lange (1936: 60–71), Lavoie (1985), Block *et al.* (2002: 53–54).
13 These are versions of socialism that lie in between socialism and the free-market system (Hayek 1945: 521).
14 In what follows we shall base our analysis on the following papers: Hayek (1935a; 1935b; 1945; 1948a; 1948b; 1978).
15 For these issues see also Kirzner (1992; Chapters 6 and 8).
16 See Hayek (1948a, 1978). See also Kirzner (1992; Chapter 8), Lavoie (1985).
17 See Polanyi (2001), Milios and Sotiropoulos (2009).
18 See Moggridge (1992: 573), Keynes (1982: 233). The same paper was also published by the journal *The New Statesman* immediately after the World Economic Conference of 1933.
19 In this regard see Crotty (1983).
20 See Helleiner (1994: 33–38), Bryan and Rafferty (2006: 111–113).
21 See Keynes (1973: Chapter 24).
22 For instance, Hayek and Mises (see Hayek 1935b and Mises 1935) attacked the ideas of Otto Bauer, who argued that the anarchy of capitalist production was responsible for the economic recessions and demanded planning of production and finance.
23 For an introduction to Lacan's conceptual system see Žižek (2006), Sean (2005).

6 Episodes in finance

1 In describing the historical details for this episode we draw heavily upon Hoffman *et al.* (2007: 149–151), Rajan (2010: 120).
2 This line of reasoning is very close to Foucault's formulations (1977: 23–4).
3 Over-the-counter (OTC) or off-exchange trading involves non-standardized products which are negotiated bilaterally between two different parties. This type of transaction gives investors the opportunity to tailor-make contracts close to their risk appetites but with low liquidity and a higher credit risk.
4 We follow here the argument of Borio *et al.* (2012: 10) and Dooley (2009).
5 These definitional issues with regard to options can be found in any elementary textbook; for instance see Hull (2011; Chapter 9).
6 One example of such disqualifiers is a bad credit rating, that is to say delays of more than ninety days in paying instalments. Other examples include having an income insufficient to justify the taking out of a loan of such high value, or being employed in a job which does not guarantee a regular flow of payments, or lacking suitable documents that could justify the size of the loan in relation to the client's declared income, etc.
7 A more complete and elaborated version of the argument of this section can be found in Sotiropoulos (2012b).
8 See Buiter *et al.* (1998), Eichengreen (2007), Volz (2006).
9 See Garber (1998), Volz (2006).
10 We have implicitly assumed that exchange rate risk premiums are zero. For the argument see Svensson (1992), Volz (2006), Buiter *et al.* (1998).
11 The logarithms can be explained by the fact that continuous interest rate compounding has been implicitly assumed.
12 When $S^e > S$, one unit of the foreign currency is expected to correspond to more units of domestic currency in the future. This is practically a depreciation of domestic currency.
13 See Bryan and Rafferty (2006; Chapter 5), Obstfeld *et al.* (2008).
14 For the development of this point see Buiter *et al.* (1998: 69).
15 For a general account of contemporary foreign exchange investment strategies including carry trade see Gyntelberg and Schrimpf (2011).
16 See Buiter *et al.* (1998: 25).
17 See for this example Easley *et al.* (2012: 7–8), Buiter *et al.* (1998: 57–58).
18 See Easley (2012: 8).

7 Fictitious capital and finance: an introduction to Marx's analysis (in the third volume of *Capital*)

1 Special Report on Financial Risk, *The Economist*, 13 February, 2010, p. 3.
2 To set up this figure we have been inspired by the analysis of Nitzan and Bichler (2009: 171).
3 See our analysis in Chapter 1. For this reading of Keynes see Wray (1998), Minsky (1975).
4 For a very interesting account of approaches that share this viewpoint see Streeck (2009). In this category someone might include many other authors than those mentioned before in this book: for instance Jameson (1997), LiPuma and Lee (2004), Duménil and Lévy (2011), Toporowski (2009).
5 For a general presentation of the underconsumptionist argument and related debates see Milios and Sotiropoulos (2009: Chapter 1).
6 Husson (2012: 16) suggests that we should "go beyond the 'purely financial' explanation of the crisis." Wages decline, the rate of profit increases, profitable investment opportunities are scarce and therefore "finance is not a parasite on a healthy body but a means of 'filling the gap' in the reproduction of neoliberal capitalism" (ibid.: 25). For Resnick and Wolff (2010: 176–177), "starting from the late 1970s and continuing thereafter," real wages of industrial workers stopped following the rise in productivity. This generated a great amount of surplus value in the hands of capitalists while the rapid growth in financial enterprises "enabled capitalists with rising surpluses to lend a good proportion of them to workers" (ibid.: 181). In this sense capitalists had, "although without acknowledging the fact, substituted rising loans to their workers in place of the rising real wages their workers had enjoyed for the previous century" (ibid.: 182). In exactly the same way, Mohun (2012: 23) sees the 2008 crisis as a market-based one in which: "too much surplus value is produced relative to demand, and, since wages are too low because of rising inequality, surplus value is channelled into speculation rather than investment."
7 The key idea of this group is captured by Foster and Magdoff (2009: 108): "financialization is merely a way of compensating for the underlying disease affecting capital accumulation itself."
8 We must also notice the puzzling issue that each author usually comes up with his/her own calculations which do not agree with the others.
9 A very interesting approach of modern financialized capitalism and its recent crisis can be found in Albo, Gindin and Panitch (2010). The authors put emphasis on the leading role of the USA in the global capitalist economy and they analyze contemporary capitalism in a different analytical way from our argument. Yet, many of their conclusions are really close to ours.
10 In fact, we assume that: $E_t[R_{t+1}]=R$. In other words, at every moment the expectation of next period's return is constant. This is a rather "brave" and unrealistic assumption which is only useful for our exposition.
11 This general pricing formula is based on the assumption that stock price is not expected to grow forever at rate R of faster (see Campbell *et al.* 2007: 255–256).
12 In a more philosophical formulation: "Substance has no existence apart from the attributes in which it is expressed and therefore cannot be said to pre-exist its own expression, through which alone, on the contrary, it can come into existence" (Montag 1989: 94). This Marxian type of "structural causality" was first articulated by Althusser (1997: 187–190).
13 On this issue see LeRoy (1989), Shiller (2000), Campbell *et al.* (2007), Bryan and Rafferty (2006)
14 We follow the analysis of Campbell *et al.* (2007: 30–31), LeRoy (1989), and Samuelson (1965). We must note that there is a difference between the random walk model and the martingale one, which is a less restrictive version of the former. For reasons of simplicity, in this text we shall ignore this distinction. We shall continue referring

to the random walk but in principle we shall analyze the martingale model, which from Samuelson's famous paper of 1965 has replaced the restrictive random walk model in mainstream discussions (see Samuelson 1965).

> Unlike the random walk, the martingale model does constitute a bona fide economic model of asset prices, in the sense that it can be linked with primitive assumptions on preferences and returns which, although restrictive, are not so restrictive as to trivialize the claim to economic justification. [...] The word *martingale* refers in French to a betting system designed to make a sure franc. Ironically, this meaning is close to that for which the English language appropriated the French word *arbitrage*. The French word *martingale* refers to Martigues, a city in Provence. Inhabitants of Martigues were reputed to favour a betting strategy consisting of doubling the stakes after each loss so as to assure a favourable outcome with arbitrary high probability.
>
> (LeRoy 1989: 1589, 1588)

15 For an elementary discussion on all these issues see Malkiel (2011).
16 For all these issues see Chapter 1.
17 In what follows we draw heavily upon Althusser (1997: 34–40).
18 The theory of the ideological state apparatuses stresses also the fact that the economy does not constitute the genetic code for *all* ideological forms (such as, e.g., German, US or Greek nationalism, racism, sexism), but an element, which is combined with the political and the ideological element in the complex structured whole of the capitalist mode of production.
19 "Sensible supersensible thing" (Marx 1990: 163); Balibar (1995: 64).
20 For the same line of reasoning see Milios and Sotiropoulos (2009: Chapter 9), Sotiropoulos (2011).
21 For an interesting reading of Veblen in this light see Nitzan and Bichler (2009).
22 This point was properly grasped by Hilferding (1981: 149): "On the stock exchange capitalist property appears in its pure form, as a title to the yield, and the relation of exploitation, the appropriation of surplus labour, upon which it rests, becomes conceptually lost."
23 For a thorough discussion on Marx's concept of fetishism and the different interpretations see Althusser (2006); Balibar (1995); Milios *et al.* (2002: Chapter 4).
24 Marx extended his reasoning to other aspects of capitalization as well, e.g., the financing of both state expenditure and private consumer expenditure, reminding us that capitalization does indeed tend to encompass every aspect of daily life (Marx 1991: 597–599). In this regard, he pointed out that the potential for securitization is inherent in the circulation of capital as such and could be generalized as a process applying to every possible movement of revenue (financialization of daily life, as Martin (2002) has called it; see also Martin 2007 and Bryan *et al.* 2009).
25 We borrow some of Marx's expression from the first volume of Capital (Marx 1990: Chapter 1, §4).
26 These formulations belong to Balibar (1995: 66–67).
27 In this section we draw upon Milios and Sotiropoulos (2009: 179–183).
28 We understand the latter in the light of the analysis of Milios and Sotiropoulos (2009: Chapter 10).
29 See also Chapter 2, Milios and Sotiropoulos (2009: Chapters 6, 10 and 11).

8 Financialization as a technology of power: incorporating risk into the Marxian framework

1 We have to stress here that prices as signals can be mostly "wrong," but it is the pricing criteria that really matters, that is to say, the context (representation) upon which any "information" is judged.

2 In the light of our reasoning it can be argued that there is some sense of homogeneity due to the fact that the subjective estimations are based on the interpretation offered by capitalist ideology. Nevertheless, this fact does not seccure the singularity of the different perspectives.

3 We do not intend to embark upon a discussion of the rather naive theoretical premises of CAPM. We shall just mention that in spite of its appeal to investors, this model has been largely discarded in mainstream academic discussions due to poor econometric evidence. One might suggest that in the framework of CAPM the term "beta" carries out a quantified estimation of every asset's riskiness. In this sense, different groups of risks (that are linked to a particular asset) can be measured against each other. So, all securities with a given "beta" could be seen as perfect substitutes from the viewpoint of risk. As we mentioned above, this is not a real development in the workings of finance, but a simplifying assumption of the model itself, which is accompanied by poor empirical results. Even given this naiveté of homogeneous expectations, CAPM does not hold for every concrete risk involved but only for the resulting total risk that drives the asset returns. But even if someone suggested that "beta" is a good measure for every single risk embodied in a security, this would not be enough to commensurate them because "beta" is a calculation which is not necessarily accepted by everyone, while the monetary value of derivatives is an "objective" measure faced by every market participant in daily market transactions.

4 We understand the problematic of empiricism in the light of Althusser's analysis (see Althusser 1997: 34–46).

5 For these issues, see our analysis of the role of ideology in the previous chapter. See also Althusser (1990: 27–29), Althusser (2006), Balibar (1995).

6 Here we build upon the argumentation of Ewald (1991).

7 For a very nice, but not so easy introduction to Foucault's line of thought, see Deleuze (1986).

8 This issue was properly analyzed by Althusser (1997); see also Milios and Sotiropoulos (2009).

9 It "does not simply do away with the disciplinary technique, because it exists at a different level, on a different scale, and because it has a different bearing area, and makes use of very different instruments" (Foucault 2003: 242).

10 Our viewpoint about the role of the state can be found in Milios and Sotiropoulos (2009: Chapters 4, 5, 7, and 10). See also Althusser (2006).

11 In all these examples we are necessarily schematic.

12 On these issues see Althusser (2006: 126–139), Milios and Sotiropoulos (2009: Chapter 5).

13 See Martin (2002: 105) and Ewald (2002).

14 The picture of finance is much more complex. Nevertheless, we think that this example captures its essential structure. Its details have been taken from the analysis of Mehrling (2010).

15 Since they have different overall risks, this implies that they are linked to different income streams (in magnitude and maturity). None of these technical details will concern us in the context of this example.

16 Nevertheless, we shall agree with Fabozzi and Markowitz (2002: 28) that: "prior to the development of portfolio theory, while investors often talked about diversification in these general terms," they did not possess sophisticated analytical tools by which to guide their investing practices.

17 For reasons of simplicity we do not take into consideration transaction costs: derivatives have lower transactions costs than the underlying bundle of assets (see Steinherr 2000: 18).

18 Black and Scholes (1973: 649–650), see also Miller (2000: 13). The no-free-lunch principle means that the replicating portfolio pays off the same amount as the

derivative. The seeking of arbitrage profits will eliminate any possible divergence between them.

19 In the relevant literature it is striking how rare are the analyses that attempt to touch upon the issue of the commensurability of different concrete risks (Rescher 1983 and LiPuma and Lee 2004 are worthy of mention as remarkable exceptions).

20 We agree with Bryan *et al.* (2009: 460) that the "ramifications of financialization are extensive" and thus can only be addressed in general terms in the analysis of a chapter. At the same time, all these financial developments are "trends rather than universal re-definitions" (ibid.). First, "these trends are not all necessarily new, but they are accelerated and take on new meaning in the context of 'financialization'" (ibid.). Second, "they are not empirically uniform in their individual or spatial impacts" (ibid.).

21 For our point about value-form analysis see Chapter 2.

22 As we mentioned above in the text, LiPuma and Lee (2004) draw attention to this line of thought. Their analysis motivates ours but also differs in many ways, which will become clear in the rest of this section.

23 While the influential intervention of Bryan and Rafferty (2006) is important for the understanding of contemporary capitalism and the organization of financial markets, the argumentation of this chapter differentiates itself in a crucial way: derivatives should not be conceived as the new global money.

24 Indeed, this is quite similar to the following remark of Marx: the necessity "to express individual labour as general labour is equivalent to the necessity of expressing a commodity as money" (Marx 1974: 133).

25 The more or less accurate pricing of a derivative always comes after its ability to bear a price. Every derivative issued has a price, even those that belong to the over-the-counter (OTC) market and conform to a particular portfolio's needs: this is enough to place them in the dimension of abstract risk. Their initial pricing has been based on a systemic assessment of the concrete risks involved. These titles are not always marked-to-market, that is, they are not always openly traded. But even in this case, the internal portfolio testing made by firms themselves always reckons the possible gains or losses. In any case, these discussions belong to a different level of abstraction.

26 For a critical assessement of the approach of these authors see Sotiropoulos and Lapatsioras (2012, 2014).

9 Towards a political economy of monetary unions: revisiting the crisis of the Euro area

1 We take the distinction between "good" and "bad" imbalances from Eichengreen (2010).

2 For an analytical account of the econometric evidence with regard to intra-European current account imbalances see Stockhammer and Sotiropoulos (2012).

3 Mainstream econometric research offers evidence which supports one of the three following arguments: (1) mere differentiations from Blanchard and Giavazzi's neoclassical point, (2) Eichengreen's counter argument, and (3) approaches which highlight the imbalance of competiveness as explanation of the current account imbalances. For a discussion of these approaches see Stockhammer and Sotiropoulos (2012).

4 In this equation we follow the trivial notation: Y stands for national income, C for consumption, I for investment and G for government spending.

5 Net savings equals saving minus investment.

6 For a critique of this approach see Milios and Sotiropoulos (2009: Chapters 2 and 8), Milios and Sotiropoulos (2011).

7 For a critique of this long standing approach in international political economy see Milios and Sotiropoulos (2009).

8 See Althusser (1969; 1997).
9 For an analytical development of all these issues see Milios and Sotiropoulos (2009 and 2011).
10 The basic idea was perceptively summarized by Busch (1978) in the context of more or less the same discussion, albeit in a different historical context.
11 We will not revisit here the historical episodes that led to the rise of the idea of the common currency. For a more or less convincing account of the historical background see Buiter *et al.* (1998) and Eichengreen (1997). See also our comments in Chapter 6.
12 Here we are referring to the *Trans-European Automated Real-time Gross Settlement Express Transfer System* (Target2), which is similar to the US Federal Reserve's Fedwire system – and which is:

> a recording, clearing and settlement system used by both public and private market participants and operated by the ECB. While the net balances of other members are settled daily or even in an intra-day fashion, Eurozone NCBs can build up gross and net claims and liabilities vis-à-vis Target2 over time, in principle without limit. In other words, Eurozone NCBs can borrow from or lend to other Eurozone NCBs through Target2.
>
> (Buiter *et al.* 2011: 1)

An interesting description of how the crisis of 1992–1993 led to the need to Target2 can be found in Garber (1998). Target2 was designed, in the first place, to protect the EMU from "speculative" attacks. Unlimited inter central bank credit can be used to accommodate capital flight out of one or more EMU member countries into other member countries (for this point see Garber 1998). In the case of a crisis, a flight of capital or a *re*-specification of private capital flows could occur independently, to some extent, from the overall adjustment of the current account balance. This mechanism makes the adjustment process less severe and the project of the common market more stable. The current account balance (let's say the trade balance), reflects the reproduction needs of an economy and cannot be as flexible as the financial flows. The Target2 system intermediates the adjustment in the balance of payments by making the current account less sensitive to the shifts of the financial flows.
13 See in this connection Eichengreen (1997: 249–256) and Wyplosz (2006).
14 See Bryan and Rafferty (2006), Obstfeld, Shambaugh and Taylor (2005), Milios and Sotiropoulos (2011).
15 Characteristic is the analysis by Bryan and Rafferty (2006: 121–123). Also see McKinnon (1993).
16 Milios and Sotiropoulos (2011: Chapter 12).
17 We shall mention one more time that this reasoning must be read in the light of our general argument with regard to finance.
18 Among the EA countries Luxemburg and Ireland have been excluded from the panel. The first is an exceptional case of a *sui generis* economy. For the second there are important limitations in the data provided by AMECO with regard to the corporate sector. Cumulative current account positions have been estimated as the simple sum of annual positions as ratios of GDP. As an index for absolute profitability we use the net primary balance of the corporations, plus other taxes, minus other subsidies on production. Practically this is equal to what is left to corporations if we abstract wages and we add net property income. From this variable we get two alternative definitions of profit ratios when we divide it, first, by GDP (profitability 1), and, second, by the gross value added of the corporate sector as a whole (profitability 2). Cumulative profitability is the rough sum of these ratios in each case. With the available data, it is very difficult to measure the Marxian profit rate for all these cases during the same time period. That's why we introduced two other alternative profit rate proxies in order to make our point. The fact that both are positively correlated with growth

proves that the profitability of the "periphery" was higher, both in sectoral and economy-wide terms.

19 In the next chapter, we shall touch upon these institutional reasons for the convergence emerging out of the monetary structure of the EA.

20 Another important tendency that may add to the build up of the financial imbalances is portfolio diversification. International investors and hedge fund managers could include assets in their portfolios from a wider range of choices now encompassing the countries of the so-called European "periphery." In this section we will not exhaust the issue but focus on one of its main aspects.

21 In many cases access to cheap loans contributed to a revival in the housing market. Between 1999 and 2005, house prices in the EA increased at around the same rate as the corresponding figures in the USA (moving around levels approximately 40 percent higher than the corresponding average for the last thirty years), while in specific areas such as e.g., Ireland and Spain, price inflation was higher than the corresponding figure for the USA (we should also note that, in these countries, the proportional contribution of house building to the GDP was higher than in the USA). Indeed, in 2005 and 2006, when the runaway increases in house prices reached their peak in the USA, the corresponding increases, not only in Ireland but also in Spain and Belgium, were even higher (see Eichengreen 2009).

22 At the beginning of the crisis, overall private sector debt in Portugal amounted to 239 percent of GDP, that is to say 29 units higher than in neighboring Spain and 116 units higher than in Greece (the corresponding debt levels in France and Germany are 130 percent and 140 percent). It is characteristic that short-term real interest rates in the 1990s for Greece averaged around 5.4 per- cent but, after 2000, fell almost to 0 percent and for long periods went even lower (see Deutsche Bank 2010).

23 For an early critique of these models see Dooley and Isard (1987), Borio and Disyatat (2011).

24 See Milios and Sotiropoulos (2010), Milios and Sotiropoulos (2011).

25 This idea can also be found in the analysis of Dooley *et al.* (2007a: 109).

26 Dooley *et al.* (2007a) apply a similar reasoning to the case of imbalances between the USA and China. At the same time, the economies of the "centre" finance (to some extent) the development in the European "periphery" (with their current account surpluses) contributing to the boost of demand there and, in this sense, indirectly encouraging their own exports. It is true that one of the reasons Germany and France have played such an important role in defusing the crisis is the overexposure of their banks to the countries of the "periphery." In 2010, the direct exposure of German banks to Greece, Spain, Portugal, and also Ireland and Italy, comes to 20–23 percent of German GDP, in the order of 3.6 trillion dollars. The exposure of French banks to the same countries is calculated to 27–30 percent of the GDP of France, in the order of 2.8 trillion dollars. It should be noted that this borrowing also includes the sovereign debt (yet, government debt accounted for a smaller part of the Euro area Banks' exposures to the countries facing market pressures, compared to claims on the private sector). The states in the EA borrow primarily from the banking systems of the EA. Indeed, at the end of September 2009, the foreign claims of European banks against the public sector of member countries amounted to 2.1 trillion dollars, corresponding to more than 60 percent of the total foreign bank claims against the states of the EA (see BIS 2010).

10 European governance and its contradictions

1 This section must be read in line with the general argument of this book as developed in previous chapters.

2 See Althusser (2006: 54–150) and Milios and Sotiropoulos (2009).

3 For a nice summary of this viewpoint see Obstfeld and Taylor (2004), Rajan (2010).

4 See for instance Dooley *et al.* (2007b).
5 See Borio and Disyatat (2011).
6 This point must be read with regard to the argument outlined in Part III.
7 Under the Emergency Liquidity Assistance (ELA) – an integral part of the European System of Central Banks – national central banks can in exceptional circumstances provide liquidity (against collateral) to distressed credit institutions under terms which are not publicly disclosed. During the recent crisis this liquidity channel was put in motion, with the cases of Germany and Ireland being the most indicative examples.
8 For this argument see Kopf (2011: 2).
9 At this stage of our analysis we are not interested so much in the roots of this shift in the perception of markets.
10 See Kopf (2011: 4–5).
11 We have excluded Luxemburg from this sample. Ireland has also been excluded from 2a, 2c, and 2d. This does not change the message of the charts.
12 Here we treat the group of EA countries as a panel. We are interested in isolating the general trend despite the different institutional settings that hold for any single country, particularly with regard to sovereign debt dynamics.
13 For a thorough discussion of the three following points, see Lapatsioras, Milios and Sotiropoulos (2011).
14 See Strauss-Kahn (2010).
15 The tax coefficients for firms have fallen to 25 percent in 2007 from their previous value of 40 percent. The implicit tax rate on capital is by far the lowest in Europe: it is around 15 percent, while the European average exceeds 25 per- cent. The reduction of capital taxes after 2000 is extraordinary, turning the Greek economy into a sort of a tax paradise. According to the OECD's data, the 11 percent reduction in tax factors for firms between 2000 and 2006 was one of the greatest among OECD countries (see Lapatsioras, Milios and Sotiropoulos 2011: 135–137).
16 This is a hypothetical exercise – an abstract "illustration" – because we assume a different system for secondary macroeconomic distribution while keeping all other factors stable. In other words, we base our estimates on the hypothesis that a big change in the forms and terms of the expansive reproduction of the Greek social formation (a fact that in its own right presupposes a different correlation of class power) would not affect public expenditure and economic growth rates. Nevertheless, while we acknowledge the limitations of our estimations, we must also emphasize that they are not *over*simplifications of the reality. This is because the increase in the taxation of capital and rich households would by no means endanger the high growth rate of the Greek economy (or, at least, the evidence to the contrary is poor and highly disputable even within mainstream research).
17 We have excluded Luxemburg from the sample. Ireland has also been excluded from 2a, 2c and 2d. This does not change the message of the charts.
18 See for instance Stockhammer and Sotiropoulos (2012).

Conclusion: a theoretical and political project for the future

1 In this last chapter we shall repeat arguments which have already been developed in the previous chapters. Therefore we shall not use references.

References

Acworth, W. (1925) *Financial Reconstruction in England: 1815–1822*, London: P. S. King & Son.

Akerlof, G. A. and Shiller, R. L. (2009) *Animal Spirits: How Human Psychology Drives the Economy and Why It Matters for Global Capitalism*, Princeton: Princeton University Press.

Albo, G., Gindin, S., and Panitch, L. (2010) *In and Out of Crisis: The Global Financial Meltdown and Left Alternatives*, Oakland (CA): PM Press.

Allen, L. (2001) *The Global Financial System 1750–2000*, London: Reaktion Books.

Althusser, L. (1969) *For Marx*, London: The Penguin Press.

Althusser, L. (1976) *Essays in Self-Criticism*, London: New Left Books.

Althusser, L. (2006) *Philosophy of the Encounter: Later Writings, 1978–1987*, London and New York: Verso.

Althusser, L. and Balibar, E. (1997) *Reading Capital*, London: Verso.

Arrighi, G. (1999) "Globalization, State Sovereignty, and the 'Endless' Accumulation of Capital," in D. A. Smith, D. J. Solinger. and S. C. Topik (eds) *States and Sovereignty in the Global Economy*, London and New York: Routledge.

Arthur, C. (2002) *New Dialectic and Marx's Capital*, Leiden-Boston-Köln: Brill Academic Publishers.

Atkinson, A. B., Piketty, T., and Saez, E. (2011) "Top Incomes in the Long Run of History," *Journal of Economic Literature*, 49(1): 3–71.

Balibar, E. (1995) *The Philosophy of Marx*, London and New York: Verso.

Balibar, E. (1997) *La Crainte des Masses*, Paris: Éditions Galilée.

Barone, E. ([1908] 1935) "The Ministry of Production in the Collectivist State," in F. A. Hayek (ed.) *Collectivist Economic Planning: Critical Studies on the Possibilities of Socialism*, London: Routledge and Kegan Paul Ltd.

Baskin, J. B. and Miranti, P. J. (1997) *A History of Corporate Finance*, Cambridge: Cambridge University Press.

BIS (2010) *Quarterly Review: International Banking and Financial Markets Developments*. Available online at: www.bis.org/publ/qtrpdf/r_qt1003.htm (accessed 19 November 2012).

Black, F. and Scholes, M. (1973) "The Pricing of Options and Corporate Liabilities," *Journal of Political Economy*, 81: 637–659.

Blanchard, O. and Giavazzi, F. (2002) "Current Account Deficits in the Euro area: The End of the Feldstein-Horioka Puzzle," *Brookings Papers on Economic Activity*, 2: 148–186.

Block, W., Barnett, W., and S. Wood (2002) "Austrian Economics, Neoclassical Economics, and Finance," *The Quarterly Journal of Austrian Economics*, 5(2): 51–66.

Borio, C. (2007) "Change and Constancy in the Financial System: Implications for Financial Distress and Policy," *BIS Working Papers*, no. 237. Available online at: www.bis.org/publ/work237.pdf (accessed 10 August 2012).

Borio, C. and Disyatat, P. (2011) "Global imbalances and the financial crisis: link of no link," *BIS Working Papers*, no. 346. Available online at: www.bis.org/publ/work346.pdf (accessed 12 August 2012).

Borio, C., Drehman, M., and Tsatsaronis, K. (2012) "Stress-testing Macro Stress Testing: Does it Live up to Expectations?," *BIS Working Papers*, no. 369. Available online at: www.bis.org/publ/work369.pdf (accessed 12 August 2012).

Brealey, R. A., Myers, S. C., and Allen, F. (2011) *Principles of Corporate Finance*, New York: McGraw-Hill/Irwin.

Brenner, R. (2002) *The Boom and the Bubble: The US in the World Economy*, London and New York: Verso.

Bryan, D. and Rafferty, M. (2006) *Capitalism with Derivatives: A Political Economy of Financial Derivatives, Capital and Class*, New York and London: Palgrave Macmillan.

Bryan, D. and Rafferty, M. (2009) "Monetary Equivalence and Functionalism: Implications for Central Banking," *Money – Interdisciplinary Perspectives (Freie Universität Berlin*. Available online at: www.polsoz.fu-berlin.de/soziologie/moneyworkshop/participants/dateien/BryanRafferty_Monetary_Equivalence_and_Functionalism.pdf (accessed 16 November 2012).

Bryan, D., Martin, R., and Rafferty, R. (2009) "Financialization and Marx: Giving Labor and Capital a Financial Makeover," *Review of Radical Political Economics*, 41(4): 458–472.

Buiter, W. (2008) "Can Central Banks Go Broke?," *CEPR*, Policy Insight no. 24. Available online at: www.cepr.org/pubs/policyinsights/PolicyInsight24.pdf (accessed 22 November 2012).

Buiter, W. H., Corsetti, G., and Pesenti, P. A. (1998) *Financial Markets and European Monetary Cooperation: The Lessons of the 1992–93 Exchange Rate Mechanism Crisis*, New York: Cambridge University Press.

Buiter, W., Rahbari, E., and Michels, J. (2011) "The Implications of Intra-Euro area Imbalances in Credit Flows," *CEPR*, Policy Insight no. 57. Available online at: www.cepr.org/pubs/policyinsights/PolicyInsight57.pdf (accessed 22 November 2012).

Busch, K. (1978) *Die Krise der Europäischen Gemeinschaft*, Frankfurt/M: Europäische Verlagsanstalt.

Callinicos, A. (2010) *Bonfire of Illusions. The Twin Crises of the Liberal World*, Cambridge: Polity Press.

Callon, M. (ed.) (1998) *The Laws of the Markets*, Oxford: Blackwell.

Campbell, J. Y., Lo, A. W., and MacKinley, A. C. (2007) *The Econometrics of Financial Markets*, Princeton: Princeton University Press.

Chancellor, E. (2000) *Devil Take the Hindmost*, New York: Plume Books.

Chomsky, N. (2012) *Occupy*, London: Penguin Books.

Crotty, J. R. (1983) "On Keynes and Capital Flight," *Journal of Economic Literature*, 21(1): 59–65.

Davidson, P. (2002) *Financial Markets, Money and the Real World*, Cheltenham (UK) and Northampton (USA): Edward Elgar.

Deleuze, G. (1986) *Foucault*, Minneapolis: University of Minnesota Press.

Deutsche Bank (2010) *Global Markets Research. Greece: A Herculean Adjustment Task*, Report, 10 March, 2010.

Dillard, D. (1942) "Keynes and Proudhon," *The Journal of Economic History*, 2(1): 63–76.

Dillard, D. (1980) "A Monetary Theory of Production: Keynes and the Institutionalists," *Journal of Economic Issues*, 24: 255–273.

Dooley, M. (2009) "Central Bank Responses to Financial Crises," *BIS working paper*. Available online at: www.bis.org/publ/bppdf/bispap51g.pdf (accessed 5 August 2012).

Dooley, M. P. and Isard, P. (1987) "Country Preferences, Currency Values and Policy Issues," *Journal of Policy Modeling*, 9(1): 65–81.

Dooley, M. P., Folkerts-Landau, D., and Garber, P. (2007a) "Direct Investment, Rising Real Wages and the Absorption of Excess Labor in the Periphery," in R. H. Clarida (ed.) *G7 Current Account Imbalances: Sustainability and Adjustment*, Chicago: University of Chicago Press.

Dooley, M. P., Garber, P., and Folkerts-Landau, D. (2007b) "The Two Crises of International Economics," *NBER Working Paper Series*, no. 13197. Available online at: www.nber.org/papers/w13197 (accessed 20 August 2012).

Duménil, G. and Lévy, D. (2011) *The Crisis of Neoliberalism*, Cambridge (USA) and London (UK): Harvard University Press.

Duncker, H., Goldschmidt, A., and Wittfogel, K. A. (1930) *Arbeiterschulung*, Berlin-Wien: Verlag für Literatur und Politik [Reprint: Erlangen 1970].

Durbin, M. (2010) *All About High-Frequency Trading*, New York: McGraw Hill.

Easley, D., López de Prado, M. M., and O'Hara, M. (2012) "The Volume Clock: Insights into the Higher Frequency Paradigm." Available online at: http://papers.ssrn.com/sol3/papers.cfm?abstract_id=2034858 (accessed 28 November 2012).

Eatwell, J. (1983) "The Long-Period Theory of Production," *Cambridge Journal of Economics*, 7: 269–285.

Economakis, G. and Sotiropoulos, D. P. (2010) "Why Did Scarcity Triumph Over Technology in Ricardo's Thinking?," *Bulletin of Political Economy*, 4(2): 109–128.

Eichengreen, B. (1997) *European Monetary Unification: Theory, Practice and Analysis*, Cambridge (USA) and London (UK): MIT Press.

Eichengreen, B. (2007) *The European Economy Since 1945*, Princeton and Oxford: Princeton University Press.

Eichengreen, B. (2009) "The Crisis and the Euro," *Working Paper, Elcano Royal Institute*. Available online at:: http://elsa.berkeley.edu/~eichengr/crisis_euro_5–1–09.pdf (accessed 19 November 2012).

Eichengreen, B. (2010) "Imbalances in the Euro Area." Available online at: http://elsa.berkeley.edu/~eichengr/Imbalances_Euro_Area_5–23–11.pdf (accessed 10 May 2012).

Emmanuel, A. (1972) *Unequal Exchange. A Study of the Imperialism of Trade*, London: New Left Books.

Engels, F. (1989) "The Socialism of Mr. Bismarck," in K. Marx and F. Engels, *Collected Works, vol. 24, Marx and Engels: 1873–1874*, New York: International Publishers.

Ewald, F. (1991) "Insurance and Risk," in G. Burchell, C. Gordon, and P. Miller (eds) *The Foucault Effect, Studies in Governmentality*, Chicago and London: The University of Chicago Press.

Ewald, F. (2002) "The Return of Descartes's Malicious Demon: An Outline of a Philosophy of Precaution," in T. Baker and J. Simon (eds) *Embracing Risk, The Changing Culture of Insurance and Responsibility*, Chicago and London: The University of Chicago Press.

Fabozzi, F. J. and Markowitz, H. M. (eds) (2002) *The Theory and Practice of Investment Management*, New Jersey: John Wiley & Sons, Inc.

Fama, E. F. (1965) "Random Walks in Stock Market Prices," *Financial Analysts Journal*, 21(5): 55–59.

Fine, B. (2010) "Locating Financialisation," *Historical Materialism*, 18: 97–116.

Foley, D. K. (2004) "The Strange History of the Economic Agent," *New School Economic Review*, 1(1): 82–94.

Foster, J. B. and Magdoff, F. (2009) *The Great Financial Crisis*, New York: Monthly Review Press.

Foucault, M. (1977) *Discipline and Punish: The Birth of the Prison*, New York: Vintage Books.

Foucault, M. (2003) *Society Must be Defended. Lectures at the College De France 1975–1976*, New York: Picador.

Foucault, M. (2007) *Security, Territory, Population*, New York: Palgrave Macmillan.

Fox, J. (2009) *The Myth of the Rational Market: A History of Risk, Reward, and Delusion on Wall Street*, New York: HarperCollins e-books.

Friedman, M. (1953) *Essays in Positive Economics*, Chicago: University of Chicago Press.

Fumagalli, A. (2010) "The Global Economic Crisis and Socioeconomic Governance," in A. Fumagalli and S. Mezzadra (eds) *Financial Markets, Social Struggles, and New Political Scenarios*, Los Angeles: Semiotext(e).

Garber, P. M. (1998) "Notes on the Role of Target in a Stage III Crisis," *NBER Working Paper*, no. 6619. Available online at: www.nber.org/papers/w6619 (accessed 11 September 2012).

Garegnani, P. (1979) "Notes on Consumption, Investment and Effective Demand: II," *Cambridge Journal of Economics*, 3: 63–82.

Garnett, R. (1995) "Marx's Value Theory: Modern or Postmodern?," *Rethinking Marxism*, 8(4): 40–60.

Goodhart, C. (1989) *Money, Information and Uncertainty*, 2nd edn, London: Macmillan Education Ltd.

Goodhart, C. (1991) *The Evolution of Central Banks*, Cambridge (MA) and London: The MIT Press.

Goodhart, C. (1998) "The Two Concepts of Money: Implications for the Analysis of Optimal Currency Areas," *European Journal of Political Economy*, 14: 407–432.

Graeber, D. (2011) *Debt: The First 5,000 Years*, Brooklyn (New York): Melville House Publishing.

Gramsci, A. (1977) *Quaderni del carcere*, Torino: Einaudi.

Grossman, S. and Stiglitz, J. (1976) "Information and Competitive Price Systems," *American Economic Review*, 66(2): 246–253.

Grossman, S. and Stiglitz, J. (1980) "On the Impossibility of Informationally Efficient Markets," *American Economic Review*, 70(3): 393–408.

Gyntelberg, J., and Schrimpf, A. (2011) "FX Strategies in Periods of Distress," *BIS Working Paper*. Available online at: www.bis.org/publ/qtrpdf/r_qt1112e.pdf (accessed 26 November 2012).

Harcourt, G. (1972) *Some Cambridge Controversies in the Theory of Capital*, Cambridge: Cambridge University Press.

Hardt, M. (2010) "The Common in Communism," in C. Douzinas and S. Zizek (eds) *The Idea of Communism*, London and New York: Verso.

Harvey, D. (2010) *The Enigma of Capital and the Crises of Capitalism*, London: Profile Books Ltd.

Hayek, F. A. (1931) *Price and Production*, London: Routledge.

Hayek, F. A. (1935a) "The Nature and the History of the Problem," in F. A. Hayek (ed.) *Collectivist Economic Planning: Critical Studies on the Possibilities of Socialism*, London: Routledge and Kegan Paul Ltd.

Hayek, F. A. (1935b) "The Present State of the Debate," in F. A. Hayek (ed.) *Collectivist Economic Planning: Critical Studies on the Possibilities of Socialism*, London: Routledge and Kegan Paul Ltd.

Hayek, F. A. (1945) "The Use of Knowledge in Society," *American Economic Review*, 35(4): 519–530.

Hayek, F. A. ([1946] 1948a) "The Meaning of Competition," in F. A. Hayek (ed.) *Individualism and Economic Order*, Chicago: The University of Chicago Press.

Hayek, F. A. ([1940] 1948b) "Socialist Calculation III: The Competitive Solution," in F. A. Hayek (ed.) *Individualism and Economic Order*, Chicago: The University of Chicago Press.

Hayek, F. A. (1960) *The Constitution of Liberty*, Chicago: University of Chicago Press.

Hayek, F. A. ([1968] 1978) "Competition as a Discovery Procedure," in F. A. Hayek (ed.) *New Studies in Philosophy, Politics, Economics and the History of ideas*, London: Routledge.

Hayek, F. A. (1979) "Towards a Free Market Monetary System," *Journal of Libertarian Studies*, 3(1): 1–8.

He, D. and McCauley, R. (2012) "Eurodollar Banking and Currency Internationalization," *BIS Working Paper*. Available online at: www.bis.org/publ/qtrpdf/r_qt1206f.pdf (accessed 27 November 2012).

Heinrich, M. (1999) *Die Wissenschaft vom Wert*, Berlin: Westfaelisches Dampfboot.

Heinrich, M. (2009) *Wie das Marxsche "Kapital" Lessen?*, Stuttgart: Schmetterling Verlag.

Helleiner, E. (1994) *States and the Reemergence of Global Finance: From Bretton Woods to the 1190s*, Ithaca and London: Cornell University Press.

Hilferding, R. ([1904] 1949) "Böhm-Bawerk's Criticism of Marx," in P. M. Sweezy (ed.) *Karl Marx and the Close of His System* by Eugen Böhm-Bawerk and *Böhm-Bawerk's Criticism of Marx* by Rudolf Hilferding, New York: Kelley.

Hilferding, R. (1981) *Finance Capital*, London: Routledge and Kegan Paul.

Hobsbawm, E. J. (1999) *Industry and Empire*, London: Penguin Books.

Hoffman, P. T., Postel-Vinay, G. and Rosenthal, J.-L. (2007) *Surviving Large Losses: Financial Crises, the Middle Class, and the Development of Capital Markets*, Cambridge (USA) and London: Harvard University Press.

Howard, M. (1983) *Profits in Economic Theory*, New York: The Macmillan Press Ltd.

Hull, J. C. (2011) *Fundamentals of Futures and Options Markets*, Edinburgh: Pearson Education Limited.

Husson, M. (2012) "Where is the Crisis Going?," in F. Leplat and Ö. Onaran (eds) *Capitalism: Crisis and Alternatives*, London: Resistance Books.

Ingham, G. (2008) *Capitalism*, Cambridge and Malden: Polity Press.

Itoh, M. and Lapavitsas, C. (1999) *Political Economy of Money and Finance*, London: Macmillan.

Jameson, F. (1997) "Culture and Finance," *Critical Inquiry*, 24(1): 246–265.

Jameson, F. (2011) *Representing Capital*, London and New York: Verso.

Jensen, M. C. (2001) "Value Maximisation, Stakeholder Theory, and the Corporate Objective Function," *European Financial Management*, 7(3): 297–317.

Keynes, J. M. (1933) "National Self-Sufficiency," *The Yale Review*, 22(4): 755–769.

Keynes, J. M. (1971) *The Collected Writings of John Meynard Keynes, Vol. 4. A Tract on Monetary Reform*, London: Macmillan for the Royal Economic Society.

Keynes, J. M. (1973) *The General Theory of Employment, Interest and Money*, Cambridge: Cambridge University Press.

Keynes, J. M. (1982) *The Collected Writings, Volume XXI (Activities 1931–1939: World Crises and Policies in Britain and America)*, D. Moggridge (ed.), Cambridge: McMillan and Cambridge University Press.

Kirzner, I. M. (1992) *The Meaning of Market Process: Essays in the Development of Modern Austrian Economics*, London and New York: Routledge.

Kleiner, D. (2010) *The Telekommunist Manifesto*, Amsterdam: Institute of Network Cultures.

Kliman, A. (2012) *The Failure of Capitalist Production*, London: Pluto Press.

Kopf, C. (2011) "Restoring Financial Stability in the Euro Area," *CEPS*, Policy Brief, no. 237. Available online at: www.ceps.eu/book/restoring-financial-stability-euro-area (accessed 22 November 2012).

Krippner, G. R. (2005) "The Financialization of the American Economy," *Socio-Economic Review*, 3: 173–2008.

Krugman, P. (2008) *The Return of Depression Economics and the Crisis of 2008*, London: Penguin Books.

Lange, O. (1936) "On the Economic Theory of Socialism: Part One," *The Review of Economic Studies*, 4(1): 53–71.

Lapatsioras, Milios and Sotiropoulos, D. P. (2008) "Marxism, Class Struggle and Ideology. Problems and Opportunities Raised by the Multi-cleavage of Marxism," paper presented at the 9th Annual Conference of *Historical Materialism*, University of London, 7–9 November 2008.

Lapatsioras, S., Milios, J., and Sotiropoulos, D. P. (2011) "Voyage in Defeat: Policies of Dealing With the Crisis or Policies of Taking Advantage of the Crisis? Thoughts for a Left strategy (Part II)," *Theseis*, 116: 117–146.

Lapavitsas, C. (2008) "Financialised Capitalism: Direct Exploitation and Periodic Bubbles," *working paper*, Department of Economics, SOAS, University of London. Available online at: www.soas.ac.uk/economics/events/crisis/43939.pdf (accessed 5 June 2010).

Lapavitsas, C. (2009) "Financialised Capitalism: Crisis and Financial Expropriation," *Historical Materialism*, 17(2009): 114–148.

Lapavitsas, C. and Dos Santos, P. (2008) "Globalization and Contemporary Banking: On the Impact of New Technology," *Contributions to Political Economy*, 27(2008): 31–56.

Lavoie, D. (1985) *Rivalry and Central Planning: The Socialist Calculation Debate Reconsidered*, New York: Cambridge University Press.

Lavoie, M. (2011) "Money, Credit and Central Banks in Post-Keynesian Economics," in E. Hein and E. Stockhammer (eds) *A Modern Guide to Keynesian Macroeconomics and Economic Policies*, Cheltenham (UK) and Northampton (USA): Edward Elgar.

Lazzarato, M. (2012) *The Making of Indebted man*, Los Angeles: Semiotext(e).

Lenin, V. I. (1913) "Three Sources and Three Component Parts of Marxism," in V. I. Lenin (1977) *Collected Works, Volume 19*, trans. G. Hanna, Moscow: Progress Publishers. Available online at: www.marxists.org/archive/lenin/works/1913/mar/x01.htm (accessed 30 November 2012).

LeRoy, S. F. (1989) "Efficient Capital Markets and Martingales," *Journal of Economic Literature*, XXVII: 1583–1621.

Lestition, S. (2000) "Historical Preface to Max Weber, 'Stock and Commodity Exchanges'," *Theory and Society*, 29(3): 289–304.

Le Trosne, G. F. (1777) *De l'intérêt social, par rapport a la valeur, a la circulation, a l'industrie et au commerce intérieur et extérieur*; reprinted in M. E. Daire (1846) *Physiocrates*, part II, series: *Collection des principaux Économistes*, vol. II, Paris: Guillaumin.

Lintner, J. (1965) "The Valuation of Risk Assets and the Selection of Risky Investments in Stock Portfolios and Capital Budgets," *The Review of Economics and Statistics*, 47(1): 13–37.

LiPuma, E. and Lee, B. (2004) *Financial Derivatives and the Globalization of Risk*, Durham and London: Duke University Press.

Luhmann, N. (2003) *Risk: A Sociological Theory*, New Brunswick and London: Transaction Publishers.

MacKenzie, D. (2004) "Globalization, Efficient Markets, and Arbitrage." Available online at: http://bscw.cs.ncl.ac.uk/pub/bscw.cgi/d57441/MacKenzie%20-%20Globalization,%20Efficient%20Markets,%20and%20Arbitrage.pdf (accessed 4 June 1997).

MacKenzie, D. and Milo, Y. (2003) "Constructing a Market, Performing Theory: The Historical Sociology of a Financial Derivatives Exchange," *American Journal of Sociology*, 109(1): 107–145.

McKinnon, R. I. (1993) "The Rules of the Game: International Money in Historical Perspective," *Journal of Economic Literature*, 31(1): 1–44.

Malkiel, B. G. (2011) *A Random Walk Down Wall Street*, New York: W. W. Norton & Company.

Marazzi, C. (2010) "The Violence of Financial Capitalism," in A. Fumagalli and S. Mezzadra (eds) *Financial Markets, Social Struggles, and New Political Scenarios*, Los Angeles: Semiotext(e).

Markham, J. W. (2002a) *Financial History of the United States. Volume I: From Christopher Columbus to the Robber Barons*, New York: M. E. Sharpe.

Markham, J. W. (2002b) *Financial History of the United States. Volume II: From J. P. Morgan to the Institutional Investor*, New York: M. E. Sharpe.

Markowitz, H. (1952) "Portfolio Selection," *The Journal of Finance*, 7(1): 77–91.

Martin, R. (2002) *Financialization of Daily Life*, Philadelphia: Temple University Press.

Martin, R. (2007) *An Empire of Indifference. American War and the Financial Logic of Risk Management*, Durham and London: Duke University Press.

Martin, R. (2009) "The Twin Tower of Financialization: Entanglements of Political and Cultural Economines," *The Global South*, 3(1): 108–125.

Marx, K. (1974) *Theorien Über Den Mehrwert*, MEW (Marx Engels Werke), vol. 26.3, Berlin: Dietz Verlag.

Marx, K. (1981) *A Contribution to the Critique of Political Economy*, London: Lawrence and Wishart.

Marx, K. (1989) "Original Text of Second and Beginning of Third Chapter of Contribution to Critique of Political Economy," *MECW*, vol. 29: 430–507, London: Progress Publishers in collaboration with Lawrence & Wishart.

Marx, K. (1990) *Capital, Volume I*, London: Penguin Classics.

Marx, K. (1991) *Capital, Volume III*, London: Penguin Classics.

Marx, K. (1992) *Capital, Volume II*, London: Penguin Classics.

Marx, K. (1993) *Grundrisse*, London: Penguin Classics.

Marx/Engels Gesamtausgabe (MEGA) (1983) *"Das Kapital" und Vorarbeiten, Marx, Das Kapital, Erster Band, Hamburg 1867*, II,5, Berlin: Dietz Verlag.

Marx–Engels–Werke (MEW) (1972), Band 23, *Karl Marx – Das Kapital. Band I*, Berlin: Dietz Verlag.

Mattick, P. (1980) *Marx and Keynes*, London: Merlin Press.

Mayer, M., Möbert, J., and Weistroffer, C. (2012) "Macroeconomic Imbalances in EMU and the Eurosystem," in H. W. Sinn (ed.) *The European Balance of Payments Crisis*, CESifo, vol. 13.

McNally, D. (2009) "From Financial Crisis to World-Slump: Accumulation, Financialisation, and the Global Slowdown," *Historical Materialism*, 17(2009): 35–83.

Mehrling, P. (2010) "Credit Default Swaps: The Key to Financial Reform," in S. Griffith-Jones, J. A. Ocampo, and J. Stiglitz (eds) *Time for a Visible Hand: Lessons from the 2008 World Financial Crisis*, Oxford and New York: Oxford University Press.

Merton, R. C. (1994) "Influence of Mathematical Models in Finance on Practice: Past, Present and Future," *Philosophical Transactions: Physical Sciences and Engineering*, 347(1684): 451–463.

Milanovic, B. (2011) *The Haves and the Have-Nots*, New York: Basic Books.

Milios, J. (1988) *Kapitalistische Entwicklung, Nationalstaat und Imperialismus. Der Fall Griechenland*, Athens: Kritiki Verlag.

Milios, J. (2001) "Diminished Profitability and Welfare Decline (Reflections on the Irreformability of Capitalism in the 1990s)," in T. Pelagidis, L. Katseli, and J. Milios (eds) *Welfare State and Democracy in Crisis. Reforming the European Model*, England: Ashgate Publishing.

Milios, J. and Sotiropoulos, D. P. (2009) *Rethinking Imperialism: A Study of Capitalist Rule*, London and New York: Palgrave Macmillan.

Milios, J. and Sotiropoulos, D. P. (2010) "Crisis of Greece or Crisis of Euro? A View from the European 'Periphery'," *Journal of Balkan and Near Eastern Studies*, 12(3): 223–240.

Milios, J. and Sotiropoulos, D. P. (2011) *Imperialism, Financial Markets and Crisis*, Athens: Nissos [in Greek].

Milios, J., Dimoulis, D., and Economakis, G. (2002) *Karl Marx and the Classics, An Essay on Value, Crises and the Capitalist Mode of Production*, England: Ashgate Publishing Limited.

Mill, J. S. ([1871] 1976) *Principles of Political Economy*, New Jersey: Augustus M. Kelley Publishers.

Miller, M. H. (1992) "Financial Innovation: Achievements and Prospects," *Journal of Applied Corporate Finance*, 4(4): 4–11.

Miller, M. H. (2000) "The History of Finance: An Eyewitness Account," *Journal of Applied Corporate Finance* 13(2): 8–14.

Minsky, H. P. (1975) *John Maynard Keynes*, New York: Columbia University Press.

Minsky, H. P. (1993) "Schumpeter and Finance," in S. Biasco, A. Roncaglia and M. Salvati (eds) *Market and Institutions in Economic Development: Essays in Honor of Sylos Labini*, New York: St. Martin's Press.

Mises, L. ([1920] 1935) "Economic Calculation in the Socialist Commonwealth," in F. A. Hayek (ed.) *Collectivist Economic Planning: Critical Studies on the Possibilities of Socialism*, London: Routledge and Kegan Paul Ltd.

Moggridge, D. E. (1992) *Maynard Keynes: An Economist's Biography*, London and New York: Routledge.

Mohun, S. (2006) "Distributive Shares in the U.S. Economy, 1964–2001," *Cambridge Journal of Economics*, 30: 347–370.

Mohun, S. (2012) "Rate of Profit and Crisis in the US Economy: A Class Perspective." Available online at: http://courses.umass.edu/econ804/Mohun.pdf (accessed 20 October 2012).

Montag, W. (1989) "Spinoza: Politics in a World Without Transcendence," *Rethinking Marxism*, 2(3): 89–103.

Montag, W. (2003) *Louis Althusser*, New York: Palgrave Macmillan.

Neal, L. (1990) *The Rise of Financial Capitalism: International Capital Markets in the Age of Reason*, New York: Cambridge University Press.

Negri, A. (2010) "Postface," in A. Fumagalli and S. Mezzadra (eds) *Financial Markets, Social Struggles, and New Political Scenarios*, Los Angeles: Semiotext(e).

Nitzan, J. and Bichler, S. (2009) *Capital as Power: A Study of Order and Creorder*, London and New York: Routledge.

Norfield, T. (2012) "Derivatives and Capitalist Markets: The Speculative Heart of Capital," *Historical Materialism*, 20(1): 103–132.

Obstfeld, M., Shambaugh, J. C., and Taylor, A. M. (2005) "The Trilemma in History: Trade-offs Among Exchange Rates, Monetary Policies and Capital Mobility," *The Review of Economics and Statistics*, 87(3): 423–438.

Obstfeld, M., Shambaugh, J. C., and Taylor, A. M. (2008) "Financial Stability, the Trilemma, and International Reserves." Available online at: http://emlab.berkeley.edu/~obstfeld/OSTreserves.pdf (accessed 25 November 2012).

Obstfeld, M. and Taylor, A. M. (2004) *Global Capital Markets*, New York: Cambridge University Press.

O'Hara, P. A. (2006) *Growth and Development in the Global Political Economy*, London and New York: Routledge.

Onaran, O., Stockhammer, E. and Grafl, L. (2011) "Financialization, Income Distribution and Aggregate Demand in the USA," *Cambridge Journal of Economics*, 35(4): 637–661.

Palloix, C. (1977) "The Self Expansion of Capital on a World Scale," *Review of Radical Political Economics*, 9(2): 1–28.

Persaud, A. (2002) "Liquidity Black Holes," *World Institute for Development Economics Research*, Working Paper, no. 2002/31. Available: http://archive.unu.edu/hq/library/Collection/PDF_files/WIDER/WIDERdp2002.31.pdf (accessed 30 November 2012).

Polanyi, K. (2001) *The Great Transformation: The Political and Economic Origins of Our Time*, Boston: Beacon Press Books.

Postone, M. (2003) *Time, Labour, and Social Domination*, New York: Cambridge University Press.

Pouliopoulos, P. (2004) *Notes on Political Economy during Exile [1938–42]*, Athens: Courier Publishing [in Greek].

Proudhon, P.-J. (1849–1850) *Letters to Bastiat*. Available online at: http://praxeology.net/FB-PJP-DOI.htm (accessed 23 November 2012).

Rajan, R. G. (2010) *Fault Lines: How Hidden Fractures Still Threaten the World Economy*, Princeton/Oxford: Princeton University Press.

Rescher, N. (1983) *Risk: A Philosophical Introduction to the theory of Risk Evaluation and Management*, New York: University Press of America.

Resnick, S. and Wolff, R. (2010) "The Economic Crisis: A Marxian Interpretation," *Rethinking Marxism*, 22(2): 170–186.

Roberts, B. (1996) "The Visible and the Measurable: Althusser and the Marxian Theory of Value," in A. Callari and D. Ruccio (eds) *Postmodern Materialism and the Future of Marxist Theory: Essays in the Althusserian Tradition*, Middletown: Wesleyan University Press.

Rotman, B. (1987) *Signifying Nothing: The Semiotics of Zero*, Stanford: Stanford University Press.

Rubin, I. I. (1972) *Essays on Marx's Theory of Value*, Detroit: Black and Red.

Rubin, I. I. (1989) *A History of Economic Thought*, London: Pluto Press.

Rubin. I. I. (2012) *Studien zur Geldtheorie von Marx*, in *I. I. Rubin, Marxforscher – Ökonomie Verbannter (1886–1937)*, Beiträge zur Marx-Engels-Forschubg Noue Folge Sonderband 4.

Rubinstein, M. (2006) *A History of the Theory of Investments*, New Jersey: John Wiley & Sons.

Samuelson, P. A. (1965) "Proof That Properly Anticipated Prices Fluctuate Randomly," *Industrial Management Review*, 6(2): 41–49.

Schapiro, J. S. (1945) "Pierre Joseph Proudhon, Harbinger of Fascism," *The American Historical Review*, 50(4): 714–737.

Schumpeter, J. (1994) *History of Economic Analysis*, New York: Oxford University Press.

Sean, H. (2005) *Jacques Lacan*, London and New York: Routledge.

Shaikh, A. M. and Tonak, A. E. (1994) *Measuring the Wealth of Nations: A Political Economy of National Accounts*, New York: Cambridge University Press.

Sharpe, W. F. (1964) "Capital Asset Prices: A Theory of Market Equilibrium Under Conditions of Risk," *The Journal of Finance*, 19(3): 425–442.

Shiller, R. J. (2000) *Irrational Exuberance*, Princeton: Princeton University Press.

Shiller, R. J. (2012) *Finance and the Good Society*, Princeton and Oxford: Princeton University Press.

Smith, A. (1981) *An Inquiry into the Nature and Causes of the Wealth of Nations*, Indianapolis: Liberty Classics.

Sotiropoulos, D. P. (2011) "Kalecki's Dilemma: Toward a Marxian Political Economy of Neoliberalism," *Rethinking Marxism*, 23(1): 100–116.

Sotiropoulos, D. P. (2012a) "Hilferding on Derivatives," *Economics Discussion Paper (Kingston University)*. Available online at: http://eprints.kingston.ac.uk/23342/1/DP-03–2012.pdf (accessed 16 November 2012).

Sotiropoulos, D. P. (2012b) "Revisiting the 1992–93 EMS Crisis in the Context of International Political Economy," *Economics Discussion Paper (Kingston University)*. Available online at: http://eprints.kingston.ac.uk/23864/1/Sotiropoulos-P-23864.pdf (accessed 16 November 2012).

Sotiropoulos, D. P. (2015) "Hilferding on Derivatives," *The European Journal of the History of Economic Thought* [forthcoming].

Sotiropoulos, D. P., and Lapatsioras, S. (2012) "Financialization and Marx: Some Reflections on Bryan's, Martin's and Rafferty's Argumentation," *Economics Discussion Paper (Kingston University)*. Available online at: http://eprints.kingston.ac.uk/23341/1/DP-02–2012.pdf (accessed 16 November 2012).

Sotiropoulos, D. P. and Lapatsioras, S. (2014) "Financialization and Marx: Some Reflections on Bryan's, Martin's and Rafferty's Argumentation," *Review of Radical Political Economics*, [forthcoming].

Sotiropoulos, D. P., Milios, J., and Lapatsioras, S. (2012) "Demystifying Finance: How to Understand Financialization and Think of Strategies for a Good Society," in J. Marangos (ed.) (2012) *Alternative Perspectives of a Good Society*, New York: Palgrave Macmillan.

Steinherr, A. (2000) *Derivatives: The Wild Beast of Finance. A Path to Effective Globalization*, Chichester: John Wiley and Sons Ltd.

Stockhammer, E. (2012) "Financialization, Income Distribution and the Crisis," *Investigacion Economica*, 71(279): 39–70.

Stockhammer, E. and Sotiropoulos, D. (2012) "The Costs of Rebalancing the Euro Area," *Working Paper, Post-Keynesian Economics Study Group*. Available online at: www.postkeynesian.net/downloads/wpaper/PKWP1206.pdf (accessed 21 November 2012).

Strauss-Kahn, D. (2010) "Greece's Economy at a Crucial Crossroads." Available online at: www.imf.org/external/np/vc/2010/121210.htm (accessed 30 November 2012).

Streeck, W. (2009) "Four Books on Capitalism," *Socio-Economic Review*, 4(7): 741–754.

Svensson, L. E. O. (1992) "The Foreign Exchange Risk Premium in a Target Zone with Devaluation Risk," *Journal of International Economics*, 33: 21–40.

Thompson, W. (1824) *An Inquiry Into the Principles of the Distribution of Wealth Most Conducive to Human Happiness; Applied to the Newly Proposed System of Voluntary Equality of Wealth*, London: Longman.

Toporowski, J. (2009) "The Economics and Culture of Financial Inflation," *Competition & Change*, 13(2): 145–156.

Tversky, A. (2004) *Preference, Belief, and Similarity: Selected Writings*, (ed.) E. Shafir, Cambridge (USA) and London: The MIT Press.

van der Pijl, K. (1998) *Transnational Classes and International Relations*, London and New York: Routledge.

Veblen, T. (1958) *The Theory of Business Enterprise, A Mentor Book*, New York, The New American Library of World Literature.

Veblen, T. (1997) *Absentee Ownership*, New Brunswick (USA) and London (UK): Transaction Publishers.

Vercellone, C. (2010) "The Crisis of the Law of Value and the Becoming-Rent of Profit," in A. Fumagalli and S. Mezzadra (eds) *Financial Markets, Social Struggles, and New Political Scenarios*, Los Angeles: Semiotext(e).

Volz, U. (2006) "On the Feasibility of a Regional Exchange Rate System for East Asia: Lessons of the 1992/93 ERM Crisis," *Journal of Asian Economics*, 17(2006): 1107–1127.

Weber, M. (1978) *Economy and Society, Volume I and II*, Berkeley, Los Angeles and London: University of California Press.

Weber, M. ([1924] 2000) "Stock and Commodity Exchanges," trans. S. Lestition, *Theory and Society*, 29: 339–371.

White, L. H. (1999) "Hayek's Monetary Theory and Policy: A Critical Reconstruction," *Journal of Money, Credit, and Banking*, 31(1): 109–120.

Wigan, D. (2009) "Financialisation and Derivatives: Constructing an Artifice of Indifference," *Competition & Change*, 13(2): 157–172.

Wray, L. R. (1998) "Preliminaries to a Monetary Theory of Production: The Labour Theory of Value, Liquidity Preference and the Two Price Systems," in R. Bellofiore (ed.) *Marxian Economics: A Reappraisal*, New York: Macmillan Press Ltd.

Wray, R. (ed.) (2004) *Credit and State Theories of Money: The Contributions of A. Mitchell Innes*, Cheltenham (UK) and Northampton (US): Edward Elgar.

Wyplosz, C. (2006) "European Monetary Union: the Dark Sides of a Major Success," *Economic Policy*, 21(46): 207–261.

Žižek, S. (2006) *Lacan*, London: Granta Books.

Žižek, S. (2012) *The Year of Dreaming Dangerously*, London and New York: Verso.

Index

Page numbers in *italics* denote tables, those in **bold** denote figures.

www.ingramcontent.com/pod-product-compliance
Ingram Content Group UK Ltd.
Pitfield, Milton Keynes, MK11 3LW, UK
UKHW010956180926
475701UK00004B/393
* 9 7 8 1 1 3 8 9 0 1 1 1 7 *